T. Thomas

FORTUNE

NEGRO AMERICAN

BIOGRAPHIES AND

AUTOBIOGRAPHIES

John Hope Franklin/Series Editor

T. Thomas

F O R T U N E

MILITANT
JOURNALIST

Emma Lou Thornbrough

The University of Chicago Press

CHICAGO AND LONDON

2-27-74

The University of Chicago Press, Chicago 60637
The University of Chicago Press, Ltd., London
© 1972 by The University of Chicago
All rights reserved. Published 1972
Printed in the United States of America
International Standard Book Number: 0-226-79832-1
Library of Congress Catalog Card Number: 73-175305

CONTENTS

[v]

CONTENTS

EDITOR'S FOREWORD

THE LAST YEARS OF THE NINETEENTH CENTURY AND THE opening years of the twentieth century were a period of great testing for Negro Americans. With virtually no support from government at any level and with the hostility of whites increasing steadily, blacks had only their own resources, meager as they were, to sustain them. Happily, their own institutions—churches, schools, benevolent societies, and a host of social organizations—had emerged and were gaining strength. A large number of articulate leaders, moreover, were representing the views and aspirations of the group to their fellows and to the larger community. Among such leaders the essayists, historians, and the editors of the Afro-American press were almost as influential as the religious leaders. T. Thomas Fortune was surely preeminent among the secular black leaders of his time.

Some contemporary observers regarded Fortune as the most

influential Negro American from the decline of Frederick Douglass to the rise of Booker T. Washington. Surely he was the most articulate. His life spanned a portion of the careers of both Douglass and Washington, and his talents and approaches were unique in many ways. As a crusading editor and as author of such important works as *Black and White: Land, Labor, and Politics in the South* and *The Negro in Politics*, Fortune spoke out clearly and fearlessly on the most important issues of the day. As founder of the Afro-American Council, he anticipated by two decades the NAACP and the National Urban League. In dozens of other activities that marked his colorful career he was constantly searching for a solution to the problem of color and race in American society.

Miss Thornbrough, the author of *The Negro in Indiana* and numerous other historical studies, brings to this work a thorough mastery of the period in which Fortune lived and the numerous problems he faced. Her research on Fortune covered almost two decades. She has written about Fortune and his times with critical understanding of the forces that made him at once a powerful and a tragic figure. The manner in which Miss Thornbrough has portrayed Fortune in this first full-length biography illuminates a whole era in the history of Negro Americans and, indeed, in the history of this country.

John Hope Franklin

PREFACE

CONTEMPORARIES OF T. THOMAS FORTUNE AGREED THAT HE was the most brilliant Negro journalist of his age. But today few people have ever heard of Fortune, and little has been written about him. As editor of the paper which was first the *New York Globe*, then the *New York Freeman*, and finally the *New York Age*, he made significant contributions to racial thought and action from the early 1880s to 1907. Much of what he wrote is apposite to our own times. He also established a place for himself in the field of "white" journalism, as a reporter and editorial writer for the *New York Sun* and the *Boston Transcript*.

He was the prime mover in the founding in 1890 of the National Afro-American League, an organization which anticipated the program and methods of the Niagara Movement and the National Association for the Advancement of Colored

People. Fortune was proud of his reputation as "Afro-American agitator"—champion of complete racial equality and unremitting foe of all efforts to weaken political, legal, and manhood rights. In his writing and his speeches he was consistently uncompromising and militant. And yet he developed a seemingly paradoxical intimacy with Booker T. Washington and was for years confidant, ghost writer, publicist, and loyal defender of the Tuskegee Wizard. He was sometimes impatient with Washington for being too apologetic and equivocal. Nevertheless, for reasons of personal and financial expediency, he cooperated in attempts to silence other Negroes who challenged Washington and his ideology and methods. As a consequence he incurred the scorn of the anti-Tuskegee intellectuals.

Fortune's importance to later generations lies in his writing and speeches. His contributions to racial ideology were original and influential. But I have tried to make this biography more than an exercise in intellectual history. I have tried to present the *man*, brilliant, sensitive, and humane, but sometimes arrogant and inconsistent, and possessed of more than his share of human weaknesses. I have also tried, so far as possible, to deal with his personal relationships. His intimacy with Booker T. Washington was crucial in shaping his life. It is fortunate that voluminous correspondence has been preserved which gives the details of this friendship and of Fortune's relations with other members of the Tuskegee circle. Unfortunately, correspondence between Fortune and other friends and political associates, which would have made possible a more complete and balanced picture of his activities, has not survived. A few letters which Fortune wrote to his wife throw important light on some aspects of his domestic life, but on the whole there is relatively little evidence on this subject. Regretably, there are lacunae in the story of his life which it is impossible to fill.

A number of persons have helped facilitate the research embodied in this book. I am especially grateful to Mr. Hallowell

Preface

Bowser, Fortune's grandson, for permitting me to use letters and a scrapbook of Fortune's writings for the *New York Sun* which were in his possession. An interview with Mr. Aubrey Bowser, Fortune's son-in-law, the husband of Jessie Fortune, was also helpful. Mrs. Alfreda Duster, daughter of Ida Wells Barnett, made some of her mother's notes available to me and permitted me to read some of the galley proofs of the autobiography of her mother which she was editing for publication by the University of Chicago Press. Mrs. Dorothy B. Porter, in addition to helping me locate materials on Fortune in the library of Howard University, also suggested other sources of information. Mrs. H. Florine Williams of the Soper Library of Morgan State College generously gave time to search the Emmett J. Scott Papers for correspondence between Scott and Fortune. The members of the staff of the Manuscript Divison of the Library of Congress and the Schomburg Collection of the New York Public Library were most helpful. Mr. Milton Meltzer permitted me to use a photograph of Fortune from his collection.

Since I began my research on Fortune, a number of scholars have published books and articles which have thrown important light on the period in which he lived and on some of the persons with whom he was associated. I am especially indebted to the research of August Meier for pioneer work in unravelling the complexities of Booker T. Washington, for illuminating the racial thought of the era of Washington, and for vignettes of some of the personalities of the period. I am grateful to John Hope Franklin for encouraging me to complete this biography.

I began the research for this book while I held a Ford Foundation Faculty Fellowship. Part of the writing was done during a sabbatical leave from Butler University.

T. Thomas

FORTUNE

T. THOMAS FORTUNE IN 1885
By permission of Milton Meltzer

I

Florida Youth

H E WAS BORN A SLAVE. THE TIME WAS OCTOBER 3, 1856—
the place, Marianna, Florida. He was the first born son of
Emanuel and Sarah Jane, slaves of Ely P. Moore. They be-
stowed upon him the impressive name Timothy Thomas. The
father, Emanuel, had been born in Marianna in 1832 to a slave
mother who was the daughter of a mulatto slave mother and a
Seminole Indian. Emanuel's father was an Irishman, Thomas
Fortune. According to family tradition, Fortune was an educated but hot tempered man, recently arrived in the United
States, who hated the hauteur of the planter class. He was killed
by a pistol shot in a duel when Emanuel was an infant. After the
Emancipation Emanuel and his family took the name Fortune.

During his boyhood Emanuel belonged to a family named
Russ who had a son, Joseph, exactly the same age. The two boys
spent much time together and developed a strong affection and

loyalty toward each other. It was no doubt this association which gave Emanuel the opportunity to learn to read, a rare privilege for a slave. Because he was exceptionally intelligent, he was also taught a trade—that of shoemaker and tanner. Later he was sold to Ely P. Moore and put in charge of a tannery. In view of the attachment of Emanuel and Joseph Russ, it appears probable that he was sold in order to enable him to marry Sarah Jane who was the property of Moore. Like her husband, Sarah Jane was of mixed blood. Her father was an Indian, while her mother was the child of a white father and a slave mother. Born in Richmond, Virginia, in 1832, Sarah Jane had been brought to Florida as a child. She was a small but wiry woman, with a graceful figure and beautiful face, and a strength of character that left an indelible impression on her children. Timothy, who was her third child but her first son, was always her favorite. There were two sisters older and one younger than Tim and a baby brother, Emanuel, Jr., born in 1863.[1]

In the 1850s Marianna, the seat of Jackson County, was a sleepy little village of five or six hundred persons. Although Florida had been the first part of the United States to be settled by Europeans, it was the last of the slave states to be admitted to the Union. It was the most sparsely populated and least wealthy of these states. But Jackson County, in the northwestern part of the state, was one of the largest and most populous counties. Although it retained frontier characteristics, it was beginning to show some of the features of the plantation society of the older cotton states of the Deep South. In 1850 the slave population was slightly greater than the white.

When Timothy was four years old the Republican Abraham Lincoln, a name as yet unknown to the slave population, was elected president of the United States, and soon afterward a

1. Cyrus Field Adams, "Timothy Thomas Fortune: Journalist, Author, Lecturer, Agitator," *The Colored American Magazine*, January–February 1902, p. 225.

convention meeting at Tallahassee, following the lead of the older slave states, voted that Florida should secede from the Union. But these events and even the war which followed had little immediate effect upon the life of the small boy. During the early stages of the war there was tremendous enthusiasm among the whites of Marianna to enlist in the Confederate cause, and no doubt Tim watched companies of young men in gray uniforms as they marched away amid the cheers of the onlookers. The resulting absence of so many men caused apprehensions among the whites over the possibility of slave uprisings and brought increased patroling and more controls over the activities of slaves, but these had little effect on the child. Only once, in September 1864, did the fighting actually touch Marianna. A Union force of a few hundred mounted troops, including some Negro soldiers, crossed Pensacola Bay and, after raiding Eucheanna, headed for Jackson County. In Marianna about three hundred irregular troops—mostly old men and boys—tried to defend the place but were dispersed by the Union forces. The Episcopal church was set afire by the invaders; eighty-one white prisoners were taken; and about six hundred slaves as well as cattle and horses, were carried off. Some of the slaves were enlisted in the Union Army, including perhaps, a few of . Timothy's relatives, four of whom gave their lives in the Union cause.[2]

The end of the war ushered in a new era in Marianna. Gradually some of the young men in gray who had marched away so gayly a few years before straggled back, but more impressive was the presence of a garrison of troops in blue uniforms, and the most striking evidence of the new order was the fact that some of these Union soldiers were Negroes. On May 14, 1865, the Union general in command of the area which embraced Florida issued an emancipation order. As news of the order was

2. William Watson Davis, *The Civil War and Reconstruction in Florida* (New York: Columbia University Press, 1913), pp. 54, 233, and passim; *The New York Freeman*, June 13, 1885.

circulated, many masters called their slaves together and told them of it. No doubt it was in this way that Emanuel learned that he and his family were free.[3] During the months of change and adjustment that followed the end of the fighting, Union soldiers and agents of the recently organized Freedmen's Bureau acted as guardians of the newly emancipated slaves. They helped to arrange terms of employment between the freedmen and their former masters and in other ways tried to protect them against exploitation and discrimination.

The white population of Marianna, already discouraged and bitter over the loss of the war, regarded the presence of the Union troops as a symbol of the humiliation and degradation imposed upon a conquered people. By many means they let the soldiers know that they resented their presence. No Union soldiers were invited into white homes; instead, they were treated as social outcasts.

On the other hand the Negroes showed unbounded admiration and enthusiasm for the troops, who represented the protecting arm of the federal government and who were also, in some instances, the first white men to manifest any humanitarian interest in the freedmen. One of the first steps taken by the federal officers in Marianna was to encourage marriage ceremonies to legalize the unions of former slaves, since under the slave system marriage contracts had been prohibited. Bibles were distributed —one became an heirloom in the Fortune family—in which Union officers recorded the marriages and birthdays of members of the freedmen's families.[4]

The first school for Negroes in Marianna was organized by

3. Joe M. Richardson, *The Negro in the Reconstruction of Florida 1865–1877*, Florida State University Studies no. 46 (Tallahassee, 1965), p. 9 and passim; T. Thomas Fortune, "After War Times," *Norfolk Journal and Guide*, July 30, 1927.

4. Fortune, "After War Times," July 30, 1927. Richardson, *The Negro in the Reconstruction of Florida*, p. 30.

the Freedmen's Bureau and was taught by two Union soldiers, a Sergeant Smith and a Private Davenport. The pupils, crowded together in the little Negro church, were a motley lot, including adults as well as children. All of them were anxious to master Webster's speller, which would unlock for them the mysteries of the printed page. Among the most eager of the pupils was Timothy Fortune, who recalled in his old age that it was in this school that he "got the book learning fever," which was to remain with him all his life. The school for former slaves caused some resentment among the white population, and on more than one occasion Negro children on their way to school were stoned by white bullies, but these unpleasantnesses did not deter them in their quest for learning.

The Union soldiers who taught in the school were among Tim's boyhood idols, and one of his closest friends was Johnny Smith, the son of one of the teachers. Johnny had the distinction of being the drummer boy for the company of Union soldiers stationed in Marianna. For the Negro folk of the village, the dress parades of the troops were exciting events. The children especially were enraptured by the beat of the drums and the blare of the bugles.[5]

On the whole those years immediately after the war were good ones for the Fortunes and Timothy treasured the memories of them throughout his life. After Emancipation, Emanuel left his master, Moore, and moved onto land owned by the friend of his boyhood days, Joseph Russ. Here he was able to grow a little cotton for a cash crop and abundant food for his growing family. In the open fireplace, where she did all the cooking, Sarah Jane prepared a variety of foods. In addition to the standard corn pone and salt pork, there were yams and other vegetables, chicken, and fish. There were always plenty of fresh fruits and molasses and raw sugar from the neighboring farms. Wheat flour was almost unknown, and fresh meat was a luxury,

5. Fortune, "After War Times," August 6, 1927.

but fish were abundant in the nearby streams. Nearly every Saturday Tim went fishing with his father. These weekly catches made Sunday morning breakfast a feast.

Besides the fishing expeditions with his father, there were many diversions. He went fishing, hunting, and swimming with other boys of his own age. In the village he played "shinny" and shot marbles with them. The latter sport, at which he excelled, was his especial weakness. If his parents sent him to the village, he was likely to become involved in a marble game and forget the errand on which he had been sent. On one occasion, when he returned home at sundown, richer in marbles, but without having done what his father had requested, the irate Emanuel gave him one of the rare floggings of his boyhood. Like most lads, he had a penchant for mischief and adventure. His friend Johnny Smith, who was wise beyond his years, taught him many things, including the taste of tobacco. On one occasion Johnny attempted to tatoo the Union flag on Timothy's arm, but the latter rebelled because of the pain. Another time Johnny gave his friend some brass caps of the type which were used in army guns. When Tim tried to explode them, he received a badly injured knee and frightened his mother almost to death.[6]

The boy also spent much time with his younger brother, Emanuel. Although there was a difference of seven years in their ages, the bonds between the two boys were strong. When he was a very small child, Emanuel suffered from an illness diagnosed then as pneumonia, but which was probably poliomyelitis, and which left him partially paralyzed on his left side. The affliction of the younger boy caused the older brother to care for him with protective tenderness.

As in the days of slavery, the Christmas season was always a gala one. The black folks took time from their usual work to

6. Adams, "Timothy Thomas Fortune," pp. 225–26; Fortune, "After War Times," September 10, September 17, 1927.

go hunting and fishing and to attend cane grindings. For the children the grinding of the sugar cane was an especial delight. Tim was never able to get his fill of drinking the hot, sweet syrup made during the production of raw sugar. On one particularly memorable Christmas two years after the war, Timothy was allowed to visit his Uncle John on another, larger Russ plantation, where he had numerous relatives and where there were many children his own age. Here he spent several days in hunting, playing games, and feasting, climaxed by a possum hunt.

Life was not all play by any means. As Timothy grew older, he was expected to perform tasks about the house and to work in the garden. He also learned to pick cotton and became expert at this occupation which required long supple fingers and a supple body. During the picking season he found that he was able to earn almost as much as the grownups. In these years just after the war he also began to learn the rudiments of the trade that was to determine his life work. One never-to-be-forgotten day he wandered into the office of the *Marianna Courier*, the weekly country newspaper. He was so fascinated by what went on in the office that he became a fixture there and was soon learning to stick type. This was the first of several printing offices in which he worked and in which he acquired a broader education than his limited opportunities for schooling afforded him.[7]

To the end of his life he cherished the memories of these boyhood years—his devoted parents and a closely knit family, the beauties of the untouched woods and streams of Florida, the benign climate. But even during these carefree days there were dark portents of events that for a time were to eclipse these happy memories. At first Timothy was oblivious to or only vaguely aware of signs that alarmed his father.

In Florida, as in the rest of the defeated South, the aftermath

7. Fortune, "After War Times," August 13, August 27, September 10, 1927; T. Thomas Fortune, Preface, *Dreams of Life: Miscellaneous Poems* (New York, 1905).

of the war brought a political revolution, followed by a counter-revolution. For a few years Radical Republican governments, supported by Negro votes, controlled the state. But the years of Radical-Negro power were followed quickly by a return to white supremacy, which was achieved by resort to lawless force and intimidation. It was Emanuel Fortune's lot to be caught up in this revolution.

The extremes of the Radical revolution were due in part to the unwillingness of the former Confederates to recognize that the Union victory meant a new era in race relations. A constitutional convention elected in the months following the war, when President Andrew Johnson was in the ascendancy, was dominated by men whose election the *New York Tribune* described as "a formal declaration that the Negro should be a social and political outcast." The constitution which they wrote gave Negroes a few rights which they had not possessed as slaves, but it established a white man's government. The first legislature elected under the constitution enacted the Black Code, which, among other provisions, permitted Negroes who were convicted of crimes or misdemeanors to be punished by whipping, and which provided for the binding out to service of idle persons and the children of such persons.[8]

The efforts to circumscribe the rights of the Negroes met at once with opposition from the Freedmen's Bureau. The state commissioner of that agency issued an order invalidating the provision in the Black Code which permitted whipping as a punishment. Bureau agents throughout the state were active in protecting the rights of the freedmen in the framing and enforcement of contracts with white employers. They also intervened when it appeared that Negroes were denied their rights in the local courts. All of these activities made the bureau an offense in the eyes of a large part of the white population.

8. Davis, *The Civil War and Reconstruction in Florida*, pp. 361, 365, 417–21; Richardson, *The Negro in the Reconstruction of Florida*, pp. 132–35.

Two of the local agents most vigorous in behalf of the rights of the former slaves served in Jackson County—Captain Charles M. Hamilton and Lieutenant W. J. Purman. Both were young men, still in their twenties, who came to Florida from Pennsylvania as bureau agents and remained to become political leaders. Both brought with them an intense hatred of slavery and a desire to better the condition of the freedmen, coupled with a deep distrust of Southern whites. Both were in turn detested by the latter group. To compel white employers to observe their contracts with their former slaves, Purman at one time asked for and received military assistance to "awe and *force*, if necessary, those who are not inclined to do so, into just settlements with their employees." Hamilton made himself equally objectionable to former Confederates by hailing two young white women into a bureau court and publicly reprimanding them for removing flowers from the graves of Union soldiers buried near Marianna.

When Congress authorized the enrollment of Negro voters early in 1867, the state commissioner of the bureau issued orders that not only should Negroes be registered but that agents should take "measures for their quiet instruction . . . in their rights and duties under the reconstruction acts." Hamilton and Purman were especially active politically. At Marianna they organized meetings of a discussion group for freedmen at which they informed the Negroes of their new rights and indoctrinated them with Republicanism, and at the same time encouraged them to express themselves. Largely as the result of the work of the bureau agents more Negro voters than whites were registered. Knowing that they were outnumbered, many whites boycotted political activity, with the result that the Republicans swept the state in the election of delegates to a constitutional convention and in the subsequent election of a state legislature.[9]

9. George R. Bentley, *A History of the Freedmen's Bureau* (Philadelphia: University of Pennsylvania Press, 1955), p. 149 and passim; Fortune, "After War Times," August 6, 1927. Emphasis as in original.

In Emanuel Fortune the two Yankees found an apt political pupil and a loyal ally who also had a flair for public speaking. Even before the Emancipation he had acquired a certain leadership among the slaves because of his natural intelligence and educational advantages. In the election of delegates to the constitutional convention which met in January 1868, Fortune was one of two Negroes chosen from the district which included Jackson County. Purman, although a bureau agent, was also elected as a delegate. In the election of the first legislature following the adoption of the constitution, Purman was sent to the Florida Senate, and Fortune to the House of Representatives. In the convention eighteen of the forty-six delegates were Negroes; in the legislature the ratio of Negroes to whites was about the same. In both bodies the white men were divided about equally between northerners and native whites. Leadership lay principally with the northerners, who were for the most part able, although sometimes unscrupulous and bitterly divided among themselves. Probably the most highly educated and cultivated member of the convention was a Negro, Jonathan Gibbs. Born in Pennsylvania of free parents and educated at Dartmouth College, he had been a Presbyterian minister before coming to Florida. Most of the other Negroes were former slaves with little education who followed the lead of the more experienced white men and were frequently used by them as pawns.

From the meager accounts which survive, it appears that Fortune made a creditable record in both the convention and the House. A contemporary historian said of him that "whenever he believed he was right, neither money nor promises could move him from his position." In the convention, which was split into bitterly opposing factions, most of the Negroes followed the lead of Liberty Billings, a Radical Republican, recently come from New Hampshire. Fortune stubbornly resisted efforts to swing him to this group and supported instead the faction including Purman and led by Thomas Osborn, formerly state commissioner of the Freedman's Bureau. Partly because of Fortune's refusal to join the Radicals, the Osborn faction was ultimately able to control the convention. The constitution which the Osborn group wrote was a relatively moderate document, which did not proscribe the native whites and which apportioned representation in such a way as to prevent the heavily Negro counties from dominating the state legislature.[10] As a member of the legislature, Fortune followed a moderate and independent course, refusing to be dominated by some of the more extreme Republicans. But his moderation did not win him the support of white constituents in Jackson County. Instead he found that simply because he dared to participate in politics he was regarded as a "dangerous nigger." His white neighbors resented especially the fact that he played an active part in the campaign in which Charles M. Hamilton was elected to the United States House of Representatives. He traveled over the state with Hamilton, speaking to groups of Negroes and vigorously defending their right to take part in politics. Hamilton's opponent in the campaign, a man named Barnes, was an outspoken champion of white supremacy and reputed to be a leader in the mysterious and dreaded Ku Klux Klan, about which there began to be rumors during the latter part of 1868.

By the autumn of that year the bitterness of the native whites of Jackson County, which had been seething and smoldering since the end of the war, was ready to erupt. Part of the bitterness was engendered by the interference of the Freedmen's Bureau agents in relations of white employers and former slaves. There was also resentment over the fact that some of the Yankees, including Purman, the bureau agent, appeared to be mak-

10. Davis, *The Civil War and Reconstruction in Florida*, pp. 493, 511; Richardson, *The Negro in the Reconstruction of Florida*, pp. 136, 152–57; John Wallace, *Carpet Bag Rule in Florida* (Jacksonville, 1888), p. 55.

[13]

ing money by purchasing lands of former Confederates which were being sold because of failure to pay taxes. But most intensely of all, the whites resented the political activity of their former slaves. Feeling was strong against the "carpetbaggers" like Purman, who had organized the Republican party, the few native whites who had joined them, and the Negroes who followed the lead of the white Yankees and had the effrontery to vote and enter politics.

Bitterness at the new order of things caused nearly all of the native white population, including elements formerly opposed to each other, to unite. Former Whigs now joined despised Democrats in the common purpose of restoring white supremacy. More ominously, heretofore law-abiding men joined in, or at least countenanced, a resort to lawlessness and violence to overthrow the new order. The prime movers were young men of the relatively well-to-do class, but older men, who might have restrained them, failed to do so, either because they did not wish to or because they were afraid.

Patrols of armed horsemen had been a part of the slave system. Now groups of "regulators" were once again organized and constituted themselves into a kind of rural police who took the law into their own hands. They went about at night in groups, sometimes wearing masks, watching the movements of Negroes and white Republicans, and issuing warnings. There were rumors of a plot to assassinate Purman, and several Negroes who were active in politics were threatened. Emanuel Fortune heard indirectly that his life was in danger—that if he did not cease his political activities, "he would be missing some day and no-one would know where . . . [he] was."[11]

As the situation became increasingly ominous, Fortune stopped going away from home at night for fear of being shot from ambush. He had learned to shoot accurately and had a

11. U. S. Congress, *House Reports*, 42d Congress, 2d Sess., no. 22, pt. 13, p. 94; Fortune, "After War Times," September 3, 1927.

reputation for personal courage which made it less likely that he would be attacked in his home, but he took steps to prepare for any eventuality. In the event of an attack, the children had instructions to hide upstairs; Sarah Jane was to open the door to the intruders, using it as a shield to protect herself, while Emanuel would open fire from a barricade he had prepared in the center of the house.

The anticipated attack on Fortune did not occur, but one night in February, 1869, as Purman was walking across the open square in Marianna in the company of the county clerk, Dr. Finlayson, a native white Republican, shots were fired out of the darkness. One shot, intended, no doubt, for Purman, struck Finlayson, killing him instantly. Another hit Purman, wounding him seriously, but not fatally. The attempted assassination of Purman signalled the complete breakdown of law and order in Marianna and the beginning of a period of terror which lasted for months. Apparently no attempt was made to apprehend the murderers. The sheriff of Jackson County, a Republican, confessed to Purman that public opinion was so strongly against him that he feared for his own life and would no longer go out of town to serve legal papers. A committee of armed Negroes came secretly to the wounded Purman and told him that Negroes were ready to sack the town in reprisal, but Purman dissuaded them, and at his insistence they swore that they would not resort to violence. Attacks on both whites and Negroes went unpunished by the authorities, but the Negro victims far outnumbered the white. There appeared to be an organized campaign to kill, drive out, or intimidate all leaders or potential leaders among the freedmen. There were also killings which were mere acts of wanton cruelty and several which were accidental. One of the intended victims of the whites was Calvin Rogers, the Negro constable of Marianna. Another Negro man and a little boy were killed when shots intended for Rogers were fired out of a woods on a group of Negro picnickers, which included Rogers. A posse of Negroes scoured the woods all night but were unable to locate the assassins. The following day two more Negroes were fired upon and wounded near Marianna.

Tragedy struck again when the Negroes attempted a reprisal by plotting the killing of two of the alleged Ku Klux leaders, J. P. Coker and Colonel McClellan. The two men were fired upon from a distance as they sat upon the piazza of the village hotel. McClellan was wounded, but the bullet intended for Coker struck McClellan's daughter and killed her. The killing of the innocent woman threw the white population into a frenzy. A mob assembled, with the intention of killing Calvin Rogers, who was suspected of complicity in the shooting. When they did not find Rogers, they looted a hardware store, thereby increasing their supply of arms, and carried another Negro out of town and shot him. The owner of the hardware store, a Jewish merchant who had lived in Marianna for twenty years, was also carried out of town by an armed group and ordered not to return because he had shown an inclination to support the rights of the Negroes. A week later his body was found about twenty miles from town, where he had apparently been shot while attempting to get back to his family. About the same time another Negro and his wife and little son were taken out of town and shot, and their bodies thrown into an old lime sink.[12]

As the terror mounted, Purman and other white Republicans called in vain upon Governor Harrison Reed to declare martial law in Jackson County, but he demurred. He apparently feared that to send militia into the area would merely inflame the situation still more, and he probably feared the political consequences of such a step. In the face of mob rule, Purman himself

12. U. S. Congress, *House Reports*, 42d Congress, 2d Sess., no. 22, pt. 13, pp. 146–48, 155; Davis, *The Civil War and Reconstruction in Florida*, pp. 567–79, 583–84; Adams, "Timothy Thomas Fortune," pp. 225–26; Fortune, "After War Times," September 24, 1927.

left Marianna and did not feel safe to return for more than a year. By this time several other Republicans, white and Negro, had fled. Among them was Emanuel Fortune, who had gone into temporary hiding soon after the killing of Finlayson. Once he tried to come back and got as far as Live Oak, a few miles away, but was warned by friends not to try to return home. For Sarah Jane those were months of prolonged horror. Before Emanuel's departure she lived in fear of an attack on their home by the Ku Klux Klan. Night after night she lay awake, fearing a knock on the door and the appearance of masked figures who would carry off her husband. After Emanuel left it was even worse. Uncertainty as to his whereabouts and safety and the fear that he would be killed trying to get back home were devastating to her. Those months also left an indelible impression on young Timothy, who in the absence of his father was the oldest male member of the household. The constant fear, the stories of outrages against other Negroes whom he knew, the sight of his once high-spirited mother gradually breaking under the strain of anxiety—all these had a lasting influence on the development of the sensitive and imaginative boy.

At the urging of some of his white friends, including Purman, Hamilton, and Joseph Russ, Emanuel decided to leave Marianna permanently and take his family to Jacksonville, where he could find employment and where there had been as yet no serious race troubles. The move meant a financial sacrifice, for in his years as a farmer since Emancipation he had acquired livestock which he was now unable to sell. In Jacksonville he would have to make a completely new start, but there he could live unafraid as a free man, and that had become impossible in Marianna, where to live in safety a Negro had to sacrifice some of his manhood. Sometime after the move to Jacksonville, Fortune encountered J. Q. Dickinson, a Vermont-born carpetbagger, who was justice of the peace in Marianna. Dickinson urged him to return to Marianna and assured him he thought he could now live there without being molested. Fortune asked him: "Could

I go back there and be a free man as I was when I was there before; . . . use freedom of speech and act in politics as a man would want with his own people—will I be safe to do that?" Dickinson replied that he was afraid that if he returned he could not hope to be active politically or to have the same freedom of speech that he had formerly enjoyed. Fortune thought the price too high and remained in Jacksonville.[13]

Ironically, the same Dickinson was one of the last victims of the terror in Marianna. A stubborn and courageous man, he had stuck to his post in the face of repeated threats against his life. Finally, in April 1871, he was shot by an assassin's bullet in the exact spot where Dr. Finlayson had been killed two years before. With Dickinson, the Republican cause in Marianna also died. By the time of his death, all the other Republican leaders, white and black, had fled or were dead or intimidated into silence. After Dickinson's death, it was reported that one of the Democrats in Marianna wrote a friend that "they have things their own way there now; that there is not a damned nigger that dares to speak in Jackson County; that Purman dare not go back again; and that they are going to have peace and prosperity there; that Dickinson was the last leader among the Republicans there, and he being away, that there were no more damned niggers to make speeches; no more white Republicans dare go there."

In the reestablishment of white supremacy in Jackson County, the number of outrages committed was greater than in any other part of Florida. An unknown number of persons died in the period of the terror. Estimates of the number of murders varied from seventy-five to more than twice that number. The vast majority of the victims were Negroes. The identity of some

13. Fortune, "After War Times," October 1, October 22, 1927; Richardson, *The Negro in the Reconstruction of Florida*, pp. 170–74; U. S. Congress, *House Reports*, 42d Congress, 2d Sess., no. 22, pt. 13, p. 95.

of the murderers was well known, but not a single person was ever indicted for any of the crimes.[14]

These events, in Jackson County, occurring during his most impressionable years, were an unforgettable part of the education of Timothy Fortune. The next chapter in his education took place in Tallahassee immediately after his departure from Marianna.

When Emanuel Fortune and his family left Marianna for Jacksonville, Tim was left temporarily in Tallahassee, where he had an appointment to serve as a page in the state senate. The Florida capital was a town of less than five thousand, but to a boy who had spent his thirteen years in rural Marianna it seemed a big city. And indeed, during the months of the legislative sessions, it was the scene of much activity. Florida, as yet one of the least developed states in the Union, was an especially fertile field for the activities of lobbyists from the North who were eager for legislative favors in promoting railroad building and the exploitation of timber lands. The headquarters of the lobbyists was the Capitol Hotel, where they openly plied the legislators with champagne, whisky, and free meals, while behind the scenes they arranged more substantial cash inducements.

Tim found life in Tallahassee amusing and exciting. He was a handsome and precocious lad, who was a general favorite. Most of the pay of three dollars a day (in scrip) which he received as a page he sent to his father, who was impoverished as the result of the move from Marianna. But he always managed to pick up spending money by making himself useful to the legislators, white and black. As he blacked their boots and performed other services for them, he observed them and formed estimates of their character.

14. U. S. Congress, *House Reports*, 42d Congress, 2d Sess., no. 22, pt. 13, p. 156; Richardson, *The Negro in the Reconstruction of Florida*, pp. 169–70.

[19]

Among the political figures whom he admired was the Negro
Jonathan Gibbs, who was at this time secretary of state. His
son Thomas was one of Tim's best friends. Thomas later attended Oberlin and received an appointment to West Point
which he was prevented from accepting because of his race.
Thereafter he returned to Florida where he became an educator.
Tim also knew the adjutant of the militia, General Josiah T.
Walls, who was soon to become the only Negro from Florida
elected to the United States House of Representatives and on
whose staff Tim later served. Another friend was the state
printer, a newspaperman from the North, who published the
Sentinel. Tim spent much of his spare time in the *Sentinel* office,
learning more of the printer's trade and listening to the talk
about state and national politics.

At the four sessions of the legislature at which he served as
a page, young Fortune received an education in the sordid
realities of Reconstruction politics which he never forgot. In
Marianna he had seen the outrages committed by white men
who were avowedly hostile to the rights of the freedmen. In
Tallahassee he saw the members of his race being duped and
exploited by white men who professed to be their friends. He
also observed the weaknesses and baseness of some of these white
politicians—their heavy drinking and gambling and their
corruption and venality—and he developed a distrust of white
politicians which he retained throughout his life. "The carpetbagger of Florida," he later wrote, "was typical of his species—
oily mercenary, hypocritical, cowardly—" and yet was looked
up to and trusted by most of the Negroes.[15]

Not all of the Negroes in the legislature were corruptible,
but many of them through ignorance or avarice became tools of

15. Fortune, "After War Times," October 1, October 8, October 15, 1927; *New York Sun*, December 29, 1895; T. Thomas Fortune, *The Negro in Politics* (New York, 1886), p. 36.

the unscrupulous whites. As Tim shrewdly observed, the bribes received by the black lawmakers were petty compared to those which went to the white members. Twenty-five years later, when he was a correspondent for the *New York Sun*, he wrote with some bitterness of the failure of the white carpetbaggers to take advantage of their opportunities to reshape the governments of the South and to teach the freedmen lessons of good citizenship. "They had a new race of voters," he wrote, "to mould into citizenship. They had governments to rehabilitate which had been devastated by war . . . they were sustained by the predominant public opinion of the republic." But they failed. Their failure was usually blamed on the ignorant Negro, but Fortune pointed out that the Negro was usually the dupe of the white man. "These Afro-Americans did not devise the elaborate system of looting State treasuries which bankrupted every state controlled by their votes; it was done by the white carpet-baggers, in whom they placed the wealth of their faith and newly acquired liberties." After Reconstruction the Negro politicians became almost pariahs, but the white carpetbaggers continued to live in wealth while "the black tools and dupes" were forced to make their living by manual labor. Said Fortune:

The one is respected, in the main, by his neighbors because of his bank account, and the other is despised because in a condition in which dishonesty was regarded as a virtue he was ignorant enough to be honest beyond a $100 or $200 limit, . . . while others of the race, too honorable to join in looting the State or in betraying their constituents, were still rated as venal and therefore enemies of the common good. . . .

The men of the carpet-bag period who are poor and despised to-day are the blacks who were too ignorant to steal or too honest to do so, while those who are respected by their neighbors and are prominent in business and professional walks, in the North and South, are the white ghosts of the carpet-baggers or their descendants who did not scruple to pocket the hard cash and valuable franchises that came within their reach.[16]

During his first legislative session in Tallahassee, the first great tragedy of Tim's life occurred. Sarah Jane Fortune died at the age of thirty-six. The nature of her last illness is not known, but the anxieties and terrors of the last year in Marianna, which had left her broken and old beyond her years, certainly contributed to her untimely death. The loss of the mother whom he had loved passionately and whose favorite he had been was a blow which hastened the development of Tim from a boy to a man.[17]

Meanwhile in Jacksonville Emanuel had found work as a carpenter. The first years in the new environment were hard ones, but after a while he earned enough money to build his own home and to make some modest investments in real estate in the growing city. By the eighties he was reported to have property valued at more than ten thousand dollars. In Jacksonville, where the Negro population exceeded the white and where Negro political activity continued after it was suppressed in most of the South, he became prominent in Republican circles. At various times between his move to Jacksonville and his death in 1897, he was elected city marshal, county commissioner of Duval County, and clerk of the city market. He attended three Republican national conventions as an alternate delegate.[18]

Before the move to Jacksonville, Tim's attendance at school had been limited to one term in the school at Marianna sponsored by the Freedmen's Bureau just after the war. Now in his teens he enrolled for two sessions at Stanton Institute, one of the better schools established by the bureau. There he was

16. *New York Sun*, March 3, 1895.

17. Fortune, "After War Times," October 22, 1927.

18. U. S. Congress, *House Reports*, 42d Congress, 2d Sess., no. 22, pt. 13, p. 95; *New York Globe*, April 26, May 17, 1884; *Cleveland Gazette*, February 6, 1897; *New York Sun*, January 28, 1897.

taught by two New England women, the Misses Williams, for whom he had a warm regard. His scholastic record at Stanton was excellent, but the greater part of his education was acquired outside the classroom. He enlarged his knowledge by reading avidly anything which came his way and from various jobs which he held during this period of his life. As a printer's devil on the *Jacksonville Daily Union*, he became an expert compositor. When a change in the ownership of the paper caused him to be out of work temporarily, he found a job as office boy and later as clerk in the Jacksonville post office. But he quit rather than endure what he regarded as an insult from his superior and returned to work in the printshop of the *Union*. At the age of seventeen he received an appointment as a mail-route agent on the line between Jacksonville and Chatahoochee. This position was secured for him through the efforts of W. J. Purman, who in 1872 had been elected to the United States House of Representatives from the second district of Florida. The mail route was interesting but not without its hazards. The railroad bed and tracks were in bad condition because it was difficult to maintain them on the sandy soil. During the few months that Tim worked on the line, he was involved in at least two railroad accidents but escaped unscathed from both of them. The following year Congressman Purman, whom Fortune with reason regarded as the best friend of his youth, secured for him another appointment, as a special inspector of customs in Delaware.[19]

In this first experience outside the deep South, young Fortune discovered that racial lines were drawn almost as tightly in Delaware as in Florida. On his arrival he took a room in a small hotel which appeared to furnish the only accommodations available. Two days later the proprietor, having realized belatedly

19. Adams, "Timothy Thomas Fortune," 1902, p. 226; W. J. Simmons, *Men of Mark* (Cleveland, 1887), pp. 785–86; *Norfolk Journal and Guide*, January 12, 1924; Fortune, "After War Times," October 22, 1927.

that the young man was "colored," ordered him to leave. But in spite of his race he was able to get a part-time job on the local weekly paper, setting type and writing copy. The stay in Delaware lasted only a few months because Fortune had taken the post for the purpose of earning more money so that he could attend Howard University. Accordingly he resigned from the position and set off for Washington, D. C., to enroll for the winter term of 1874.[20]

In the nation's capital Fortune found a large black population. Beginning with the influx of "contrabands" during the Civil War, the number of Negroes had increased from a mere fourteen thousand at the beginning of the war to about sixty thousand. Already in 1876 they constituted almost half of the total population of the city.

Howard University, named after the head of the Freedmen's Bureau, and one of the lasting monuments of that agency, had been in operation less than ten years when Fortune enrolled. The school was located on hills just north of the city, at the head of Seventh Street, on land that had recently been a farm. By 1876 University Hall, containing classrooms, library, and a chapel, a medical department building, and Freedmen's Hospital had been built, as well as Miner Hall, the dormitory for women students, and Clark Hall for men.[21]

When he entered Howard, Tim had less than three years of formal schooling, and his education had been spotty, to say the least. He had read a great deal on a variety of subjects but was totally untrained in some fundamentals. Many of the students who came to Howard had similar deficiencies, and for them the preparatory department was maintained. In this department Fortune was enrolled in Latin, algebra, grammar, and history

20. Fortune, "After War Times," November 19, 1927; Simmons, *Men of Mark*, p. 786.
21. *Catalogue of Officers and Students of Howard University*, June 1874 to February 1876.

classes. The authorities also attempted to put him in music and drawing, but he resisted. Most of his courses he enjoyed. Outside the classroom he read a great deal—mostly history, biography, and verse—and he participated in debating activities. His fellow students remembered that he was especially interested in history and that he discussed history and politics "with the head of an older man."

He rebelled at one feature of student life—what he termed the "religious tyranny," which was imposed on the resident students. Fortune certainly was not irreligious. In Florida he had regularly attended church and Sunday school and had learned to love the Scriptures. All his life he was to work with church groups and ministers and to manifest a genuine, if somewhat unorthodox, religious feeling. But he found the extreme emphasis upon religion at Howard stifling and depressing, and he was convinced that it induced a spirit of hypocrisy among the students. There were two chapel services daily, a Bible reading and repetition of grace before every meal, and at least five religious societies with which the students were expected to affiliate. Fortune decided that the emphasis upon religion, which was always accompanied by references to the obligation of the students to devote their lives to uplift their race, merely led to an outward conformity and that it caused some students to make a career of hypocrisy—to use the cause of religion and race-uplift merely as a means of bettering their own condition. For a young person like Fortune, sensitive, introspective, and already given to fits of melancholy, the constant talk of sin and preparation for the hereafter was also depressing and unwholesome. Writing of this experience in later years, he said that he contended that he "did not matriculate at the college for the purpose of learning how to die, but how to live, and that the requirements of the religious observances took up so much time as to leave little for the prescribed course of studies, while the religious atmosphere was so intense as to make worldly matters seem inconsequential, inducing a mental depression which amounted to habitual sadness, if lived in long enough." After a few months he left the dormitory to live in a private home, where he had more freedom and was much happier.[22]

The staff at Howard at this time was small enough that the students learned to know the members well. One of the first persons whom Fortune met after his arrival was John Mercer Langston, the dean of the law department and for a time acting president. Born in Virginia of a slave mother, Langston had been freed as a child by his white master, who was also his father, and sent to Ohio to be educated. After graduating from Oberlin he had practiced law and been the first member of his race to be elected to public office in that state. During the Civil War he had played an important role in the recruitment of Negro troops, and after the war, before joining the Howard faculty, he had been inspector of the schools founded by the Freedmen's Bureau. Next to Frederick Douglass he was generally regarded as the most distinguished Negro in the United States. But although he was made acting president of Howard, his Negro ancestry kept him from the presidency, since it was felt that a white man should occupy that position. To Fortune, just arrived from Florida, Langston was a most impressive figure. He recalled that he had never seen a man of his race "who approached Mr. Langston in polish and grace of manners, in faultlessness of dress, and in consciousness of superiority to all things around him."[23] In later years, when he had come to know Langston better, Fortune did not revise this opinion. He continued to admire the older man but always regarded him as slightly pompous. Of the staff at Howard, the two members whom Fortune remembered with the greatest affection were women, Miss Martha Briggs, a teacher in the preparatory school,

22. Simmons, *Men of Mark*, p. 786; T. Thomas Fortune, "A False Theory of Education," *Colored American Magazine*, July 1904, p. 476.

23. *New York Sun*, November 21, 1897.

and Mrs. Keith Bozeman, who invited him into her home and introduced him into the black society of Washington.[24]

During his first year at Howard, one of those blows of malevolent chance that seemed to stalk him throughout his life struck Fortune. The Germania Bank, in which he had deposited the savings which he expected would see him through the law course at Howard, failed, leaving him penniless. In his hour of need he was befriended by the Masons, the family with whom he lived. Mrs. Mason allowed him to earn his meals by doing chores for her. Once more Congressman Purman came to his aid with an appointment as a messenger in the Treasury Department, but the money which Tim was able to save from this work was not enough to pay his expenses for a second year at Howard. He decided to take a job in the print-shop of the *People's Advocate*, a recently established Negro weekly, and to attend law classes at night. The law department at Howard was as yet very small and no doubt fell far short of the impressive course of study described in its catalog, but nevertheless, in his brief attendance there Fortune gained an understanding of fundamentals, especially in American consti-tutional law, which was reflected in his writings in later years. His great love would always be journalism, but he was fas-cinated by the law and sometimes expressed regret that he had not completed the law course and gone into practice.[25]

Among the students at Howard in those years were several young men who were to become racial leaders and with whom

24. *Norfolk Journal and Guide*, January 12, 1924; Fortune, "After War Times," November 26, 1927.

25. Fortune, "After War Times," December 3, 1927; *Catalogue of Officers and Students of Howard University*, March 1876 to March 1878, p. 8; *New York Age*, September 13, 1890; *Norfolk Journal and Guide*, June 9, 1928. After Reconstruction Purman moved to Boston where Fortune visited him in 1891. Fortune said that Purman was "the best friend I ever had" (*New York Age*, June 30, 1891).

Fortune was later to be associated. These included John C. Dancy of Tarboro, North Carolina, who had already begun a career in journalism and politics; George H. White of Wilmington, North Carolina, a future member of Congress; William D. Crum of Charleston, South Carolina, a medical student who became not only a successful physician but a political leader; Jesse Lawson from New Jersey, a future lawyer of some note; and Hugh M. Browne, who became a well-known educator.[26]

The experience at Howard and the other associations which he made in Washington expanded Fortune's horizon and contributed greatly to his development socially and intellectually. Through faculty members at Howard and friends in government offices, he was introduced to black society and became acquainted with the leading political figures of his race. Most notable of these was Frederick Douglass, the former slave, now marshal of the District of Columbia, and the undisputed leader among Negro Americans. Douglass liked young people and frequently entertained groups of Howard students and their friends at his spacious home, Cedar Hill, in Anacostia. Now about sixty years old, he was a striking figure—over six feet tall, with a strong, handsome face and leonine head of white hair. Like everyone else who met him, Fortune was strongly attracted to this gracious, eloquent man, and retained a warm admiration and affection for him although in later years he sometimes disagreed with him over political questions.[27]

From his experiences and associations during his work on the *People's Advocate*, Fortune learned much. John Wesley Cromwell, the editor and proprietor, was a scholarly man, noted for his knowledge of English literature, who was at various times a teacher, lawyer, and civil servant. He had been born a slave in

26. *Catalogue of Officers and Students of Howard University,* June 1874 to February 1876.
27. *Norfolk Journal and Guide,* February 19, 1927.

Virginia in 1846, but his parents had been freed in 1851 and moved to Philadelphia, where the boy attended public schools and the Institute for Colored Youth. After his graduation in 1864 he taught school for a few years in Pennsylvania and Virginia before coming to Washington, where he held various government clerkships. In 1874 he was graduated from the law department of Howard and was admitted to the bar. In 1876 he started the publication of the *People's Advocate* in Alexandria. Like many other Negro editors he did not devote his full time to the paper but continued to earn a living through teaching or practicing law in addition to publishing the paper. The *Advocate*, like most Negro papers, was chronically in financial difficulties, but Cromwell persisted in the venture, perhaps with some assistance from funds from the Republican party. In 1877 he bought some secondhand printing equipment, moved the publication to Washington, and put Tim Fortune in charge of the mechanical end of the paper. Fortune also wrote a column for the paper under the nom de plume Gustafus Bert. Why he chose this name we do not know, but Bert was the name by which his future wife and some of his intimates knew him.

The literary quality of the "Caty," as the paper was popularly called, was high, and its contributors included some of the most distinguished and scholarly Negroes of the nation's capital. Frederick Douglass occasionally wrote for it under the initials M.D.C.—for the Marshal of the District of Columbia. Other contributors were Bishop Alexander Crummell and Richard T. Greener, the first Negro graduate of Harvard College, who had earlier been associated with Frederick Douglass in the publication of the *New National Era* and who was at this time on the law faculty at Howard.[28]

During the period of his association with the *Advocate*, For-

28. Simmons, *Men of Mark*, pp. 898–907; I. Garland Penn, *The Afro-American Press and Its Editors* (Springfield, Mass., 1891), pp. 154–58.

tune also made the acquaintance of two young journalists of his own age whom he was to know the rest of his life. One was John E. Bruce, who had been born a slave in Maryland in 1856. When John was three years old, his father was "sold south" to Georgia and never saw his wife and son again. The boy and his mother won their freedom at the beginning of the Civil War simply by attaching themselves to a regiment of Union soldiers which was marching through Maryland and by following them to Washington. Bruce received little formal education and began his training in journalism as an office boy in the Washington office of the *New York Times*. In 1879 he established his own paper, the *Argus*, which like several other ventures with which he was associated, went bankrupt almost immediately and passed into other hands. Bruce never founded a successful publication, but throughout his lifetime he managed to eke out a living by holding an assortment of government jobs and doing free-lance writing, usually under the nom de plume of Bruce Grit. He was a six-footer, casual to the point of slovenliness in his dress, with a broad homely face and a heartwarming smile.

The second young man was W. Calvin Chase, who had a talent for invective and for the use of methods approaching blackmail that was probably unmatched by any other Negro newspaperman of his generation. He had been born in Washington in 1854 and was largely self-educated, but he had attended the Howard preparatory school for a time and had mastered the printer's trade. When scarcely twenty years old he had quarreled publicly with Frederick Douglass over the alleged failure of the latter to secure him an appointment in the government printing office. As editor of the *Argus*, renamed the *Free Lance*, after Bruce's departure, Chase began a series of attacks on public figures which were so vicious that the owners of the paper were afraid of libel suits, but they were even more afraid of the consequences of firing Chase. When they solved their problem by selling the paper, Chase found another mouthpiece by starting a paper of his own, the *Bee*, which he published until his death.[29]

During the period he was employed at the *Advocate*, Fortune was married. Although there were many girls in Washington who were eager for the attentions of such an attractive young man, and although he was by no means indifferent to their charms, there was a girl in Florida whom he could not forget. Apparently by this time he had decided to try to make a career of journalism and not to finish the law course. Certainly the responsibilities of taking care of a wife meant that he could not continue his schooling, but love was stronger than his interest in formal education. His bride was Carrie C. Smiley, and we know little about her except her name.[30] She was younger than Fortune—a mere girl of sixteen or seventeen at the time of her marriage. Her picture shows a very pretty face with beautiful dark eyes and a gentle, thoughtful expression. Her skin was light, although her face gave more evidence of her Negro ancestry than did that of her husband. At the time of his marriage, Fortune was a handsome young man, striking in appearance. He was tall and slender and rather delicate looking—so slender that his friend John E. Bruce sometimes referred to him as "Slimothy." This was a characteristic that he retained all of his life. It was an event worthy of note when his weight reached 140 pounds. All of the pictures of him before middle age give the impression of an intense, proud young man. He had an aquiline nose, flashing black eyes, and a high forehead surmounted by a mane of long black hair. Like many other young men of the period, he sometimes wore a drooping mustache,

29. Penn, *The Afro-American Press*, pp. 287–90, 344–47; *Indianapolis Freeman*, April 4, 1903. *Globe*, August 2, 1884; Sketch of John E. Bruce, Catalogue of Manuscripts, Schomburg Collection, New York Public Library.

30. Adams, "Timothy Thomas Fortune," p. 226; *Norfolk Journal and Guide*, January 12, 1924.

but at other times was clean shaven. Early in life he began to have difficulties with his eyes, and most pictures show him wearing glasses.

He and Carrie were much in love, and their first years together were on the whole happy ones, in spite of the fact that Fortune's financial prospects took a turn for the worse almost as soon as they were married. The *Advocate* suffered reverses which brought a cut in his wages, and his efforts at getting a government position to supplement this income proved futile. By this time the influence of the political leaders from Florida whom he knew had almost vanished as a result of the overthrow of the Republican regime in 1876. Purman had not been reelected to the House, and Fortune apparently was not in the good graces of Simon B. Conover, the Republican senator. In later years, when Fortune had become a political independent, W. Calvin Chase charged that his disenchantment with the Republican party arose from his failure to get an appointment in Washington at this time, and he accused Fortune of attacking Conover in the columns of the *Advocate* out of pique.[31]

Whether this charge was true or not, Fortune and Carrie decided to leave Washington and return to Florida, at least temporarily. The move was also probably dictated in part by Carrie's desire to return home for the birth of their first child. In Florida Fortune tried teaching for a time in schools in Duval and Madison Counties, but he found conditions insufferable. The pay was miserable—about thirty dollars a month—and the terms lasted only three or four months. About twenty percent of his pay was deducted by the county treasurer as a political assessment, and Negro customers were exploited by the store where they were compelled to trade. In addition the teachers were subjected to indignities by the superintendent and trustees —indignities to which Fortune would not submit. Later, after

31. *Washington Bee*, August 25, 1883.

he had moved North, he declared that rather than teach again in a southern school he would drive a dray.³²

After his brief excursion into teaching, Fortune returned to the printer's trade in the office of the *Jacksonville Daily Union*, where he had worked before going to Washington. But the routine work did not satisfy his restless and ambitious temperament, and he found the caste system of the South increasingly galling. Even though there had been segregation in Washington, Negroes there were not treated as pariahs, as he felt they were in the South. In Washington there had been intellectual stimulation and an opportunity to associate with other persons with interests similar to his own. Having once lived in such an environment, Fortune found the atmosphere of Florida so degrading and stifling that it aroused in him a spirit of rebellion which he said made him feel more like "a revolutionist than a patriot."³³ Since the prospects of successful revolution were nonexistent, he decided to leave at the first opportunity. He did not have long to wait. The way to a new life in the North was opened by the offer of a job as a printer in the office of a weekly newspaper in New York.³⁴

So he left Jacksonville in 1881. After the move to the North, he wrote of the dilemma of the talented and educated Negro in the South, admitting that such a person could probably accomplish more for his people by remaining in the region where most of the Negro population lived. But he asserted that for such a person the very air he breathed was "poisonous," that his position was "odious and infamous." He declared: "We have been there and we know how it feels and how we felt. It feels like a dagger against the heart and we felt like using dagger against dagger. Instead of doing this we moved out."³⁵

32. *Globe*, March 17, September 22, 1883.
33. *New York Freeman*, February 28, 1885.
34. Ibid., May 28, 1887.
35. Ibid., February 28, 1885.

The years of his Florida youth helped to shape Fortune's attitudes for the rest of his life. From personal experience he remembered the transition from slavery to freedom and the high hopes and shattered dreams which followed Emancipation. He was an eyewitness to the terrors and political chicanery of Reconstruction and the degradation of southern Negroes in the post-Reconstruction period. But he also remembered the natural beauties and sunny climate of Florida. He never resided again in the South, but he always felt a nostalgia for the state of his birth. Nor did he forget the plight of the millions of Negroes in the South, and as a journalist in the North he waged an unceasing campaign to arouse public opinion in their behalf.

II

New York:
Editor of the "Globe"

WHEN FORTUNE ARRIVED IN NEW YORK, THE CITY WAS already a bustling metropolis of 1,700,000. The heavily populated part of Manhattan was concentrated south of Forty-Second Street. Business had not yet expanded north of Twenty-Eighth Street, and Fifth Avenue from Washington Square to Central Park was still lined with private brownstone residences. The Brooklyn Bridge was under construction but not completed, and travel between Manhattan and Brooklyn was by ferry. Horse-drawn streetcars still operated in some sections of the city, but the elevated trains which were already running from the Battery to the Harlem River would soon cause a northward shift of population.

In 1880 United States census figures showed a total of only 28,815 Negroes in New York City—13,093 in Manhattan and 9,153 in Brooklyn—or only 1.6 percent of the whole. The great northward migration of southern blacks had not begun. Most of New York's black population was descended from slaves and free Negroes who had been in the North before the American Revolution. In Manhattan much of this population was concentrated in an area south and west of Washington Square, but a movement northward was in process. By 1890 almost 8 percent of Manhattan's black residents lived north of Fourteenth Street, many of them in the Tenderloin district of the west twenties and thirties. In the Greenwich Village area increasing numbers of Italian immigrants were displacing Negroes. But Harlem was still a village remote from the bustle of lower Manhattan. The trains which rattled back and forth to the elevated terminal at One Hundred Twenty-Fifth Street passed sparsely settled areas.[1] In Brooklyn a sizeable Negro colony, including many of the more prosperous, was found in an area extending from the Brooklyn Navy Yard to the Bedford Stuyvesant section and a part of the Williamsburg section. The movement to Brooklyn had begun during the Civil War years when the Draft Riots caused thousands to flee.

In spite of the riots of 1863 and an occasional minor disturbance, New York Negroes as a rule lived in peace with their white neighbors. They voted freely and sent their children to public schools. As the result of the riots of 1863 the Common School Act of 1864 had permitted local schools to provide separate facilities for Negro children, but by the Civil Rights Act of 1873 the state legislature opened all schools to Negroes. Nevertheless a number of "colored" schools continued to operate.[2]

A factor which probably deterred blacks from coming to

1. James Weldon Johnson, *Black Manhattan* (New York, 1930), p. 59 and passim; Seth M. Scheiner, *Negro Mecca: A History of the Negro in New York City, 1865–1920* (New York, 1965), pp. 17–18.
2. Scheiner, *Negro Mecca*, pp. 23–24, 160–62.

New York was the presence of large numbers of European immigrants who competed for jobs usually open to Negroes. Most Negroes had traditionally been employed in domestic service and as common laborers. But by the eighties and nineties they were being replaced in some cases by Irish and Italians. Negroes were seldom employed in the skilled trades, and as soon as Fortune reached New York, he found that race prejudice was not confined to the South and that in some respects economic proscription was more intense than in Florida. When he arrived, he began work as a compositor in the print shop of the *Weekly Witness*, a religious paper published by John Dougall, a white man. Walter Sampson, another Negro, with whom he had worked on the *People's Advocate*, and who was also employed by Dougall, secured the job for him. But the employment of two black printers caused the white employees to go on strike in protest. However, Dougall stood firm, and eventually the strikers returned. Fortune and Sampson continued to work on the *Witness* for about a year.[3]

Fortune's introduction to the great city, and especially to its newspapers, opened a new world to him and fired his ambition. In New York he met other young Negroes with intellectual interests similar to his own. One of them was George Parker, who had recently begun publication of a little weekly tabloid which he called *Rumor*. Parker was in financial difficulties, and Fortune and Sampson agreed to join him in trying to salvage the paper. Apparently Fortune was immediately designated managing editor. For several months he and Sampson continued to work for the *Witness* during the day, while at night they wrote copy and set type for *Rumor*. At Fortune's insistence the name of the paper was changed to the *Globe*, apparently in

3. *People's Advocate*, April 17, 1880; *New York Freeman*, August 28, 1886; *Norfolk Journal and Guide*, December 12, 1924; Adams, "Timothy Thomas Fortune," pp. 226–27.

July, 1881.[4] The *Globe* was launched at a time when the number of Negro newspapers was multiplying rapidly. Prior to the Civil War there had been a few papers—notably John B. Russwurm's *Freedom's Journal* and Frederick Douglass's *North Star*. Their number increased after Emancipation, and especially after 1880. Estimates as to numbers vary widely. Fortune himself said that by 1885 over one hundred had been started, but few survived. Negro papers were conspicuous for their rapid proliferation and their high mortality rate. So short-lived were many that no records—not even their names—survive.

Although the vast majority of Negroes lived in the South, the most influential and enduring race papers were published in the cities of the North. Race was their raison d'être. They were published by black men for black readers. With varying degrees of militancy, all protested against racism in their editorial pages and publicized racial achievements and acts of racial injustice in their news columns.

All of them were weeklies. Some were owned by a single individual; others by a small group who pooled their resources to start a paper. The same person was likely to be publisher, editor, and sometimes typesetter, since it was not uncommon to enter journalism via the printer's trade as Fortune did.

4. Beyond these few facts nothing is known of *Rumor* or the establishment of the *Globe*. No known copies of *Rumor* exist, and the early issues of the *Globe* have also disappeared. See *Favorite Magazine*, Autumn 1920, quoted in Frederick C. Detweiler, *The Negro Press in the United States* (Chicago, 1922), p. 55; Adams, "Timothy Thomas Fortune," p. 227; T. Thomas Fortune, *The New York Negro in Journalism*, New York State Commission, National Negro Exposition, Richmond, Virginia (n.p., 1915); N. W. Ayer and Sons, *American Newspaper Annual*, 1881, p. 65; *People's Advocate*, July 23, 1881. By November 1881, the *People's Advocate* said that the *Globe* was on its way "to secure a vantage ground of superiority from which it can be dislodged only with great difficulty" (*People's Advocate*, November 26, 1881).

Negro papers were invariably launched with high hopes but meager financial resources, and the high mortality rate reflected the inability of most to establish themselves as viable business enterprises. Even the few which survived were nearly always in chronic financial difficulties. Partly because of the large number of papers, circulation figures were always small, and since income from circulation and advertising was inadequate, the papers which survived did so because they were subsidized in one way or another. One source of income, at least during political campaigns, was the Republican party and individual Republican politicians. Nearly all Negro editors and papers were strongly partisan. Some papers were founded simply as party organs and frequently survived only one campaign. Among the better established papers income from political advertising and government printing contracts awarded for political services were important sources of income. After Republican victories, the faithful sometimes received government jobs, and Negro editors frequently used income from these appointments to make up deficits which their papers suffered. Many editors were able to continue publication only because they had income from other sources—usually a second job, such as teaching or the practice of law. Others were printers and used income from job printing to make up deficits which their newspaper incurred.[5]

The *Globe* (which subsequently became the *Freeman* and the *Age*) proved an exception to the rule and had one of the longest histories in Negro journalism, surviving until 1960. At almost the same time it began publication, a number of Fortune's contemporaries were launching similar papers. In several cases the life of the paper coincided with that of the publisher-editor

5. *Freeman*, June 17, 1885. See Emma Lou Thornbrough, "American Negro Newspapers, 1880–1914," *Business History Review*, 40, no. 4 (Winter 1966): 467–90 for a more detailed treatment of the Negro press in this period.

and ended with his death. The result was a personal brand of journalism unknown in a later age. Editorials gave expression to the personal experiences, philosophy, and prejudices of the owners, and the columns of the papers were used to air their private rivalries and feuds.[6]

As early as 1880 John W. Cromwell of the *People's Advocate* had taken the initiative in calling a convention of Negro editors and publishers which met in Louisville. This resulted in the formation of the Colored Press Association (later the Afro-American Press Association, and after 1907 the Negro Press Association). The organization included editors of religious publications, which were numerous, as well as editors of commercial, lay publications. Its annual conventions, which were usually lively, and sometimes tumultuous, gave members an opportunity to know each other and to discuss common problems. Fortune was a member of the association and through it became acquainted with other editors. During the 1890s he served as its president and chairman of the executive council. But he was critical of it because of its close identification with the Repub-

6. The following were the most influential and long-lived Negro newspapers which were founded at about the same times as the *Globe*: *Chicago Conservator*, founded in 1878 by Ferdinand Barnett, an attorney; *Washington Bee* (1883–1925), founded by W. Calvin Chase; *Cleveland Gazette* (1883–1945), founded by Harry C. Smith, later a member of the Ohio legislature; *Richmond Planet* (1884–1945), founded by John P. Mitchell, Jr., who served on the Richmond city council and became president of the Richmond Mechanics Savings Bank; and the *Philadelphia Tribune*, founded in 1884 by Christopher Perry, who later served six terms as a member of the Philadelphia city council. The *Tribune* is the ony one of the papers which survives today (1971). See Penn, *The Afro-American Press*, pp. 145, 183–87, 280–82; *Cleveland Gazette*, January 7, 1905; *New York Age*, January 9, 1892; Simmons, *Men of Mark*, p. 231; August Meier, *Negro Thoughts in America, 1880–1915* (Ann Arbor: University of Michigan Press, 1963), p. 231.

lican party and because he did not consider some of its members bona fide journalists.[7]

Far more important to his own intellectual growth and to his development as a journalist were certain associations which he made in New York. One of these was with John F. Quarles, who was about ten years older than Fortune and who served as editor of the *Globe* for a few months after its founding, while the younger man served as managing editor. Although he had been born a slave, Quarles had attended Westminister College in Pennsylvania after Emancipation and had studied law at Howard University under John Mercer Langston. During Reconstruction he had practiced law and been politically active in both Georgia and South Carolina. During the 1870s he had served as United States consul in Minorca and Malaga and had married the daughter of the French consul at the latter port. In 1880 he returned to New York and took up the practice of law. He helped in the establishment of the *Globe* and wrote some of the editorials which first established its reputation. After a few months he relinquished the editorship to Fortune in order to devote himself entirely to his law practice. Quarles was a man of scholarly tastes, widely read and widely traveled, and fluent in several languages. Fortune admired his intensely and learned much from him.[8]

But a more important influence on the *Globe* editor was a white journalist, John Swinton, who at the time Fortune arrived in New York was chief of the editorial staff of Dana's *Sun* and reputed to be the highest paid newspaperman in the city. Swinton had been born in Scotland and had spent his boyhood in Montreal and New York, where he had acquired the printer's trade as well as an academic education. In the 1850s, as a young

7. *People's Advocate*, July 31, September 4, 1880; August 27, 1881; *Globe*, January 13, June 9, 1883; August 9, 1884.

8. *People's Advocate*, July 23, 1881; *Freeman*, January 31, February 7, February 14, 1885.

man, he had taken part in the free-soil emigration to Kansas and had briefly edited the *Lawrence Republican*. He soon returned to New York, where he became chief of the editorial staff of Raymond's *Times* before going to work on the *Sun* in 1875. In New York he became interested in the labor movement, while maintaining his old-time abolitionist concern for the rights of Negroes. He was the first white journalist, Fortune later recalled, "who extended to me the right hand of fellowship," soon after the founding of the *Globe*. It was the beginning of an enduring friendship.

In 1883 Swinton resigned from the *Sun* to begin the publication of *John Swinton's Paper*, which declared itself to be "The Only Paper in New York City for the Rights of the Whole People."

In explaining his purpose in founding the paper, Swinton said: "The curse of the New York press is intellectual timidity. The chief editors are overawed by the ruling powers of society. . . . If any man of the press has strong convictions, . . . he must start a paper of his own, and run it while his locker holds out or as long as he can find subscribers to support it." Such men, he predicted, might have a hard time and run the risk of death in a poor house, "but what a glorious enjoyment it is," he exulted, "as long as it lasts, to give free play to your faculties and forces!"[9]

The paper was strongly tinctured with the views of Henry George, whom Swinton greatly admired. It warned the American people against "the treasonable and crushing schemes of Millionaires, Monopolies and Plutocrats, and against the coming Billionaire whose shadow is now looming up." It attacked convict labor, contract labor, and the exploitation of immigrants. It endorsed Greenbackism, the eight-hour day, and federal aid to education. Swinton cried: "A plague on both your houses," to the major political parties and called for a new party. He

9. *Age*, November 16, 1889; *John Swinton's Paper*, March 22, 1885.

labeled the Republican and Democratic platforms of 1884 as "shams" and the parties as "twin relics of barabarism."

Fortune frequently commended Swinton's paper in the columns of the *Globe*, and he was sometimes accused of slavishly imitating it. Certainly Swinton's influence in shaping his views on the role of the newspaperman and on certain specific subjects was powerful. This is most obvious in the economic views which Fortune proclaimed during the eighties—his attacks on monopoly and plutocracy and his insistence on mutuality of interests of all labor, black and white. Swinton, who remained a staunch Calvinist in spite of his economic radicalism, was probably a factor in Fortune's brief espousal of prohibitionism in 1886. More significantly, Swinton's influence was undoubtedly important in Fortune's advocacy of political independence and his attacks on the major parties. Finally, Swinton, who as a writer was described as having "a rare sense of word values" and being a "master of the language of opprobrium" both in "vehement invective and in biting sarcasm," must have influenced the development of Fortune's literary style.

Swinton brought to his publication long experience in newspaper work but found that the work of publishing and editing his own paper was the most arduous he had ever undertaken. Subscribers were few, and pecuniary losses were greater than he had anticipated. On the first anniversary of *Swinton's Paper* (at a time when the *Globe* faced financial ruin), on the subject of financial losses, Fortune exclaimed: "We know all about it, Mr. Swinton. Men who fight for principles are always misunderstood—crippled by enemies as well as those who should be friends. . . . May *John Swinton's Paper* long live, the scourge of unjust capitalism, of corruption and hypocrisy." Swinton replied with an editorial to "our brilliant contemporary, the *Globe*," and encouraged Fortune to "peg away" in his own journalistic crusade.[10]

10. *John Swinton's Paper*, March 9, November 9, December 28, 1884; "John Swinton," *Dictionary of American Biography*.

Although so different in background and experience, Swinton and the youthful editor of the *Globe* published papers which in some respects were similar, and both faced some of the same problems. But the *Globe* was first of all a race paper and shared the characteristics and problems of its Negro contemporaries. Like all the Negro papers of the period, the *Globe* was a four-page weekly. It was published in its own printshop by Negro printers who worked under Fortune, himself an expert printer, and was remarkably free of the grammatical and typographical errors which marred most Negro papers. Like most of its white contemporaries (but unlike *Swinton's Paper*), the *Globe* accepted patent medicine advertisements. It also printed advertisements directed especially at Negro readers which promised to straighten kinky hair and lighten black skin.

The *Globe* declared that its aim was "to supply the place of a National Journal for the colored people of the United States," and it claimed to be the only race paper with a national reputation. It carried some news of New York City, but its point of view was national and racial rather than local. By 1883 it claimed to circulate in every state in the Union. Negro papers did not enjoy news-gathering facilities comparable to the white press, since they were not admitted to membership in the Associated Press or its predecessors. But the *Globe* had a staff of able correspondents in many cities in the North and South who reported news of race conditions and political developments related to race. News letters from smaller communities reported local trivia including activities of churches and fraternal organizations. Among the occasional contributors was sixteen year old Willie Du Bois who wrote of the news in Great Barrington, Massachusetts, and also served as agent for the *Globe* in that community.[11] The *Globe* also published portraits and biographical sketches of prominent Negroes. A more unusual feature for

11. *Globe*, January 13, May 5, 1883; July 12, 1884; Ayer, *American Newspaper Annual*, 1884, p. 63.

a Negro publication, which reflected the interests of the editor and staff, was a column devoted to book reviews and reviews of articles in the leading literary journals of opinion.

But the prestige which the *Globe* enjoyed among other race papers, and which elicited favorable comment even in the white press, rested on the quality of its editorials, which, after the departure of Quarles, were usually written by Fortune or reflected his views. Fortune was scornful of the "patent insides" used by many weekly papers, white and black. Throughout his life he held the view that the editorial page was the most vital part of any newspaper. When at one point it was necessary as an economy measure to reduce the size of the *Globe*, he announced that other matters would be decreased, but the editorial page would remain intact.[12]

In an early essay on Negro journalism, Fortune declared that if the Negro did not "carry with him in his face a proclamation of his race and previous condition of servitude, . . . a half century would have sufficed to obliterate from the minds of men the fact that slavery once prevailed." But the "mark of Color" remained and made its possessor "a social pariah, to be robbed, beaten and lynched,—and a political nondescript, who has got his own salvation to work out, of equality before the laws, with almost the entire white population of the country arrayed against him" The reasons for a Negro press, he added, were "that white men have newspapers; that they are published by white men for white men; give, in the main, news about white men, and pitch their editorial opinions entirely in the interest of white men." There were white papers which professed to love colored citizens, but this, he said, was purely for partisan reasons. The entire white press of the South was "leagued against the negro and his rights," and it was "reinforced by quite two thirds of the press of the North and West." "How are we to overcome this tremendous influence?" he asked. "Are we

12. *Globe*, July 5, 1884.

to prevail aginst our enemies *not* as other men prevail against theirs? Can we reasonably expect other men to use their lungs to cry out for us when we are wronged and outraged and murdered? If we do, let us look at the white papers of the South and learn from them the necessary lesson, that the only way we can hope ever to win our fight is to arm ourselves as our opponents do, support those newspapers alone that support us, and support those men alone that support us."[13]

Consistently with these views, the *Globe* adopted a militant and uncompromising position on civil rights. At the time the paper was founded, the power of Congress to protect the rights of Negroes was being steadily circumscribed by decisions of the federal courts. After a part of the Ku Klux Klan Act of 1871 which dealt with voting rights was declared unconstitutional by the Supreme Court on the grounds that it invaded areas reserved to the states, Fortune pointed out that the courts were saying in effect, that although Congress and the people had adopted the Fourteenth and Fifteenth Amendments, Congress lacked the power to enforce the amendments. In a *Globe* editorial, January 27, 1883, he said:

> Verily ours is a disjointed constitution. It makes a fraction greater than the whole—it makes one state greater within its prescribed territory than the Union of States. . . . The United States is simply a puppet which each state treats with contempt or reverence as the spirit moves it.
>
> There is no law in the United States for the Negro. The whole thing is a beggaredly [*sic*] farce.

When a judge in Texas declared that the public accommodations provisions of the Civil Rights Act of 1875 were unconstitutional and beyond the power of the federal government, Fortune protested that to leave such matters to the jurisdiction of

13. T. Thomas Fortune, "The Editor's Mission," in Penn, *Afro-American Press*, pp. 481–83. The spelling "negro" is in the original. Hereafter in quotations the spelling will be as in the original.

the states was a mockery.[14] A few weeks later in the Civil Rights Cases, the Supreme Court, with only one dissenting vote, declared the act invalid on the grounds that the Fourteenth Amendment did not give Congress the power to enact such substantive legislation, nor did the amendment prohibit actions by private individuals. A *Globe* editorial, October 20, 1883, declared:

> The colored people in the United States feel today as if they have been baptized in ice water. . . .
> Having declared that colored men have no protection from the government in their political rights, the Supreme Court now declares that railroad corporations are free to force us into smoking cars or cattle cars; that hotel keepers are free to make us walk the streets at night, that theater managers can refuse us admittance to their exhibitions for the amusement of the public. . . .
> Then, what is the position in which the Supreme Court has left us? Simply this—we have the ballot without any law to protect us in the enjoyment of it; we are declared to be created equal, and entitled to certain rights . . . but there is no law to protect us in the enjoyment of them. We are aliens in our own land.

In another editorial Fortune recalled the loyalty of Negroes to the Union cause during the Civil War and the contributions of Negroes to Union victory. "The honor of citizenship was not conferred upon us because men loved us," he said, "it was conferred upon us because our conduct in the war, when men's nerves and souls were tried, earned it." Therefore, "we do not ask the American government or people for charity . . . ; we do not ask any special favor from the American government or people. But we do demand that impartial justice which is the standard of reciprocity between equals."[15]

14. *Globe*, June 23, 1883.
15. Ibid., October 27, 1883. Fortune presided at a meeting in

But if dominant white opinion did not support the black man's demand for justice and protection of his rights as a citizen, what recourse was there? Earlier, on June 23, 1883, Fortune had pointed out the fatuity of leaving these questions to the states and warned:

> If we find that the law of the United States has no power to shield us from robbery and violence, and if we find that the States' law will give us no redress, we will fall back upon the time-honored remedy of being a law unto ourselves. Once establish in the minds of colored people that . . . [they] have no recourse in law or equity of Federal or State courts from the robbery of corporations and the insults and rough treatment of the minions and scullions of these, and the colored men will show the very same disposition to fight for their rights as any other people.

When a Georgia judge upheld the right of a railroad conductor to require all Negro passengers to ride in the smoking car on the grounds that this was the "custom," Fortune warned that such decisions were "full of dynamite." His own instinct, he said, in the face of a decision which gave a railroad the right to give only two dollars worth of accommodation when he had paid for a five dollar ticket would be "to knock down any fellow who attempts to enforce such robbery." Black men tended to be too servile and docile.

> We do not counsel violence; [he said] we counsel manly retaliation. We do not counsel a breach of the law, but in the absence of law, in the absence of proper police regulation, we maintain that the individual has every right, in law and equity, to use every means in his power to protect himself.

After a race riot in Danville, Virginia, which was alleged to have started when a Negro shoved a white man off a sidewalk,

---

Manhattan called to protest the Supreme Court decision in the Civil Rights Cases. After hearing the opinion of the Court dissected by John F. Quarles, the meeting passed resolutions condemning the decision and praising Justice John M. Harlan for his dissent (Ibid.).

a *Globe* editorial explicitly defended the right of Negroes to resist force with force. "If white men are determined upon shooting whenever they have a difference with a colored man, let the
colored man be prepared to shoot also. . . . If it is necessary for
colored men to turn themselves into outlaws to assert their manhood and their citizenship, let them do it."[16]

This editorial brought a spate of protests in the white press,
including an editorial in the *Jacksonville Herald*, written by a
man Fortune knew and admired. The *Herald* declared that Fortune was giving Negroes bad advice, that in a race war Cauca-
sians would inevitably demonstrate their superiority. In reply
in an editorial December 1, 1883, entitled "The Stand and Be
Shot or Shoot and Stand Policy," Fortune asserted that almost
invariably in the South it was white men who first resorted to
violence and who incited other white men. From personal experience in his Florida boyhood he had seen how some of the
"best" white men had inflamed ignorant whites to violence
against Negroes. He declared:

> It is only because the whites resort to violence, to assassina-
> tion and murder, that we advise colored men to "stand their
> ground." We have no disposition to fan the coals of race dis-
> cord, . . . [But] when colored men are assailed (they are very
> seldom the aggressors) they have a perfect right to "stand
> their ground," and in such riots as the white mobs are pleased
> to foment the blacks will not be exterminated. If they run
> away like cowards they will be regarded as "inferior" and
> worthy to be shot; but if they "stand their ground" manfully,
> and do their honest share of the shooting they will be re-
> spected, and by so doing they will lessen the propensity of
> white roughs to incite to riot.

Some Negro papers also assailed Fortune. In reply to one editorial which called him an incendiary, he declared that the man
or race which would not resist insult and defend its rights was
"a coward worthy only of the contempt of brave men." He

16. Ibid., March 1, March 31, November 10, 1883.

insisted that whites imposed upon Negroes only because they considered them cowards. In reply, the *Cincinnati Afro-American* declared that it was joining "the list of cowards" and added that it was "better for the colored man to stand and be shot than to shoot and stand."[17]

Fortune also outraged white Americans (and some Negroes) by defending the right of whites and Negroes to intermarry. When Frederick Douglass married a white woman, the *Globe* declared that it was entirely a personal matter and deplored the criticism heaped upon Douglass, especially by members of his own race. "We are always prating about the unreasonable prejudices of other people," he said, "and yet show, when occasion presents itself, prejudices just as narrow and unreasonable." He added:

> We are surprised at the amount of gush which intermarriage inspires in this country. It is in strict keeping with all the sophistries kept alive by the papers and the people about the colored people. It is the ceaseless but futile effort to show that the human nature of the black man and the human nature of the white man differ in some indefinable way, when we all know that, essentially, human nature is, in fundamental respects, the same wherever mankind is found.

This elicited an exchange between the white *Wilmingtonian* and the *Globe* in which the former asserted that God had created racial barriers which man should not transcend and criticized the *Globe* and "rabid journals of this class" for demanding miscegenation as their prerogative. Fortune replied, "We do demand miscegenation as our prerogative. . . . We are American citizens pure and simple, and there is no right a white man enjoys as a citizen to the full and equal enjoyment of which we are not entitled. We are all equal alike under the Constitution, and the little State of Delaware can't rub it out."[18]

17. Ibid., January 19, February 9, 1884.
18. Ibid., February 2, March 1, 1884.

In news columns and editorials, the *Globe* publicized discrimination and racial injustice in the North and the South. When the *Atlanta Constitution* asserted that Negroes in the North had no more rights than those in the South, Fortune disagreed vehemently. If this were true, he said, he would still be in Florida. "The editor of the Globe," he proclaimed, "enjoys in the North the same measure of freedom and immunity that any other well regulated man enjoys." But elsewhere he admitted that discrimination existed even in the northern states which had adopted public accommodations laws. He also admitted that Negroes in New York were systematically victimized in the matter of housing. Negroes were not free to live where they chose but were restricted by real estate agents and public opinion to certain localities "not noted for respectability or healthfulness." They were charged exorbitant rents for run-down houses which whites would not occupy, and all kinds of people —"the decent, the rowdy and criminal"—were crowded together, and there was no escape.[19]

But the emphasis in the *Globe* was on the worsening plight of southern Negroes. In one editorial Fortune said that the only solution in South Carolina was to remand the state to territorial status until abuses were corrected.[20] In the *Globe*, March 17, 1883, he wrote a lengthy reply to a series of articles on southern Negroes in the *New York Sun* which were written by Frank Wilkeson, whom Fortune described as "brim full of the milk of human vindictiveness." Among other items which he sought to refute was the assertion that all Negro women were "wenches and strumpets." He pointed out that the laws of the South put a premium upon lewdness by prohibiting lawful marriage. In the South, in the past, white women had "preserved their chastity at the expense of the involuntary corruption of colored women."

19. Ibid., July 28, 1883; January 19, August 9, 1884.
20. Ibid., January 20, 1883.

In reply to the assertion that the Negroes of the South were a "shiftless, thievish, improvident race," he asked who produced the cotton, rice, corn, and tobacco and who did all the work in the homes, on the railroads and steamboats, and on the turpentine farms? The white man did not do it, but he swindled the Negro out of his share, and thus kept him poor and improvident. "Study the labor system," he said, "the account system kept at cross-road groceries, see how these are worked to oppress and defraud one class to enrich another in the South, and then talk about the 'shiftlessness, thievishness, and improvidence of the Negro!' Lastly study the public school system of the South." Negroes had been free only eighteen years. They had emerged from slavery burdened with poverty, illiteracy, "and the nameless vices which are fostered in a state of involuntary servitude." The problem of the southern Negro was a vast one, one which the South alone was incapable of solving. The whole nation was responsible for its existence, and the whole nation should aid in its solution.[21]

In a lengthy report which he prepared at the request of the Senate Committee on Education and Labor, which was headed by Henry W. Blair of New Hampshire, he called for the creation of a special commission to investigate the status of southern Negroes. He called attention to abuses in the administration of justice—the barring of Negroes from juries and the double standard under which a white man who shot a Negro always went free, while a Negro who stole a hog was sent to the chain gang for ten years. Especially he denounced the convict lease system, which, he declared, was not equalled in inhumanity and deliberate fraud outside Siberia. He also presented from personal observation evidence of the inequities of the crop-lien system which victimized many Negro sharecroppers, compelling them to pledge future crops as security in return for credit to buy necessities.

21. Ibid., March 17, 1883.

But he labeled mass illiteracy as the greatest misfortune of southern blacks and cited statistics on the comparative expenditures for schools for whites and Negroes and the number of children of both races enrolled as evidence of the total inadequacy of the existing system. He insisted that the remedy lay in the creation of a federal bureau of education and appropriations by Congress which would be distributed to the states on the basis of the rate of illiteracy.[22]

In answer to critics (like the *New York Herald*) which deplored putting responsibility for education in the hands of a federal agency, Fortune declared:

> It is useless to talk about leaving the matter to the states. *The South will not educate the black child; it does not educate the white child. The two grow up in ignorance and vice and stupidity. And so the whites grow up to lawlessness and the blacks to crime.* . . . When the states virtually abdicate authority, as is the case in the South, the entire network of government is threatened with entanglements horrible to contemplate; and it is the part of wise policy, of judicious statesmanship, to take the matter in hand and work off the impending crisis.[23]

On the subject of education Fortune had an exchange with the editor of the Macon, Georgia, *Telegraph,* who asserted that white people in Georgia would refuse to pay taxes to educate Negroes. Education, he asserted, did not usually serve the purpose of making Negroes into industrious, honest, useful citizens. Instead the Negro who demanded education usually did so, "not as a stepping stone to useful and honorable employment—but that he may reach full social equality with whites." He cited

22. Ibid., September 22, 1883.
23. Ibid., March 1, 1884. Emphasis as in the original. Some white newspapers, among them the *Boston Herald,* supported Fortune's plea for federal aid. The *Herald* spoke of Fortune as an "intelligent colored man" (*Globe,* September 29, 1883).

Fortune as an example of an educated Negro who was exercising a pernicious influence and warned: "Negroes who may be taught their personal and political duties by such as he, will be certain to find a place in the penitentiary, or to meet a fate more summary still." In reply Fortune denied that the Negro sought education in order to achieve social equality. "No colored man that we know of," he said, "desires to force himself upon any white man who does not want his society. What every colored man wants, and what we unhesitatingly and emphatically demand, is, the concession of every right given to the white man under the laws of the United States. . . . Call this social equality if you will."[24]

But while defending the right to pursue education on exactly the same terms as whites, Fortune also emphasized the need for practical, vocational training. The idea of "industrial education," as it was usually called, enjoyed a great vogue in the eighties. In an editorial on "True and False Education," which sounded very much like later utterances of Booker T. Washington, the *Globe* said that the fundamental error in current education was that it was "too intensely theoretical" and did not prepare students for life-work. The result was the development of "a class too superciliously educated" to fit into the society in which they had to live. A system of education which made men unwilling to do farming, carpentry, blacksmithing and other practical and necessary work was a false system. The disposition of Negro youths to make sacrifices to secure higher education was commendable, but the professions for which higher education prepared them were already overcrowded or closed entirely to members of their race.[25]

Along with his uncompromising demands for full civil and political equality, Fortune stressed the importance of economic

24. *Globe*, May 5, May 19, 1883.
25. Ibid., April 7, 1883.

progress in the attainment of equal rights. He frequently asserted that power resided with the group that owned the land—an idea which he may have derived from his interest in Henry George, but which also was consistent with the ideology later expressed by Booker T. Washington. He urged the readers of the *Globe* to acquire homesteads. "A mass of black voters, penniless, soilless and illiterate are absolutely at the mercy of land owners," he declared. Other editorials showed a striking similarity to doctrines identified with Washington in later years. "Let us put more money in the banks. Let us spend less hours in the pursuit of destructive pleasures," the *Globe* urged. "Let us venture to invest more in the business enterprises of the community. Take care of the pennies and the dollars will take care of themselves." Fortune reported that a white journalist had said to him if there were one or two Negro merchants on Broadway and one or two black bankers in Wall Street, sentiment with regard to color would be revolutionized. "The observation was just," he said, "and that there was any justification to it cut us to the quick."[26]

But although appeals to thrift and industry written by Fortune in the eighties sounded like the Washington of the nineties, Fortune espoused, at this period, an economic radicalism which was completely alien to Washington's laudatory approach to capitalism. In editorial after editorial the *Globe* attacked special privilege and the power of monopolies in language which sounded like John Swinton. The *Globe* was especially critical of the protective tariff, which it said victimized the poor, and of land grants to railroads. Congress, it declared, was composed of "blood-sucking men who are handcuffed to the moneyed interests of the country—the interests which thrive by crushing the poor man." "A People's prosperity," said Fortune, "should be measured by the general

26. Ibid., February 17, February 24, August 25, 1883.

diffusion, not the concentration of wealth. And all governments have concentrated wealth by taxing the body of the people in the interest of the few."[27]

To Fortune no subject was entirely sacred. In some respects he was deeply religious and was a member of the African Methodist Episcopal Church, but he was highly critical of conventional religion. He assailed white churches as "arsenals of narrowness, subterfuge and caste." He resented the patronizing attitude of white religious groups toward blacks. "We get a great deal of charity," he remarked, "but most of it tends to our degradation." The religion of the white South was "largely a sham," and he predicted that the number of white Christians who would be snubbed when Gabriel called the roll would "make somebody's head swim." "The white minister who finds it uncomfortable to sit in the church or conference with a colored minister may just as well make up his mind now that God will make no special provisions for him in Heaven on account of his tallow complexion."[28]

Negro journalists with few exceptions agreed that the *Globe* was the most distinguished race paper and Fortune the most brilliant member of their fraternity. W. Calvin Chase might call him the "crank of the colored press," but the *Cincinnati Afro-American* declared that Fortune was "without peer or superior as a colored journalist." If Fortune and Chase were white men, it said, Fortune would be editor of the *New York Times* and Chase would be lucky to enoy a position higher than that of printer's devil. The *People's Advocate*, on which Fortune had worked as a printer, called the success of the *Globe* "phenomenal."

The *Globe* also attracted comment in the white press. Some papers, including the *New York Sun*, the *Boston Herald*, and

27. Ibid., February 24, March 31, 1883.
28. Ibid., June 7, 1884; April 14, 1883.

the *Springfield Republican,* spoke favorably of it. Other white publications regarded the *Globe* and its editor as dangerous, but the fact that papers like the *Macon Telegraph* were critical of Fortune was evidence that his paper was being read. The Sunday *New York World* paid Fortune the compliment of printing an interview with a fictitious Negro named "Martune," who was obviously intended to be a parody on the editor of the *Globe* and which ridiculed his interest in the "culchah of his race." The *Sun* countered by speaking unfavorably of the parody.[29]

Best of all the *Globe* appeared to be in sound financial condition. By 1883 it claimed a circulation of more than 6,000, which was large for a Negro paper. There were four members on the editorial staff, and in the print shop, which did job printing as well as printing the paper, there were seven employees. In May 1883 the size of the *Globe* increased from six to seven columns per page. The editor asserted that income was derived entirely from subscriptions and advertising and that "we owe no man a cent."

Yet less than a year later the rival *New York Progressive American* was hinting that the *Globe* was in serious financial difficulties. This was strongly denied, but in July it was announced that the size of the paper was being reduced to the old six column format. And in November the *Globe* abruptly ceased publication.[30]

It is impossible to unravel all the details which led to the paper's untimely demise, but certainly its political attitude was an important factor. Fortune's militancy on civil rights, his defense of interracial marriages, his economic radicalism might offend some Negroes and horrify some whites, but they stimulated interest in the *Globe.* But his lack of political orthodoxy

29. *Washington Bee,* March 17, 1883; *Cincinnati Afro-American* quoted in *Globe,* October 14, 1884; *People's Advocate,* May 17, 1883; *Globe,* June 30, July 7, 1883.

30. *Globe,* May 5, 1883; July 4, 1884.

and his outspoken attacks on the Republican party and certain of its leaders contributed to a financial debacle.

At the time the *Globe* began publication, Negro voters, with few exceptions, gave unquestioning allegiance to the party of Lincoln, and nearly all Negro newspapers were partisan sheets, subsidized in one way or another by Republicans. But as early as 1872 a few northern Negroes had espoused local Liberal-Democratic coalitions and had followed Charles Sumner in the Liberal Republican movement.

By the time the *Globe* was launched, a small group of older Negro leaders in the North had already defected or were about to defect from the Republican party. While calling themselves "independents," they were ready to cooperate with the Democrats. One of the first was Peter H. Clark, principal of a Negro high school in Cincinnati. More distinguished and more influential probably was George T. Downing of Rhode Island, a successful caterer and restaurateur who had been a close friend of Sumner's. In Pennsylvania, William Still and Robert Purvis, both of whom had been conspicuous in Underground Railroad activities before the Civil War, took the lead in the independent movement which helped to defeat the Republican machine in 1882. In New York, James C. Matthews of Albany was one of the earliest and most influential defectors from Republicanism, while in Boston, James Monroe Trotter, who had fought in the Massachusetts Fifty-Fourth Regiment during the Civil War and had held a political appointment in the post office for years thereafter, left the Republicans in 1883.

Among Fortune's friends and contemporaries John F. Quarles and T. McCants Stewart, both of whom had been active Republicans, were identified with the independent movement.[31]

The *Globe* was listed as an "independent" paper. In an advertisement it proclaimed: "We do not advocate any man or

31. Meier, *Negro Thought*, pp. 28–30; *Washington Bee*, February 10, February 17, 1883; *Globe*, August 4, 1883.

any party. . . . To properly defend a people's interest, a newspaper at this juncture should be non-partisan."[32] Although he was himself never an important figure in politics, through his editorials and speeches Fortune indicted the Republican party and its leaders for their betrayal of the Negro and developed an ideological basis for political independence and a division of the Negro vote. To him, breaking away from blind loyalty to Republicanism was a step in the maturation of black people and in their assimilation into the mainstream of American life. In the face of the extreme partisanship of most Negro leaders and especially of the Negro press, his course required courage, even audacity. It put him in opposition to the most powerful men of his race, especially the venerable Frederick Douglass, for whom he had not only respect but personal affection.

In a speech, "The Colored Man as An Independent Force in Politics," before a meeting of the Colored Press Association in Washington in June 1882, he presented a plea with cogency and restraint. He urged that for Negroes political strength lay in diversity rather than unity. He also asserted that the interests of Negroes and whites were basically identical. He pointed out that most Negroes lived in the South and that it was in the South that "the problem of their future usefulness as American citizens must have full and satisfactory, or disastrous and disheartening demonstration." The Republican party had forgotten the principles of Lincoln and Sumner and had abandoned southern Negroes and shown itself powerless to protect them in the exercise of their political rights. For these reasons he did not "deem it binding upon colored men further to support the Republican party when other more advantageous affiliations" could be formed. While castigating Bourbon Democracy as a "curse" and

32. *Globe*, January 27, 1883. An editorial in *Rumor* in 1880 had declared that in order to develop power and to make necessary progress, Negroes must "cut loose from the galling thralldom of party rule" (Quoted *People's Advocate*, December 11, 1880).

declaring that no Negro could ever be a Bourbon Democrat, Fortune said he could be "an independent, a progressive Democrat."

"The Independent colored man, like the Independent white man, is an American citizen who does his own thinking," he said. The preservation of liberties and consummation of citizenship of Negroes could be attained only by "imbibing all that is American, entering into the life and spirit of our institutions, . . . feeling the full force of the fact that while we are classed as Africans, just as the Germans are classed Germans, we are in all things American citizens, American freemen." "To preach the independence of the colored man," he emphasized, was "to preach his Americanization." Negroes had tried political unanimity and it had failed. Now it was time for them to do their own thinking. "The color of their skin must cease to be an index to their political creed." Negroes and whites were destined to live side by side in the South. Therefore Negroes should try to "hasten the day when politics shall cease to be the shibboleth that creates perpetual warfare." Instead of paying so much attention to national party labels and national politics, Negroes would do well to interest themselves in local questions and vote for the candidate and party which would best serve them and their race at that level. "Let there be no aim of solidifying the colored vote," he warned, because "the massing of black means the massing of white by contrast." He predicted: "When the colored voters differ among themselves and are found to be on *both sides* of local political contests, they will begin to find themselves of some political importance, and their votes will be sought, cast, and *counted*."[33]

Fortune expressed doubts as to whether southern Democrats were capable of cooperating with Negroes even though Negro

33. T. Thomas Fortune, *Black and White: Land, Labor and Politics in the South* (New York, 1884), pp. 115, 118–19, 126–27, 129–30. Emphasis as in original.

disenchantment with the Republicans offered them a rare opportunity. In an editorial in which he labeled the Democrats the "party of stupidity" which "learns nothing and forgets nothing," he said that to succeed in recruiting black votes Democrats must be prepared to give Negroes a fair share of offices, admit them to juries, devise an honest penitentiary system, pay more attention to their education needs, and abolish proscription on common carriers and in hotels. "We hardly believe," he observed, "there is any Democrat in the South whose mind is broad enough to concede one half of our demand, though it is grounded in justice."[34]

But his sharpest attacks were directed at Republicans whom he repeatedly assailed for betraying their black supporters. In 1876 he said, in order to put the "prating, vainglorious, nerveless" Hayes into the White House, "the Republican party sacrificed the black vote of the South. . . . It cut itself loose from the issues on which the war was fought and won." In the North, Fortune averred, the Republican party had always considered itself a "white thing," although not openly proclaiming the fact. And by the 1880s even in the South a "white Republican" movement was developing. Its leaders were saying that Negroes had proved themselves incapable of intelligent participation in politics and that the Republican party could not succeed until it had "thrown off the incubus of Negro leadership."

Republicans were also blamed for the erosion of Negroes' constitutional rights because the Supreme Court was dominated by members of the party. After the decision in the Civil Rights Cases in 1883, the *Globe* declared:

> The Republican party has certainly tried the faith of the colored man. It has gradually stripped him of all the rights which had been given him for his valor in the field and his patriotism in time of peace. We maintain that the Republican party has made an infamous use of the power which our

34. *Globe*, March 17, 1884.

votes aided to bestow upon us; we maintain that it has betrayed us at every point, and that it stands today denuded
of its successful hypocrisy, a mean, cunning, treacherous
organization.[35]

At a meeting of the Bethel Literary and Historical Society
of Brooklyn, at which the topic of discussion was "That we
owe no party a debt of gratitude," he denied that Lincoln had
issued the Emancipation Proclamation out of humanitarian motives but had been forced to do so by military exigencies. He
reiterated this in numerous editorials and also declared that the
Fourteenth and Fifteenth Amendments had been adopted
largely out of political expediency. "These amendments," he
asserted, "have always been as distasteful to the Republican
party as to the Democratic party." Republicans had consistently
used the Negro for their own ends, and during the Grant administration, when the federal government was entirely controlled by them, they had not made a sincere effort to punish
southern whites who were guilty of outrages.[36]

In 1883 Fortune and John F. Quarles participated in an effort
to organize Negro Republican workers in New York City into
an "independent" movement with the purpose of exerting pressure on the Republican organization for greater recognition.
Fortune also endorsed the idea of a national Negro convention
which was called as the result of mounting dissatisfaction with
the Arthur administration. But he opposed holding the meeting
in Washington, where it would be dominated by officeholders.
The *Globe* advised against endorsing Arthur or anyone else for
the presidency. Fortune took an active part in the convention
which met in Louisville in October. Even Frederick Douglass,
who served as permanent chairman, made concessions to the

35. Ibid., October 20, October 27, 1883; April 12, 1884.
36. Ibid., March 17, 1883; March 28, 1884. In a long letter to the
New York Times, reprinted in the *Globe*, August 18, 1883, Fortune
summarized the Republican record and reasons for Negro dissatisfaction with the party.

"independents" in his address. "If the Republican party cannot stand a demand for justice and fair play it ought to go down," he declared. Resolutions which were introduced endorsing the Republican party were referred to a committee but never voted on, and a resolution endorsing the Arthur administration was tabled. However, in a letter to the press after the convention, Douglass made it clear that if he was to be classed as an "independent" it was an independent in the Republican party. "I can have all the independence I want inside of the Republican party," he said. "My advice to colored men everywhere is to stick to the Republican Party." As Fortune had already observed, Douglass was too old to change his politics. His partisanship was "bone of his bone and flesh of his flesh," and nothing could shake it.[37]

As the political campaign of 1884 approached, Fortune himself appeared to be following a course which was erratic and inconsistent. In December 1883 he was guest of honor at a reception in Boston which was sponsored by the Sumner National Independents, a group which indicated that it might support Democratic candidates. In January some of the leading Negro Republicans in Washington, including former Senator Blanche K. Bruce, gave a dinner in his honor, which was interpreted in some quarters as an effort by officeholders to woo Fortune and insure that the *Globe* would support the Republicans in the coming election. But an editorial in February declared: "We are not the subsidized champion of the Democratic hag or the Republican nightmare." From among the Republican presidential aspirants, Fortune expressed a preference for John A. Logan to James G. Blaine. But he strongly opposed the endorsement of any Republican candidate by a Negro convention which met in Pittsburgh in May.[38]

37. *Globe*, April 7, May 12, June 2, August 18, September 1, September 8, September 29, October 20, 1883.

38. Ibid., December 29, 1883; January 12, January 19, February

After Blaine was nominated, the *Globe* gave him rather grudging endorsement. "Mr. Blaine," it said, "for many reasons, is objectionable to us. We have not admired his style of statesmanship, nor have we been unmoved by the many charges brought against his methods to put money in his purse." But as a member of Congress Blaine had been a consistent friend of the Negro. "There are many weak elements in Mr. Blaine's record —and who of us is perfect?—but we candidly believe that these weaknesses have been unduly magnified." The *Globe* branded the conduct of independent Republicans who refused to support Blaine as "babyish." But the same issue in which the editorial appeared contained a news story of a meeting of Negro voters in Brooklyn at which Fortune had prevented the adoption of a resolution endorsing Blaine's nomination. The *New York World* predicted that Fortune intended to support the Democratic nominee. This he denied, stating categorically: *"I shall not support the nominees of the Democratic Party as against Blaine and Logan."* But he added that the nomination of Blaine was not the best that could have been made, and that he felt free to say so.[39]

After the Democrats nominated Cleveland and Hendricks, the *Globe* spoke of Cleveland as a weak candidate who had antagonized powerful groups while serving as governor of New York and who had had no experience in national affairs. Hendricks it described as "a bigoted Democrat of the ancient school" and pliant tool of the Southern Democracy. "Until the Democratic party is rejuvenated in fact, until the solid South ceases to stand for all that is vile and infamous in republican govern-

---

9, May 3, May 10, 1884. The *Washington Bee*, which equated Fortune's independence with sheer inconsistency, praised Fortune for endorsing Logan, but warned that he might change his mind and endorse Jefferson Davis the next week (*Washington Bee*, January 19, 1884).

39. *Globe*, June 14, June 21, 1884. Emphasis as in original.

ment," said the *Globe*, Negroes would vote for Republicans at the national level.[40]

Later in the campaign Fortune wrote a letter to the *New York Herald* (which it failed to print) in which he accused that paper of fomenting race feeling by emphasizing that the Negro vote would be solidly for Blaine, apparently with the hope that this would win white votes for Cleveland. It was not surprising, said Fortune, that Negro voters were Republicans since whatever rights they possessed had been obtained from Republicans. The record of the national Democratic party was nothing but a record of oppression so far as Negroes were concerned. In the present campaign, he said, he could discover no issues except the personal character of the candidates and the spoils of office. But the party of Blaine had been "more of a friend of good government and the race with which I am identified than the party for which Mr. Cleveland stands," and therefore he would vote for Blaine, and his feelings were probably identical with those of most Negro voters.[41]

In spite of his public and repeated, if unenthusiastic, statements in support of Blaine, rumors that Fortune was in reality supporting the Democratic party and was in their pay persisted. It appears that behind the scenes the editor was engaged in a struggle with his partners. George Parker, who like Fortune, owned a fourth interest in the *Globe* and was listed as publisher, wished the paper to be avowedly Republican.

In August a reorganization of the *Globe* was announced. The Reverend William B. Derrick, an active Republican with whom Fortune had previously feuded, was reported to have purchased Parker's interest in the paper. In the columns of the *West Indian Abroad*, a Negro paper which had sprung up during the campaign and which Derrick controlled, it was reported

40. Ibid., July 19, August 9, 1884.
41. Ibid., September 13, 1884.

that he had acquired a controlling interest in the *Globe* and that henceforth it would be a Republican paper. But Fortune hotly denied this and said that as long as he was editor he would determine the editorial policy. Faced with failure to receive much needed financial support from the Republican sources, he asserted that the paper had always been "Republican in sentiment" but that he had had "the nerve to arraign his party for its falsehoods and corruption and its *base desertion of the Black Republicans of the South.*" At that very moment, he added, the party "treats with contempt the black vote of this country, proceeding upon the assumption that the black men are loyal to the party and cannot be alienated from it." The editor of the *Globe*, he asserted defiantly, could not be coerced into retracting the truths which he had spoken "by any bull of excommunication which the National Republican Committee may hurl at him." Nor, he added, was he interested in any public office which Blaine might offer him. He would prefer "to edit a paper on bread and water in defense of the rights of his race than be bribed into silence."[42]

The *Washington Bee* reported gleefully that the Republican organization had repudiated Fortune and would deal only with Derrick, who was the real "proprietor" of the paper. "We pity you, Bro. Fortune," it said, "but chickens always come home to rest." The National Republican Committee, added the *Bee*, had taught Fortune a lesson.

The last issue of the *Globe* appeared on November 8. Fortune returned to the office one night to find that the presses and other property had been removed. The details are not entirely clear, but according to Fortune's account, when Derrick had been admitted to partnership, he had, without Fortune's knowledge, given George Parker some sort of mortgage on the *Globe* property. Immediately after the election, Parker's attorneys

42. Ibid., August 16, September 13, 1884. Emphasis as in orignal.

foreclosed. Fortune insisted that the proceedings were irregular, but he did not fight them in court.[43]

In three short years the *Globe* had won national recognition and its editor had gained the reputation of the most brilliant, fearless, and uncompromising journalist of his race. The *Washington Bee* attributed the untimely demise of the *Globe* to "the fatal malady of too much independence." But out of the ashes of the *Globe* came the *Freeman*, a paper of which Fortune was sole owner, which continued the independent, uncompromising policies of its predecessor.

43. *Washington Bee*, September 20, October 4, November 15, 1884; *Freeman*, November 22, 1884.

III

"Freeman" Editor and Political Independent

DURING THE MONTHS WHEN THE *Globe* WAS TOTTERING ON the brink of financial collapse and Fortune·was feuding with George Parker and the Reverend Derrick in particular and Republicans in general, he was also engaged in writing *Black and White: Land, Labor and Politics in the South*, a book of some 250 pages. James Weldon Johnson, a Florida lad recently moved to New York who had known Fortune in Jacksonville, recalled in his autobiography seeing Fortune at work on the book. Young Johnson was a playmate of children who lived in a house in the Williamsburg district of Brooklyn which Fortune shared. Sometimes the youngsters would see him as he "sat at a desk writing, covering sheet after sheet that he dropped on the floor, and all the while running his fingers through his long hair." The children were usually playing parchesi on the floor, and when they annoyed the writer too much he chased them away, but they stood in no awe of him.[1]

The book appeared a few weeks before the demise of the *Globe*, and attracted some comment. Bruce Grit declared that in the book Fortune, whom he called *"the most prominent and brilliant young Negro in America,"* handled his subject in "that terse vigorous and manly style characteristic of one who has no foes to fear or friends to reward, and what is really remarkable he tells the thing just as it is. Stranger,—you ought to get Black and White and read it carefully." The *Nation*, which reviewed Fortune's book jointly with Albion Tourgée's *Fool's Errand*, commented on the similarity between Fortune's views on land and labor and the views of Henry George. It also quoted at length and with approbation his advocacy of political independence of Negroes. The *Springfield Republican* printed a lengthy and favorable review. Fortune, it said, "speaks his mind very freely, sometimes bitterly and defiantly. He gives notice that the Negro is here to stay—an American not an African, and an American citizen who is biding his time and intends to be counted."[2]

The book gives the impression of having been written in haste by an angry but reasonable young man. Parts of it were obviously based on Fortune's testimony before the Blair committee and some of his speeches and newspaper articles. Two distinct and somewhat contradictory threads run through the book. One is race and the race problem—and the parts of the book dealing with these subjects are pure Fortune, and Fortune at his best. The chapters on economics bear a strong resemblance to Henry George and John Swinton and are buttressed

1. James Weldon Johnson, *Along this Way: The Autobiography of James Weldon Johnson* (New York, 1933), p. 48.

2. *Washington Grit*, September 20, 1884, emphasis in original; *Nation*, no. 1013, November 27, 1884, pp. 462–63; *Springfield Republican*, quoted in *Freeman*, December 20, 1884.

by lengthy quotations from such books as William Goodwin Moody's *Land and Labor in the United States.*

In the first chapter, entitled "Black," the author assailed the distorted picture of Negroes and Negro history in books written by white men.

> The books which have been written in this country—the books which have molded and controlled public opinion—during the past one hundred and fifty years have been written by white men, in justification of the white man's domineering selfishness, cruelty, and tyranny. The white man's story has been told over and over again, until the reader actually tires of the monotonous repetition. . . . The honest reader has longed in vain for a glimpse at the other side of the picture so studiously turned to the wall.
>
> Even in books written expressly to picture the black man's side of the story, the author has been compelled to palliate . . . the ferocity and insatiate lust and greed of his race. He has been unable to tell the story as it was, because his nature, his love of race, his inborn prejudices and narrowness made him a lurking coward.[3]

The treatment of Negroes—and Indians—by the white press was equally distorted, said Fortune:

> The Negro and the Indian, the footballs of slippery politicians and the helpless victims of sharpers and thieves, are wantonly misrepresented—held up to the eyes of the world as being incapable of imbibing the distorted civilization in the midst of which they live and have their being. They are placed in the attic, only to be aired when somebody wants an "issue" or an "appropriation."[4]

In the chapter entitled "White" and subsequent chapters Fortune said some bitter things about the white race and the

3. T. Thomas Fortune, *Black and White: Land, Labor and Politics in the South* (New York, 1884), pp. 11–12.

4. Ibid., pp. 13–14.

Constitution and government of the United States. "Under our government," he said, "all the peoples of the world find shelter and protection—save the African . . . and the industrious China-man. . . . That great document [the Constitution], while con-stantly affirmed to be the most broad and liberal compact ever devised for the government of man . . . cannot shield a black man, a citizen . . . in any common, civil or political right which usually attaches to citizenship." Civil War, Emancipation, and Reconstruction had failed to "decide the rights of States, or the measure of protection which the National Government owes to the individual members of the States." In the South the spirit of Hayne and Calhoun was still alive. It had been absurd for the formulators of Reconstruction policy to expect the master class to accept the political equality of the former slave or to expect the freedmen to be able to bear successfully the responsibili-ties suddenly thrust upon them. Reconstruction policy was arraigned as "one of the hollowest pieces of perfidy ever per-petrated upon an innocent, helpless people," and the Republican party was arraigned "for base ingratitude, subterfuge and hy-pocrisy to its black partisan allies."[5]

Again and again Fortune assailed the impotence of the fed-eral government. When black men appealed to the Supreme Court, they were told to go to the state authorities, which was absurd since they would not have appealed to the one had the other given them the protection to which their citizenship en-titled them. "Practically," he declared, "there is no law in the United States which extends its protective arm over the black man and his rights." Again:

What shall we say of that government which has not the power or inclination to insure the exercise of those solemn rights and immunities which it guarantees? To declare a man free, and equal with his fellow, and then to refrain from en-acting laws powerful to insure him in such freedom and

5. Ibid., pp. 18–19, 25–26, 97–99.

equality, is to trifle with the most sacred of all the functions of sovereignty. Have not the United States done this very thing?[6]

But Fortune emphasized that he and fellow Negroes were *Americans.* "As an American citizen," he declared, "I feel it born in my nature to share in the fullest measure all that is American. I sympathize in all the hopes, aspirations and fruitions of my country. . . . In a word, I am an American citizen. I have a heritage in each and every provision incorporated in the Constitution of my country." He rejected and ridiculed proposals of expatriation to Africa, declaring:

The colored man is in the South to stay there. He will not leave it voluntarily and he cannot be driven out. He had no voice in being carried into the South, but he will have a very loud voice in any attempt to put him out. . . . The talk about the black people being brought to this country to prepare themselves to evangelize Africa is so much religious nonsense boiled down to a sycophantic platitude. . . . The Colonization society has spent mints of money and tons of human blood in the selfish attempt to plant an Anglo-African colony on the West Coast of Africa. The money has been thrown away and human lives have been sacrificed in vain. The black people of this country are Americans, not Africans; and any wholesale expatriation of them is out of the question.[7]

In *Black and White* Fortune emphasized the need for education of black Americans and the obligation of white Americans to fill this need. He maintained that "the people of this Nation who enslaved the black man, who robbed him of more than a hundred years of toil, who perverted his moral nature, and all but extinguished in him the Divine spark of intelligence, are morally bound to do all that is in their power to build up his shattered manhood, to put him on his feet, as it were, to fit him

6. Ibid., pp. 28–29, 32.
7. Ibid., pp. 121–22, 143.

[73]

to enjoy the freedom thrust upon him so unceremoniously." He spoke scathingly of the unwillingness of white Southerners to pay taxes to support schools. "They think it a sounder principle, of government," he observed, "to equip and maintain vast penal systems—with chain gangs, schools of crime, depravity and death than to support schools and churches." School teachers were paid twenty-five dollars a month for three months a year, prison guards fifty dollars a month for a twelve month year. He also spoke of the absurdity of the separate school system. Although the South was as poor as "Job's turkey," she supported the dual system to gratify prejudice. And the bills which had been introduced into Congress by Northerners for federal aid to education did not propose to interfere with the dual system —"thereby, in effect, giving the national assent to a system repugnant to the genius of the Constitution."[8]

While expressing gratitude for the humanitarianism of northern whites during Reconstruction, Fortune spoke satirically of some of the efforts of white missionaries and philanthropists. In some respects they had done incalculable injury to the black man. "Indeed," he said, "there have been times when I have seriously debated the question, whether the black man had any manhood left, after the missionaries and religious enthusiasts had done picturing, or rather, caricaturing his debased mental and moral condition." The misrepresentations in which missionaries indulged in order to raise money in his behalf had the effect of spreading "broadcast over the land a feeling of contempt for him as a man and pity for his lowly and unfortunate conditions; so that throughout the North a business man would much rather *give a thousand dollars* to aid in the education of the black heathen than to give a black scholar and gentleman an opportunity honestly to *earn a hundred dollars*."[9]

Partly as the result of misguided philanthropy there existed

8. Ibid., pp. 63, 71, 76.
9. Ibid., pp. 66, 79. Emphasis as in original.

in the South too many "colleges" financed out of private charity instead of common schools maintained by taxes. Fortune questioned the multiplication of these institutions for the "higher education of colored youth." Were theology and the classics, he asked, the studies best suited to and most needed by a people most of whom lacked rudimentary elementary education and whose "immediate aim must be that of the mechanic and farmer?" Any education was "false," he insisted, which was not suited to the conditions and the prospects of the student. He said:

> I do not inveigh against higher education. I simply maintain that the sort of education the colored people of the South stand most in need of is *elementary and industrial.* They should be instructed for the work to be done. Many a colored farmer boy or mechanic has been spoiled to make a foppish gambler or loafer, a swaggering pedagogue or a cranky homiletician. Men may be spoiled by education, even as they are spoiled by illiteracy.

Advocacy of practical training for the rank and file did not rule out higher education for those with capacity to benefit from it. "Genius will take care of itself. . . . It is therefore that I plead, that the masses of the colored race should receive such preparation for the fierce competition of every day life that the odds shall not be against them."[10]

In discussing economic conditions Fortune assailed the concentration of wealth and the tyranny of capital. He sought to

10. Ibid., pp. 81–82, 85. Emphasis as in original. Advocacy of industrial education enjoyed a great vogue among Negro spokesmen in the 1880s. Fortune's views were influenced by T. McCants Stewart, who had returned from Liberia to make a study of the system of education at Hampton Institute (Ibid., pp. 87–90). The comments of Fortune quoted above bear a strong resemblance to statements in the writings and speeches of Booker T. Washington which appeared subsequently to Fortune's book.

demonstrate. he said, that *"the condition of the black and white laborer is the same, and that consequently their cause is common."* At the same time he spoke disparagingly of the poor whites of the South. The Ku Klux Klan had been largely recruited from "this idle, vicious, ignorant class." He added:

> It is safe to say, that the peasantry of no country claiming to be civilized stands more in need of the labors of the schoolmaster and preacher, than the so-called "poor white trash" of the South. On their account, if no other, I am an advocate of a compulsory system of education, a National Board of Education, and a very large National appropriation for common school and industrial education.[11]

In contrast, the blacks, whose intelligence and morality had been hampered by two hundred years of slavery and who had been turned loose upon the land after Emancipation without a dollar in their hands, had made immense progress in less than a generation. The great hope of the blacks, he said, lay in acquiring land. "For the man who owns the soil largely owns and dictates to the men who are compelled to live upon it and derive their subsistence from it." He predicted that in the future, landlords and capitalists of the South would not be confined to the white race.[12]

Considering the condition of the freedmen at Emancipation, it was surprising that "the race did not turn robbers and highwaymen, and in turn, terrorize and rob society as society had for so long terrorized and robbed them." Instead black men *went manfully to work* to better their own condition and repair the ravages of war. On the other hand:

> *the white men of the South, the capitalists, the land sharks, the poor white trash, and the nondescripts, with a thousand years of Christian civilization and culture behind them, . . .*

11. Ibid., pp. 174, 200, 201. Emphasis as in original.
12. Ibid., p. 207.

these white scamps, who had imposed upon the world that
they were paragons of virtue and the heaven-sent viceregents
of civil power, organized themselves into a band of outlaws,
whose concatenative [sic] chain of auxiliaries ran throughout
the entire South, and deliberately proceeded to murder inno-
cent men and women for POLITICAL REASONS and to
systematically rob them of their honest labor because they
were too accursedly lazy to labor themselves.[13]

On the question of the future and the manner in which the
problems with which he dealt would be resolved, Fortune displayed a certain ambivalence. At times he appeared to foresee
racial harmony, at others bloody revolution, but whether the
revolution would be one of races or classes was not clear.

On the subject of politics he included as one chapter in the
book the address on the political independence of the Negro
which he had delivered before the Colored Press Association.
He advised Negroes to think for themselves, to abandon their
blind loyalty to the Republican party, to recognize that blacks
and whites had common interests in the South, and to use their
"voting power in independent local affairs with some discrimination more reasonable than an obstinate clinging to a party
name." In turn whites must show "colored men that they accept
the Constitution as amended, and are earnestly solicitous that
they should prosper in the world and become useful and respected citizens." He admonished the white South to spend less
money on penitentiaries and more on schools, to "use less
powder and buckshot and more law and equity." He predicted:
"Time and education will give proper adjustment to the politics
of the South." But elsewhere he said that denial of constitutional
rights and violations of the rights of citizenship would breed
revolution. "The white man having asserted his superiority in
the matters of assassination and robbery, has settled down upon

13. Ibid., pp. 239–40. Emphasis as in original.

a barrel of dynamite, as he did in the days of slavery, and will await the explosion with the same fatuity and self-satisfaction true of him in other days."[14]

But he seemed to say that the problems of the South were fundamentally economic rather than racial and political. The "so-called 'war of races' " would pass away as the Negro made economic progress.

> When the lowly condition of the black man has passed away; when he becomes a capable president of banks. . . ; when he has successfully metamorphosed the condition which attaches to him as a badge of slavery and degradation, and made a reputation for himself as a financier . . . his color will be swallowed up in his reputation, his bank-account and his important money interests.[15]

In conclusion he asserted that the future struggle in the South would be "not between white men and black men, but between capital and labor, landlord and tenant." Basically the problems of the South were the same as those of the rest of the country. In a reversion to the Henry George theme he declared:

> The hour is approaching when the laboring classes of our country, North, East, West and South, will recognize that they have a *common cause*, a *common humanity* and a *common enemy*. . . . When the issue is properly joined, the rich, be they black or be they white, will be found on the same side; and the poor, be they black or be they white, will be found on the same side.[16]

The *Globe* ceased publication on November 8, 1884. Two weeks later the first issue of the *Freeman* appeared, with Fortune

14. Ibid., pp. 129, 145–46, 176, 234, 240.

15. Ibid., pp. 180–81. Fortune's predictions that economic progress by Negroes would lead to the elimination of race prejudice—especially the paragraph quoted above—sound very much like later statements of Booker T. Washington.

16. Ibid., p. 242. Emphasis as in original.

as sole proprietor and editor, and chief printer as well. In speaking of the demise of the former paper he said:

> "The Globe is dead! Long live
> THE FREEMAN!"

As editor of the new paper, he declared he would continue "the battle for justice and fair play for the race," and that he would be "the plastic tool of no man or party." "I am my own master," he proclaimed. The paper began publication simply as the *Freeman*, but in less than a month had become the *New York Freeman*.[17]

How Fortune managed to assume the financial burden of launching the paper and avoid the responsibility for some of the debts incurred by the defunct *Globe* is not entirely clear. At least one law suit was brought against him, by a former reporter for the *Globe*, for payment of $600, but the jury rendered an unconditional verdict in favor of Fortune. The costs of publishing a four page weekly were relatively modest. Fortune estimated his expenditures at about $7,000 a year. But from the outset the *Freeman* (and Fortune) were in financial difficulties. In a plaintive editorial early in 1885 he commented on the lot of the Negro editor. Of the more than 100 race papers, he said he doubted that as many as three were financial successes. Some of them survived, but they paid no dividends. He complained:

> The editors cannot afford the luxury of New Year's turkey, and their children seldom have any stocking to hang up to invite the generosity of Santa Claus, and their wives cannot rusticate at Long Beach or Atlantic City, during the sultry days of July. If they get any fresh air it is such as finds its way into the third story window of their tenement house homes. . . . [The editor's] days are spent in anxious expectation of subscriptions which never come and dodging creditors who always dog his footsteps.

17. *Freeman*, November 23, December 13, 1884.

He declared: "I say candidly, I need money," and pleaded with persons who owed him money (including delinquent subscribers) to pay him. At the end of the first year the *Freeman* was holding its own and had a circulation of about 5,000, but subscriptions had not increased as much as he had hoped. Part of the deficits which were incurred in publishing the paper were offset by a job printing business which was run in connection with it.[18]

In starting the new paper, Fortune had emphasized that it was published for Negroes, that it spent money in the Negro community, that all its employees were Negroes, and that therefore it deserved the financial support of the black community. But at the beginning of 1886 he announced that he had entered into an arrangement with two white men (whose identities he did not disclose) to give him financial backing for his printing business while leaving him complete freedom in management of the *Freeman*. When another Negro paper commented that because of his dependence on white money the name of the *Freeman* should be changed to "The Bondsman," Fortune replied that for five years, while seeking to publish a race paper, he had been compelled repeatedly to borrow from white men because Negroes did not support him and because he received no subsidy from a political party.[19]

But in spite of financial difficulties (which were chronic and endemic in Negro journalism) the *Freeman* claimed to have a stronger staff of correspondents than any other race paper. It regularly carried dispatches from several places in the South and the major cities in the North. Its readers were entertained by a humorous column by Bruce Grit, and in 1885 Mrs. N. F.

18. Ibid., January 17, April 4, June 10, November 21, 1885. Fortune was represented in the law suit by Louis P. Post, who was closely associated with John Swinton.

19. Ibid., January 10, 1885; January 2, January 16, 1886.

Mossell of Philadelphia, a strong advocate of women's rights, began to edit a women's department. Reviews of books (usually on subjects in which Fortune had an especial interest) and reviews of articles from the leading magazines appeared frequently.

As in the case of the *Globe* the reputation of the *Freeman* rested principally on its editorials. With Fortune as editor-in-chief, the editorial page reflected his views and was written in part by him, but Jerome Peterson, who had been associated with the *Globe*, and T. McCants Stewart, Fortune's closest friend, also contributed. Some of the editorials reflected Fortune's current interest in economics and socialism and his admiration for such radicals as Henry George and John Swinton. He advocated a "reasonable but iron-clad tax" on incomes above $5,000. As in *Black and White* he frequently expressed concern over the exploitation of labor by capital and predicted that "a more equitable distribution of the net results of labor" was inevitable.[20]

During 1886, a year of labor unrest, he watched with interest the growth of the Knights of Labor, especially their overtures to black workers. He vigorously criticized Negro papers which urged black workers to act as strikebreakers. He said:

> We lay it down dogmatically that the colored laborers cannot afford to antagonize the interests of white laborers, for the interests of the one and the other are identical in every particular. . . . We must not get on the wrong side of this labor fight, just now begun in earnest. . . . The black man who arrays himself on the side of capitalism as against labor would be like a black man before the war taking sides with the pro-slavery as against the anti-slavery advocates.

On this point Fortune differed from many members of his race,

20. Ibid., January 16, May 8, 1886; January 8, 1887.

[81]

including Stewart, who urged Negroes to take advantage of strikes by white unions to benefit themselves.[21] But he and Stewart (both of whom were moving in the direction of an alliance with the Democrats) strongly opposed the protective tariff.

Fortune's understanding of economics was not profound, and his interest in radicalism temporary. The question of most intense and lasting concern, and the one which evoked the best use of his talents, was always racial justice. By the mid-eighties the consequences of the Compromise of 1877 were plain for all to see, and Fortune devoted much space to scathing denunciation of whites, North and South, who were responsible. A favorite target was Henry W. Grady of the *Atlanta Constitution*, arch-prophet of the New South and darling of northern businessmen. When Grady came north to address the New England Club at Delmonico's on December 22, 1886, Fortune commented: "It takes a very small amount of Southern taffy, judiciously distributed, to fire the enthusiasm of the North. . . . Mr. Grady spoke on 'The New South.' He should have called his speech 'The White South.'" Earlier Fortune had refuted paragraph by paragraph Grady's article, "In Plain Black and White," which was published in *Century Magazine* as a reply to George W. Cable's "Freedman's Case in Equity," which had been published in the same journal.

Grady's assertion that the course of instruction given in Negro schools in the South was as thorough and the school term as long as that in white schools was labeled by the *Freeman* as a "bold and unscrupulous attempt to impose upon the credulity and ignorance of the American people." And Grady's contention that travel accommodations for members of both races were equal was declared an "unqualified falsehood." To the assertion that blacks preferred their own separate churches, Fortune replied: "They would be fools not to," pointing out

21. Ibid., May 1, May 22, 1886.

that when Dwight L. Moody had carried his "religious menagerie" to Richmond and Washington, black men had been confined to the galleries. Such practices made religion appear more a "parody" than anything else. "If the religion of the blacks is largely innoculated with illiteracy and superstition," he said, "that of the whites is no less so with cant, hypocrisy, and snobbery and we doubt if God has more toleration for one than the other."[22]

Fortune dissected Grady's statements further in an article entitled, "Civil Rights and Social Privileges," in the *A.M.E. Church Review* in January 1886. Grady had insisted that "the South must be allowed to settle the social relations of the races according to her own views of what is right and best," that her very existence depended upon this, and that this implied "the clear and unmistakable domination of the white race." This, he said, was simply the "assertion of the right of character, intelligence and property to rule." This, retorted Fortune, was an effort by Grady to confuse two things which were quite distinct for "the very obvious purpose of giving a bare semblance of rationality for the absurd prejudices he rushed forward to champion." "Civil rights," said Fortune, "are all such as affect the whole people, and are regulated by them in their collective capacity as a government. Social privileges, on the contrary, are regulated wholly by individual tastes and inclinations, and are in no sense subject to the cognizance or supervision of government." Negroes could win social privileges only through economic and intellectual progress. To Grady's appeal to the North to leave the race question to "us" and that "we" will settle it, Fortune replied:

> So *we* will; but the *we* Mr. Grady had "in his mind's eye" will not be permitted to settle it alone. Not by any means, Mr. Grady. Not only the white *we*, but the colored *we* as well, will demand a share in that settlement. . . . We protest

22. Ibid., January 1, 1887; April 11, 1885.

against the current treatment of this momentous question by which we are completely counted out, or regarded as other than passive or acquiescent factors. Unlike in times past, *we have a voice; and we propose to make that voice heard*, in all future phases of the discussion of the race question.[23]

Another object of Fortune's wrath was the white liberal "mugwump" who acquiesced in turning the solution of the "southern problem" over to southern whites. He denounced "The New South," a pamphlet published by Carl Schurz after a visit to the former Confederate States in 1885. It was an apology for the "White South," he said, which epitomized the "Let the South alone" attitude of the mugwumps. "The 'Black South' only comes in incidentally," he complained, "as a chicken thief, an ignoramus, a fellow indisposed to work (however small the wages or to what extent he is robbed of them), and a political nuisance, which must be ruled by wealth and intelligence because he cannot rule himself." Many northern papers, including the *New York Times*, said Fortune, made

a speciality of showing up the worthlessness and hopelessness of the Negro character. The prime object, of course, is to show that the whites of the South . . . are the natural and proper rulers; and that majorities, constitutional guarantees, inherent fundamental manhood rights, if these be claimed by black men, don't amount to a ginger-snap. Fraternity of North and South, in the interest of commerce and good government (based upon usurpation and maintained by tyrannical practices), must be fostered by all means.[24]

Fortune also differed sharply with those northern whites who urged implementation of the second section of the Four-

23. Henry W. Grady, "In Plain Black and White," *Century Magazine*, n.s. 8 (November, 1884–April, 1885): 916–17; T. Thomas Fortune, "Civil Rights and Social Privileges," *A.M.E. Church Review*, January, 1886, pp. 125–27, 131. Emphasis as in original.

24. *Freeman*, June 13, 1885.

teenth Amendment which provided for the reduction of representation in Congress for states which denied the right to vote to Negro citizens. After his defeat in his bid for the presidency in 1884, James G. Blaine had said that reduction of representation would "at least establish the equality of white men under the National Government, and . . . give to northern men who fought to preserve the Union, as large a voice in its Government as may be exercised by the Southern men who fought to destroy the Union." Frederick Douglass praised Blaine's speech and said it should be made the keynote for the Republican campaign in 1888. But Fortune dissented. The stand of Blaine and Douglass, he argued, amounted to acquiescence in disfranchisement. It meant that if Negroes were denied the right to vote, the federal government, which had already demonstrated its inability to enforce the right to vote, had "the right to disfranchise the voters so denied their rights explicitly guaranteed in the Constitution." Instead, said Fortune, "we want a man, a Supreme Court, and a party which will enforce the Constitution as amended, instead of curtailing, denying or subverting the rights conferred upon us by the Constitution."[25]

As sole owner of the *Freeman* Fortune was entirely free, as he had not been as editor of the *Globe*, to express unorthodox political views. An advertisement declared:

While professedly Republican in Politics The Freeman makes paramount the Rights and Interests of Colored People, independent of parties, and counsels the adoption and prosecution of such policy as will best conserve the important features of citizenship. The Freeman recognizes that Parties are made by men, not men by Parties, and maintains that

25. Ibid., June 5, 1886. In later years Fortune continued to oppose reduction of representation. This was an issue over which he differed sharply with W. E. B. Du Bois and members of the Niagara Movement. See below p. 272.

Party allegiance is binding in so far as Parties maintain the just rights of the People and administers the Government justly and economically.[26]

The election of Grover Cleveland and the demise of the *Globe* occurred almost simultaneously. Fortune later asserted that he had wanted to support Cleveland's candidacy but that his Republican partners had insisted that the *Globe* support Blaine, but while his support of the Republican candidate had been merely lukewarm, there is no evidence that he felt any enthusiasm for Cleveland prior to his election. But immediately after it became clear that for the first time since Emancipation a Democrat had been elected to the presidency, Fortune expressed confidence that Negroes need not be fearful since Cleveland would attempt to check the reactionary tendencies of his party. At the beginning of the new administration the *Freeman* expressed guarded praise, saying that Cleveland's choices for the Cabinet were "as strong in brains and as liberal and progressive in sentiment as it was possible for him to select from the material from which he had to draw." Fortune reluctantly admitted that public opinion had dictated Hayes' southern policy—that people had grown weary of the "bloody shirt" and wanted whites and blacks of the South to be left alone to solve their own problems. It was a difficult lesson for Negroes to understand, and it was even more difficult to understand that the politicians "who had professed so long to love us for ourselves, really loved us for our votes, and had not love to give when there were no more votes to offset the affection." The painful lesson for the Negro to learn from this was that he could not look to the federal government for protection and that "unless he can make himself useful to politicians he cannot expect politicians to make themselves useful to him." The question of the black man and his rights was no longer a live political issue; instead new issues such as the tariff and civil service reform had arisen, whether

26. Ibid., November 24, 1884.

Negroes liked it or not. Old alignments had lost their meaning in the face of the changed political situation, and, Fortune suggested, it would be advantageous to Democrats to start cultivating Negro votes, especially in doubtful northern states where they held the balance of power. "If the Democratic party pursues a broad, liberal and honorable course towards us," he said, "there is no reason whatever why such support [of Democrats by Negroes] may not be expected with reasonable assurance." When it was reported that some Negroes had voted a straight Democratic ticket and even more had voted split tickets in the state elections in New York in 1885, the *Freeman* said that this showed that "colored voters of the Empire State are growing in political wisdom." Before the end of Cleveland's first year in office, some Negro papers were accusing Fortune of using the columns of the *Freeman* to "white-wash" Cleveland. Others were suggesting that he was angling for a political appointment.[27]

During 1886 Cleveland strengthened his position with Negroes by a number of appointments, but especially by his efforts on behalf of James C. Matthews of Albany, whom he named to succeed Frederick Douglass as recorder of deeds for the District of Columbia. The Senate Committee on District Affairs rejected the appointment by a vote of five to two, and the chairman of the committee was reported as saying that members voted as they did "because the Republicans do not like a Democratic nigger and the Democrats don't like any nigger." In spite of opposition from Washington Democrats and the press of the city, Cleveland commissioned Matthews the day after Congress adjourned.[28]

The *Freeman* praised Cleveland for rising above party in his

27. *Age*, August 8, 1888; *Globe*, November 4, 1884, *Freeman*, March 7, March 14, March 21, May 16, October 31, November 7, November 28, 1885; *Washington Bee*, April 25, 1885.

28. *Freeman*, March 13, March 27, July 3, August 7, August 14, 1886; Simmons, *Men of Mark*, p. 966 ff.

determination to see that justice was done. "Indeed," it said, on this and other issues, "the President has set the mark for his party . . . and the Democratic party will have either to come up to the high ground taken by the President or suffer defeat at the polls, simply because the President has the people with him." As early as June 1886, Fortune expressed the hope that the Democrats would renominate Cleveland. He was watching political parties like a hawk, he said, and emphasized that Democrats could not escape the fact that in the North the Negro vote counted. "On what side of the scale this vote will be thrown in the next Presidential election will be determined by the policy the Democratic party shall pursue in Congress towards the policy advanced by the President on matters affecting us." T. McCants Stewart, who had worked for Blaine in 1884, also expressed his support of Cleveland. George T. Downing praised Cleveland and predicted that more and more Negroes would come to support him. He criticized Frederick Douglass for condemning Negroes who left the Republican party as "ingrates."[29]

Fortune devoted most of an Emancipation Day Address delivered at Oswego and attended by Negroes from all over western New York, which had been Douglass's home territory, to the subject of politics. Douglass, he said, knew the Republican record as well as any man, and yet he condemned Negroes like Downing for deserting the party. "We have not deserted any party," he declared, "the party has deserted us. . . . We are sick of the farce and we propose to work a change." To his black listeners he said: "You are simply a political cipher in the South and a voting machine in the North; and your Douglasses, Lynches, Bruces, Langstons and the rest have no more influence on the politics of the country nor the policies of the parties than so many Aunt Dinahs. . . . Why is this true? It is because this million and a half voters are Republicans and not Negro-

29. *Freeman*, May 29, June 5, June 12, August 14, August 21, September 11, September 18, 1886.

wumps." As for himself, he was neither a Democrat nor a Republican, he said, but simply a Negro-wump. But he closed his address with remarks of approbation for Cleveland.[30]

In the mayoralty campaign in New York City in 1886 Fortune supported the Democratic candidate Abram S. Hewitt in a contest in which the other candidates were Theodore Roosevelt and Henry George. This was somewhat surprising in view of his frequent advocacy of some of George's views and the fact that John Swinton supported George, but he dismissed the author of *Progress and Poverty* as too much of a theorist to be able to govern effectively.[31]

Meanwhile he had published a pamphlet entitled *The Negro in Politics*, in which he traced once more the record of the Republican party and its exploitation of Negro voters. The essence of the pamphlet was a plea to put race before party—to discard sentimentalism and to recognize that there was no essential difference between the Republican and Democratic parties. From the time white politicians had first begun to turn to the Negro question, it had been used as "a leverage to advance selfish individual and partisan ends." And so-called race leaders had acquiesced and all too often deserted the Negro masses and "sold out" to white leaders.

> Instead of loving the race, . . . each one of us seeks to get as far away from his African origin as circumstances will permit. The majority of us no sooner mount to giddy heights on the shoulders of the race than we desert the cause and live henceforth oblivious, apparently, that the struggling mass needs brains and wealth and leadership to master the situation in which it finds itself. . . . [Men who claim to be race leaders] have swallowed without a grimace every insult to their manhood or their rights which pseudo friends and avowed enemies have heaped upon them. The slaves of one set of sharpers, and browbeaten, shot and roundly abused by

30. Ibid., August 14, 1886.
31. Ibid., October 23, 1886.

another, they have accepted the situation with a resignation really laughable and to some extent inexplicable—on no other hypothesis than that they hoped, often not in vain, that the cunning hand that had the dispensation of public patronage would dole out a bone to them.[32]

And yet, in spite of betrayals, the mass of Negroes continued to vote the Republican ticket. "There has not been a time since the war," he said, "when the race has not been ruled almost entirely by sentimental politics,—weighted down with a sense of infinite obligation to somebody for the God-given right to be free and the constitutional right to vote—or, oftener, to be shot in attempting to vote." But while Negroes had continued to give unswerving support to the Republican party for twenty years, their political position had steadily deteriorated. The reason, said Fortune, was that:

We have confided implicitly in the leadership of white men, whose main purpose was, not to see justice done to us, but to secure all the notoriety and emolument for themselves our votes gave them an opportunity to scoop in. . . . While the colored man was hurrahing himself into a state of frenzy and getting shot on all sides for his sentimental loyalty, the politicians were smiling in their sleeves at his supreme ignorance and gullibility. . . . I have never met a white Republican in the North or South, who did not talk and act as if I belonged to him and his party, body and soul, simply because my face was colored, and just in proportion as this spirit has obtruded itself upon me have I felt indignant and disgusted and rebellious.[33]

Early in 1887 at a dinner at Trenton, New Jersey, which was attended by a number of Negro notables, Fortune once more reiterated the record of the Republican party, including the Re-

32. Fortune, *The Negro in Politics*, pp. 10–11, 17–18.
33. Ibid., pp. 34, 60.

publican dominated Supreme Court. Without committing himself as to his position in the election of 1888, he spoke warmly of Cleveland and declared that colored men no longer looked, in the language of Frederick Douglass, to the Republican party as the ship and all else as the sea. The speech attracted a considerable amount of attention in the white press. The *Trenton Daily Emporium* characterized it as a "masterpiece of oratory," Fortune as one of the "able men of the country," and the *Freeman* as "the acknowledged organ of the race." Even the Montgomery, Alabama, *Advertiser* spoke highly of Fortune for his commendation of Cleveland.[34]

But while Fortune appeared to be moving in the direction of endorsement of Cleveland and open affiliation with the Democrats, he was at the same time engaged in a curious flirtation with the Prohibitionists. The crusade against strong drink was one which received support from the Negro clergy, and resolutions adopted at Negro conventions frequently assailed the use of liquor as an impediment to race progress. Several Negro newspapers were strongly Prohibitionist in the eighties. It was not uncommon for the *Freeman* to advocate temperance in editorials. In an editorial in 1885 entitled "Prohibition and Crankyism," it spoke of the liquor traffic as a disgrace and declared that the good of society demanded restrictions on the manufacture and sale of intoxicants. The Prohibition party, it declared, was a "good thing" and had "a noble mission," but it warned that Prohibitionists should not forget that the people would not submit to extreme restrictions. Later in an interview in the *Weekly Voice*, the Prohibition organ in New York, Fortune lauded efforts of the Prohibitionists in the South. He attributed much of the lawlessness of that region to drinking by both whites and blacks. "Take away the rum power," he said, "and you destroy the apology for lynch law and assassination on the part of the

34. *Freeman*, February 12, February 19, 1887.

whites, and the propensity of the colored people to engage in low brawls and to commit crimes upon persons and property."[35]

While declaring that he was not ready to espouse the Prohibition party, Fortune declared editorially that it was the only party of the day which had "a high and noble object; . . . the only party laboring for the attainment of an object for the good of humanity, and not for the personal advancement and aggrandizement of its individual members." In this respect he considered it like the old abolitionist parties. By August 1887 he had become a registered lecturer of the National Prohibition Bureau and had attended the state Prohibition convention at Syracuse, where he spoke in favor of a constitutional amendment. The prestigious *Springfield Daily Republican* thought this of sufficient importance to take note of it. It declared that the Prohibitionists had gained a strong ally in Fortune, who was "easily at the head of the Negro journalists of the country," who was "intelligent, independent, brave, determined," and whose "influence is of the growing sort."[36]

When other Negro papers accused Fortune of allying himself with the Prohibitionists for purely mercenary reasons, he reiterated his disenchantment with the old parties. It was impossible for Negroes to win a place of respect in them, he said. "*We have got to make our own status*, and this can only be done in a new party, where brains are needed and votes are rated at a premium." But he soon became disillusioned. When he urged a union of the Prohibition and Labor parties, the Prohibitionist *Voice* repudiated the suggestion.[37]

35. Ibid., December 12, 1885; November 6, 1886. During the eighties several other Negro papers and Negro spokesmen endorsed the Prohibition party.

36. Ibid., July 24, 1886; September 3, September 10, 1887; *Springfield Republican*, quoted in *Freeman*, September 17, 1887.

37. *Freeman*, September 17, October 1, October 8, 1887. Emphasis as in original

While saying in October 1887 that he intended to vote for the Prohibition candidate for president in 1888, he continued to have kind words for Cleveland and some northern Democrats. "As far as the Democratic party of the North is concerned," he said in December, "it is vastly better in many respects than its opponent, and not one-tenth as hypocritical in its practices toward colored men." In a letter to the *New York Evening Post* in February 1888 he said that Cleveland had a better record in dealing with Negroes than any recent occupant of the White House. In May, in a letter to the *New York Sun*, he announced that he would support the Democrats in the forthcoming campaign—a step which his friend T. McCants Stewart had already taken the previous October.[38]

Both Fortune and Stewart were active in the ensuing campaign,[39] in which for the first time the national Democratic organization made a serious bid for the Negro vote. Fortune was conspicuous in the proceedings of a meeting of "Indepen-

38. *Age*, October 15, November 12, December 3, February 11, June 2, 1888. In the letter to the *Sun*, Fortune repeated once more the record of Republican betrayal of the Negro. "Republican leaders have admitted time and again within the past decade that there is no power in the Federal Government to correct the conceded irregularities of the suffrage in the South. . . . Now, this is the straw that breaks the camel's back, as far as intelligent colored voters are concerned. . . . If the question of race rights be taken out of the Republican platform; or if it remains there as a glittering generality, why should I or any other intelligent colored citizen continue to hurrah for the Republican party and vote for its candidates?" Since the tariff and civil service reform appeared to be the real issues, and since the Democratic position on them more nearly coincided with his own, Fortune said he would support the Democrats.

39. In October 1887, as seen below, the *Freeman* had become the *Age*, and Fortune had left his editorial position to engage in free-lance journalism.

[93]

dents" and Democrats in Indianapolis in August. In all, about sixty persons from fifteen states and the District of Columbia took part in the convention. George T. Downing was not present but sent a message endorsing the purpose of the meeting. Peter H. Clark of Cincinnati was elected permanent chairman, while Fortune was chairman of the committee on resolutions. The most significant action taken was the adoption of a declaration that: "This Negro Democratic national conference endorses the administration of Grover Cleveland, and that it will do all in its power to secure the election of Cleveland and Thurman."[40]

The convention was also notable for Fortune because it was here that he first met Ida Wells, who was at that time teaching school in Memphis and writing under the pen name of Iola. From Indianapolis he went to Chicago, where he was hospitably entertained and met a number of leading Negroes, including attorney Ferdinand L. Barnett, editor of the *Conservator*, another political independent and future husband of Ida Wells; S. Laing Williams, another attorney; and the surgeon, Dr. Daniel Williams.[41]

From Chicago he went to Cincinnati where he worked for the Democratic organization during the remainder of the campaign. His most important responsibility was editing the *Cincinnati Afro-American*, which Peter H. Clark had founded a few years earlier. Fortune's good friend and fellow journalist, John Durham, expressed regret that he had thrown in his lot with the Democrats. Nevertheless, said Durham, in editing the *Afro-American* he would "demonstrate to whites and blacks in Ohio and Indiana that honesty, ability and energy can be united in Negro leadership. And the country needs a demonstration of that sort more than it needs torchlight processions." Nevertheless, he warned his errant friend to stick to his journalistic career

40. *Indianapolis Freeman,* July 28, 1888.
41. *Age,* August 11, 1888.

in New York and not to lose his head and be carried away by the allurements of leadership. After the November elections, Durham predicted, the average colored Democrat would "not make a decent door mat."[42]

As editor of the *Freeman* Fortune was considered not only the leading Negro journalist, but one of the most promising leaders of his race.[43] But in spite of the prestige which the *Freeman* enjoyed, it was never a financial success. Fortune was constantly seeking ways of supplementing his income. He was in great demand as a speaker—his reputation as an orator was second only to his reputation as a journalist—and he frequently addressed Emancipation Day celebrations, religious conventions, and other groups. But he soon found that there was not enough money in this sort of thing to make it feasible to go on lecture tours.[44] He also attempted free-lance journalism on a small scale from time to time.

In October 1887 Fortune announced that he was severing his connection with the *Freeman* to take up other work, and that henceforth the paper would be edited by Jerome B. Peterson, while his brother, Emanuel, would become business manager. Simultaneously, Peterson announced that the name of the paper was being changed to the *New York Age* and that it would be Republican in politics since Republican views most nearly coincided with the views of most Negroes. But he added

42. *Indianapolis Freeman,* September 8, 1888; *Age,* September 15, 1888.

43. In his book, *The Afro-American Press,* published in 1891, I. Garland Penn said: "The most noted man in Afro-American journalism is T. Thomas Fortune of New York" (p. 133). In 1886 a group of Negroes who acquired land in Flordia along the route of the Flordia Southern Railway which they hoped to make into a colony of fruit and vegetable growers named the settlement Fortune, in honor of the journalist (*Freeman,* July 24, 1886).

44. *Age,* October 22, 1887; *Freeman,* March 14, 1885.

that color would not be the index of political affiliation and urged readers to make their own judgments.[45]

It appears that the decision to reorganize the paper was motivated by a number of considerations. Obviously under existing conditions income from the *Freeman* was not sufficient to support both the Fortunes and Peterson. Moreover, the withdrawal of the elder of the Fortune brothers, who had made himself objectionable to the Republican organization, would open the way for financial support from Republican sources while leaving him free to pursue his own independent political course. Indeed, although the *Age* was officially Republican and supported the GOP and its candidates in the campaign of 1888, it also regularly published signed columns by T. Thomas Fortune and T. McCants Stewart, both of whom were working actively for Cleveland.

An additional factor which may have influenced Fortune to seek another way of earning a livelihood was the decision of John Swinton in August 1887 to cease publication of his paper, which had proved to be a financial disaster. This helped to convince Fortune of the hopelessness of making a success of a small weekly. Swinton's return to the staff of the *Sun* also probably helped pave the way for a place for Fortune on that paper. At any rate, at the time he decided to withdraw from the *Freeman*, Fortune approached Amos Cummings, editor of the *Evening Sun*, for a job. Cummings told him brusquely that the only salaried employees were the editors. Reporters were expected to "hustle" for themselves and find their own stories and were paid according to the amount of their copy which was published. He added that he did not like "long-winded articles." Fortune accepted the conditions and went to work at once. Fortunately for him, Cummings liked his style, and he was quite successful in having his copy accepted. His contributions were varied. In fact, he wrote for every department of the *Sun* except the one

45. *Freeman*, October 8, 1887; *Age*, October 15, 1887.

on Wall Street. He also succeeded in getting stories into the morning *Sun*, which was edited by Charles A. Dana, whom he admired intensely and whose views he was prone to emulate. Swinton warned him that Dana was a severe critic. "Fortune," he said, "when you get your first editorial into the morning edition of the *Sun* through Mr. Dana you can go out and buy a gold pen with a diamond point." The younger man was accordingly greatly elated a few weeks later when his first editorial appeared.[46]

In spite of chronic financial uncertainty, those early years in New York were years of achievement, adventure, and bright promise for Fortune, but they were also years clouded with personal tragedy. An infant son had died in Florida, and a second infant son was to die soon after the move to New York. The second son, who was named Stewart after his father's closest friend, was born in 1884, a year after their daughter Jessie.[47]

Except for the fact that Fortune lived in various rented quarters in Williamsburg and Brooklyn, little is known about his living arrangements. He and Carrie appear to have shared some interests and activities. She was a member of the Brooklyn Literary Institute and of various musical groups. She had a good voice and enjoyed singing. Sometime after her arrival in New

46. *Age*, November 5, 1887; September 13, 1890; *Indianapolis Freeman*, January 18, 1890. After he was employed by the *Sun*, Fortune wrote that that paper had always opened its columns to him and that it had employed other colored reporters. The *New York World*, the *Evening News*, and the *Star* (all Democratic papers) had all employed Negroes. Among independent papers the *Evening Post* employed a Negro bookkeeper, and the *Herald* had employed Negro reporters. But the Republican *Tribune* had not employed a Negro. "It is remarkable," Fortune said, "that the Republican papers which have done the most preaching about the equality of colored men should be the last to put their preaching into practice" (*Age*, November 12, 1887).

47. *Age*, May 17, 1890.

York she became a member of the Protestant Episcopal Church, but her husband was a member of the African Methodist Episcopal church. In spite of his frequent diatribes against religion, he took part in church affairs and in 1884 served as a lay delegate to the A.M.E. General Conference in Washington, D. C.

Husband and wife were frequently apart for long periods of time. Both missed the sunny climate which they had left and family and friends in Florida. At least twice, and probably more often, Carrie and the children spent the entire winter with Emanuel Fortune, Sr., in Jacksonville. During their absences Fortune wrote a number of poems expressing his loneliness for them. In 1888 the family remained in New York, and Stewart fell a victim of the great blizzard of that winter. He contracted pneumonia and was under a doctor's care for many weeks. In May, on the advice of the doctor, Carrie took him to the country in New Jersey, but he failed to rally and died a week later.[48]

Although he died a year later, Emanuel Fortune, Jr., was also a victim of the terrible winter of 1888. Soon after his graduation from Cookman Institute in Jacksonville he had come north to work in the office of the *Globe*. Like his brother he was interested in politics and oratory but less inclined to repudiate the Republicans. He was a handsome youth, and in spite of his physical handicap he gained a reputation as a public speaker. When Tim Fortune withdrew from the editorship of the *Freeman*, as already shown, the younger brother became the business manager of the *Age*. But during the great blizzard of the winter of 1888 he contracted pneumonia and never completely regained his health. Early in 1889 he returned to Florida to recuperate, but he survived for less than a year, dying in March 1890.

In his anguished grief at the snuffing out of a life so young and full of promise the elder brother wrote a long poem, "Emanuel."

48. Ibid., May 23, June 1, 1889.

It seems not true to me; it seems not true,
That one so gifted and so young could die—. . . .
Serious he was, and passing cold and stern;
For life is serious, and its work, to those
Intent to do their share, to those who yearn
To serve the race, is hard, and harder grows. . . .
He was my brother, younger far than I,
And shared with me the sports of happy youth,
In that reposeful village where my eye,
Still constant, pleading ever, turns, forsooth,
To scenes of guileless innocence and truth!
It is a memory! . . .
Those days will ne'er return to us again,
For one is dead—a broken link in life's short chain!
  .   .   .   .

He little dreamed in those delightful hours
The changes that the future years would bring;
He little dreamed the sunshine and the showers
That make our Southern life an endless Spring
Whose joys the mocking bird delights to sing,
Would merge into the storms of Northern life
Intense, and wither him—a blasted thing!
The tropic plant, before the North Wind's strife,
Too often falls a victim to Death's pruning knife.[49]

After the deaths of Stewart and Emanuel, Jessie was all the more dear to Fortune, and he lavished affection on her. On her eighth birthday he published a poem telling her of his devotion.

And may each birthday bring to thee
The gladness thou has brought to me.
May length of years be thine to live
To enjoy the love to thee I give.

A few months later a son, Frederick White Fortune, was born. Fred was to be very close to Carrie, and no doubt a con-

49. Fortune, *Dreams of Life*, pp. 21–28.

solation for the other sons she had lost, but Jessie remained the special object of her father's love.[50]

Friendships—and especially the friendship with T. McCants Stewart—helped assuage grief over the loss of Emanuel. Stewart, who was four years older than Fortune, had been born of free parents in Charleston, South Carolina. Although it was rumored that blood of some of the most aristocratic white families flowed in his veins, he was very dark skinned and short and wiry. During the Reconstruction era he had received both an A.B. and law degree from the University of South Carolina. He had also studied theology and was an ordained minister of the A.M.E. Church. He came to New York at about the same time as Fortune and for a few years combined law practice and a pastorate. In 1882 he had gone to Liberia to join the staff of Liberia College with the pretentious title of Charles Sumner Professor of Belles Lettres, History and Law. But the college proved to be a feeble affair, and Stewart became convinced that its future lay in emphasizing industrial training. He returned to the United States to study the methods of education in use at Hampton Institute, but after a few months he abandoned plans to return to Liberia and decided to settle down in New York and practice law. He opened an office on Cedar Street and joined Fortune in writing editorials for the *Freeman*.[51]

Stewart was invariably cheerful, even in the face of adversity, and his sunny disposition was a wholesome influence on Fortune who was given to fits of depression.[52]

Stewart was the only person besides Carrie who called Fortune "Bert," and no other friend was so close or exerted so much influence on him, but there were many other friends of con-

50. *Age*, May 3, August 1, 1891.

51. Simmons, *Men of Mark*, pp. 152–53; *Freeman*, October 24, 1885; January 10, 1886. Stewart wrote a series of letters describing his trip to Europe en route to Africa and letters describing West Africa which were published in the *Globe* in 1884.

52. *Age*, August 13, 1890.

genial tastes. Among them was Jerome Peterson, three years younger than Fortune. Peterson, who had a "Spanish complexion" and a "French mustache of remarkable luxuriance," was a native of Brooklyn. While working in an office in a bank, he had started contributing to the *Globe*. When the *Freeman* became the *Age*, he became a partner and editor. [53] There was also John S. Durham, who spent most of his time in Philadelphia but who came to New York frequently. Durham, a native of Philadelphia, had worked his way through the University of Pennsylvania, earning a degree in civil engineering and also studying law. In the 1880s he entered journalism, working as a reporter and editorial writer on the *Philadelphia Bulletin*. Fortune maintained a long friendship with Durham, who later became minister to Haiti and manager of a sugar plantation in Santo Domingo.[54]

Another lasting friendship which began in this period was with Robert H. Terrell of Washington, D. C. Terrell had been born of slave parents but graduated cum laude from Harvard College in 1884. Thereafter he taught in the Negro high school in Washington for a few years before receiving a law degree at Howard and entering legal practice. The acidulous *Washington Bee* described Terrell as quite "Harvard"—which, it said, meant the "ability to study, row, play baseball and cricket and waltz with the d-e-a-r g-i-r-l-s, in the latest style." But the Harvard Club of Washington refused to accept him as a member. Fortune liked Terrell immensely—partly since he did not put on airs because of his academic distinctions—and predicted that he would become a race leader.[55]

53. *Colored American Magazine*, June 1904, p. 456.

54. *Washington Bee*, March 22, 1902; *A.M.E. Review*, May, 1920, p, 522. In 1897 Durham married Constance MacKenzie, a daughter of Shelton MacKenzie, editor of the *Philadelphia Press*.

55. *Globe*, May 31, August 16, 1884; *Washington Bee*, September 20, 1884; October 15, 1898; *Age*, October 6, 1888; August 22, 1891.

One of Fortune's chief pleasures was the Bethel Literary and Historical Society (later the Brooklyn Literary Union) which he helped to organize soon after his arrival in New York. Programs consisted of the presentation of a paper followed by discussion. Subjects ranged from literature to economics and debates on such questions as: "Is society right in compelling a woman to wait for a proposal of marriage?" (Fortune took the negative position.) Sometimes there was a guest speaker—on one occasion Mayor Seth Low of New York, who read a paper "Libraries, Ancient and Modern."[56]

Fortune and Peterson (and Durham when he was in New York) and a few other congenial souls also organized "The Innocents," a social club which brought them together once a month to "Dine off wit and humor and deviled bits of wisdom, with here and there a succulent beefsteak."[57]

On the more frivolous side, Fortune admitted to having succumbed to the roller-skating craze while still in Florida. After coming to Brooklyn he and Carrie belonged for a time to a skating club. Occasionally he and Stewart went to a horse race at Coney Island, if the black jockey, Isaac Murphy, who had won the Kentucky Derby three times, was riding.[58]

He also found time to write poetry, especially during periods of emotional stress. His verses frequently appeared in the *Freeman* and the *Age* and occasionally in other papers, including the *Springfield Sunday Republican*.

The illness and death of his younger brother caused Fortune to abandon his plans for a full time career on the *Sun*. In February 1889 he became editor of the *Age*, a position he held until 1907. But for many years he continued to supplement his income

56. *Globe*, June 2, 1883; *Freeman*, April 17, June 5, 1886; May 28, 1887; *Age*, February 14, March 7, 1891.

57. Ibid., February 28, 1898.

58. *Freeman*, March 28, 1885; *Age*, July 5, 1890.

by writing for the *Sun*, for the *Age* was never sufficiently prosperous to support both Peterson and him.

Soon after his return to the *Age*, and less than a year after
Cleveland's defeat, Fortune also recanted his political apostasy
of 1888 and renounced his brief affiliation with the Democrats.
In a signed editorial in the *Age*, August 31, 1889, he remarked
that since the defeat of Cleveland southern Democrats and
northern Mugwumps had opened up an unprecedented fusilade
of abuse of Negroes. He quoted with approval an editorial in
the *New York Sun* which said that southern newspapers were
"breathing wrath against Negro suffrage" and which admonished Democrats: "You are not taking the best way to bring
colored voters to the Democracy." Under the circumstances,
said Fortune: "Whenever the question is reduced to 'shall the
Negro enjoy his full rights under the Constitution?' only the
mercenary Negro will be found in the future on the Democratic side of the fence in national and congressional elections."[59]

Personal ambitions and frustration no doubt were partly
responsible for Fortune's political tergiversations, as his critics
charged. The number of Negro "leaders" identified with the
Republican party was legion. In the Democratic party or a new
third party a young man of Fortune's talents would be more
conspicuous and perhaps more likely to receive an appointment
or other reward than at the hands of the Republicans. But more
important was the fact that he was above all a "race" man—and
a maverick—who deeply resented the Republicans' record
toward his race and who sought ways to break the impasse and
indifference which contributed to the continuing deterioration
in the political condition of the blacks. In commenting on his
achievements as editor of the *Freeman*, Fortune said: "I helped
to break the backbone of the 'eternal gratitude' business, and to
smash the life out of the sentimental politics Mr. Douglass im-
mortalized in his remark that 'the Republican party is the ship

59. *Freeman*, November 21, 1885; *Age*, January 10, 1891.

and all else is the ocean.' There are few of us today who subscribe to the soundness of this apotheosis of political hum-
buggery."[60]

As sole owner and editor of the *Freeman* Fortune enjoyed
greater independence than at any other time in his career. He
was free to express his personal views—to attack and defend as
he thought fit. This brand of journalism attracted attention—
favorable and unfavorable—but the *Freeman* was not a financial
success, and Fortune decided to try to make his way in the larger
world of white journalism. But the illness and death of Emanuel
Fortune brought him back to race journalism as editor of the
Age. Likewise his campaign for political independence, which
led to an endorsement of Cleveland and an alliance with the
Democratic party, was short lived. Thereafter he was nominally
a Republican and at various times worked for the party and for
individual candidates. But he continued to criticize—sometimes
bitterly—and Republican politicians, white and black, tended to
distrust and suspect him because of his independence and his
deviation in 1888.

60. *Age*, October 22, 1887.

Afro-American Agitator

Duction and influence as a journalist, race spokesman, and champion of civil rights. It is unfortunate that the files of the *Age* are lost for most of the decade and that the correspondence between Fortune and Booker T. Washington which throws light on his later career became voluminous only in the late nineties. But from the fragmentary evidence which survives, it is possible to construct a fairly complete account of the variety of his race activities and his contribution to racial thought.

Perhaps his most important contribution, next to his journalism, was his attempt to organize the National Afro-American League. That he had conceived the idea for such an organization as early as January 1884 is shown from a speech which he delivered before a racially mixed audience at the annual dinner of the Charles Sumner Union League at Hartford. In his opening remarks he observed that Connecticut and Massachusetts were probably the only states in which such a gathering could occur. "I know," he said, "that it has become the fashion to hoot out of the politics of the North the race question; I know that men and parties have entered into a compact to treat with silence and indifference the wails of sorrow and distress that come up hourly from our Southland." And even in New York, Connecticut, and Massachusetts, he said, "a black man lurks about the doors of theaters and churches, and school houses, reluctant to enter lest his constitutional right to do so be peremptorily denied." He suggested that the Sumner Union League make itself a central organization, from which would radiate kindred organizations "devoted to the progress and uncompromising defense of the race with which we are identified and for which Charles Sumner labored to such great and beneficent purpose." "Let us agitate! *agitate!* AGITATE!" he cried, "until the protest shall awake the nation from its indifference."[1]

Three years later in an editorial in the *Freeman*, May 28, 1887, he called for the formation of a national organization to carry on the work he had suggested in the Hartford speech, but by this time he apparently envisioned an all-black organization. Every day, he said, the white press reported outrages against Negroes in the South, outrages frequently perpetrated by the "best people." The same papers daily denounced British misgovernment in Ireland while failing to condemn the white ruffians in the South or to express sympathy for their black victims. The reason was that the Irish were vocal in airing their grievances, and the Irish vote was an important factor in American politics. Said Fortune:

> We think that it has been thoroughly demonstrated that the white people of this country have determined to leave the colored man alone to fight his battles; especially is this true of the treacherous, self-seeking politicians. There is no

1. *Hartford Telegram* reprinted in *Globe*, January 19, 1884.

dodging the issue; we have got to take hold of this problem ourselves, and make so much noise that all the world shall know the wrongs we suffer and our determination to right these wrongs.[2]

He proposed a National Afro-American League modeled on the Irish National League which would incorporate local and state organizations from all parts of the United States. The following week he amplified on this proposal and listed the principal grievances against which the league should work. First in importance was the suppression of the vote in the South —the denial of a voice in government in the states in which Negroes were most numerous. Second was the reign of lynch and mob law. Other grievances were inequities in the distribution of school funds; "the odious and demoralizing penitentiary system of the South, with its chain gangs, convict leases, and indiscriminate mixing of males and females"; the discrimination and indignities in transportation to which southern Negroes were subjected; and the denial of accommodations in such places as inns, hotels, and theaters. Since grievances were most acute in the South, the league should have its stronghold in that region. In the North its role would be to exert political pressure and stir up public opinion. Fortune did not minimize the dangers and difficulties of organizing in the South, where free speech and free press were not tolerated and where physical violence was a daily occurrence. "We propose to accomplish our purposes by the peaceful methods of agitation, through the ballot and the courts," he said, "but if others use the weapons of violence to combat our peaceful arguments it is not for us to run away from violence. A man's a man, and what is worth having is worth fighting for."[3]

The proposal met with a favorable response from much of the Negro press, especially in the North, and a number of

2. *Freeman,* May 28, 1887.
3. Ibid., June 4, 1887.

prominent Negroes and Negro organizations endorsed the idea. From Tuskegee, Alabama, the youthful Booker T. Washington wrote an enthusiastic letter. "Push the battle to the gate," he urged. "Let there be no hold-up until a League shall be found in every village. God bless you. God bless the proposed League."[4]

The *People's Choice* of Macon, Georgia, cried: "With all our soul we say go on Brother Fortune," but other Negro papers in the South dissented. The *Standard* of New Orleans said that if Fortune desired a "redivivus of the white league, kuklux klan, and all sorts of things, let him proceed with his league." From Fortune's old home, the *Southern Leader* of Jacksonville said that the league would intensify rather than alleviate race troubles in the South, and other Negroes agreed.[5]

As might be expected, white newspapers in the South which deigned to comment were opposed to the league proposal. The *Charleston News and Courier* said that colored people had nothing to gain by such an organization—that it would merely perpetuate racial divisions in politics and give added ammunition to those who opposed the privileges and rights which the

4. Ibid., June 18,1887. In the *People's Advocate* John Cromwell traced the history and failure of earlier attempts to form permanent protest organizations. In 1864 a national convention meeting at Syracuse, over which Frederick Douglass presided, had voted to form the Equal Rights League with John M. Langston as national president. A number of local and state leagues had been formed, but the organization had soon died out. In 1879 at the National Colored Convention at Nashville, a proposal had been made for the creation of an Afro-American Protective Society, but the organization had never become operative. Cromwell warned against calling a national convention to organize the league which Fortune proposed. Instead he urged that the league should be built on local organizations (*People's Advocate* reprinted in *Freeman*, July 9, 1887).

5. *Freeman*, June 25, 1887.

league would demand. The *Atlanta Constitution* said the organization could do no good and might do harm. "Our opinion is that the negroes are getting along as well as could be expected under the circumstances," it added. "The prejudices that exist against them are natural and inevitable." Fortune hotly replied that Negroes were not getting along "as well as can be expected." Nor, he added, were injustice natural and infamy inevitable. Hence the need for the league.[6]

Traditional race prejudice and "the instinctive unwillingness of intelligence to submit to the domination of ignorance viciously and corruptly controlled," which were the causes of the suppression of political rights, were not remedial by law, declared *Harper's Weekly*. To this Fortune answered: "We propose to cease not from the work until we have demonstrated to our own satisfaction at least that 'traditional class prejudice and intelligence' have no constitutional right to usurp authority and to rob and outrage eight million people."[7]

On September 10, 1887, Fortune published a proposed constitution which stated that the league would attempt to educate public opinion and would appeal to the courts for redress of legal and constitutional rights. In spite of his earlier statement that league members should not run away from violence, the constitution declared: "Any member who shall provoke and participate in any violent demonstration or disorder shall, after a fair hearing and conviction, be denied all privileges of membership, the purpose of the League being to secure the ends desired through peaceable and lawful means." Another article declared that the League would be politically nonpartisan. *Harper's Weekly* expressed agreement with the general purposes stated in the constitution but warned that the success of the league would depend on ability to bring suits at law and

6. Ibid., July 23, October 8, 1887.

7. *Harper's Weekly* 31 (June 21, 1887): 450; *Freeman*, July 2, 1887.

that this would necessitate the raising of large sums of money to employ able legal counsel.[8]

During 1888, while Fortune was deeply involved in political activity, the proposal for the league was dormant; but after the defeat of Cleveland, Fortune renewed his call for the organization of local leagues. In November 1889 he issued a call for all societies which had as their objective the securing of rights denied because of race to send delegates to a national convention the following January. The original plan to meet in the South, at Nashville, Tennessee, was abandoned because of the lack of suitable hotel accommodations and the hostility of the white population of that city, and the meeting place was changed to Chicago.[9]

But although a spirit of caution might dictate meeting in the North, Fortune made it very clear that the league was intended to be a militant force. On the eve of the convention, December 21, 1889, he published an editorial in praise of the "Afro-American Agitator" (a term which Henry W. Grady had recently coined and had used in his last speech—probably with Fortune in mind). This new creature, Fortune said, had come into being with the idea of the Afro-American League. His appearance marked "the death knell of the shuffling, cringing creature in black who for two centuries and a half had given the right of way to white men" and proclaimed "in no uncertain voice that

8. *Freeman*, September 10, 1887; *Harper's Weekly* 31 (October 1, 1887): 703.

9. *Age*, December 15, 1888; November 7, November 30, 1889. During 1887 there were reports of the organization of local leagues in most of the towns in the vicinity of Boston, in Connecticut, Illinois, Minnesota, Kansas, Virginia, and Georgia (*Freeman*, September 10, October 8, 1887). During 1889 several more leagues were reported—in San Francisco, Philadelphia, Baltimore, and Charleston. In the weeks immediately preceding the national convention, local leagues proliferated—in places as remote as Helena, Montana (*Age*, January 4, January 11, 1890).

a new man in black, a freeman every inch, standing erect and undaunted, an American from head to foot, had taken the place of the miserable creature." What did he look like? *"He looks like a man!* He bears no resemblance to a slave, or a coward, or an ignoramus." His mission was to force the concession of absolute justice under state and federal constitutions. The Afro-American Agitator had come to stay until his work, like that of the abolitionists of an earlier generation, had been crowned with success in every corner of the Republic.[10]

The call for the convention was signed by eighteen persons from thirteen states and the District of Columbia. Among the signers were several Negro editors—John Mitchell, Jr., Harry C. Smith, Ferdinand L. Barnett, and W. Calvin Chase—and educators and clergymen, including J. C. Price and Alexander Walters. But the names of the nationally known political figures such as John M. Langston, P. B. S. Pinchback, John Lynch, and Blanche K. Bruce were notably absent.[11] Probably the most important politician to sign the call was "Colonel" William A. Pledger of Georgia, who served as permanent chairman of the Chicago convention and who became one of Fortune's closest friends.

The son of a white master, Pledger was a handsome man who dressed well and looked like a rather flamboyant version of the typical gentleman of the Old South. For many years he was

10. *Age*, December 21, 1889. Emphasis as in the original. See also Fortune's article, "The Race Problem: The Negro Will Solve It," in *Belford's Magazine* 4 (June 1890): 489–95.

11. *Age*, November 30, 1889. The *Age* listed eighteen persons and "others" as signers of the call. Alexander Walters, *My Life and Work* (New York, 1917), listed nineteen and "others," p. 97. Earlier Fortune and T. McCants Stewart had met with Pinchback and some other leaders to discuss the possibility of inviting John M. Langston to head the league, but although at first it was reported that he was receptive to the proposal, Langston did not sign the call and took no part in the league (*Age*, October 5, 1889).

the most influential Republican in Georgia, serving as chairman of the state executive committee. He also practiced law and edited various Negro newspapers and had served as the president of the Afro-American Press Association. Pledger, whom Fortune characterized as "the unterrified and irrepressible," had organized an Afro-American League in Georgia and as a newspaperman had consistently denounced the convict lease system and outrages against Negroes. His activities caused the *Augusta Evening News* to remark: "Some of these days Pledger's smartness will lead him to take a step that will bring him to the end of his career very suddenly," a statement which the *Age* had said sounded like an invitation to assassination.[12]

The credentials committee reported one hundred thirty-five delegates from twenty-three states assembled in Chicago. From the South there were seven from Georgia and one each from North Carolina, South Carolina, Tennessee, Virginia, and Texas. Five came from New York and five from Pennsylvania but only one from Massachusetts. There was also a delegate from Colorado, but as would be expected, the largest numbers were from Illinois and the neighboring states.[13]

Fortune as temporary chairman made a long, carefully prepared address in which he recounted the sufferings and injustices to which blacks had been subjected. "We have been robbed

12. *Age*, September 28, December 14, 1889; Cyrus Field Adams, "Col. William A. Pledger," *Colored American Magazine*, June 1902, pp. 146–49; *Washington Colored American*, March 17, 1900. For details of Pledger's political activity see Clarence A. Bacote, "The Negro in Georgia Politics, 1880–1908," (Ph.D. thesis, University of Chicago, 1955), passim.

13. *Age*, January 25, 1890; *Indianapolis Freeman*, February, 1, 1890. According to Bishop Walter's account, there were 141 delegates from 21 states (Walters, *My Life and Work*, p. 135). Although it was an all-black meeting, the constitution which was adopted said that membership in the league was open to persons eighteen years of age or older without regard to race or sex.

of the honest wages of our toil, we have been robbed of the substance of our citizenship by murder and intimidation; we have been outraged by enemies and deserted by friends," he said. "And because in a society governed by law we have been true to the law, . . . it has been charged upon us that we are not made of the stern stuff which makes the Anglo-Saxon race the most consummate master of hypocrisy, of roguery, of insolence, of arrogance, and of cowardice in the history of races." It was time to call a halt. "We have been patient so long that many believe we are incapable of resenting insult, outrage and wrong; we have so long accepted uncomplainingly all the injustice and cowardice and insolence heaped upon us, that many imagine that we are compelled to submit and have not the manhood necessary to resent such conduct."

Because of the wrongs suffered, the present convention had met to perfect an organization whose mission would be to right these wrongs "by every reasonable and legal means" until no right guaranteed by the Constitution was denied. "We shall no longer accept in silence," he declared, "a condition which degrades our manhood and makes a mockery of our citizenship." In outlining a program for the league, Fortune mentioned the creation of an Afro-American bank, a bureau of emigration to help Negroes disperse themselves over the entire country, and a bureau of technical and industrial education; but the main thrust of his speech was the demand for constitutional and political rights. To the criticism that whites would make against an all-black organization, Fortune pointed out that whites had drawn the color line in politics, in religion, in education, and in moral reform movements. "If the white man cannot rescue our drunkards and evangelize our sinners except by insulting us, let him keep away from us," he said.[14]

14. T. Thomas Fortune, "Why We Organize a National Afro-American League," *Afro-American Budget*, 1, no. 8 (February, 1890): 229–40.

Pledger followed Fortune with a speech on conditions in the South. At the bottom of the "race" problem and the "southern" problem, he said, was "a spirit of disobedience to the Constitution." Of the "trinity of evils" of the South—"state sovereignty, slavery and secession"—two had been eliminated by the sword, but the first survived in pristine vigor. The federal government was powerless in many parts of the South. "We do not desire Negro supremacy," said Pledger, "but as loyal citizens we do yearn for constitutional supremacy."[15]

The convention adopted a constitution which said that the national league was to consist of state leagues. The purpose of the national organization was to encourage and assist state and local leagues in the efforts to attain full citizenship and equality. The objects of the league were to be attained by the creation of healthy public opinion through the press and pulpit and public meetings and by appeals to courts of law, "the purpose of the league being to secure the ends desired through legal and peaceable means."

In his opening address Fortune had warned against permitting the league to become a partisan instrument. "I have served the republican party, the prohibition party, and the democratic party," he said, "and I speak with the wisdom of experience when I declare that none of them cares a fig for the Afro-American further than it can use him." He recommended that local leagues be free to pursue whatever political course local conditions might warrant, but in national affairs the league should not commit itself to any party. The constitution as adopted declared that the league was nonpartisan and that any officer who was elected or appointed to a political post must resign his league office.[16]

15. *Indianapolis Freeman*, February 1, 1890.

16. *Afro-American Budget*, 1, no. 8 (February 1890): 233–34, 247–49. In his address, while stressing the denial of constitutional and legal rights, Fortune had also recommended a number of measures

Although southerners were in a minority at the convention, a southerner, J. C. Price, was elected president of the league. Fortune, Price, and J. A. Brackett of Massachusetts were nominated for the office. On the first ballot Price received 44 votes, Fortune 43, and Brackett 33. When the second ballot produced the same results, Fortune asked that his name be withdrawn. Brackett then followed suit, and Fortune moved to make the election of Price unanimous. Thereafter Fortune was nominated for secretary and elected on the first ballot. The failure to elect Fortune president was no doubt due in part to his abrasive and sometimes arrogant personality, to his reputation for extreme militancy, and to his political vagaries. During the period when nominations were being made, he was bitterly assailed by one delegate. In Price the convention chose a president who was noted for his sunny, conciliatory personality and one who had never been active in politics. Price, who was a full-blooded Negro, six-feet-two inches tall, and weighing almost three hundred pounds, was president of Livingstone College, an institution of the A.M.E. Zion church in North Carolina. After graduating from Lincoln University in Pennsylvania and entering the ministry, he had gained a reputation as an orator. He spoke in many pulpits in the northern states and in England, where he was sent as a delegate to the World's Methodist Council. As president of Livingstone he showed some of the same

---

to improve the economic and educational status of the race. These included an Afro-American bank, a bureau of emigration to assist in dispersing the Afro-American population more widely throughout the country, a system of farmers' cooperatives, and a program of technical, industrial education. An "Address to the Citizens of the Republic" prepared by a committee headed by H. C. Astwood which was adopted by the convention, released to the press, and presented to President Harrison, contained all of these proposals. It also spoke of the denial of constitutional rights and deplored the atrocities committed against blacks, but it was less militant in tone than was Fortune's address (*Age*, January 25, 1890).

ability to win support of northern philanthropists for which Booker T. Washington of Tuskegee was notable.[17]

The proceedings at Chicago attracted some attention in the white press, much of it unfavorable. *The Nation* accused Afro-Americans of seeking "class legislation." The attempt to organize the league, it said, would merely strengthen growing resentment against Negroes and their leaders. The *St. Louis Republic* said that the convention was the work of " a few northern Negro agitators" who did not represent "the decent Negroes of the South." The *Chicago Tribune* spoke of Fortune as "the New York coon," who had made an "oily" and "tricky" speech and who was in reality working for the Democratic party. The *New York Sun*, in contrast, found Fortune's speech "eloquent and scholarly," and it found the attempt to degrade Fortune merely degrading to the *Tribune*. The members of the convention were merely "exercising their rights as American citizens to organize, agitate, cooperate," it said.[18]

Fortune left Chicago fired with optimism. One task which remained was to bring into the league other civil rights groups which had remained aloof, and to win the support of nationally known politicians. Sometime before the Chicago convention a call had been issued for a national colored convention to meet in Washington, D. C., in February. Whether this was a deliberate attempt to draw support away from the Afro-American League is not clear. Some persons, such as W. Calvin Chase, who had endorsed the league, were also active in promoting the Washington meeting. John Mitchell was also present in Washington. It seems probable that some New England groups sent delegates to Washington rather than far-off Chicago, but a large part of the group which assembled in the capital city was made up

17. *Age*, January 25, 1890; *Indianapolis Freeman*, February 1, 1890; *Indianapolis World*, January 25, 1890; Simmons, *Men of Mark*, pp. 754–58; W. J. Walls, *Joseph Charles Price* (Boston, 1943), passim.

18. *Nation* 50 (February 13, 1890): 123; *Age*, February 8, 1890.

of Negro politicians and persons who held or had held government jobs. Pinchback, Langston, Bruce, James M. Townsend, the recorder of deeds, and many lesser political figures were present. But Price, who had recently been elected president of the Afro-American League, was chosen chairman of the convention. He urged the two groups to unite. A resolution asking that steps be taken to unite with the league was adopted, but in the meantime Pinchback had been elected president of the American Citizens Civil Rights Association of the United States, established by the Washington meeting, and the convention had voted to hold annual conventions.[19]

A few months after the Chicago meeting, Fortune gained public attention for himself and for the league when he became involved in a civil rights case in New York City. When he went into the bar in the Trainor Hotel on Thirty-third Street and attempted to buy a beer, he was refused service by the waiter. He then called the proprietor, who also refused to serve him. Thereupon Fortune sat down and announced he would not leave until served. The proprietor called upon another patron to help in forcibly ejecting him and called a policeman to arrest him. Fortune demanded that the policeman arrest the other two men for assault. The trio went to the local police station where Fortune was charged with disorderly conduct and held in jail for three hours without being permitted to call a lawyer. The following day in police court the case against him was dismissed.[20]

Whether Fortune deliberately provoked the incident will never be known, but it furnished an opportunity to rally public

19. *Age*, February 15, 1890. The Washington group was called at various times the American Citizens Civil Rights Association and the American Citizens Equal Rights Association. Its connection with the earlier Equal Rights Association of the Reconstruction era was tenuous.

20. Ibid., June 7, 1890.

opinion and to give the league a test case. In a signed article in the *Age* he recounted his humiliation and cried: "Close up the line, and let us fight for our civil as well as our political rights. Hold up the hands of the Afro-American League. Put money in its treasury. Let us stand together and fight." He announced his intention of suing the proprietor of the saloon for $10,000 in damages and appealed to the membership of the league for money to carry on the legal fight.

As news of the outrage spread, indignation meetings were held in a number of places and expressions of sympathy poured in from the Negro press all over the country. Some ministers preached sermons on Fortune's behalf. Some papers objected to helping Fortune because his arrest had occurred while he was trying to buy beer, but some of the religious papers supported him. The *American Baptist* declared: "While we would prefer that Mr. Fortune abstain from the use of such a beverage, yet it is a shame that a man of his ability and position should be refused entertainment on account of color." President Price called upon Afro-American leagues throughout the country to come to Fortune's aid—declaring that he had been thrust into a felon's cell because he claimed his rights as an American citizen.[21]

The case was finally tried in November 1891. At the trial the manager of the hotel testified that Fortune had not been ejected because of his color but because the hotel had instructed its employees not to serve anyone who was disorderly or who was objectionable to other guests. The defense also asserted that Fortune had threatened to mop up the floor with anyone who laid hands on him. But Stewart had on hand reserve witnesses

21. Ibid., June 7, June 14, June 21, June 28, July 5, July 12, 1890. The *Star of Zion*, another church paper, said that the point was not that Fortune had tried to buy beer but that he was suing on account of false imprisonment and that a principle was involved which was vital to the race (*Age*, August 2, 1890). In spite of the publicity and the expressions of indignation, financial contributions to aid Fortune were small.

who were ready to testify that it was a policy of the saloon to refuse service to Afro-Americans. The jury took only fifteen minutes to decide that force had been used in ejecting Fortune and in returning a verdict in his favor. It agreed to award him $825 in damages plus costs, bringing the total to $1,016.23. The trial had attracted widespread attention in the black community, and the courtroom was crowded with persons who rushed forward to congratulate Fortune and Stewart.

The defense appealed, and it was not until 1894 that the New York Court of Appeals upheld the verdict of the trial court. The Negro press exulted. The *Indianapolis Freeman* declared that Fortune had set an example that others should emulate. "The Negro's greatest fault is in being a magnificent sufferer," it declared.[22]

But although the outcome was a sweet personal triumph for Fortune and for Stewart, who had represented him throughout the litigation, the case had not served to strengthen the Afro-American League as Fortune had hoped. Indeed the league had expired before the final appeal.

During 1890 and 1891 a number of state leagues were formed which showed some vitality, but in other places state and local leagues which had been organized earlier languished and disappeared. A convention was held in Rochester in May 1890 to complete the formation of the New York league, which included twenty-two local leagues. A second annual convention was held at Albany the following year at which delegates from only eight leagues were present. Fortune served as president of the state league both years.

The New York leagues endorsed a bill introduced into the state legislature in 1890 to strengthen the existing civil rights law, but the measure did not pass, partly because of the opposi-

22. *Age,* November 14, 1891; *Indianapolis Freeman,* March 21, 1894; *Washington Bee,* March 24, 1894. Among those present to congratulate Fortune and Stewart was Booker T. Washington.

tion of the hotel keepers lobby. Efforts to outlaw discriminatory treatment by insurance companies were more successful. The legislative committee of the state Afro-American League had a part in drawing up a bill (modeled on a Massachusetts law) which was passed in 1891. Both Fortune and Stewart lobbied in Albany for the adoption of the law which prohibited insurance companies from "making any distinction and discrimination between white and colored persons . . . as to the premium or rates charged for policies."[23]

But in spite of some local success, the prospects of the National League were not bright as it assembled for its second convention in Knoxville, Tennessee, in July 1891. One weakness which had not been overcome was the reluctance of the nationally known political leaders to identify themselves with the league. Frederick Douglass had not joined, nor had such lesser luminaries as Langston, Bruce, or Pinchback. An even more serious weakness was lack of financial support. Some delegates were unable to come to Knoxville because local leagues were without funds. Financial reports given at the convention showed that neither Price nor Fortune had received any payment for their services. Delegates were present from only Georgia, North Carolina, New York, Wisconsin, Michigan, Minnesota, and Tennessee.

Fortune was elected president of the organization and served as chairman of a committee which recommended a change in the constitution to relax the prohibition against partisan activity on the part of officers and to permit the organization to endorse political candidates—a move to try to attract the support of the politicians.

The question which aroused the most intense feeling at the Knoxville meeting was separate-coach laws which had recently been adopted in several states. The enactment of the Tennessee

23. *Age*, April 12, April 26, May 17, May 31, 1890; May 9, 1891; Scheiner, *Negro Mecca*, p. 189; *Laws of New York*, 1891 (Albany, 1891), 1: 288.

law on the eve of the convention was thought to be one reason for the small attendance by northern delegates. Several persons who did attend reported trouble with insolent railroad employees. In his address to the convention Fortune condemned separate-coach laws as a "gratuitous indignity." On his return to New York he declared, "We all know how the pinch of the shoe feels, since we have felt it, and are enlisted for the war to break up the infamous injustice." On her trip home from Knoxville to Memphis, Ida B. Wells was forced to ride in a Jim Crow car and to sit in a Jim Crow waiting room. She wrote to Fortune calling upon the league to take action against this evil.[24]

About the same time the Reverend William H. Heard, a minister of the A.M.E. church in Philadelphia, and a member of the Afro-American League, who had boarded a Pullman car at Nashville, was forced to leave the car and ride in the Jim Crow coach even though he had paid for a first class reservation. Heard informed Fortune of the incident and asked his help in securing legal redress. Fortune suggested to Judson Lyons, who had been named legal counsel for the league, that a case be instituted against the Pullman Company and the Nashville, Chattanooga, and Saint Louis Railroad if an amicable arrangement could not be worked out. Subsequently, Heard and Fortune met with representatives of the Pullman Company who agreed to dismiss the conductor who had ejected Heard and to reimburse Heard for his ticket and pay him damages of $250. This settlement was a personal vindication for Heard, but it established no legal precedent or protection against future offenses. Thereafter Fortune advised Lyons to proceed with a suit against the railroad, but the effort was dropped because of lack of funds. It was, said Fortune, "simply tomfoolery to institute [a] suit against a railroad without money to prosecute it."[25]

So hopes of winning a test case were abandoned. Some local

24. *Age*, July 11, July 25, August 8, 1891.
25. Ibid., September 19, October 10, 1891.

leagues had limited success in winning civil rights suits, but the National League was never able to institute a suit in a federal court. Although some local leagues continued to exist for several years, the national organization failed to hold a convention in 1892, and in August 1893 Fortune announced the demise of the league. It was defunct, he said, because of lack of funds, lack of mass support, and indifference of race leaders. Fortune declared that he was thoroughly disillusioned and convinced that the race was not ready for such an organization.[26]

In spite of the failure of the league Fortune continued to wage his own personal crusade against racial discrimination and to champion other individuals who were making the same fight. In 1896 the New York legislature passed the Malby Law, which was intended to strengthen earlier civil rights legislation; but a few months later Fortune found that discriminatory practices still persisted when he and a friend tried to buy tickets at a Brooklyn theater. A long line of white persons were sold tickets, but when Fortune reached the ticket window he was told that there was standing room only. When he protested, the ticket salesman called the manager and a special policeman who escorted him to the sidewalk. Once outside, Fortune got in line again, and the same performance was repeated when he reached the ticket window the second time. When Fortune refused to leave, he was arrested for obstructing the sidewalk. He was taken to the station house, the arresting officer brandishing his club all the way and threatening to make use of it. He would have been locked up in jail all night if the friend who was with him had not reached T. McCants Stewart. At the trial the judge found Fortune guilty but suspended sentence.

In the columns of the *Sun* Fortune wrote an account of the incident and denounced the management of the theater for evasion of the intent of the Malby Law and the police for their brutality toward Afro-Americans. The theater, he said, did not

26. *Indianapolis World*, August 26, 1893.

sell orchestra seats to Afro-Americans, and when all balcony seats were sold, members of the race were told that they could buy standing room or nothing. When the victims protested, the policemen obligingly escorted them to the sidewalk, waiting to make the arrest until they were outside the theater in order to protect the theater management from an action for false arrest and false imprisonment. "The police justice accepts the story of the policeman and the theater people, and the honest citizen who has been wronged and outraged from the beginning to end is adjudged guilty of violating a city ordinance and he is held up to the public as a lawbreaker, with much damage to his good name and reputation." The only recourse of the victim was to spend time and money in appealing the case. It was the only way to teach policemen and police justices that ordinary citizens had certain rights; but regardless of the outcome, the arrested man suffered in his personal feelings and reputation because the public seldom learned the true facts. "It sees that a citizen is arrested and railroaded by the police and the police justice, and naturally concludes that the citizen is no better than he ought to be, and that he got not more than he deserved."[27]

More dramatic was the case of Ida B. Wells whom Fortune attempted to help when she was forced to leave Memphis for her denunciation of lynching. Miss Wells, who had been born in Holly Springs, Mississippi, four years after the end of the Civil War, had started teaching in the rural schools at the age of fourteen in order to support her younger brothers and sisters when both her parents died. At the same time she managed to attend Rust College. She later came to Memphis, where she taught in the Negro schools and helped in the publication of the *Memphis Free Speech*. She was not reappointed to her teaching position in 1891 because of criticism of the school board which she had made in her paper. In *Free Speech* she also began to

27. *New York Age* reprinted in *Richmond Planet*, November 6, 1897; *New York Sun*, November 1, 1897.

speak out against lynchings, commending retaliatory measures which Negroes in Georgetown, Kentucky, attempted after a lynching. This caused the *Tribune and Sun* of Jackson to demand that the people of Memphis muzzle Miss Wells.[28] A few months later three young Negroes who were owners of a grocery store in Memphis were lynched after they had resisted depradations on their property. In *Free Speech* Miss Wells declared that after the lynching there was nothing for Negroes to do but leave Memphis, a town "which will neither protect our lives nor our property, nor give us a fair trial in the courts, but takes us out and murders us in cold blood when accused by white persons." She also encouraged Memphis Negroes to boycott the street railroad because of humiliating treatment. A few weeks later, after five Negroes accused of raping white women had been lynched, she said in another editorial: "Nobody in this section believes the old threadbare lie that Negro men assault white women. If Southern white men are not careful they will over-reach themselves and public sentiment will have a reaction; a conclusion will then be reached which will be very damaging to the moral reputation of their women." This caused the *Memphis Daily Commercial* to shriek: "The fact that a black scoundrel is allowed to live and utter such loathsome and repulsive calumnies is a volume of evidence as to the wonderful patience of Southern whites. . . . There are some things that the Southern white man will not tolerate, and the obscene intimations of the foregoing have brought the writer to the very outermost limit of public patience. We hope we have said enough."

Soon after the publication of this editorial a mob stormed the offices of the *Free Press*, forcing Miss Wells' partner to flee for his life. Fortunately she herself was on a northern trip when the mob descended. Fortune, who learned of the destruction of the *Free Press* office before she did, met her in Jersey City

28. *Age*, September 19, 1891.

and warned her not to return to Memphis. Instead he took her to New York where he gave her a job on the *Age* and an opportunity to continue her fight against lynching.[29]

In June 1892 the *Age* carried a seven column article on lynching, giving dates and the names of victims, and exploding the fallacy that rape was the cause of most lynchings. Ten thousand copies of the issue were distribtuted—one thousand of them in the city of Memphis. Fortune also helped Miss Wells secure lecture engagements, and she soon found herself a nationally known figure. Late in 1892 she sailed for England in response to an invitation of the Anti-Caste Society in which Miss Catherine Impey, with whom Fortune had long been corresponding, was a leading figure. On this and a second trip to England, Ida Wells aroused much interest. One British clergyman said that nothing since *Uncle Tom's Cabin* had taken such a hold on public opinion as the antilynching crusade. In the United States antilynching leagues were organized in a number of cities to raise funds to support Miss Wells's efforts. In 1895 she published a pamphlet, *A Red Record*, which contained a statistical record of lynchings and their causes. In it she called upon churches and organizations like the Y.W.C.A. and the W.C.T.U. to join the antilynching crusade. The same year she married Ferdinand Barnett, the Chicago attorney and editor of the *Conservator*.[30]

29. *Free Speech*, May 21, 1892, quoted in Ida B. Wells, *A Red Record: Tabulated Statistics and Alleged Causes of Lynchings in the United States* (Chicago, 1892), p. 12; *Memphis Daily Commercial*, quoted in Ida B. Wells, *United States Atrocities: Lynch Law* (London, 1892), p. 2; Alfreda M. Duster, ed., *Crusade for Justice: The Autobiography of Ida B. Wells* (Chicago, 1970), pp. 61–71, 77–78. The author is indebted to Mrs. Duster, the daughter of Ida Wells Barnett, for an interview and for permission to use some of the clippings in her possession.

30. Arna Bontemps and Jack Conroy, *Anyplace but Here* (New York, 1966), pp. 97–101.

Fortune warmly admired Ida Wells as he did all women who showed courage and ability. Another remarkable woman with whom he was closely associated in these years was Victoria Earle Matthews, who had been born a slave in Georgia in 1861. Her mother, who was cruelly mistreated by her master, ran away, leaving nine children behind. After the war she returned to Georgia and reclaimed the children and took them to New York, where she had been working. In New York Victoria attended public schools for a few years until she was forced to leave school and go to work. But she continued her studies and began to write. She was employed as a reporter for the *Globe* and the *Age* and other Negro papers and also did reporting for several white papers and published short stories in women's magazines. In 1897 she started the White Rose Mission as a social center for the Negro migrants who settled in the tenements of New York's upper east side. She started a program of mother's clubs, sewing classes, and classes to train girls for domestic service. Fortune had no money with which to help her in the project, but he helped persuade Booker T. Washington to take an interest in the mission and to speak at a fund raising meeting. When Washington visited the mission a few months later and saw the derelicts who lived in the neighborhood, Fortune reported that he said to Mrs. Matthews: "My friend I wouldn't change fields with you,"[31] and went away looking depressed.

Meanwhile Mrs. Matthews played a leading part in the founding of the Federation of Afro-American Women, a movement which Fortune observed and reported on with sympathy and approbation. When he was trying to organize the Afro-American League, he had urged the participation of women,

31. Lawson A. Scruggs, *Women of Distinction* (Raleigh, N. C., 1893), pp. 30–32; Penn, *The Afro-American Press*, pp. 375–76; *Age*, April 22, June 17, 1897; *New York Sun*, September 14, 1897, and undated clipping from *New York Sun*, 1898, in Scrapbook, Booker T. Washington Papers, Manuscript Division, Library of Congress; Fortune to Washington, April 14, May 28, 1897, Washington Papers.

declaring that they should have equal rights and responsibilities. "In the League," he said, "a women is just as good as a man. Out of it she is usually much better." In general, he pointed out, Negro women were better educated than Negro men because economic necessity usually forced boys to leave school at the earliest possible age. Therefore women were often better equipped than men to play a role in race uplift.

Fortune went as a reporter and participant to the Negro Women's Convention in Boston in July 1895—the first meeting of its kind. It was a meeting, he said, which "linked Boston of the time when George Thompson was chased all over the city and William Lloyd Garrison was rotten egged for pleading the cause of the slave, with Boston of the time when no slave exists in all the land, and the schools have transformed the slave women of the plantation into the educated and cultivated woman of the home and school room of to-day." Fifty-two delegates, representing Negro women's clubs all over the United States, attended. The only male participants were William Lloyd Garrison, Henry B. Blackwell, and Fortune, who took part in a session on "Political Equality."

In the final session, after there had been agreement to form a permanent organization, there was a discussion over the adoption of a name. The Bostonians opposed both "Afro-American" and "Negro" and preferred "Colored." But on the motion of Mrs. William D. Crum of South Carolina the name National Federation of Afro-American Women was adopted, to Fortune's gratification. Mrs. Booker T. Washington of Alabama was chosen president of the federation, and Mrs. Victoria Matthews chairman of the executive committee.[32]

The organization founded at Boston, which soon consolidated with a rival group, the League of Colored Women, became the largest and most influential Negro women's orga-

32. *Age*, May 30, 1891; *New York Sun*, August 7, August 11, 1895.

nization. In 1897 Mary Church Terrell, wife of Fortune's long-time friend Robert Terrell, and who was to have a long career as a champion of women's rights and civil rights, was elected president.[33]

Fortune came away from the Boston meeting much impressed with the manner in which it had been conducted and with the earnestness of the participants. It was carried on "with a deliberateness, courtesy, and fidelity to parliamentary procedure in striking contrast with the turbulence, rudeness and disregard of rules which usually characterize[d] a convention of their sons and brothers." The questions over which the delegates showed the deepest concern were temperance and "social purity." The most heated discussion was provoked by the reading of a statement of white journalist who had said, in connection with the lynching question, that Negro women were without honor or moral purity—an assertion frequently made by white writers. "It was worth-while to travel a long way," Fortune commented, "to see fifty women as indignant as these were over . . . the slander."[34]

Fortune himself consistently sought to refute the widely held assumption of the low sexual morals of black women. The principal reason for his oft-repeated opposition to antimiscegenation laws was the effect which such laws had on the legal and moral position of black women. This, he told a white reporter on one occasion, was one of the most serious elements of the race problem. "Until our womanhood is properly protected by law as white womanhood is we shall have a larger volume of immorality and crime than belongs to us, and those who are responsible for the unfortunate results talk longest and loudest in condemnation of them." The presence of 2,500,000 mulattoes and "variations of black and white" in the population of the United States "ought to blister the tongues" of those who spoke

33. *Sun*, July 5, 1896; May 17, 1897.
34. Ibid., August 7, 1895.

most frequently on the dangers of mixed marriages. "If all the white men in the South who have reared common-law families by Afro-American women were made to support them, if they were not protected by miscegenation laws," he said, "while the women and children were left to shift for themselves, or become public charges, there would be a vast gain to southern morality and much decrease in the volume of crime."[35]

While not advocating mixed marriages, Fortune championed the right of persons of different racial backgrounds to fall in love and marry if they wished—a conviction which he tried to help put into practice in the case of a Scotch girl, Maggie Woods, and her fiancé, Martin Hamilton, an American Negro. The two had become engaged while Hamilton, a resident of Newark, New Jersey, had been working in Edinburgh. After Hamilton returned to the United States, Maggie followed him to New York, where they expected to be married. But when she arrived, she was detained by immigration officials, who refused to release her to Hamilton and who tried to dissuade her from marrying him. Hamilton in turn appealed to Fortune and to an attorney, Macon Webster. The immigration commissioner called in a Presbyterian minister who tried to convince Maggie that the marriage would be a mistake, and she was taken on a tour of some of the "tough" parts of the Negro areas in New York to give her an idea of what her life would be like, although Hamilton lived in New Jersey where he owned a house. She was shocked by what she saw, but when Hamilton, accompanied by Fortune, appeared at the immigration office, she flung herself into his arms, crying, "Oh, I canna think of anything or anyone but Martin. I love him, indeed I do, and I will marry him if I have to go back to Scotland to do it." Fortune and Webster threatened to seek a writ of habeas corpus in federal court if the girl was detained longer. Hamilton reappeared accompanied by a Negro Presbyterian minister (who

35. *Boston Globe*, January 14, 1899.

had a white wife), and carried her off to the minister's home where the marriage ceremony was performed, with Fortune acting as best man.[36]

Fortune not only defended the right to intermarry, he predicted the eventual assimilation of the black minority with the white majority in the United States. In a signed article in the *New York Herald* he took exception to the statement of Charles A. Dana that since Emancipation Afro-Americans were growing darker in color and also to the opinion of James Bryce that social relations between the races were becoming less intimate every year. If Afro-Americans were growing darker and social relations were less intimate, this was merely evidence that "the demoralizing license of the slavery period" was giving way to "a higher regard for marital relations on the part of both races." But Afro-Americans were already a mixed race. The process of absorption had already gone so far that nothing but expatriation could "avert the ultimate extinction of the African as an integral race type in the United States." This result might be delayed, but it could not be prevented, since the existing Afro-American minority was not likely to be reinforced by new immigrants from Africa. Another factor which would lead to ultimate absorption, he predicted, would be the diffusion of the Afro-American population throughout the whole United States, and the eventual repeal of the "iniquitous and demoralizing miscegenation laws" of the southern states.[37]

36. *New York Sun*, September 13, September 14, 1898; *Washington Bee*, September 17, 1898. Fortune not only defended the right to enter into interracial marriage, he also defended the right of light-colored persons of Negro blood to "pass" into the white community. In an early editorial he declared: "Our opinion of the matter is, that the man or woman who is so white as not to be distinguishable as colored has a perfect right to get over on the white side and stay there. When such remain in the colored camp and turn up their noses at black people they should be made to get over into the white camp" (*Freeman*, February 28, 1885).

37. *New York Herald*, July 9, 1893.

Although Fortune always described himself as a *race* man, he was at the same time, obviously, an *integrationist* and *assimilationist*. Some of his views which were shocking to whites were also repugnant to blacks like Bishop Alexander Crummell and John E. Bruce who wanted to preserve black identity and resisted assimilation. Bruce not only opposed racially mixed marriages but also opposed mixed schools and racially integrated teaching staffs, two objectives for which Fortune had fought from his arrival in New York. Bruce declared that he opposed mixed schools because Negro youths who attended them were "educated away from the race, that the ideals set before them . . . [were] white." But when they began the real business of life as Negroes, "no amount of association with the white race, whether in school, college, or church can make them other than Negroes in the estimation of their late associates." The American Negro Academy, organized in 1897 by a group of intellectuals under the leadership of Crummel (who had a low opinion of Fortune) to promote Negro culture and unity, emphasized "the integrity and perpetuity of the black race as such." The academy rejected the use of the term *Afro-American*, which Fortune was seeking to promote.[38]

Although the academy did not ostensibly seek to separate blacks and mulattoes, Fortune thought that the emphasis upon racial integrity would have a divisive effect. In an article entitled "The Latest Color Line," he pointed out that historically, during slavery and since Emancipation, mulattoes and others of

38. Alexander Crummell to John E. Bruce, September 29, 1897, and Bruce to Crummel, December 15, 1897, John E. Bruce Papers, Schomburg Collection, New York Public Library; *Washington Colored American*, November 26, 1898; T. Thomas Fortune, "The Latest Color Line," *Liberia*, November, 1897, pp. 62–65. Bishop Alexander Crummel, rector of St. Luke's Episcopal Church in Washington, D. C., a native of New York, had graduated from Queen's College, Cambridge. After leaving England he spent twenty years in Liberia as a pastor and teacher. He was proud of his unmixed Negro ancestry.

mixed blood had enjoyed a favored position in the eyes of whites and had had opportunities denied those of darker color. Consequently blacks protested over the fact that persons of mixed blood held nearly all the teaching positions and government appointments. Fortune asserted that persons of mixed blood, even those who could have "passed" into white society, had always stood between whites and blacks, softening the prejudices and acting as a kind of connecting link. He warned that protests by blacks over the favored treatment of mulattoes could presage a situation similar to that in the West Indies, where lines were sharply drawn between blacks and persons of mixed blood—to the detriment of the former. "No friend of the Afro-American race can fail to regret," he said, "that the black and yellow people of the United States will have their problem of manhood further complicated by a color line in a color line. They have enough trouble as matters now stand without borrowing more."[39]

Fortune did not invent the term *Afro-American*, as he freely admitted, but he probably did more to publicize and popularize it during the nineties and the first years of this century than any other person. In advocating the term he made it clear that it included all persons of African ancestry and not merely those of mixed blood. But he considered *Negro* a misnomer, since only a minority of persons of African descent were all-black. He denied the assertion of Senator John T. Morgan of Alabama that the use of the term was intended to secure "incorporation, by marriage" into the white families of the country. The term, he said, was "the most comprehensive and dignified term in sight to cover all the shades of color produced by the anxiety of the white men of the South to 'secure their incorporation' without marriage into the black families of the country!"[40]

39. Fortune, "The Latest Color Line," pp. 62–65.

40. T. Thomas Fortune, "The Afro-American," *The Arena* 3 (December, 1890): 115–18. Fortune's article was in reply to an article by Senator Morgan, "The Race Problem in the United States," in the same journal.

The debate over *Afro-American* went on for several years. Fortune tried, without success, to convert Booker T. Washington. After the address at Atlanta, September 18, 1895, which brought the principal of Tuskegee national prominence, Fortune asked Washington: "Can't you see your way to use the term Afro-American when speaking of the race as a whole? We are not all black and colored and yellow, but we are all Afro-American." But Washington continued to use *Negro*. W. E. B. Du Bois also chose to use *Negro* and declared that the destiny of persons of Negro blood was "*not* absorption by white Americans."[41]

The debate was revived in 1906 when J. W. E. Bowen, professor in Gammon Theological Seminary, published an article entitled, "Who Are We?" in *The Voice of the Negro*. He endorsed the use of *Negro* and called *Afro-American* the "least satisfacory and the least sensible" of designations. It was "an hybridity in philosophy and history" and therefore "absurd." In an article in reply Fortune said that time, habitat, and blood mixture had produced a new race, more American than African. Moreover, the term *Negro* could never be given dignity. It would never be made a proper noun in popular usage. "We are African in origin and American in birth," he insisted, and "therefore, by the logic of it, Afro-Americans." Until a suitable race designation was adopted, "we shall be kicked and cuffed and sneered at as a common noun, sufficiently and contemptuously characterized by the vulgar term 'negro.' " In an extemporaneous address which he made a few months later at the national convention of Booker T. Washington's National *Negro* Business League, Fortune told his audience,

41. Fortune to Washington, September 26, 1895, Washington Papers; W. E. B. Du Bois, "The Conservation of Races," in American Negro Academy, *Occasional Papers*, no. 2 (Washington, D. C., 1897), reprinted in John H. Bracey, Jr., August Meier, and Elliott Rudwick, eds., *Black Nationalism in America* (Indianapolis and New York, 1970), p. 256.

You can take your choice of names, BUT I AM AN "AFRO-AMERICAN." All the white newspapers of this country regard you as "negroes" and write Negro with a little "n." ... They regard you as a common noun. ... Now I get around that undesirable title by adopting "AFRO-AMERICAN," which calls for the use of two big capital "A's." (Laughter and applause.) I AM A PROPER NOUN, NOT A COMMON NOUN!

Fortune rejected the term *colored* as lacking geographical or political significance. He considered it "a cowardly subterfuge," an attempt to convey the impression that the person so designated had no race that he wished to acknowledge. "I always feel a sort of merciful contempt," he said, "for the goody-goody Afro-American who insists that he is a 'colored person.' "[42]

The attempt to establish the National Afro-American League, although abortive, was nevertheless of lasting significance. It represented a vision which would be revived and would influence later civil-rights organizations. The league and his

42. J. W. E. Bowen, "Who Are We?" *Voice of the Negro* 3 (January 1906): 32; T. Thomas Fortune, "Who Are We?" *Voice of the Negro* 3 (March 1906): 197–98; National Negro Business League, *Report of the Seventh Annual Convention*, (Boston 1906), p. 156. Partly as the result of the articles in *The Voice of the Negro* and partly because of questions raised over a bill pending in Congress which referred to the "colored race," the *New York Tribune* took a survey among 20 prominent Negroes as to the term which they preferred. Eleven were found to prefer *Negro* spelled with a capital *N* and only two to prefer *Afro-American*. Among those favoring *Negro* were Booker T. Washington, Judge Robert Terrell (although he objected strongly to the term Negress), Judson Lyons, George Knox, and Charles W. Anderson. Of those questioned only Fortune and Professor W. S. Scarborough of Wilberforce University unequivocally favored *Afro-American* (*New York Tribune*, June 10, 1906).

other efforts as Afro-American agitator Fortune regarded as preludes to ultimate racial integration and assimilation, which he thought were inevitable. But pending these developments, which would occur in the distant future, he was convinced that Negroes would have to fight their own battles. And in an effort to instill a feeling of dignity among members of his own race and to win greater respect from whites, he carried on his campaign for the use of the term *Afro-American*.

Southern Travels: Early Relations with Booker T. Washington

DURING THE NINETIES FORTUNE TRAVELED EXTENSIVELY IN the South writing for the *Sun* and *Age* and other papers and observing at first hand the worsening plight of southern Negroes. During these years he paid several visits to Tuskegee and cemented the bonds with Booker T. Washington which were to be a decisive influence in his career.

On all his travels Fortune wrote of conditions in the South for the *Sun*, but his most comprehensive reportorial tour was made in the winter of 1894–95 when he spent five months in the southern states and traveled 10,000 miles. He wrote thirty signed articles for the Sunday *Sun* as well as numerous news dispatches. His articles covered such diverse subjects as the Tillman movement in South Carolina, the songs which Negro workers sang as they loaded cotton onto a ship in Charleston harbor, the role of Afro-American preachers in southern politics, the Back-to-Africa movement, and the evils of the chain gang and convict lease system. In the *Sun* of April 14, 1895, appeared the results of a survey which Fortune had made among leading Afro-Americans in the South, among them Booker T. Washington, Norris Wright Cuney of Texas, and John Mitchell, Jr., of Virginia. In a circular letter he asked their views about the status of racial discrimination and the economic status of Negroes. From the survey and from his own observations, Fortune declared that discrimination was much more intense than it had been twenty years earlier. Economic opportunities were becoming more restricted, and few jobs other than menial ones were open to Negroes.[1]

The next winter he was in Atlanta to visit the Cotton States and International Exposition. Atlanta, he found, was a "new" and "gawky" city where "prejudice of race" was "more general and pronounced than in any other city of the South." He was unable to find a social, civil, or political right to which a black man was entitled and which white men could control, that had not been abridged or denied. To expect the fullest development of the members of either race under such conditions was "to expect a stream to rise above its source." At the exposition Fortune observed many examples of the rural white southerner— "the backbone of the South"—the man "who did most of the fighting in the war," and who "does most of the fighting now." His type was seldom elected to Congress, but he was a force in the state legislatures and was responsible for the Jim Crow coach laws and the constitutional conventions which disfranchised Negroes. "He heads the lynching party and thinks he is bigger than the sheriff, and he is." The jails and chain gangs were not instituted for such as he. The white masses know they can commit any sort of excess without fear of punishment. "The

1. *New York Sun*, April 14, 1895. For details about Cuney see pp. 149–50. John Mitchell, Jr., as already noted, was editor of the *Richmond Planet* and a successful banker.

black masses, on the other hand, know that the chain gang and convict camp are eternally yawning for them," a fact which drives them to desperate action. "Contempt of the law in the South on the part of the white masses breeds contempt on the part of the black masses." But the records show only the crimes of the blacks; the crimes of the whites go unrecorded and unpunished.[2]

Fortune wrote satirically of the visit of evangelist Dwight L. Moody, who spent four weeks in Atlanta during the exposition, preaching in a tabernacle built especially for him. Moody, said Fortune, was a kind of circus, "sought after by the religious and curiosity seekers of the community, as the rest of mankind seek after Barnum's greatest show on earth." But of the 100,000 persons living in Atlanta, there were 40,000 who were not permitted to look upon Mr. Moody's red whiskers and face and hear him lift up his voice in song and exhortation "unless they would consent to pocket their self-respect and accept seats reserved in a corner of the tabernacle made with hands." All of these were persons who had been reared in the Christian faith. Some, perhaps half, were "as black as the Cyrenian who helped the Master bear his cross to Calvary's brow." Others were yellow; others were as white as Moody himself—but all were Afro-Americans, and on that account "unable to drink in the word of Life as it percolated from Mr. Moody's lips in his big tabernacle without placing themselves on exhibition as proscribed members of society and of the great Christian family." It was but fair to say, he added, that few Afro-Americans went to hear Moody. They stayed away, leaving him "free to wrestle with the white sinners, fully conscious of the size of the job." But those who tried to hear Moody and who objected to being seated in the Jim Crow section were faced with charges of disorderly conduct—and the Fulton County jail.[3]

2. *New York Sun*, December 15, 1895.
3. Ibid.

Fortune himself experienced at first hand increasing discrimination in transportation. In April 1890 he began a tour which took him to Tuskegee and to Jacksonville, where he had not been for twelve years and where he was royally entertained. He traveled first class from New York to Montgomery, Alabama, without any unpleasantness. But in the railroad station at Montgomery, where he bought a ticket for Tuskegee, he found separate ticket windows for "white" and "colored" and was forced to ride in the Jim Crow coach. When he left Montgomery for Jacksonville, he again purchased his ticket at the "colored" window but then boarded a Pullman car and bought a berth without any difficulty. As yet the Pullman Company usually treated Negroes equally with whites. But, after this trip, Fortune branded the railroad system of the South as a whole "a monumental fraud, outrage and swindle" on Afro-Americans. The Jim Crow coaches in which blacks were forced to ride in no way approximated coaches for white passengers. The next year, when he left the Afro-American League convention in Knoxville, he, along with a friend, took a seat in the common smoking car. The conductor ordered the two men to leave. Fortune protested so vehemently that the conductor left, but the two Afro-Americans, anticipating more trouble, transferred to the Pullman car. Their pleasure in the trip through the mountains was spoiled by the incident. "There are some laws which no self-respecting person should be expected to obey," Fortune declared. "No man is compelled to obey a law which degrades his manhood and defrauds him of what he paid for. When I willingly consent to ride in a 'Jim Crow Car' it will be when I am a dead Afro-American Leaguer."[4]

On every trip which he made, he found conditions more degrading. Even Pullman travel became increasingly difficult, the more so after the United States Supreme Court enunciated the "equal but separate" doctrine in 1896. No man could accept

4. *Age*, April 26, May 10, May 17, 1890; August 1, 1891.

travel conditions in the South, he declared in a letter to the *New York Evening Post*, without feeling outraged. There was "no self-respecting Afro-American" who had ever been forced to submit to "the vile application" of separate coach laws who did not "hate the malicious, cowardly men who put them on the statute books." When the Supreme Court placed the seal of constitutionality on such laws, "it made violation of solemn contract permissible and justifiable, where Afro-American citizens are the victims, and sowed the seeds of hatred in the breast of ten million freemen who, 200,000 strong, helped to crush the head of the Southern rebel snake and to save the Union of the States from disruption!"[5]

Fortune frequently advocated the diffusion of the Negro population of the South to other parts of the Union. As part of the program of the Afro-American League, he proposed the creation of a bureau to help persons emigrate to the North. But for all the bitterness which he expressed toward the federal government and the discouragement he felt over the conditions in the South, Fortune rejected emigration to Africa as a solution for southern Negroes.

During his travels he observed some of the manifestations of the Back-to-Africa movement which swept parts of the South in the nineties. What he saw strengthened his earlier conviction that African emigration schemes were a delusion and that the men who promoted them were at best misguided. Although in one early editorial in the *Globe*, he had expressed the opinion that emigration to Africa, which Bishop Henry M. Turner of Georgia was already advocating, or to some other place, might

5. *New York Evening Post*, November 25, 1903. In 1896 in the case of *Plessy* v. *Ferguson* (163 U.S. 537) the United States Supreme Court upheld the constitutionality of a Louisiana law which required railroads to provide "equal but separate accommodations for the white and colored races" and imposed penalties upon persons who failed to comply with the act.

be the solution for southern Negroes who were denied the protection of the United States Constitution, on the whole he strongly opposed emigration proposals. The reports which T. McCants Stewart brought back from Liberia strengthened his opposition to colonization. In 1884 he declared that there had been "no more lamentable failure" than the attempt to colonize American Negroes on the west coast of Africa. Negroes were *Americans* who were here to stay.[6]

Fortune excoriated the West Indian born Bishop Edward Wilmot Blyden, who came from Liberia to the United States to carry on a campaign for the American Colonization Society, as a "hireling and spy." He denounced Blyden's derogatory characterization of mulattoes as "mongrels who set themselves up as leaders" and accused him of fomenting discord among Afro-Americans in order to delude them into going to Africa. His opposition to emigration schemes and to the propaganda of the American Colonization Society was intensified early in 1892 when a group of 200 destitute blacks from Oklahoma

6. *Globe*, January 13, 1883; September 6, 1884. In *Black and White*, as already seen, Fortune strongly rejected African colonization (see chapter 3 above). Bishop Henry M. Turner (1834–1915) of the A.M.E. Church was the most important black advocate of African colonization in the years between the Civil War and World War I. Turner, who had been stationed in Georgia as a chaplain of the Freedmen's Bureau, played an important part in the formation of the Republican party in that state during Reconstruction and was elected to the Georgia Constitutional Convention of 1867 and to the state legislature in 1868. He, along with the other black members, was expelled from the legislature by the white majority. After this experience he became increasingly disillusioned over the prospects of Negroes in the United States and began to urge emigration. He became one of the vice-presidents of the American Colonization Society. An excellent recent account of Turner's activities is contained in Edwin S. Redkey, *Black Exodus: Black Nationalist and Back-to-Africa Movements, 1890–1910* (New Haven, 1969).

arrived in New York City. They came expecting the Colonization Society to provide funds and transportation to Liberia but
found themselves stranded. They had arrived without authori-
zation from the society and found that there were no ships
available. Fortune and Stewart joined local ministers of the
A.M.E. church in trying to raise money to help care for the
would-be emigrants and to return them to Oklahoma. At a
public meeting and through the columns of the *Age* and the *Sun*
he assailed the American Colonization Society and Bishop
Turner for their responsibility for what he considered exploitation of ignorant and helpless victims.[7]

Fortune was, of course, skeptical about the expedition of
the *Horsa*, a small ship which sailed from Savannah in March
1895, carrying some 200 blacks to Liberia. A year later, after
interviewing some of the emigrants who had returned, he reported that most of those who had gone were disillusioned by
their African experience and wanted to return to the United
States, but few had the money to do so. He insisted that during
a four months trip through the South he was unable to find any
genuine enthusiasm for emigration to Africa. Such interest as
there was, he was sure, was "artificial, stimulated by fanatical or
selfish people."[8]

Bishop Henry M. Turner was a frequent target of For-
tune's journalistic attacks. In one article in the *Sun* he said that
Turner and others who claimed that the future of blacks in the
United States was hopeless were too impatient and short-sighted
—that they did not realize that the race problem in the United
States would be solved only by a slow, evolutionary process.
They expected a slave caste that had been in existence for 250

7. *Age*, January 4, January 11, January 18, 1890; Redkey, *Black
Exodus*, pp. 122–24. For an accont of Blyden see, Hollis R. Lynch,
Edward Wilmot Blyden, Pan Negro Patriot, 1832–1912 (London,
1967).

8. *New York Sun*, April 5, 1896.

years to become a masterful, free caste in the short space of a quarter of a century. American Negroes were better off than Turner thought they were, said Fortune, and would be still better off if men like Turner "would play less with their tongues and saw more wood with their hands." He denounced Turner, who himself continued to live in the United States, for calling Negroes who did not choose to go back to Africa such names as "scullions," "cowards," "sneaks," and "menials."[9]

While rejecting emigration as a solution to the race problem in the United States, Fortune was by no means indifferent to Africa. He was deeply concerned about the exploitation of the continent by white colonial powers and sometimes wrote scathing editorials on the subject. "If it should be deemed necessary to their thieving purposes in Africa, the European powers will not hesitate a moment to destroy every black woman and child on the continent of Africa," he declared. "Such are the practices of great nations which profess the Christianity of Jesus of Nazareth." But he also predicted the ultimate redemption of the continent from the oppressors:

> Bloodshed and usurpations, the rum jug and the Bible—these will be the program of the white race in Africa, for, perhaps, a hundred years. . . . But, in the course of time, the people will become educated not only in the grasping and cruel nature of the white man, but in the knowledge of their power, their priority ownership in the soil, and in the desperation which tyranny and greed never fail to breed for their

9. Ibid., August 30, 1896. Booker T. Washington shared Fortune's opposition to emigration and his opinion of Turner and encouraged Fortune to derogate the bishop's schemes. When, a few years later, Turner once again castigated as contemptible those Negroes who would not go to Africa, Fortune replied in an editorial in the *Boston Transcript*, May 10, 1900, entitled, "A Prophet of Unrest," saying that Negroes in the United States would accept the advice of Washington, who opposed emigration, as a safer guide and better authority than the wails of Turner.

own destruction. Out of the convulsions which are sure to come an African Confederation, not unlike that of Germany, will certainly be evolved. . . . So out of toil and privation and long agony good will will eventually come to the swarthy millions of our Fatherland.

He was sympathetic to proposals for missionary work in Africa by the African Methodist Episcopal church, and as early as 1896 suggested that the time was ripe for an "association of Africans and the descendants of Africa from all parts of the world."[10]

In 1895 both Fortune and Turner participated in a conference on Africa held under the sponsorship of Gammon Theological Seminary in Atlanta. Participants were white and Negro clergy and laymen, including representatives of the American Colonization Society. The theme which ran throughout most of the papers presented was "the relation of the American Negro to the civilization and redemption of his Fatherland." Many of the speakers expressed the view that Providence had caused the Negro to be brought to America in order that he might return to Africa to carry on missionary work. Bishop Turner declared: "The Negro was brought to this country in the providence of God to a heaven-permitted if not a divine-sanctioned manual laboring school, that he might have direct contact with the mightiest race that ever trod the face of the globe." In the United States, he insisted, *"there is no manhood future . . . for the Negro."* To him it seemed practical to transport two or three million American Negroes to the "fatherland."

Fortune's paper "The Nationalization of Africa" was somewhat of an incongruity at such a gathering. In it he stressed the unity of the human race and once more expressed his assimilationist views. "Color of the skin, texture of hair, differences of language and of habitation avail nothing," he said, "against the

10. *Globe*, January 13, 1883; *Freeman*, January 15, 1887; *Age*, June 28, 1890; *Age*, March 22, 1906

demonstration that all mankind proceeded from the same cause;
. . . that their origin and their destiny are as interlocked and as
inseparable as life and death." In time the whites who were presently subduing Africa and imposing their civilization would
begin "to be absorbed and assimilated by the vast black majority." The inevitable destiny of the white minority in Africa was
absorption and assimilation by the blacks, just as the destiny of
blacks in America was ultimate assimilation by the white majority. "I know," said Fortune, "that to many this is an abhor-
rent view of the question, but we are dealing with the philosophy of recorded history and the invariable laws of human
conduct and not with the prejudices of men." Rigid laws
adopted by the English, Germans, French, and Belgians to keep
the native population in "their place" would prove ineffectual
in the long run. But, he thought, the Christian religion would
supplant other religious systems in Africa because it was the
"best code of moral philosophy ever given to man."[11]

During his travels Fortune observed political conditions and
became acquainted with the southern Negro political leaders.
After his return to the Republican fold, he was active in Republican politics in New York, and prior to the 1896 presidential
nomination he was involved in the game of Republican politics
in the South.

Fortune strongly supported Republican efforts during the
Harrison administration to enact the Lodge Federal Elections
Bill which was introduced in 1890. An editorial in the *Age* con-

11. *Africa and the American Negro: Addresses and Proceedings
of the Congress on Africa. Held under the auspices of the Stewart
Missionary Foundation for Africa of Gammon Theological Seminary in connection with the Cotton States and International Exposition, Dec. 13–15, 1895* (Atlanta, 1896), pp. 13–14, 198–99, 203–04,
and passim. Emphasis as in original.

tended that if states were unable to secure honest elections, Congress had an obligation to act. To argue that there was no remedy to fraud was to admit the failure of the democratic process. When the Democratic press in the North took up the cry of "Federal bayonets in the bill!" Fortune declared that the provisions of the Lodge bill were merely an answer to "the shotguns and the Winchester rifles with which the Democracy usurped and maintained power in the South." He was critical of white Republicans for not campaigning vigorously for the bill, but not even all northern Negroes favored it. William Still of Philadelphia was reported as saying that it was wisest for the race to concentrate on making money to improve its status and to forget about politics. Fortune replied that black men could not afford to sit back quietly and accept the denial of constitutional rights. More interesting, in the light of later developments, were differences between Fortune and the youthful W. E. B. Du Bois, who had recently won a scholarship at Harvard. Du Bois was quoted as saying at a meeting in Boston that the whole idea of the Federal Elections Bill was wrong. The idea that merely passing a law could cure evils was absurd. "We must ever keep before us the fact that the South has some excuse for its present attitude," said Du Bois. "We must remember that a good many of our people south of Mason and Dixon's line are not fit for the responsibility of republican government. When you have the right sort of black voters you will need no election laws. The battle of my people in the South must be a moral one, not a legal or physical one." To this Fortune replied that Mr. Du Bois was still young and did not know as much about some things as he thought he did. The Federal Elections Bill was based on the Fifteenth Amendment. What Mr. Du Bois had to say was "humbug based upon no provision of the Constitution and at war with all the principles predominant in our system of government." Southern newspapers might praise Du Bois's remarks, but such remarks represented "simply the opinions of a very young man who will think and talk differently a few years hence."[12]

As it became apparent that the bill would not pass, some northern newspapers began to urge reduction of southern representation, but Fortune opposed this strategy as he previously had done and continued to do. "Once take away the representation based upon the Afro-American vote," he warned, "and it will be a full century before the Afro-American regains the right to vote in the South." When the Lodge bill was finally killed by the vote of eight Republican senators who voted against cloture, the *Age* declared that once more the Republican party had betrayed Afro-Americans. The treachery of the Hayes administration was being repeated.[13]

But in spite of his bitterness, Fortune did not desert the party, largely, no doubt, because the Democratic party, dominated by southern white supremacists, was a greater evil. Democrats were responsible for the movement for complete disfranchisement which began with the adoption of the Mississippi Constitution of 1890. A series of editorials in the *Age* was highly critical of the Mississippi convention and expressed doubts as to the wisdom of Isaiah Montgomery, the only Negro delegate, who made a speech in which he indicated acquiescence in the abdication of political rights while expressing hope that the convention, in return for this abdication, would give Negroes some assurances of improved race relations. The speech, the *Age* declared, was not in the best interests of the race. In any "compromise" the white man invariably got the better of the black. Fortune predicted that the constitution would not be fairly administered. "Can a thief be just to the man he has robbed?" he asked. Nor did he agree with the view (expressed by Booker T. Washington and others) that the "understand-

12. *Age*, November 30, 1889; July 19, August 9, 1890; June 13, 1891.

13. Ibid., September 6, 1890; January 10, 1891.

ing" requirements in the suffrage clause would serve as a spur to Negroes to gain an education in order to qualify themselves to vote.[14]

During the presidential campaign of 1892, the *Age* supported Harrison for reelection and received financial aid from the Republican organization. Fortune's most important link with the Harrison administration and with white Republicans was General James S. Clarkson, who served for a time as assistant postmaster general. Clarkson, an old time abolitionist, was editor of the *Des Moines Register*. Like Fortune, he had entered journalism via the printer's trade. He was one of the dwindling number of northern Republicans who continued consistently to champion the rights of southern Negroes. As dispenser of patronage in the Post Office Department he was able to bring about the appointment of more than 1100 Negroes—a fact of which he was proud but which brought protests from white Republicans. A warm friendship developed between Clarkson and Fortune, and Fortune apparently had some influence through Clarkson in the selection of Negro appointees by Harrison.[15]

During his travels Fortune came to know most of the Negro political leaders in the South, a fact which made him valuable to Clarkson. Probably the most influential of these was Norris Wright Cuney of Texas. Cuney, the child of a Virginia planter and a slave mother, had been taken to Texas as a child and enjoyed unusual educational opportunities for a slave. After the Civil War he settled in Galveston and acquired substantial wealth as contractor for the employment of Negro stevedores. He was the most powerful Republican in Texas and held the

14. Ibid., September 27, October 25, November 29, 1890.

15. Ibid., November 19, 1892; *National Cyclopedia of American Biography* (New York, 1899), 2: 118; James W. Clarkson to Washington, February 7, 1896, Washington Papers; James Dean to Bruce, August 8, 1891, Bruce Papers.

post of national committeeman for years in spite of efforts of Lily Whites to oust him. He was close to General Clarkson and through the latter's influence was appointed Collector of the Port of Galveston, the most important post which Harrison conferred upon a Negro. Fortune observed that in most southern states the real leadership was vested in white men, but in Texas Cuney exercised genuine independent leadership over the black voters and enjoyed greater confidence of the blacks than any other Negro leader in the South. In Texas, Fortune also met a young man named Emmett J. Scott, who was closely associated with Cuney. Scott, who had been born in Houston in 1873, had entered newspaper work after graduating from Wiley University. In 1893 he began publication of the *Texas Freeman* in Houston. In 1897 he went to Tuskegee to become private secretary to Booker T. Washington.[16]

During his visits to Atlanta, Fortune renewed his friendship with William A. Pledger, who was for many years the most influential Negro among Georgia Republicans. He served as chairman of the state central committee and was a delegate to every national convention from 1876 to 1900. He maintained a law office with Henry Lincoln Johnson and dabbled in journalism, but his true vocation was politics. Like Fortune, he was a convivial soul with a weakness for strong drink. Fortune loved him because he possessed an "abundance of those exuberant qualities of head and heart which grapple men to the heart and keep them there," and because of his courage and refusal to yield "an iota of manhood rights or personal dignity."[17]

16. Fortune wrote an article on Cuney and Texas Negroes in the *New York Sun*, December 23, 1894. See also Maude Cuney Hare, *Norris Wright Cuney: A Tribune of the Black People* (New York, 1913), passim. For account of Scott's early life see *Indianapolis Freeman*, March 26, 1904,

17. *Washington Colored American*, March 17, 1900; Adams, "Col. William Pledger," *Colored American Magazine*, June, 1902, pp. 146–49.

During the winter of 1895–96 Pledger and Fortune were actively engaged in the business of rounding up Negro delegates to the Republican National Convention. In a dispatch to the *Sun* in 1895 on the state of southern politics, Fortune had commented on the impotence of the Republican party in the South, where since 1876 most state organizations did not even nominate candidates for office. But southern Republican politicians (who were predominantly Negro) made the most of their limited opportunities by seeking appointment to federal jobs and sending delegates to the national conventions. These delegates were much sought after by presidential aspirants, a fact which gave southern Republicans their only real power. It was a system which, as Fortune admitted, "bred scandals." Nevertheless, he said, southern Negroes would resist any move by the national Republican organization to deny votes in the national convention to states which were unable to deliver electoral votes—a reform proposal which was being made by some northern Republicans.[18] In fact he himself had a part in rounding up Negro delegates during the 1896 campaign.

In January 1896 a meeting of leading Negro Republicans from the states of the Deep South was held in New Orleans. Among those present were Cuney and Emmett Scott of Texas, Pinchback of Louisiana, Pledger of Georgia, and the venerable Emanuel Fortune of Florida. The younger Fortune was the only northerner present. He told the press that the group had discussed methods of securing an honest count of Negro votes and had also considered presidential candidates. It seems probable that the meeting was called partly at the instigation of General Clarkson and that one of the purposes was to develop a strategy to circumvent Mark Hanna, who was already engaged in a campaign to round up southern delegates favorable to the nomination of William McKinley of Ohio. Fortune was put in charge of coordinating the movement in Florida, Alabama,

18. *New York Sun*, August 23, 1895.

Georgia, and Louisiana. Charles W. Anderson was later sent from New York to help him. Clarkson favored the nomination of Senator William B. Allison. In Texas Cuney supported Allison, but in Louisiana Pinchback supported Speaker Thomas B. Reed. In Georgia Pledger and his partner, Johnson, both worked for Allison and later for Reed. Fortune and Anderson seem to have followed a similar course.[19] The *Washington Bee* described Fortune and Anderson as two fishermen who had gone South with "boodle bait on their hooks, fishing for Negro delegates." But they were "green in the business," and hence their luck was poor. They were using the same "bait" as McKinley's supporters, but McKinley "bait" was being used more effectively.[20]

Pledger and Fortune traveled over Georgia together seeking to round up delegates to the state convention to oppose the Hanna organization, which was headed by a white man, Colonel E. A. Buck. They dispensed whisky and cigars, and no doubt money, as part of their persuasive tactics. But in spite of their

19. *New Orleans Picayune*, January 11, 1896, quoted in *Age*, January 23, 1896; Fortune, "Passing Show," *Norfolk Journal and Guide*, January 28, 1928; *Cleveland Gazette*, March 21, 1896; Clarkson to Washington, February 7, 1896, Washington Papers. A letter from Senator T. C. Platt to Clarkson, May 27, 1896, in the James W. Clarkson Papers, Manuscript Division, Library of Congress, shows that Cuney and Fortune had received checks for $1000 and $200 respectively.

20. *Washington Bee*, March 21, 1896. Richard Greener wrote Whitfield McKinlay that he had information that the "slick and oily Timothy" Fortune was not entirely loyal to Clarkson and Allison. When informed of this, Clarkson wrote McKinlay that he still had confidence in Fortune—that he was doing good work in the South. "He has his weaknesses as you and I have," said Clarkson, "but he is wonderfully smart and I think he is loyal" (Richard Greener to Whitfield McKinlay, Februauary 20, 1896; Clarkson to McKinlay, February 29, 1890, Woodson Collection, Manuscript Divison, Library of Congress).

efforts, at the tumultous convention, which was made up largely of Negroes, a majority of the delegates favored McKinley, and Judson W. Lyons, another Negro lawyer, defeated Pledger in the vote for national committeeman. Fortune attributed Pledger's poor showing in the convention to the fact that many Negroes preferred to follow white leaders rather than men of their own race, but a recent scholar says that prior to the convention Buck, who was trying to bring the party under white control, persuaded Pledger that his cause was hopeless and that it was better for him not to contest the control of the convention, and that a deal was made between the two men.[21]

During the months which he spent in Georgia, Fortune engaged in journalistic activities as well as politics. For a time he took over the publication of a Negro paper, the *Reporter*, changed its name to the *Southern Age*, and apparently considered settling permanently in Atlanta. Mrs. Victoria Matthews, who traveled in the South during the winter of 1895–96 making a study of southern Negro women and ways to improve their condition for the Federation of Afro-American Women, was also in Atlanta. She joined in the editing of the newspaper.[22] But Fortune soon abandoned this undertaking and decided to continue to make New York his headquarters.

He traveled to the Republican national convention in Saint Louis with the black delegates from Georgia in a private Pullman car. But in Saint Louis the Negroes found the color line was drawn almost as tightly as in Atlanta. They were refused accommodations in the good hotels and forced to take quarters in private homes. At the convention, southern whites were con-

21. Fortune, "Passing Show," *Norfolk Journal and Guide*, February 25, 1928; *New York Sun*, June 28, 1896; Bacote, "The Negro in Georgia Politics," pp. 235–39.

22. Fortune to Washington, April 10, 1896, Washington Papers; *Cleveland Gazette*, May 30, 1896; *Washington Bee*, July 18, 1896; *New York Sun*, July 5, 1896.

solidated as they had not been since 1876. Cuney, who had refused to get on the McKinley bandwagon, came to the convention, claiming that he was a duly elected delegate, but was
refused a seat. Prominent political figures like Blanche K. Bruce,
John R. Lynch, and Pinchback were present simply as observers and not as delegates. The Hanna-McKinley forces were in
such complete control that the convention was a cut and dried
affair. The platform which was adopted condemned lynching
and mob action but merely stated a desire for a free and un-
restricted ballot without advocating a federal election law. It
elicited little enthusiasm from the Negro delegates.[23]

During the campaign the *Age* denounced the Democratic
party as the party of racism. Afro-Americans had more at stake
in the election than the hard money question, it declared. Fortune himself campaigned for McKinley, but he was critical of
Hanna as national chairman, claiming that the latter wanted to
relegate Afro-American Republicans to the role of "hewers of
wood and drawers of water" for the party. However, during
the closing weeks of the campaign, Fortune was sent out by the
Republican National Committee to address colored Republican
clubs in northern cities.[24]

After the election Fortune and Booker T. Washington spec-
ulated over appointments which McKinley might make. In the
press it was suggested that Washington might even be named
to the Cabinet as secretary of agriculture—a possibility which
both he and Fortune considered remote. But Washington said
that the suggestion gave him "a lot of fun." Washington said that
Fortune deserved a good appointment from the incoming administration and indicated that he wanted to do anything he

23. Fortune, "Passing Show," *Norfolk Journal and Guide*,
March 24, 1928; *New York Sun*, June 28, 1896; *Age*, quoted in *Indianapolis World*, August 1, 1896.
24. *Age* quoted in *Indianapolis World*, October 3, 1896; *Cleveland Gazette*, August 22, October 24, 1896.

could to help him in securing whatever post he wanted. Fortune was interested in the post of consul in Jamaica, or some other post which had not been held by an Afro-American. Washington predicted that either Senator Allison or Andrew D. White would be named secretary of state and that the appointment of either man would insure that Fortune would receive the kind of assignment abroad which he wanted. But when word of McKinley's choices began to leak out, Fortune expressed consternation, especially at the selection of the aged John Sherman for the State Department, an appointment which seemed to doom his personal prospects.[25]

McKinley's inaugural address, in which he promised the white South that he would do nothing, nor permit anything to be done, which would disturb the growing reconciliation between the sections, was not reassuring to Fortune. But he at first withheld criticism since he continued to hope for an appointment. Later he began to assail the president's southern policy. He expressed dissatisfaction with his failure to appoint more Negroes to office and especially with his treatment of Judson Lyons, the lawyer who was Republican national committeeman from Georgia. After proposing Lyons for the postmastership at Augusta, McKinley urged him to withdraw his name when southern whites objected to the appointment of a Negro to a post where he would have contact with whites. In a speech at the Metropolitan Methodist Church in Washington, Fortune castigated the administration for its handling of the case. He himself sought an appointment as a member of an industrial commission, an investigative body appointed by Mc-

25. Fortune to Washington, December 3, December 18, 1896; January 18, February 24, 1897; Washington to Fortune, December 15, December 26, 1896, Washington Papers. In spite of the unfavorable prospects, Fortune continued to hope for an appointment and enlisted some of his friends to intercede for him (Fortune to John E. Bruce, March 22, 1897, Bruce Papers).

Kinley, but was disappointed. No Negroes were included on the commission.[26]

Fortune's opinion of the president sank even lower as he observed McKinley's conduct on his tour of the South in the winter of 1898, even though McKinley paid a visit to Tuskegee. Fortune wrote Washington that he was glad that the visit to Tuskegee was a success, but added that the president was "no friend of us." The president's speeech at Atlanta in which there was "no word of rebuke to deviltry" and no word of encouragement to Negroes was branded as "about as cruel and cold blooded as can be imagined."[27]

By the time of McKinley's visit to Tuskegee, Fortune and Booker T. Washington were on terms of such intimacy that they wrote to each other almost daily, and sometimes more than once a day. This friendship, seemingly paradoxical, but resting nevertheless on genuine affection and respect as well as mutual self-interest, had begun in the eighties and had became much closer during the nineties, when Fortune spent long periods of time at Tuskegee.

The two men were almost exactly the same age, Washington being about six months older. Both had been born into slavery and had grown to manhood during Reconstruction. Both had achieved education and a degree of success against great odds. Both men were southerners at heart, although Fortune spent most of his time exiled in New York. They loved the region of their birth and were deeply concerned with improving the con-

26. *New York Sun*, June 20, 1897; *Washington Evening Star*, July 20, 1897; Bacote, "The Negro in Georgia Politics," pp. 251–52; Fortune to Washington, March 11, July 22, July 25, August 9, September 7, 1898, Washington Papers. Lyons was ultimately appointed Register of the Treasury when Blanche K. Bruce, who held the post, died.

27. Fortune to Washington, December 17, 1898, Washington Papers.

dition of their race in the South. Both felt that they were working toward the same goals, although they sometimes differed over methods and short-term objectives.

Washington always urged Negroes to stay in the South, while Fortune usually (though not always) thought that they should be encouraged to move northward. Fortune scorned states' rights doctrines and excoriated the United States Supreme Court decision in the civil rights cases. In contrast, in one of his early addresses in the North in 1884, Washington said that "brains, property, and character" would settle the civil rights question—that the best course to pursue with regard to civil rights in the South was to let the matter alone and it would settle itself. Good teachers would be more effective in solving race problems than civil rights bills and investigating committeees.[28] And yet when Fortune first urged the creation of the National Afro-American League, Washington gave his enthusiastic blessing.

Fortune put great emphasis on the exercise of political rights and the obligation of the federal government to protect these rights and enforce the Fifteenth Amendment. In public statements Washington's position on political rights was equivocal. At times he deprecated political activity and appeared to acquiesce in disfranchisement, but Fortune knew, as the public did not, that behind the scenes Washington worked against disfranchisement and segregation legislation. He also was aware of the limitations which residence in the South and the necessity of raising funds for Tuskegee imposed upon Washington.

Like Washington, Fortune believed, as he had stated in *Black and White*, that the interests of blacks and whites were fundamentally the same. He agreed with Washington that race

28. Booker T. Washington, "The Educational Outlook in the South," *Journal of the Proceedings and Addresses of the National Education Association, Session of the Year 1884, at Madison, Wisc.* (Boston, 1885), pp. 125–30.

progress depended upon economic progress and sometimes expressed views on education and the importance of hard work and thrift which sounded very much like those expressed by the Tuskegee principal. But as editor of the *Globe* and the *Freeman*, he held an economic philosophy very different in some respects from that of Washington and had expressed views on labor relations quite inconsistent with those of Washington. In later years he showed less interest in economic questions and labor problems, perhaps because he recognized that his earlier views were utopian. But there is no evidence that he ever condoned the use of Negroes as strikebreakers. He occasionally denounced white unions for discriminatory practices, but he urged Afro-Americans to form their own unions.

Like Washington, Fortune could be conciliatory, when he chose, in addressing a white audience. At a dinner in Connecticut in honor of George Washington Cable in 1885 he asserted the right of Negroes to equality in civil rights but warned that Negroes must not try to push themselves into prominence but should seek education and leave their social position to take care of itself.[29]

More significant was Fortune's speech "Afro-Americans in the South," made on Colored Peoples Day at Waco Cotton Palace in December 1894, almost a year before Washington made his celebrated address at Atlanta. The conciliatory note which Fortune struck bore little resemblence to some of the speeches which he made in his role of "Afro-American agitator." The theme of the speech was the progress which Afro-Americans had made since emancipation and the importance of economic foundations for continued progress. He quoted Frederick Douglass who had said that Negroes should be judged "not by the heights to which we have risen, but by the depths from which we have been dragged." The Afro-American was fighting

29. *Meridien* (Conn.) *Daily Republican*, quoted in *New York Freeman*, November 14, 1885.

bravely up from the dependent condition of the slave to the self-reliant condition of a man. The progress which he had made would have been impossible without the sympathy and assistance of whites. The interests of blacks and whites were "one and the same," and "the man who lifts a finger to disturb the good relations which should exist between them, who would put neighbor against neighbor . . . is a common enemy to the state and to the nation."[30] But although in this address and others which he gave, Fortune was careful to avoid offending his white listeners and to emphasize the interdependence of whites and blacks, he avoided the semiapologetic, deprecatory tone which Washington sometimes used. Nor did he ever tell the "darkey" stories which were an important part of Washington's stock in trade.

There were marked contrasts in appearance and personality between Fortune and Washington. The latter was a big man, with broad shoulders and large hands and feet, who always retained a certain rusticity in dress and appearance—perhaps as part of the image which he sought to perpetuate. Fortune was also tall, but extremely slender and rather delicate looking, with small hands and feet. He had a taste for expensive and fashionable clothes. Fortune was intense, impetuous, and hot tempered. Washington, on the other hand, possessed masterly self-control and the ability to disguise his feelings. In spite of his seeming simplicity and guilelessness, Washington was the more adroit and subtle of the two, and Fortune had profound respect for his friend's diplomatic skill and self-control.

The beginnings of this friendship are obscure, but the two men knew each other at least by the early 1880s, soon after Fortune had begun his journalistic career in New York and soon after the founding of Tuskegee Institute. If they had not met earlier, they became acquainted when Washington first began to come North, seeking financial aid for Tuskegee from white

30. *Dallas Morning News*, December 2, 1894.

philanthropists. During these early years Washington was concerned only with the success of Tuskegee and thought of himself only as an educator and not in the role of race spokesman and leader which he later sought to assume. In fact Fortune was the better known of the two, and his familiarity with New York, its newspapers, and some of its leading men, was no doubt useful to the young man from Alabama.

In May 1885 the *Freeman* published a long article on Washington and the establishment of Tuskegee, together with a picture of Washington which showed him wearing a heavy mustache. In 1886 the paper carried an account of a visit to Tuskegee written by Francis J. Grimké. There were other articles on Tuskegee from time to time, but in some of them Washington's name was not even mentioned. The cult of personality which characterized Washington's later career had not yet begun. On a later visit to Tuskegee in 1888 Grimké described Washington as "a quiet unassuming man, with a wise head, and a big heart, and the weight of the race problem resting upon him." He was not mentioned very much in newspapers, said Grimké, but "judged by his work he is one of the most remarkable men that the race has yet produced—a man to be proud of, and to be honored,—a man, caring nothing about notoriety, content to be unknown, so long as the work goes on, and the race goes up."[31]

Meanwhile the *Freeman* and *Age* occasionally mentioned visits which Washington made to New York and speeches which he made in northern cities, and Washington had begun to send suggestions for editorials to Fortune.[32] But it was not until 1890, when Fortune paid his first visit to Tuskegee, that he began to

31. *Freeman*, May 16, 1885; April 9, April 17, June 4, 1887; *Age*, April 7, 1888.

32. One suggestion was a letter which Henry W. Grady sent to Washington and which Fortune published in the *Age*, using it as the basis of an editorial (Fortune to Washington, January 21, April 29, 1887, Washington Papers; *Age*, January 29, 1887).

play the role of confidant and adviser and publicist for Washington. During the period when Fortune was planning the first meeting of the National Afro-American League, which he at first hoped to hold in the South, Washington invited him to come to Tuskegee to deliver two lectures. These plans did not materialize, but on his southern trip during the spring of 1890 Fortune paid a visit to Tuskegee, delivered his lectures, and fell completely in love with the school. Thereafter he sometimes expressed a desire to come to Tuskegee permanently. After his visit he published articles on Tuskegee for a number of periodicals, including the *Christian Recorder* and *Teacher*, but the editor of *Frank Leslie's* declined to publish what he wrote. Washington expressed great pleasure with the success of Fortune's efforts, and Fortune replied that he had a great many friends among journalists and was grateful that he had been able to fulfill so successfully the agreement he had made with Washington regarding the articles.[33]

Fortune apparently visited Tuskegee again in January 1895, but he was not in Atlanta for the opening of the Cotton States Exposition and he did not hear Washington give the speech on September 18, which was to make the principal of Tuskegee a national figure. Earlier, in the *Sun*, Fortune had spoken approvingly of the selection of Washington to give the opening address on Negro Day.[34] It is difficult to believe that Fortune was enthusiastic about the content of the entire speech. The reference to Negroes as "the most patient, faithful, law-abiding, and unresentful people that the world has ever seen," who would in their "humble way" be ready to lay down their lives for their white benefactors would surely have grated on his ears. The reference to a people who, "without strikes and labor wars," had

33. Fortune to Washington, November 18, 1889; March 17, April 9, April 12, April 22, May 26, 1890, Washington Papers.
34. Fortune to Washington, January 2, 1895, Washington Papers; *New York Sun*, September 1, 1895.

built railroads and mined treasures from the earth, with its implied derogation of unions and sanction of strikebreaking, was inconsistent with views on labor which Fortune had expressed. And he could not have endorsed the acceptance of segregation implicit in the address. But he was in agreement with the basic theme of the speech—the mutual interests and interdependence of the races and the importance of Negroes to the economic development of the South. And he would have applauded the plea which Washington made for the administration of "absolute justice" and "willing obedience among all classes to the mandates of law." He was gratified with the nation-wide enthusiasm which the speech evoked—and perhaps he wanted to be sure of a front seat on the Booker T. Washington bandwagon.

Fortune published the entire text of the Atlanta address in the *Age*, and wrote a congratulatory letter to Washington in which he said that he was glad that the Tuskegeean was being hailed as the successor to Frederick Douglass. "You," he said, "are the best equipped of the lot of us to be the single figure ahead of the procession. We *must have a leader*, and it ought to be [someone] in the South, and every one of us should hold up his hands."[35]

An article by Fortune in the *Sun*, October 31, on the Atlanta address was headlined by the caption: "Is He the Negro Moses?" It declared that Washington, born a slave, had become the spokesman for the entire South. The address and its reception had been an object lesson for the whole world.

It marked the reversal of the long prevalent belief in the South that the Afro-American was incapable of the mental grasp and development of the Anglo-Saxon. It was also a proclamation that the black man is a living, positive factor in the intellect and industrial conditions of the southern states

35. Fortune to Washington, September 26, 1895, Washington Papers. Emphasis as in original.

and of the republic, and entitled to the same fair and honorable consideration enjoyed by the white man.

The appearance of Washington on the platform at Atlanta was seen by Fortune as evidence that old prejudices were giving way and an omen of still greater progress for the race during the coming years.[36]

Fortune was unable to accept an invitation to spend Christmas at Tuskegee in 1895, but he visited the school the following month and was present at the commencement in May 1896 and at the annual Tuskegee Conference in February 1897. During the winter of 1897–98 he spent several weeks at Tuskegee.[37] Emmett J. Scott, the young journalist and friend of Cuney, whom Fortune had met in Texas, had recently joined the Tuskegee staff. With Scott, who was seventeen years his junior, Fortune developed a friendship which was even closer and more enduring than his relationship with Washington.

This winter visit of Fortune's occurred on the eve of the meeting of the constitutional convention in Louisiana, which, it was generally assumed, would follow the examples set by Mississippi and South Carolina and adopt some sort of article to disfranchise the black electorate. Fortune and Scott collaborated with Washington in the preparation of an open letter to the convention which was published over Washington's name in the *New Orleans Times-Democrat* and the *Picayune*. In the letter Washington disclaimed being a politician and said that he had always advised Negroes to avoid political agitation and to emphasize the acquisition of property and the development of good character as the bases of citizenship. But the question

36. Another article by Fortune on the Atlanta address appeared in *Progress of the World*, October, 1895. See Fortune to Washington, October 12, 1895, Washington Papers.

37. Fortune to Washington, December 20, 1895; February 16, 1898; Washington to Fortune, December 6, 1896, Washington Papers; *Montgomery Daily Advertiser*, May 29, 1896.

before the convention was one which would affect the civilization of both races for a long time; therefore he felt it his duty
to speak and to plead for a voting law which would be "absolutely just and fair to black and white alike." He said that the
Negro agreed that some restriction should be put on the ballot
and did not object to an educational or property test, but he
pleaded that "the law be so clear that no one clothed with
state authority will be tempted to perjure and degrade himself
by putting one interpretation upon it for the white man and
another for the black man." He also urged that "in the degree
that you close the ballot box against the ignorant that you
open the schoolhouse. . . . No state can long prosper, when a
large percentage of its citizenship is in ignorance and poverty,
and has no interest in government."[38]

Fortune later insisted that he had not agreed with the endorsement of educational and property requirements for voting,
but he published the letter in the *Age* and declared that it was
good that the race had a man of Washington's ability and courage "to speak out in trying times like these and have the Nation
for an audience." The best opinion of the country would support the plea for a voting law without ambiguity that would
guarantee equal treatment of members of both races.

But regardless of what the "best opinion of the country"
may have been, the Louisiana convention insured the elimination of black voters by literacy and property tests, while
protecting the ballot for ignorant whites by means of a "grandfather clause," which exempted those who had been entitled to
vote on January 1, 1867, and their sons and grandsons from the
requirement of these tests. Washington evidently professed to
see some merit in the work of the convention because the voting

38. Emmett J. Scott and Lyman Beecher Stowe, *Booker T.
Washington, Builder of a Civilization* (New York, 1916), p. 88;
New Orleans Times Democrat, February 21, 1898; *New Orleans
Picayune*, February 21, 1898.

requirements would be an incentive to Negroes to acquire an education. But Fortune disagreed sharply. He found "no saving grace" in the enactment. "The vicious thing about it," he said to Washington, "is that it was enacted *for the expressed purpose of disfranchising* Afro-Americans and not for the keeping of the *intelligence* of the State, a justice for which you made your plea. The enactment as it stands is entirely immoral and vicious."[39]

During the long visit to Tuskegee, Fortune and Washington discussed plans for compiling some of Washington's speeches for publication—an idea which had already occurred to Victoria Matthews, who was a close friend of Mrs. Washington and who had written some articles on Tuskegee for the *Age.*

The result was the publication in 1898 of *Black-Belt Diamonds,* the first of many books by and about the Tuskegeean. Fortune wrote the lengthy introduction and was responsible for the choice of the title, while Mrs. Matthews selected and edited the speeches. The book, Fortune assured his friend, would "contribute permanently to your reputation as a philosopher, as a wise and safe leader."[40]

In the introduction Fortune said that since the Civil War the South had produced only two men who had achieved national reputation—Henry W. Grady and Booker T. Washington—and then proceeded to compare the two men. After reading the introduction, Mrs. Matthews expressed apprehension that the comparison would offend southern whites. Fortune asked Washington to read what he had written and said he would

39. *Age,* March 3, 1898; Fortune to Washington, April 8, 1898, Washington Papers. Emphasis as in the original.

40. *Age,* January 2, 1896; Fortune to Washington, April 6, May 2, May 17, May 23, 1898, Washington Papers; *Black-Belt Diamonds: Gems from the Speeches, Addresses and Talks to Students of Booker T. Washington* . . . selected and arranged by Victoria Earle Matthews, Introduction by T. Thomas Fortune (New York: Fortune and Scott, 1898).

change it if he wished him to, but he added, "as the comparison is just and truthful to you and Grady I don't see why I should temper my thoughts to the Southern back." Washington apparently made no objection. In the published introduction Fortune said that Grady represented the white South and spoke for it alone and was dangerous because he spoke for a part and not the whole of the Southern people. Washington, on the other hand, was safe and helpful because he spoke for the whole southern people, "because he contends for the whole and not for a part of the truth, as it is related to manhood and citizenship, and to that Christian charity which embraces all the children of men."

The cornerstone of Grady's faith, wrote Fortune in the introduction, was white supremacy, which was contrary to Christian philosophy and specifically disavowed by the United States Constitution. In contrast with Grady's utterances, Fortune quoted from speeches of Washington on the mutual interests and interdependence of the races. The difference between Grady and Washington, wrote Fortune, arose from the fact that one was an Anglo-Saxon American, the other an Afro-American. One was born free, the other a slave; one was educated to believe "that God made freedom and opportunity for His white children alone, the other that he made them for all his children." Grady was dead but Washington still lived, and "the God that lifted him out of bondage has made of him a great power for good." The southern people as a whole recognized the ability and consecration to service of the man who had taken the place so long filled by Frederick Douglass. One of the strongest elements of Washington's strength and influence was the respect and confidence of the *whole* southern people.[41]

Fortune also did some editing, considerable revising, and proofreading for *The Future of the American Negro*, which

41. Fortune to Washington, May 28, 1898, Washington Papers; *Black-Belt Diamonds*, pp. vi, viii-ix, xi-xii.

was published in 1899 under Washington's name. While reading the manuscript, he gave Washington some advice on his literary style. "Your propensity to cut sentences short and to leave out qualifying clauses in subordinate sentences cannot be tolerated in a book," he said. To Scott he wrote that he was "appalled" at the literary quality of the work, that "it would ruin us" to permit the book to appear as Washington had written it. He was also dissatisfied with some of the content of the book. "I worry over your unconscious habit of apologising for the short comings of white men, as in the Reconstruction deviltry," he told Washington, "and I have qualified it where I could; otherwise you would have a tornado at your heels."[42]

In a variety of other ways Fortune worked to publicize Washington and his work. In one week in October 1896, for example, he said that he had written an editorial for the *Sun* on "Afro-American Education," which was based on a speech which Washington had given in Brooklyn; had given instructions to Mrs. Matthews on writing an article which Washington requested; and was reprinting in the *Age*, at Washington's suggestion, editorials from the *Brooklyn Eagle* and the *Boston Herald*. In August 1898 he wrote Washington that current issues of the *Boston Evening Transcript*, the *Southern Workman*, and *Zion's Herald*, all contained articles about him for which he was responsible.[43]

In the article in the *Transcript*, which was entitled "The Tuskegee Wizard," Fortune lauded Washington and sought to answer some of the charges which northern Negroes were making against him. After Frederick Douglass died, Fortune

42. Booker T. Washington, *The Future of the American Negro* (Boston, 1899); Fortune to Washington, October 13, 1899; Fortune to Emmett J. Scott, October 14, 1899, Washington Papers. After the book was published, Fortune wrote a favorable review of it which appeared in the *Boston Transcript*, December 16, 1899.

43. Fortune to Washington, October 3, 1896; August 11, 1898, Washington Papers.

said, no one had expected that his successor would come out of the Black Belt, "where mental darkness and moral perversion were believed to possess the Afro-American race body and soul." But the Atlanta speech had revealed a new leader, ready to carry on where Douglass had left off. Some Negroes criticized Washington because of his friendliness to the whites of the South. But, Fortune insisted, Washington had cultivated friendly relations "without sacrificing any interest or dignity of his race." The future of Afro-Americans in the South would be bleak, indeed, if they did not have the sympathy and help of the whites. "How to secure these in a manly way" was Washington's constant concern. Influential Afro-American thinkers criticized Washington for putting too much stress on "industrial education" to the disparagement of higher education. But Fortune said that Washington's position had been misunderstood and misrepresented. He was not opposed to higher education but believed that the masses of his race, especially in the Black Belt, needed industrial training and devoted his energies to that phase of education, believing that those who needed and were qualified for higher education would be able to secure it.[44]

Through the columns of the *Age* Fortune tried to answer the Negro editors who were critical of Washington. One of the most persistent critics was Chase of the *Washington Bee*, who had called the Atlanta address "another apology for Southern outrages," and who called Washington "an apologist and trimmer, pure and simple." Later he declared that he was merely "a money making machine for the Tuskegee Institute and an Afro-American apologist." To this Fortune replied that it was

44. *Boston Transcript*, August 6, 1898. To a Negro critic who complained that Washington put too much emphasis upon the depraved condition of Negroes, Fortune replied that the man did not understand Washington's purpose—that by directing attention to certain conditions, such as crime and illegitimacy, he hoped to arouse people to the importance of correcting them (Fortune to J. Silas Harris, October 22, 1898, Washington Papers).

necessary for Washington to be a money-making machine in order to carry on the work of Tuskegee which required almost $100,000 a year. "As to 'the Afro-American apologist gag,'— Let the editor of The Bee define what he means by it. We suppose that he means that Mr. Washington points out the race as it is and not as he wishes it was. We have reached the point where the loud mouthed glorification of race, to the utter obscuration of its short comings, should have a rest. We must be honest with ourselves." Chase replied that Washington was an apologist "in that he apologizes to the white people for the Afro-American and misrepresents the race," and that he depreciated the Afro-American in the estimation of whites in endeavoring to show that he was incapable of higher education. Fortune answered that Washington had never exaggerated the ignorance and poverty of the people among whom he labored in Alabama because it would be impossible to exaggerate their condition. "As the editor of the Bee has never lived in the South or visited there as Mr. Washington has done and the editor of the Age has done and is doing now," said Fortune, "he can have no personal knowledge of the conditions with which Mr. Washington has to deal and which he seeks with Spartan courage and woman's devotion to better." Chase continued to attack Washington and Tuskegee, but sometimes, for brief periods, he desisted. Thus, in December 1899, for example, Fortune was able to write to Washington: "I have made Chase promise to leave you alone."[45]

When Washington came to Albany to give an address, Fortune introduced him to John E. Bruce (Bruce Grit), who had been critical of Washington. Washington and his daughter Portia had dinner together with Bruce and Fortune. Bruce thereafter expressed himself as being favorably impressed with

45. *Washington Bee*, October 19, December 21, 1895; January 1, 1897; *Age* quoted in *Washington Bee*, January 1, January 30, 1897; Fortune to Washington, December 30, 1899, Washington Papers.

the Tuskegeean. Several months later Fortune (at Washington's prompting) tried to persuade Bruce to write a series of letters to various papers in support of Washington and his policies. Bruce demanded more money than Fortune was at first authorized to pay him for the assignment because, Bruce said, if he wrote the letters he would be under the necessity of continuing to appear to be an ally of Washington's. But later he did write letters which appeared in the *Springfield Republican* and in several Negro newspapers and an article which was published in *Howard's Magazine*. Washington was pleased with these efforts, and Fortune said that Bruce appeared to have developed a genuine admiration for the Tuskegeean.[46]

In his relationship with Washington, Fortune was doing what would today be considered public relations and ghost writing. Some of it he did out of friendship; for some of it he was paid, though never very generously. In accepting pay for these services he was not necessarily compromising his integrity as editor of the *Age* so long as he and Washington were in agreement over ideology and methods. But at a later time when differences arose between them, Fortune was confronted with an ethical dilemma. The financial relationship with Washington must also be viewed in the context of the finances of the *Age* and Fortune's personal life. Income from the *Age* was never sufficient to furnish a living for both Fortune and Peterson. In addition, Fortune's numerous race activities, especially the efforts to promote the Afro-American League, required both time and money. Fortune was always under pressure to supplement

46. *Washington Colored American*, July 16, 1898; *Cleveland Gazette*, September 16, 1899; Fortune to Washington, August 24, August 25, August 31, September 16, November 1, 1899; Washington to Fortune, September 16, October 28, 1899, Washington Papers. Bruce's conversion to a pro-Washington position was temporary. For the most part he continued to be critical of the Tuskegeean.

the income of the *Age*—by writing for the *Sun*, by other free-lance journalism, by speeches.

Washington evidently paid Fortune a fee for the lectures which he gave on his first visit to Tuskegee in 1890. As early as September 1891 Fortune tried to borrow two hundred dollars from Washington, explaining that the money he had spent on the Afro-American League conventions had knocked his finances "higher than Gilderoy's kite." When his friend replied that it was impossible to lend the money, Fortune replied that he knew he would help him if he could. As for himself—"It is the most uncomfortable situation in which I have found myself and I have been [and] am very much cut up by it, as I have found that it is easier to get into such a pickle than to get out of it."[47]

But Fortune was to find himself in many such "pickles," and the payments which he received from time to time from Tuskegee helped assuage his chronic financial predicaments. Washington paid him $125 for his visit to Tuskegee in January 1896 and offered to pay his expenses when he invited him to attend the Tuskegee Negro Conference of 1897. As early as 1896 Washington appears to have had an account with the *Age* for the publication of matters relating to Tuskegee.[48]

But the relationship between the two men was more than a financial one or merely one of mutual convenience. Each clearly felt a warm affection for the other, and the friendship with Washington became the more important to Fortune as

47. Fortune to Washington, November 18, 1889, April 12, 1890; September 11, September 21, 1891, Washington Papers. Earlier Fortune had appealed to William Still of Philadelphia without success for financial assistance in connection with the league (Fortune to Still, June 6, 1891, Woodson Collection).

48. Fortune to Washington, October 6, October 19, 1895; August 12, 1896; Washington to Fortune, December 6, 1896, Washington Papers.

family troubles and responsibilities, financial pressures, ill health, and the realization that his youth was past made him despondent over the future. On his birthday in 1895 he wrote a rather morbid little poem, entitled "I'm Thirty-Nine."

> I'm thirty-nine! The vanished years
> Have been all toil and pain and tears,
> With here and there a ray of sun
> When some fierce battle was won.
>
> . . . .
>
> I'm thirty-nine! The brightest days
> Of life are dead! . . .[49]

More sorrows were soon to follow. The following year his father died. Fortune spent several weeks in Jacksonville attending the old man in his last illness, during which he was unable to do any of his usual journalistic work and was without income. Washington offered to lend him money to tide him over the difficult time, and Fortune gratefully accepted. Emanuel Fortune died in January. Pledger came from Atlanta to be with the son during the funeral. Then Fortune returned to New York and hard work. He wrote to Washington in March that he was regaining his old confidence and "swing" in his work and expected soon to be "out of the woods financially."[50] But then he fell sick and was sick intermittently for several months with nervous and stomach disorders. By that time it was evident that he was not to receive the appointment which he had hoped for from the McKinley administration, and he was despondent over the future.

He was dissatisfied with the prospects for the future of the *Age*, which was worth no more than it had been ten years earlier. He was weary of the incessant outside work which was

49. *Age*, October 3, 1895.
50. Fortune to Washington, December 10, 1896; January 28, March 17, 1897; Washington to Fortune, December 26, 1896, Washington Papers.

necessary to keep his income up to expenditures. He had no time to do any of the literary work which he had always wanted to do. Worst of all was the realization that in ten years he would be fifty years old and would not have been able, if the present way of life continued, to make adequate provisions for his family's future. He wrote Washington that he was looking for some other work. "If I stick to the hard work here I shall lose my health after a while," he said, "and have nothing whatever to fall back upon." A possible way out had appeared when he was offered the presidency of Payne University in Alabama, an institution of the A.M.E. church. But after he learned more about the school, he decided that he would be worsening his position rather than improving it by accepting the offer.[51]

A few months later Washington invited him to spend the winter at Tuskegee, where, away from the tensions of the *Age* office, he could regain his health and do some writing. He wrote Washington that he was deeply affected by the letter of invitation. "The kindly spirit, the solicitude for my health and well doing, and the generous invitation are all such as I would expect of you," he said, "but the time and manner of the letter moved me more than would ordinarily be the case, for my health and spirit are much undermined." At Tuskegee he would be able to do his regular newspaper work and other work which Washington might suggest. During the visit, as we have seen, he started work on *Black-Belt Diamonds* and helped in the preparation of the letter to the Louisiana convention. After he left Tuskegee in March to go to Jacksonville, he wrote to his host: "I am sure you all do not miss me any more than I miss you all, and I shall go back to Tuskegee as soon as I can. *I would like to stay there all the time.*"[52]

51. Fortune to Washington, June 19, 1897; undated letter, July 1897, Washington Papers.

52. Fortune to Washington, November 5, November 11, 1897; March 7, 1898, Washington Papers. Emphasis as in original.

When he arrived in Jacksonville, he found that his oldest sister was dying and that his younger sister was also sick. "Sure I am having a hard row to carry in the matter of sickness in the family," he wrote Washington. "The relentless breaking of these ties" (the death of father, sister, and two other relatives in eighteen months) placed severe strain upon his "vital forces." His financial situation also remained critical. The costs of operating the *Age*, maintaining his family, paying insurance premiums, were constant and unremitting. In addition there were medical expenses for his own illnesses and those of members of his family. And the income from the *Sun* was always uncertain. Sometimes the *Sun* did not use his copy—and then he received no pay.[53]

But in spite of his personal problems Fortune was unable to resist involving himself in race matters and in other people's battles. He assumed the responsibility for the meeting at Rochester in the summer of 1898 which resulted in the formation of the Afro-American Council which is described in the next chapter. Following that there was the legal battle with the immigration officials over the right of the Scotch girl to marry her Negro fiancé, already mentioned. As the result of overwork and nervous strain Fortune fell sick again and was unable to work for some time.

Washintgon suggested that he come to Tuskegee again to recuperate, but Fortune answered, "You are very good to think of me at Tuskegee, but *I have already been too much trouble and expense to you*, and I am fearful of increasing these." He did not go to Tuskegee but accepted with gratitude a loan to tide him over the period of recuperation. By the end of November his health had improved, but he was very tired and dead broke, "as this race business steals time and cash." Nevertheless he planned to go to Philadelphia to make a speech and then to

53. Fortune to Washington, March 7, April 22, July 22, July 27, 1898, Washington Papers.

Washington for a meeting of the executive committee of the Afro-American Council. A few days later he had a bad attack of grippe, and his doctor advised him to go South. He went to the Washington meeting with the expectation of going from there to Tuskegee.[54]

In the light of Fortune's later career the ties which he established with Washington during these southern travels in the 1890s were of crucial importance. The two men shared the same goals, and their relationship was based on warm friendship and respect as well as mutual advantage. But unintentionally Fortune was entangling himself in a situation in which he became increasingly dependent upon Washington and which would create for him ideological and ethical dilemmas from which he would be unable to escape.

54. Carrie Fortune to Washington, September 20, 1898; Fortune to Washington, September 30, November 21, November 30, December 14, December 20, 1898, Washington Papers. How much addiction to alcohol, which, as we shall see became a serious problem with Fortune, was already a factor in his ill-health and fits of depression is not clear, but he had acquired a reputation of drinking to excess (*Indianapolis World*, August 22, 1896; *Cleveland Gazette*, September 12, 1896; Bruce to Alexander Crummell, November 6, 1897, Bruce Papers; emphasis as in original).

VI

The Washington-Fortune Alliance

A T THE TURN OF THE CENTURY WHITE RACISM AND JIM Crowism were reaching their apogee in the United States. By 1898 Mississippi, South Carolina, and Louisiana had incorporated articles in their state constitution disfranchising blacks. Other states of the South were preparing to follow their example. Jim Crow laws and ordinances were proliferating, and lynching and mob violence against Negroes increasing. White opinion in the North appeared not merely to acquiesce in disfranchisement but to approve it, and few voices were raised in the North in protest against lynchings. In these years Booker T. Washington's prestige among whites reached its peak. His program of hard work, thrift, and industrial education was hailed as the answer to the race problem; and whites were the more favorably disposed toward him because he spoke in conciliatory terms, seemed to deprecate political activity, to acquiesce in segregation, and to place the onus of solving race problems primarily on blacks.

In spite of the increasing futility of protest, Fortune was never more the Afro-American agitator than during this critical period. Through his journalism and especially in speeches he hurled defiance at the white South and denounced the federal government for its betrayal of its black citizens. During these years he was the most militant and articulate northern Negro. W. E. B. Du Bois, who was at Atlanta University, wrote articles for such periodicals as the *Independent* and *Atlantic*, interpreting his race and race problems to whites, but he had not yet entered the arena as a militant champion of political and civil rights. Fortune wrote regularly for the *Sun* and the *Boston Transcript* and various periodicals, and his speeches, which were frequently considered sensational, sometimes received wide coverage in the northern press. Editorials in the white press sometimes compared Fortune, "the Afro-American agitator," with the "sound" and "safe" Booker T. Washington—always to Fortune's detriment. And yet, paradoxically, the two men remained close friends. Fortune was Washington's closest confidant, and in addition to his role as northern agitator, he played the role of defender and interpreter of Washington—especially to Negro critics.

Deteriorating conditions in the South led to a movement to revive the Afro-American League. In November 1896 W. Calvin Chase of the *Bee* took the lead in calling for the resurrection of the league under the leadership of Fortune—a suggestion which was immediately taken up by several other Negro papers. Fortune, who was then in Jacksonville attending his dying father, wrote a letter to Chase, indicating his support of the suggestion but warning that the movement could succeed only "by the united efforts of the people, under the leadership of men of the largest capacity and courage and unselfishness for the race's good."[1] But, beset by sickness and financial problems,

1. *Washington Bee*, November 14, 1896.

Fortune failed to take any steps for calling a convention.

In March 1898 Bishop Alexander Walters sent an appeal to the *Age*, asking Fortune to call a meeting to revive the league. Thereafter Fortune received letters from about 150 persons endorsing Walters' recommendation, but he declined to issue a call for a general convention because he doubted that there was enough popular support for a permanent organization. But because the need for such an organization was even greater than it had been in 1890, he agreed to call a conference of race leaders to meet at Rochester, where they would be assembled for the unveiling of the Frederick Douglass monument.

On September 14 a large group assembled for the ceremonies commemorating Douglass (although the statue was not completed and could not be unveiled). An original poem by Fortune written for the occasion was included in the program. The following day a group met to consider the revival of the league. Among those present were Helen Douglass, the widow of Frederick Douglass; Susan B. Anthony; John H. Smythe, ex-minister to Liberia; John C. Dancy, collector of customs at Wilmington, North Carolina; Bishop Walters; Chris Perry of the *Philadelphia Tribune;* and Ida Wells Barnett. Prominent Negroes who had signed the call for the meeting but who did not attend included Booker T. Washington, ex-Governor Pinchback, Judson Lyons, Congressman George White, and Archibald and Francis Grimké.[2]

At the opening session, Fortune spoke on a new aspect of the race question which had emerged with the recently concluded war with Spain. He expressed apprehension over the future of

2. Ibid., August 27, 1898; *New York Sun*, September 15, 1898; *Indianapolis Freeman*, September 3, October 1, 1898; Bishop Alexander Walters, *My Life and Work* (New York, 1917), pp. 98–102. Alexander Walters (1858–1917) was Kentucky born and had served in a number of pastorates of the A.M.E. Zion church before coming to New York in 1888 to become the minister of one of the largest churches of that denomination. In 1892 he was elected a bishop at the age of thirty-four.

Cubans, Filipinos, and Puerto Ricans under the rule of the United States. He predicted that the "Southern sentiment" in race relations would be carried to the new possessions, with disastrous results.[3] But when the meeting got down to the actual business of forming a permanent organization, Fortune expressed the same doubts and ambivalence which he had shown since the question of the revival of the league had first been raised. When a report was made in favor of a permanent organization, he spoke against it, saying that Afro-Americans were not ready for such a movement and that it would be used for political purposes. Nevertheless the nominating committee recommended the election of Fortune as president of the organization. After the election of officers, he again expressed doubts about the wisdom of attempting to form a national organization. Thereupon Ida Wells Barnett arose and declared that it would be better to have as president someone who had utmost confidence in the movement. Fortune said he agreed with her and promptly resigned as president and nominated Bishop Walters, who was then elected. Mrs. Barnett was elected secretary. The group voted to adopt the name National Afro-American Council with the intention of incorporating existing religious, political, and benevolent organizations without destroying their local constitutions or autonomy. A list of objectives similar to the objectives of the earlier league were drawn up.[4]

In the weeks following the Rochester conference racial outrages increased, most conspicuously in the riots in Wil-

3. *New York Sun*, September 16, 1898.

4. Ibid.; *Washington Colored American*, September 24, 1898; Mrs. N. F. Mosell, "The National Afro-American Council," *Colored American Magazine*, August 1901, pp. 291-95. The *Washington Colored American* accused Fortune of "petulance" in not accepting the presidencey of the council. He replied that his health was not good, and that he already had more work than he could do. "I do not wish," he said, "to be burdened with the management of an organization in which the people are not interested to the extent of giving

mington, North Carolina. The call for a national meeting of the Afro-American Council in Washington, D. C., in December declared that the continuance of lynchings and other outrages made it absolutely necessary to organize for self-protection.[5]

In spite of the doubts which he had expressed earlier about the wisdom of trying to organize the council, and in spite of his own delicate health and straitened finances, Fortune agreed to attend the convention and serve as chairman of the committee which was to draw up an address to the country. Even though he was still recuperating from an attack of grippe, he decided to stay in Washington for the meeting rather than go immediately to Tuskegee. He wanted to do what he could to prevent the convention *"from doing something foolish,"* he wrote Washington, a remark which was highly ironical in the light of subsequent developments.[6]

A few days prior to the convention, Fortune was the principal speaker at a mass meeting at the Zion A.M.E. Church in Washington which was held under the auspices of the Racial Protective Association, of which W. Calvin Chase was president. Exactly what occurred and precisely what Fortune said are not entirely clear, although his speech received extended coverage

---

it proper comfort and support and which would eat up my time and earnings and health" (*Washington Colored American,* October 1, 1898).

5. *Washington Evening Star,* December 29, 1898.

6. Fortune to Washington, December 18, 1898, Washington Papers. Emphasis as in original. President McKinley, who was touring the South, had just visited Tuskegee. Fortune congratulated Washington on the speech he had made welcoming the president and said that the visit would enhance the prestige of Tuskegee. "The President's visit ought to be worth a great deal to you and your work," he said. "The President is a thoroughly despicable character and I despise him, but I am glad that he went to Tuskegee, where he ought to learn something" (Fortune to Washington, December 14, December 16, 1898).

in the press. Headlines in the *Baltimore Herald* the next day cried:

FRANTIC MR. FORTUNE

WILD UTTERANCES OF THE COLORED EDITOR

ATTACKS THE PRESIDENT

According to the account in the *Washington Times*, the meeting opened with the singing of the national anthem, after which a minister offered a prayer for President McKinley, asking the Lord to forgive him for his injustices to the Negro. Another minister stated that the object of the meeting was the preservation of the rights of southern Negroes. A lawyer then introduced resolutions, later adopted, which were critical of McKinley for not asking Congress to take action following the killing of Negro Republicans on the eve of recent elections in North and South Carolina and calling for congressional investigation of southern outrages. One member of the audience interposed that an appeal should first be made to the president, but a minister replied that nothing could be accomplished by appealing to the president as he was down South "throwing daisies over rebel graves."

At this point Fortune was introduced as the speaker of the evening. He began his remarks by saying that McKinley badly needed the blessing of his Creator because he was down South "glorifying rebellion, mobocracy, and the murder of women and children." He accused the president of betraying his Negro supporters. "I want the man whom I fought for to fight for me, and if he don't I feel like stabbing him." (Cries of "Stab him, stab him.") Fortune also expressed contempt for the Supreme Court for its decision in the Mississippi vote case.

On the subject of southern chivalry, he said: "Talk about rape. If ever there was a race of rapists it is in the white men of the South." As the result of southern chivalry, Fortune contined, there were hundreds of thousands of mulattoes in the country. The very men who had been killed at Wilmington were probably the sons and grandsons of the men who killed them. Furthermore, Negroes would never get their rights until they were willing to die for them. For every one of the thirty Negroes killed at Wilmington a white man should have been killed.[7]

The following day Fortune told a reporter that he had been misquoted in part but admitted that he had said that for every Negro killed a white man should have been killed and repeated that southern white men were organized rapists. He said that his whole speech had been predicated upon the fact that while black men were being shot down, the president of the United States was in the South adulating the hereditary enemies of blacks. An editorial in the *Washington Evening Star* declared that Fortune was an enemy of his own people, that he should be "suppressed," and that other colored people should refuse to associate with him. Chase wrote a letter to the *Star*, insisting that Fortune's remarks had been political only and that some of them had been lifted out of context, that he had not advocated "physical assassination." Fortune himself wrote a long letter in which he accused the *Star* of "twisting" his "extemporaneous remarks." He had meant to "stab" McKinley only at the ballot box. He also pointed out that in dealing with the race question, "white men should remember that black men do not always think about it as they do. Most white men argue the question as if black men had nothing whatever to do with the settlement of it."[8]

In reply the *Star* asserted that Fortune had been quoted accurately, that his protest was the "usual whimper of the man

---

7. *Washington Times*, December 20, 1898; *Washington Evening Star*, December 20, 1898. In *Williams* v. *Mississippi*, 170 U.S. 213 (1898) the Supreme Court had upheld the constitutionality of the "understanding clause," designed to disfranchise Negroes.

8. *Baltimore Herald*, December 21, 1898; *Washington Evening Star*, December 20, December 21, 1898.

who allows his tongue to run away with his head." Fortune was a capable writer who would never, said the *Star*, "put down with a pen the absurd bosh he allowed his tongue to utter and he naturally does not like the looks of his remarks in cold type." Even the Negro press was critical. The *Washington Colored American* said that Fortune had not been quoted accurately, but it regretted that Fortune had gone far enough to furnish an occasion for misconstruction. Fortune's "rash and ill judged utterances" could not be defended "by a race which has so much at stake." Bruce Grit, who agreed that Fortune had not intended to convey the impression which he did, nevertheless termed his speech "unfortunate" and "dangerous" in light of the recent racial troubles.[9]

The meeting of the Afro-American Council was almost an anticlimax after the sensation created by Fortune's speech. But it was not without its fireworks. Ida Wells Barnett made a speech denouncing mob violence and anarchy North and South. When she said that President McKinley was too busy decorating the graves of Confederate soldiers to pay attention to the rights of Negroes, she was warmly applauded. "If this gathering means anything," she said, "it means that we have at last come to a point in our race history where we must do something for ourselves, and do it now. We must educate the white people out of their 250 years of slave history." She called for reduction in southern representation in Congress and expressed opposition to United States expansion overseas. When Henry P. Cheatham, recorder of deeds, a McKinley appointee, made a plea for conservatism in reply to Mrs. Barnett, he was greeted with groans and hisses. But the audience quieted down and listened politely when he praised McKinley for appealing to the white South to forget its past prejudices. John P. Greene, another political appointee, also defended McKinley. His statement that it was upon the

9. *Washington Evening Star*, December 21, 1898; *Washington Colored American*, December 24, 1898; January 21, 1899.

advice of certain Negroes that the president had said nothing about the protection of Negroes in his last message to Congress threw the meeting into an uproar. At least a dozen men leaped to their feet. Fortune was finally recognized and demanded that Greene name the Negroes who had given McKinley that advice. His demand was greeted with cheers, and when Bishop Walters attempted to introduce the next speaker, Bishop Abraham Grant, before Greene had answered Fortune, the tumult continued. Grant said he did not intend to speak until the names of the Negroes who had advised the president were revealed. The uproar subsided when a committee was appointed to ascertain the names from Greene. When it was announced that Greene was unable to furnish the names, there was much laughter.[10]

Bishop Walters was elected president of the council, Ida Wells Barnett, secretary, and John W. Thompson, treasurer. There were eight vice-presidents and an executive committee which included representatives from both North and South. The address to the people, which was drawn up by a committee of which Fortune·was chairman, was clearly an attempt to compose differences and represent all points of view. The prefatory statement said that under present circumstances, where racial conditions were "abnormally disturbed in one section and comparatively composed" elsewhere, more than one method of dealing with problems was called for. In the South the "work of education and internal development" could "best be determined and carried out by the wise men of us in the Southern states who have done so much since the War of Rebellion to pave the way for our *future* status as men and citizens in all the walks of life." Varying local conditions and prejudices made important "a broad toleration" of differences of opinion as to methods. On the subject of political rights the address declared that the council did not oppose "legitimate restrictions" but

10. *Washington Evening Star*, December 30, 1898.

insisted that they apply alike to citizens of all states. It also called for reduction of representation in states which disfranchised Negro voters. Other articles on separate coach laws, the convict lease system, education, and mob violence and lynching were similar to those which had been part of the platform of the Afro-American League. It expressed regret that the president had failed to deal with the question of mob violence in his message to Congress. Fortune signed the address, but he did not accompany the delegation which presented it to McKinley. The statement was less militant and uncompromising than many of his statements, but he expressed satisfaction with it, perhaps because it embodied the idea of different approaches to race problems in North and South—a concept which he apparently felt he himself embodied in the North and Washington in the South.[11]

The sensational reports and the editorial denunciation of Fortune's Washington speech did not cause any rift in the relationship with Washington, although Fortune had been apprehensive that they might. He sent clippings of the newspaper reports to Tuskegee, but insisted the "newspaper scamps" had twisted what he had said.[12] He did not go on to Tuskegee from Washington as he had planned, but a few weeks later he and Washington were in Boston together, obviously on the best of terms. It may even have been that Washington was secretly pleased to have Fortune say some of the things he dared not say. Certainly his friendship with Fortune was useful to him since it would be considered by Negroes as evidence that he was not as conservative as his critics claimed. On the other hand among

11. Ibid., December 31, 1898; *Washington Colored American*, January 14, 1899; Walters, *My Life and Work*, p. 134; Fortune to Washington, January 1, 1899, Washington Papers. Emphasis added.

12. Fortune to Washington, December 20, December 23, December 27, 1898, Washington Papers.

whites Fortune's radicalism served as a useful foil to his conservatism and strengthened Washington's position in their eyes.

In an interview with a reporter from the *Boston Globe*, Fortune spoke at length on his relations with Washington and on their respective roles. The reporter remarked that the press frequently contrasted the positions of the two men and asked him whether there was any antagonism between them. Fortune replied that there was not. "There is no difference whatever on our basic views on the race question," he declared, while admitting that Washington was "naturally conservative" and he was "naturally radical."

> [Washington] speaks always from the point of view of a leader who lives and labors in the South, and who believes that in order to gain one point in manhood development something can be yielded upon another, and that we are to depend mostly upon education, property and character to pave our way to success; while I speak from the standpoint of a man who lives and labors in the North, and who does not believe in sacrificing anything that justly belongs to the race of manhood or constitutional rights.

Perhaps, said Fortune, in the long run more victories were won through the policy of moderation which Washington espoused than through "the radical and unbending policy" which he himself pursued, "but it is the temperament of the two of us, and we can neither of us change our nature." He added that Washington was the strongest and safest leader which the race had—"a wise and self-contained man," who, because he had the confidence of both the white South and the white North, could accomplish much good.[13]

In Boston there was an active and articulate group of anti-Washingtonians, among whom William Monroe Trotter was the most conspicuous. One of Washington's motives in visiting the city was to try to counteract this group. At a meeting of a

13. *Boston Globe*, January 14, 1899.

group called the Colored National League, Fortune made a speech which was in part for the purpose of effecting an affiliation with the National Afro-American Council. But the occasion was also used by some of the speakers to defend Washington and his policies. Washington was pleased with the results of the meeting, which appeared to strengthen his prestige in the community, and grateful to Fortune for the part which he had played.[14]

During the following months Fortune continued to play the complicated role of northern agitator and defender of Washington, while at the same time trying to make a living from journalism. In addition to editing the *Age* and writing for the *Sun*, he wrote numerous editorials for the *Boston Evening Transcript*. He considered giving up his other work and becoming a full time member of the *Transcript* staff and asked Washington to intervene in his behalf with Edward Clement, the editor. But Washington evidently did nothing. Fortune wrote him:

> I do not write to refresh your memory in the Transcript matter, because you always remember what you promise to remember; but I do write to emphasize the fact that I want to get away from New York and its influences and that I could do more good, while bettering my own condition, on the editorial staff of such a paper as the Transcript than in my present relationship. *But if you think otherwise, if you think I can do more good by sticking to the Age,* don't say anything to Mr. Clement, but let us talk it over further.[15]

Fortune continued to struggle along with the *Age* but took satisfaction from the publication of the editorials in the *Transcript*, some of which attracted attention and rebuttals from the *Atlanta Constitution*. On some days he had two editorials in the

14. *Boston Transcript*, January 18, 1899; Fortune to Washington, January 25, February 1, 1899, Washington Papers.

15. Fortune to Washington, March 20, 1899, Washington Papers. Emphasis as in original.

Transcript, and in June an article in the *Independent.* "It seems to me that I have entered upon a higher and stronger phase of my work as a journalist," he wrote Scott.[16] Through the columns of the *Age,* the *Transcript,* and the *Sun* and in speeches, he continued to denounce lynchings and to flay McKinley for his failure to speak out.

In an article in the *Sun* he cited evidence to show that, contrary to popular opinion, rape was not the principal cause of lynchings. "The curse of the South today," he said, "is that private white citizens will not attend to their own affairs and leave the officers of the law to attend to theirs. . . . There is never an instance where the constabulary or the courts need any such gratuitous service." A short time after Fortune's article appeared, Washington, in Alabama, give to the Associated Press a paper in which he appealed to public sentiment in the South to condemn lynching and cited evidence similar to that which Fortune had cited as to the causes of lynching.[17]

A few weeks earlier Fortune had spoken at a meeting in the A.M.E. Zion Church in New York at which he had received a standing ovation after a glowing introduction by Bishop Walters. In the speech he discussed the continuing outrages in the South and counselled against the use of violence in retaliation as futile but declared: "There is one man in Washington who has done more to breed disquiet and create these outrageous acts than anyone else. That man is William McKinley who is now in the White House. . . . He is a man of jelly who would turn us loose to the mob and say not a word." In July 1899 the *Age* announced that it opposed the renomination of McKinley, primarily because of his record on lynchings —because he had made no effective effort to curb "the reign of mob law which has terrorized the southern states ever since he

16. Fortune to Scott, June 19, June 20, 1899, Washington Papers.
17. *New York Sun* quoted in *Boston Transcript,* June 14, 1899; Associated Press release of Washington's paper, June 21, 1899.

has been in presidential office, while showering favors and rhetorical bouquets on the white Democrats who have committed or connived at these lynching murders." The president was also condemned for his reluctance to accept Afro-American volunteers in the War with Spain and his refusal to issue commissions to Afro-Americans while showering commissions on southern Democrats. This editorial elicited an answer in the *Atlanta Constitution* which said that the "educated Negro" who wrote the editorial had no understanding of the constitutional barriers which prevented the president from taking action against lynchings. Furthermore the writer of the *Age* editorial was obviously consumed with jealousy of Booker T. Washington, who was on friendly terms with McKinley.[18]

Meanwhile, during 1899 the intensity of criticism of Washington by northern Negroes mounted, and Fortune was busy trying to defend his friend. While Washington was on a trip to Europe, Fortune wrote him: "I am fighting your battles as the occasion requires," and sent him a clipping of an article he had written to "plug" Harry Smith of the *Cleveland Gazette*, a consistent critic of Washington. At a meeting of the Bethel Historical and Literary Association in Washington at which Chase had read a paper saying that Washington was not a real race leader, that he was put forward and sustained by white men, not black men, Fortune spoke in rebuttal. He then wrote an editorial in the *Transcript* in which he declared that neither whites nor blacks had placed Washington in his "preeminent but perilous position," but that he had placed himself there "by supreme devotion to the race, by persuasive eloquence, by a wisdom tempered with conservatism." The country and Afro-Americans were fortunate, he said, to have such a

18. *New York Times*, May 11, 1899; *Age* quoted in *Boston Transcript*, July 24, 1899; *Atlanta Constitution* quoted in *Boston Advertiser*, July 31, 1899. The *Washington Bee*, August 5, 1899, insisted that Fortune's animus against McKinley arose solely from his failure to receive a political appointment.

leader in a time when race relations were so strained.[19]

The mounting criticism of Washington caused Fortune to warn him not to attend the convention of the National Afro-American Council in Chicago in August. Fortune himself did not attend because of ill-health, and few nationally recognized figures went to the meeting. The politicians evidently stayed away because they feared that the convention might condemn the McKinley administration. Bishop Walters gave a presidential address in which he made no mention of Washington, but several other speakers bitterly denounced the Tuskegeean. One whole session was consumed debating resolutions condemning Washington, but the resolutions failed to pass, and friends of Washington succeeded in pushing through a resolution which said that the race honored him and wished him "God speed in his noble efforts."

W. E. B. Du Bois, who had been named a director of the business bureau of the council and who had been active in the convention, told a reporter that he deplored the attacks on Washington and that they had not been representative of the sentiment of the delegates in general. In his statement Du Bois characterized Washington as "one of the greatest men of our race." After the convention Fortune wrote a letter to the *Independent* in which he declared that Washington was too valuable a man and had accomplished too much to have his reputation and work injured by "hot headed members of his own race, who accomplished no great thing in the place where they stand, and who have neither the capacity nor force to accomplish anything."[20]

19. Fortune to Washington, June 1, 1899, Washington Papers; *Boston Transcript,* July 5, 1899.

20. Fortune to Washington, August 10, 1899, Washington Papers; *Washington Colored American,* August 26, 1899; *Indianapolis Freeman,* September 2, 1899; *Chicago Tribune,* August 20, 1899; *Independent,* August 31, 1899, clipping, scrapbook, Washington Papers; *Springfield Republican,* undated clipping, scrapbook, Washington Papers.

Although Fortune did not attend the Chicago meeting, he agreed to serve on the executive committee and as chairman of the committee which drew up resolutions for the consideration of the meeting of the executive group in December. He asked Washington to send him an abstract of what he thought should be included in the resolutions. After the meeting he expressed satisfaction with the resolutions which were adopted except the endorsement of the Crumpacker bill, then pending in Congress, which called for the reduction of southern representation—a move which Fortune continued to insist was a false step.[21]

Although Fortune consistently defended Washington in the press, not infrequently the two men assessed the race situation differently, and Fortune was sometimes impatient with his friend because he thought him too ready to make concessions to white prejudices. The differences between the two men were well illustrated by their reactions to the conference on race relations which was held at Montgomery, Alabama, in May 1900. It was an all-white meeting, called at the instigation of clergymen, educators, and political leaders—representatives of the "better class" of whites whose good will Washington so assiduously cultivated. Washington was not invited to participate but decided to attend as a spectator, sitting in a section reserved for Negroes. Privately he wrote to Fortune that he anticipated "some very radical" and "unwise" proposals at the conference but hoped that some good might come of it. Publicly he showed his usual indomitable optimism. He wrote a letter to the *Age* asking Negroes to suspend judgment, assuring them that there would be friends of the race at Montgomery. He warmly defended Edgar Gardner Murphy, the principal instigator of the conference. "No black man in the South who has had the

21. *Washington Colored American*, January 6, 1900; Fortune to Washington, December 19, December 30, 1899; January 4, February 20, 1900, Washington Papers.

opportunity to really know Mr. Murphy at his home in the South can doubt that while he may advocate a means of solving the problem, with which we are not in accord, at the same time he is a sincere friend of the Negro, as well as of the white man," said Washington. Fortune agreed to publish the letter but warned Washington that it would be accompanied by an editorial which he might not like. "But," he added, "it is *not* best *that you and I always agree* in public policy and discussion." In the editorial he said he agreed that it was a gain when influential white men discussed the race problem, but the gain would have been greater if Washington and other prominent Negroes had been asked to participate in the conference. To leave them out was "like putting Hamlet on the stage with Hamlet left out."[22]

At Montgomery, John Temple Graves spoke in favor of separation of the races and endorsed colonization. In the course of his remarks he said that there was not a man at the meeting who would invite Booker Washington to be his guest overnight. Professor Paul R. Barringer of the University of Virginia expressed the view that the Negro was fast reverting to barbarism, and that "Emancipation sounded the death knell, and he would eventually be annihilated." Hilary A. Herbert, former member of Cleveland's Cabinet, expressed the opinion that Negro suffrage was a failure. While denying that he advocated the restoration of slavery, he nevertheless asserted that Negroes had never been so industrious, law abiding, and trustworthy as they were before emancipation. Moreover Negro assaults on white women were unknown under slavery. The solution of the race problem, in his view, lay in industrial education as practiced at Tuskegee. Several other speakers urged the repeal of the

22. Fortune to Washington, May 4, 1900; Washington to Fortune, May 5, 1900; Washington Papers; *Age*, May 10, 1900. Emphasis as in original. As Episcopal bishop resident in Montgomery Edgar Gardner Murphy had taken the lead in the establishment of a Negro church. He was regarded by white contemporaries as a liberal on the race question.

Fifteenth Amendment. When ex-Governor McCorkle of West Virginia denounced "understanding clauses" and insisted that all restrictions on the franchise should be equitable and nondiscriminatory, his remarks were received with "conspicuous absence of enthusiasm."[23]

In the *Transcript* Fortune criticized the conference as "one-sided" and for failing to appeal to Negroes for cooperation. "The question," he said, "seems to be, how shall he [the Negro] be disposed of without consulting him in the matter, so as to give the least trouble to the white population; not, how shall he be uplifted so as to become of the most benefit and credit to himself and everybody else." To Washington he wrote privately: "We can't trust white men North or South to shape thoughts for us, we must do it ourselves." In characteristic fashion Washington found some good in the proceedings at Montgomery. In an article in the *Century* he said that the mere fact that the conference had been held in the former capital of the Confederacy only thirty-nine years after secession was cause for encouragement. The conference expressed "the voice of the educated, cultivated white South," which had too long been silent. He found Professor Barringer's speech discouraging, but of the nineteen speeches delivered, there were not more than four "that anyone could consider antagonistic to the higher interests of the negro."[24]

Shortly after the Montgomery conference, Washington was to deliver a speech at the Bethel Historical and Literary Association in Washington, a group which included some of his sharpest critics. He asked Fortune to send him an outline of what he

23. Isabell Barrows, "The Montgomery Conference," *Outlook*, 66 (May 19, 1900): 161; *New York Times*, May 9, 1900; *Boston Transcript*, May 10, 1900; *Springfield Republican*, May 15, 1900.

24. Fortune to Washington, May 9, 1900, Washington Papers; *Boston Transcript*, May 10, 1900; Booker T. Washington, "The Montgomery Race Conference," *Century* 60 (n.s. 38) (August 1900): 630–32.

thought he should say. One point which Fortune advised him to deal with was the subject of higher education for Negroes, which had been attacked by several speakers at Montgomery and which was under attack by other white writers and speakers, most of whom took care to endorse Washington and Tuskegee while decrying academic training for blacks. Many educated Negroes were blaming Washington, Fortune warned his friend, for the onslaught on higher education. "You have got to come out squarely on the subject," he said. "The matter is a vital one to you and the race." He also advised Washington that he must say something in a general way about political rights, and Washington replied that it would be an act of cowardice on his part to avoid the subject.

The speech as reported in the press bore evidences of Fortune's influence. In it Washington included his usual praise of industrial education, but he added that the intellectual development of Negroes should not be circumscribed in any way. The material prosperity of the South rested in large measure on Negroes, he argued, and the South could not afford to jeopardize that prosperity "by any practice that keeps alive in the negro a spirit of unrest, of fear, of suspicion, of feeling that life and property are not safe, a feeling that opportunities for education may be removed and be eventually deprived of his citizenship." On the subject of the repeal of the Fifteenth Amendment, he said that while he had never urged political activity for Negroes, when the foundation of the Negro's citizenship was under attack he felt he must speak. To deny a man the right to vote and yet expect him to support a government would undermine republican principles. Any law which permitted the ignorant white man to vote while withholding the same privilege for the ignorant Negro was an injustice to both races.[25]

25. Fortune to Washington, May 9, 1900; Washington to Fortune, May 14, 1900, Washington Papers; *Washington Post*, May 23, 1900.

In articles in the *Transcript* and the *Sun* Fortune tried to answer some of the whites who opposed higher education and to clarify Washington's position on education. Charles Dudley Warner, as president of the American Association of Social Sciences, praised industrial education and Tuskegee and said that slavery had taught Negroes to work, while college education, instead of stimulating industry and thrift, bred "idleness, indisposition to work, a vaporous ambition in politics, and the sort of conceit of gentility of which the world has already had enough." To this Fortune replied that the Afro-Americans who were achieving reputations for character and making money were not graduates of the plantations but of the academies and the colleges. The black criminals of the South were not those who had attended college; they were those in the rural districts and the city slums who had had no schooling and who had not been reached by missionary work. He quoted a statement which Washington had made in the *New York Post* in which he had said that he was not opposed to higher education and did not believe that his race was incapable of assimilating higher education—that to believe this would be "a virtual indictment of the mental capacity of my race." It was not necessary to disparage higher education for Negroes, Fortune reiterated, in order to make a case for industrial education. Both kinds of schools were needed.[26]

He undertook with more zest a campaign to counter the movement for the total disfranchisement which had been advocated at Montgomery and which seemed to be sweeping the South. When Edgar Gardner Murphy, speaking of educational requirements for disqualifying the unfit, said that public opinion in the South would never sanction the disfranchisement of illiterate Confederate soldiers because in every civilization there

26. Charles Dudley Warner, "The Education of the Negro," *Journal of Social Science* 38 (1900): 1–14; *Boston Transcript*, May 8, 1900; *New York Sun*, May 13, 1900.

was a deep and rightful regard for the men who had fought in the armies of the state, Fortune scornfully rejoined: "Of course the ignorant black and white soldiers who fought in the armies of the Union, thousands of whom reside in the Southern States, are not to be considered in the same breath with Mr. Murphy's Confederate soldier!" Murphy added that he did not seek to destroy the "potential citizenship" of the Negro and disapproved legislative subterfuge, but legislative subterfuge represented "a higher morality than the domination of the brutal and irresponsible illiteracy." The answer lay in modifying the Fifteenth Amendment so as to leave the question of suffrage to local government. "Mr. Murphy and the South display an unprecedented amount of nerve," commented Fortune, "in the light of the history of the past twenty-five years, when they ask and expect that people of the rest of the country will have any faith whatever in their professions of honesty and fair play in dealing with the Afro-American race in its political rights."[27]

During this period Fortune made a number of speeches denouncing disfranchisement and its advocates. A contemporary has left us a description of one of these performances which occurred at a Negro gathering in Chicago. At the conclusion of a dinner, Fortune was called upon to respond to a toast "Supremest Moments." "Gaunt and erect, his hair standing straight up like a bush, his eyes spitting fire, and his bony index finger beating time to his impassioned eloquence," Fortune told the assemblage that his "supremest moments" came with every opportunity to strike a blow in defense of his people, and he never let one pass. He then launched into a speech on disfranchisement in which he flayed Ben Tillman unmercifully. After he finished, "trembling and much overwrought from his effort, he sat down amid tremendous applause."[28]

A more widely publicized speech was one he delivered be-

27. *New York Sun*, May 6, 1900.
28. *Washington Colored American*, October 20, 1900.

fore the general conference of the A.M.E. Zion Church in Washington, D. C. He declared that it has cost tons of blood and money to put the Fifteenth Amendment into the Constitution, and it would take tons of blood and money to take it out. The speech, which was wildly applauded, was described by the *Washington Post,* which was consistently hostile to Fortune, as extremely sensational.[29] But the response to this speech was mild in comparison to the furor which Fortune aroused in a speech in Brooklyn shortly thereafter. The occasion was a mass meeting held in honor of the centennial of John Brown's birth. After paying tribute to the martyred Brown, Fortune declared that the Negro in the United States was on the verge of a crisis as serious as the one of Brown's day—that the first gun had been fired at the Montgomery conference where there had been serious discussion of the repeal of the Fifteenth Amendment. After repeating that it had taken blood and money to put the amendment into the Constitution and would require blood and money to take it out, he was reported as saying that if the Negro could not be a man in the South he should leave, but if he stayed he should stay as a man and fight his way up. It was useless to remain in the South and cry "Peace! Peace! when there is no peace." He added that he believed in the law, "but if the law

29. *Washington Post,* May 21, 1900; *Washington Colored American,* May 26, 1900. The *Colored American* suggested that Fortune and the editor of the *Post* should try to reconcile their differences. To this Fortune replied: "Get together? Not much! There is no man or combination of men who can construct a platform upon which the editors of the Age and Post could stand two minutes without a hand to hand fight. The two men think from two absolutely irreconcilable points of view. We shall fight it out to the bitter end, and as we have the justice and humanity side of this contention we are dead sure we will win in the end. Twenty-five years hence the editor of the Washington Post will admit that his ideal Negro was a monstrous impossibility in our republic" (*Washington Colored American,* July 28, 1900).

can afford no protection, then we should protect ourselves, and if need be die in defense of our rights as citizens. The Negro can't win through cowardice."

The speech elicited a barrage of unfavorable editorial comment in the white press. The *Hartford Post* entitled its comment "Bad Advice" and ended with the remark: "Meantime T. Thomas Fortune reminds us of Booker T. Washington—he is so different." The *New York Times* in an editorial entitled "A Very Foolish Negro" said that Fortune was a Negro "whose folly verges on crime." Resistance by force was the worst possible remedy to advise, and to urge Negroes to leave the South could lead only to suffering and distress. Blacks and whites of the South must live together; the labor of Negroes was necessary for the prosperity of the region. The best course for Negroes to follow was to follow the advice of Booker T. Washington and make themselves indispensable by improving their skills. The *Brooklyn Eagle* was somewhat more temperate. It was natural, it said, for Fortune to be aroused about talk of the repeal of the Fifteenth Amendment, although he knew quite well it would not be repealed. But though the amendment would not be repealed, its promises could not be completely fulfilled until the Negro had achieved fitness for self-government. A speech such as Fortune had given was an invitation to race conflict which would lead to annihilation of Negroes.[30]

In a letter to the *Eagle*, June 5, 1900, which represented one of his best journalistic efforts and his most effective defense of the use of retaliatory force, Fortune admitted that some of the fire of old John Brown had crept into his speech, but he defended what he had said. "If I stood in your shoes," he told the editor, "I should perhaps think as you do and reach such conclusions as you do; but I do not stand in your shoes, and there are 10,000,000 people in this country who do not. I and these

30. *New York Times*, June 4, June 5, 1900; *Hartford Post*, June 4, 1900; *Brooklyn Eagle*, June 4, 1900.

10,000,000 people are the gored oxen. You are not gored at all."
On the question of the use of force he declared:

> The blackman's right of self-defense is identically the same
> as the white man's right of self-defense. Tell me that I shall
> be exterminated, as you do, if I exercise that right and I will
> tell you to go ahead and exterminate—if you can. That is a
> game that two can always play at. And suppose you do ex-
> terminate me, what of it? Am I not nobler and happier ex-
> terminated while contending for my honest rights than living
> a low cur that any poor white sneak would feel free to kick?
> The black race is not going to be exterminated for standing
> up for its rights; the white race of the North and West will
> see that it is not. But if it continues to allow itself to be robbed
> of its manhood and womanhood rights, to be lynched and
> flayed and mutilated by frenzied mobs, to be degraded in
> legislative enactments which ramify all the relations of life;
> if it continues to be allowed all this without protest . . . then
> it will fall into . . . contempt.

He added that he believed in law and the rule of law, but
asked: "When the law does not protect me, as it does not in
the South . . . what am I to do? Accept it all meekly, without
protest or resentment? . . . Slaves do that sort of thing, and are
worthy to be slaves, but free men, American freemen! Who
expects them to do it?" He agreed with the *Eagle* that it was
essential that the black people of the South should make friends
with the whites, and that they should be law abiding and industrious, "but I go a step further," he said, "and believe that
it is equally essential to the desired result that the white people
should make friends with the black people and that the white
people should be law abiding and industrious." Talk of leaving
the solution of the race question to the white people of the South
was "the veriest rot." The whole problem must be solved "in
conformity to the Federal Constitution and the Christian sentiment which dominates the republic."[31]

31. To Washington Fortune wrote that he had raised a "news-

Later in the summer a riot occurred on Manhattan's West Side following the killing of a white plainclothes policeman by a Negro. After the slain man's funeral, whites went on a rampage in the Negro section, kicking and beating anyone whom they chanced to encounter. Blacks claimed that when they sought protection from the police they were clubbed instead. Newspaper accounts appeared to substantiate the police brutality. A delegation of Negroes protested to the mayor: "There was no race riot. The Negroes were attacked and instead of receiving protection from the police they were brutally treated by them." In fact, the police "appeared to be glad of the opportunity to club Negroes." Fortune was away from New York at the time but was named chairman of the executive committee of a Citizen's Protective League which was created to seek redress following the incident.[32]

The *Morning Telegraph*, organ of Tammany Hall, held Fortune responsible for the disorders because in his Brooklyn speech he had advised Negroes to defend their rights. Bruce Grit labeled the attack upon Fortune as "too disreputable and puerile to produce any other feeling than that of supreme contempt for its author." The kind of Negro whom the *Telegraph* editorial admired was one who was "willing to submit to outrage and insult without protest. Mr. Fortune doesn't happen to be that kind of a Negro." The real responsibility for the disorders, said Grit, lay with Tammany and the police.[33]

Fortune was absent from New York in the weeks following the riot. He was attending the meeting in Boston at which the

paper howl" and was enjoying it, although "I am pretty sure you do not favor this sort of rumpus." But he thought some good might come of it, and it would "at least show the people of the North that we can fight back" (Fortune to Washington, June 5, June 6, 1900, Washington Papers).

32. *New York Sun*, August 16, August 17, August 22, 1900; Johnson, *Black Manhattan*, pp. 127, 130.

33. *Washington Colored American*, September 1, 1900.

National Negro Business League was organized and the convention of the National Afro-American Council in Indianapolis.

The idea of an organization of Negro businessmen, which was one of Washington's most cherished projects, was not original with him. As early as 1891, J. H. Lewis, of Boston, a tailor and one of the wealthiest Negroes in the United States, had urged a conference of Negro businessmen, a proposal which was endorsed in the *Age*. In 1899 W. E. B. Du Bois had sponsored a conference at Atlanta University on "The Negro in Business," at which a proposal was drafted for a businessmen's league in every community. Local leagues would in turn be affiliated with state and national organizations. At the meeting of the Afro-American Council in Chicago, Du Bois had been made a director of a bureau on Negro business which was intended to begin the organization of the leagues.[34]

While Du Bois was gathering data and developing plans, Washington acted, sending out a call for Negro businessmen in Boston in August 1900, less than a week before the Afro-American Council was scheduled to meet in Indianapolis. The action was interpreted by Washington's critics as an attempt to undercut the council and Du Bois. Instead of going to Indianapolis and helping Du Bois and the council, charged the *Chicago Conservator*, Washington called a rival meeting which would be injurious to the council. "It looks like Mr. Washington is determined to help no movement he does not inaugurate," said the *Conservator*. At a conference of New England colored men, William Monroe Trotter, the young man who was to become

34. *Age*, December 12, 1891; T. Thomas Fortune, "The Quick and the Dead," *A.M.E. Church Review*, April 1916, p. 249; W. E. B. Du Bois, ed., *The Negro in Business*, Atlanta University Publications, no. 4 (Atlanta, 1899), p. 50; Louis R. Harlan, "Booker T. Washington and the National Negro Business League," in William G. Shade and Roy C. Herrenkohl, eds., *Seven on Black: Reflections on the Negro Experience in America* (New York, 1969), pp. 76–77.

Washington's most relentless critic, opposed a meeting devoted to a discusison of business at a time when Negroes faced a crisis over political rights. "No man is a man who thinks only of making a dollar," he said. "It is the duty of the Negro to agitate for his political rights, and when the campaign is over you can have your business meeting."[35] But Washington, undeterred by his critics and ignoring any indebtedness to Du Bois for the idea of the organization, completely dominated the proceedings in Boston where about three hundred businessmen and Washington supporters gathered.

The Tuskegee Wizard served as permanent chairman of the gathering and was elected president of the National Negro Business League, created by the gathering, a position he continued to hold until his death. He pushed through a resolution which gave the president the authority to name the chairman of the executive committee, a position to which he promptly named Fortune. The sessions were devoted exclusively to discussion of Negro-operated businesses. Washington adamantly refused to permit the discussion of political questions or even mention of riots which had recently occurred in New Orleans and Akron as well as in New York. The program at this meeting, as at later conventions of the league, consisted almost entirely of the reading of papers by men who had been successful in various lines of business. In his address "The Negro Publisher" Fortune praised Washington profusely for his leadership and for his work at Tuskegee, which was training young people to enter business and commerce. On the subject of the Negro press he said that none of the papers which had been founded "was intended to serve as a stepping stone to fortune," but rather for racial uplift—an idea somewhat inconsistent with the basic premise of the league which Washington was promoting. But, he said, the

35. *Chicago Conservator*, quoted in *Indianapolis Freeman*, July 14, 1900; *Boston Herald*, August 17, 1900.

financial success of the race press would come with the development of other successful race business ventures.[36]

From Boston Fortune went to Indianapolis, where he played a conspicuous part in the convention of the Afro-American Council, serving as chairman of the committee on resolutions. The *Indianapolis Freeman* described him as "the spoiled darling of the convention . . . brilliantly erratic . . . and theatrical." Washington did not attend the convention although he came to the city a few days later to deliver a lecture. At the council meeting the emphasis was on politics and suffrage. The address to the country which was adopted protested against the nullification of constitutional guarantees. The council, it said, did not necessarily oppose property or educational requirements for voting if they were applied to all citizens alike, but the suffrage restrictions which had been adopted were "immoral in their purpose" and contravened the Constitution. Before the convention Fortune had anticipated a move to denounce the McKinley administration, but the address which was adopted was silent on this question. Walters was reelected president of the council, with Fortune as first vice-president and Pledger as second vice-president. Ida Wells Barnett continued as secretary and Du Bois as head of the business bureau.[37]

Although the council failed to take a stand for or against the McKinley administration, the Afro-American Press Association meeting a few days earlier had warmly endorsed McKinley. It issued a statement that "the best interests of the country at large and the Afro-American people in particular, will be served by a consistent support of McKinley and Roosevelt." Fortune was listed as one of the signers. In spite of

36. National Negro Business League, *Proceedings*, 1900, pp. 157–61 and passim; Harlan, "Washington and the National Negro Business League," pp. 77–79.

37. *Indianapolis Freeman*, July 7, September 1, September 8, 1900; Fortune to Washington, August 11, 1900, Washington Papers.

all his earlier fulminations, he had decided several months before this to support McKinley, principally because there was no alternative. The ideological justification for his position was expressed in an editorial which he wrote for the *Transcript* in November 1899. After pointing out that the progress of the disfranchisement movement was the work of southern Democrats and redounded to the strengthening of the Democratic party in Congress, he asked: "How can a black man in the South support such a party and not go and hang himself immediately after voting for its candidates? On all questions of national policy, withal, Afro-Americans are, to their credit, Republicans."[38] In an editorial in the *Age* on January 4, 1900, he commended McKinley for calling attention to lynchings in his annual message, something which he had failed to do previously.

In personal and practical terms Fortune hoped by endorsing McKinley to be appointed by the Republican National Committee as head of the Afro-American Literary Bureau. Although Washington apparently interceded for him, he failed to receive the position. But in July Theodore Roosevelt, the vice-presidential candidate, wrote to Mark Hanna, the Republican national chairman, that McKinley had told him that some of the best colored men, including Booker T. Washington, thought it very important that Fortune be employed in the Literary Bureau. Fortune, he told Hanna, was "an able and rather discontented black man [who might otherwise use his journalistic talents to the detriment of the McKinley ticket?] and the President thinks it would be most useful to get him at once."[39]

Early in September Fortune was called to Republican head-

38. *Springfield Republican,* August 20, 1900; *Boston Transcript,* November 16, 1899.

39. Fortune to Washington, January 10, March 9, 1900; Scott to Fortune, January 15, 1900, Washington Papers; Roosevelt to Hanna, July 7, 1900, in Elting E. Morison, ed., *The Letters of Theodore Roosevelt,* 8 vols. (Cambridge, Mass., 1951–54), 2: 1349.

quarters in Chicago to assist Ferdinand Barnett, who was in charge of Negro affairs there. In an interview in the *Chicago Times Herald*, Fortune declared that there was no prospect that Negro voters would desert the Republican party. What the Democrats had accomplished by violence in 1876 and had maintained by violence, intimidation, and fraud ever since, he said, they were trying to legalize through disfranchising clauses in state constitutions. Whereas Bryan, the Democratic candidate, had refused to comment on disfranchisement, McKinley as president had "stood by the Constitution as he understood it in dealing with the abnormal condition of affairs which Southern Democratic cussedness had forced on the country."[40]

In addition to working in Chicago, Fortune had traveled in Indiana and Missouri during the closing weeks of the campaign. The campaign work, "the whirl and hurrah," had done havoc to his regular work, he wrote Washington, after his return to New York. But both he and Washington expected that he would be rewarded with a worthwhile appointment. When Fortune went to Chicago, Washington wrote him a letter of advice, admonishing him especially to keep on good terms with Hanna. "It will pay you to bite your tongue very often and sit down upon your dignity in order to accomplish the ends we have in view," he wrote his impetuous friend. "If you can go through the campaign and keep on smooth terms with all concerned and impress the authorities with your value I am sure that we can secure a handsome reward for you at the close of the campaign." Fortune thanked him for the advice. His conduct throughout the campaign was evidently circumspect, and his relations with Hanna appeared to be cordial. In February he went to Washington to press his case, and it appears that Washington and others endorsed him. In June he went to the capital again but was unable to see the president. Once more

40. Fortune to Washington, September 10, September 12, 1900, Washington Papers; *Chicago Times Herald*, October 1, 1900.

his hopes of a political appointment which might help him out of his chronic financial troubles were dashed.[41]

Meanwhile, behind the scenes, Fortune was almost continuously engaged in writing for Washington or doing research for and editing and revising what Washington had written. He also tried to find time—without much success—for his own literary efforts.

As Washington's fame grew, white editors were eager to publish anything which bore his name, and he was constantly approached by them for books and articles. As Fortune remarked when Lyman Abbott invited Washington to write the series of articles for the *Outlook* which later appeared in book form as *Up from Slavery*, if his friend had been able to fulfill all the requests to publish his autobiography, he would have been able to retire and live off his royalties.[42] Busy as he was administering Tuskegee, raising funds, and traveling widely on lecture tours, Washington had little time for writing and none for the research necessary for the preparation of some of the publications which appeared under his name. Consequently he relied heavily on others to gather information, to revise what he had written, and sometimes to do the actual writing. At this date it is impossible to unravel all the details and to say precisely which parts of the vast list of publications attributed to Washington were ghost written, but in some cases the evidence is clear.

For several years Fortune was deeply involved in ghosting for Washington. Sometimes Washington paid him by simply sending him the check which he received from the publisher.

41. Fortune to Washington, September 15, September 20, November 10, 1900; March 18, March 21, April 3, April 17, June 21, 1901; Washington to Fortune, September 15, 1900, Washington Papers; *Indianapolis Freeman*, February 2, 1901.

42. Fortune to Washington, January 8, 1900, Washington Papers.

For example, when Fortune wrote an article for the *New York Evening Post* which Edward Villard had requested of Washington, Washington sent Fortune the twenty dollars he recived for it. Incidentally, Fortune later quoted from the article to buttress his argument in the *Boston Transcript* that Washington did not oppose higher education for Negroes.[43]

Fortune evidently wrote *A New Negro for a New Century*, a book of more than four hundred pages, which was published in 1900. It included chapters on the part played by Negroes in the Spanish-American War, on industrial schools, colleges, and universities and other aspects of race progress and the race problem. During the spring and summer of 1899 Fortune was engaged in gathering materials and writing. The publishers were anxious for the manuscript, and the book was hastily put together. After it was published, the publisher for some reason failed to pay according to the terms to which they had originally agreed. Fortune and Washington considered a law suit to · compel payment, but there is no evidence that they did so.[44]

Fortune selected the title and did the compiling and editing of *Sowing and Reaping*, a volume of speeches which Washington had delivered to Tuskegee students. Washington sent the finished manuscript to the publisher without reading it, but

43. See above p. 196; Fortune to Washington, November 13, 1899; March 18, 1900; Washington to Fortune, March 18, 1900, Washington Papers. Fortune wrote an article which appeared in the *Chattanooga Tradesman* over Washington's name. He advised him on the contents of the article, "The Case of the Negro," which was published in the *Atlantic* in November 1899, and he wrote a draft of the article, "The American Negro and His Economic Value," published in the *International Quarterly* in December 1900 (Fortune to Washington, August 6, 1899; January 1, 1900; Washington to Fortune, March 4, 1900, Washington Papers).

44. Fortune to Washington, June 23, August 15, September 24, 1900; Fortune to Scott, November 14, 1900, Washington Papers.

Scott assured him that it was a good job. Washington had promised to pay Fortune any money he might receive from royalties.

While he was working on *Sowing and Reaping*, Fortune was also engaged in reading proof and making corrections on Washington's first autobiography, *The Story of My Life and Work*, which was published by J. L. Nichols and Company in 1900. He finished his first reading of the proof while confined to bed with chills and laryngitis. Afterwards, he wrote Washington, he realized with a shock, "that you had finished the record of your life and work without deeming it necessary to mention my name as your good friend of eight years, or any of the many signed things I have said about you. I write in great sorrow and with wounded pride because I have tried to do so much to sustain you and your work and am grieved and pained to find it amounts to so little in the summing up."[45]

In the book as it finally appeared Washington did pay high tribute to Fortune, and to Scott, but apparently only as an afterthought and because Fortune had brought it to his attention. "Mr. Fortune," he said, "in all . . . matters where he has considered my position the correct one has defended and supported me without regard to his personal popularity or unpopularity." He went on to say that although he and Fortune sometimes differed on public questions,

> we have never allowed our differences to mar our personal friendship. In all matters, pertaining to our race in the South I have always consulted him most freely and frankly. . . . I have seldom ever given any public utterance to the country that have not had his criticism and approval. His help and

45. Fortune to Washington, January 19, February 23, April 27, May 4, May 15, 1900; Washington to Fortune, May 2, May 8, May 15, 1900, Washington Papers. For the work which he did on *The Story of My Life and Work*, Fortune was paid $50.

friendship to me in many directions has [*sic*] been most potent in enabling me to accomplish whatever I have been able to do.

In the same class with Mr. Fortune I would put my private secretary, Mr. Emmett J. Scott. . . .[46]

Fortune later helped in the revision of this first autobiography, even filling in certain blank pages which the author had left in the manuscript. "Have you anything to suggest about my filling in the vacant pages of this book by you?" he asked Washington. "It is a formidable job for me." Shortly thereafter, Max Bennett Thrasher, a white journalist who also wrote for and about Washington, did yet another revision. A member of the Tuskegee staff who had been mentioned in the original version but was not mentioned in this revision complained to Scott, evidently blaming Fortune for dropping his name. Fortune answered: "I am *not* responsible for leaving Weber out. I left him in; if he is out in the Thrasher revision it was done on the instance of Mr. Washington . . . and Weber should go gunning for the author and not for any of us." Fortune had difficulty in collecting payment from the publisher for the work which he did on the book, nor was he paid for a review of Washington's second autobiography, *Up from Slavery*, which he wrote for the *Transcript* at the request of the editor, although Fortune insisted that it was customary to pay for such an article.[47]

In spite of the scramble to make a living, Fortune kept trying to find time for his own literary work. In 1898 he conceived the

46. Booker T. Washington, *The Story of My Life and Work* (Napierville Ill., and Toronto, Ontario: J. L. Nichols and Co., 1900), pp. 396–97. After reading the paragraph about himself, Fortune wrote the author that he was deeply touched and appreciative (Fortune to Washington, June 1, 1900, Washington Papers).

47. Washington to Fortune, September 11, 1900; April 17, 1901; Fortune to Washington, September 24, November 27, 1900; March 21, May 18, 1901, Washington Papers. Emphasis as in original.

idea of writing a book on the Supreme Court. He suggested that Washington finance him in doing the necessary research. "The best service you and I could render the race," he wrote his friend, "would be a judicial history by me on the attitude of the Supreme Court on the question of Civil and Political Rights from the foundation of the Government." Such a book would alert the American people to "the dangerous position which the Supreme Court holds in our government." Nothing came of this suggestion, however.

Earlier Fortune had begun a novel, "The Man without a Race," which was evidently never completed. In 1899 he started another novel, "After War Times," a book which he hoped to make an "eye-opener" about Reconstruction. In spite of the burden of all his other writing, he was resolved "to break through the difficulties in literary links" with this novel and with "work and sacrifice" to "*create*" something of lasting value. In 1901 he was still trying to find time to work on the novel, declaring, "It must be a make or bust in the literary high push this time." Eight chapters were completed when he had to give it up because of trouble with his eyes.[48]

He continued to write verses and sought to find someone who would publish them in book form. One publisher, Tennyson Neely, agreed to publish them but required Fortune to pay half the cost—two hundred dollars. John Durham advised Fortune to accept the offer, and somehow the money was raised. But almost immediately thereafter the publisher failed. "I guess my $200 has gone glimmering up salt lake," Fortune lamented. "I as as blue as indigo. There *seems to be no success for me*." Later he submitted his verses to Walter Hines Page, one of Washington's warmest admirers. Page read them and told him: "Your poetry is good; much of it, I think, very good, and our

48. Fortune to Washington, July 27, 1898; September 26, September 27, October 13, December 19, 1899; April 17, May 19, 1901, Washington Papers. Emphasis as in original.

readers agree with me in this." Nevertheless Page could not publish the verses because there was no possibility that they would be a commercial success. "It is not the kind of excellence that is popular," he said. The Abbey Press indicated a willingness to publish but required Fortune to pay half the cost, and he did not have the money.[49]

Recurring ill health, some of it undoubtedly psychosomatic (he was something of a hypochondriac), not only interfered with Fortune's hopes of doing creative writing but also added to his chronic financial problems. During the summer of 1899 he was sick almost continuously with rheumatism and other ailments and spent much of the time at Saratoga on the advice of his doctor. While there he underwent surgery for an undisclosed ailment and was confined to the hospital for several days, while doctors' fees and hospital costs added to his depression. By November he said his health was fair and his working capacity normal, but he frequently complained of other illnesses. His eyes gave him chronic trouble which sometimes prevented him from working. In May 1901 his eyes were in such bad shape that he said he was "almost blind" for ten days, but his sight began to improve under the ministrations of a doctor in Philadelphia.[50]

Except for short intervals, however, he worked continuously and frantically. The salary which he received from the *Age* covered only half of his fixed living expenses; hence special writing was an absolute necessity. Income from the *Sun* became less certain since he could not be sure that everything he submitted would be printed. Consequently he grasped eagerly any other writing assignment which came his way. In a single week, when he was in "bang-up working shape," he turned out five

49. Fortune to Washington, October 7, October 12, October 21, October 23, October 25, 1899; May 28, June 26, 1901, Washington Papers. Emphasis as in original.

50. Fortune to Washington, June 19, August 3, August 5, August 6, 1899; May 8, May 13, May 16, May 18, 1901; Fortune to Scott, November 18, 1899, Washington Papers.

special articles for newspapers besides doing his regular work for the *Age* and reading proof on Washington's autobiography. When he did not receive a check which he expected from the publisher for his work on *Sowing and Reaping*, he was "almost crazy over small debts" which could not be met. "The money problem is giving me more trouble than 16 to 1 is giving Mr. Bryan," he said.[51]

Late in 1900 he tried to supplement his income from journalism by going into the cigar business with Roscoe Simmons, nephew of Mrs. Washington. But this venture proved a fiasco and left him with some additional debts. This, plus the trouble with his eyes, left him in such straits that he was once again compelled to appeal to Washington to tide him over. "I have been making a strenuous effort to pull through my affairs without calling on you," he wrote, but now he was unable to meet pressing obligations unless his friend came to his assistance.[52]

While Fortune struggled—with little success—to avoid being financially dependent upon Washington, the personal ties between the two men remained close and affectionate. When Washington was in Europe in 1899, Fortune wrote him: "The country seems sorter empty without you"; and later, in reply to a letter which he had received: "I am pleased to learn that you miss me because we are in the same box on that score. The fact is that I feel like a fish out of water with you so far away; I shall be glad when you return." Fortune was in the hospital when Washington returned and was unable to go to New York to meet him, so Washington went to Saratoga.[53]

When Washington came to New York on Tuskegee business, as he did frequently, the two men spent much time to-

51. Fortune to Washington, September 27, 1899; March 11, May 1, May 4, May 9, May 31, June 4, 1900, Washington Papers.

52. Fortune to Scott, January 2, 1901; Fortune to Washington, May 19, May 21, 1901, Washington Papers.

53. Fortune to Washington, June 1, June 23, August 9, 1899, Washington Papers.

gether. "Been with the Wizard most of the day and thus lost 12 more hours in this shooting match," Fortune wrote to Scott during one of the visits. "*I shall have to reform*, as my affairs are going to——." When Washington was not in New York, the two friends wrote to each other almost daily, on all manner of subjects, political, racial, and personal. Fortune expressed his views on current Afro-American writers and advised Washington what to read.[54]

Washington sometimes gave Fortune advice on his personal conduct, especially his drinking as that became more and more of a problem. On various occasions, especially at conventions and banquets, Fortune was publicly drunk, and it seems likely that some of his more intemperate extemporaneous speeches were given when he had been drinking. Scott, probably at Washington's prompting, first wrote Fortune on the subject. Fortune replied: "I am glad you spoke of the drink business if it was on your mind. *And you can give men no advice that would not be good advice.*" A few weeks later he assured Washington he was sticking to his resolution to limit his drinking. "I have stopped lushing," he said, "and shall not begin again. I shall boss myself in that as in other things concerning myself. I know that I have injured myself in this matter and I regret it." While Fortune was working in Chicago during the campaign of 1900, Washington urged him to beware of friends who would tempt

54. Fortune to Scott, November, 1899; Fortune to Washington, undated letter, 1900; Charles W. Chesnutt to Washington, November 16, 1901, Washington Papers; *Washington Colored American*, November 30, 1901. Emphasis as in original. Although Fortune was a friend of Paul Laurence Dunbar, he did not admire much of his writing. One story of Dunbar's especially exasperated him. He considered it "pure niggerism from the white man's point of view hashed up by a black man." On the other hand he greatly admired Charles W. Chesnutt. He was enthusiastic about *The Marrow of Tradition*. Chesnutt, he thought, was able to portray a "genuine Negro" and despised "a good nigger" as much as he, Fortune, did.

him "to do that which I am sure you together with your system and general nervous condition cannot stand." The friends who might lead him astray would be the first, Washington noted, to criticize him for his weakness. Fortune thanked him for the advice and appears to have followed it, at least for the duration of the campaign.[55]

In these crucial years at the turn of the century, as the disfranchisement movement gained momentum and segregation became more firmly entrenched, Fortune through his writing and his speeches, continued to protest, more eloquently and vehemently than ever. His role as militant northern spokesman placed him in sharp contrast with the conciliatory, accommodating part which Washington played in public. But the intimacy between the two men continued, and Fortune cooperated with Washington in a number of ways, defending him and promoting his claims of race leadership. In his relations with Washington and in his zeal for political appointments which would ease his financial problems, the middle-aged Fortune was beginning to follow the lines of expediency which were inconsistent with the independence and idealism which he had proclaimed as the youthful editor of the *Globe*.

55. Fortune to Scott, April 16, 1900; Fortune to Washington, May 9, September 20, 1900; Washington to Fortune, September 14, 1900, Washington Papers. Emphasis as in original.

VII

Washington Becomes the Dominant Partner

THE ACCESSION OF THEODORE ROOSEVELT TO THE PRESIDENCY in 1901 raised Booker T. Washington to new heights of power and prestige as a presidential adviser. But the power which he wielded aroused the apprehensions of his black critics and led them to intensify their attacks, and Washington was compelled to strive as never before to preserve the image of unchallenged race spokesman and leader.

As Washington's star rose, Fortune's waned. He failed to receive the kind of appointment he sought from Roosevelt, and his chronic financial problems became more acute. Publicly he continued to support Washington loyally, thereby incurring the scorn of the Tuskegean's critics. But behind the scenes his relations with the Wizard deteriorated, partly for personal reasons, partly because it was increasingly difficult for Fortune to reconcile his own views on race matters and politics with the accommodationist views of Washington.

While Roosevelt was still vice-president, Fortune, before joining Washington in Chicago for the meeting of the Business League, went in August to Philadelphia for the convention of the Afro-American Press Association. In a speech which he gave at the meeting, "The Press as an Educator," he reportedly said: "We have cringed and crawled long enough. I don't want any more 'good niggers.' I want 'bad niggers.' It's the 'bad nigger' with the Winchester who can defend his home and children and wife." Pledger followed with a speech in a similar vein in which he agreed that Negroes would have to fight lynch laws with rifles.[1]

At Chicago serious differences arose between Fortune and Washington. Fortune wanted to support a resolution against a recent atrocity in Atlanta in which a man had been burned alive. He and Washington quarreled during a committee meeting because Washington refused to permit the resolution to come to the floor. Washington also was instrumental in rearranging the scheduled program to prevent Fortune from speaking from the floor. Evidently he and others were afraid that the editor of the *Age*, who probably had been drinking, would make another speech of the kind he had made in Philadelphia. Fortune insisted on speaking in spite of efforts to restrain him. There was a "mighty squally time," he wrote Scott, and Washington was deeply offended.[2] Nevertheless, Fortune and Washington went on together to Gauley Bridge, West Virginia, for a camping holiday with John S. Durham, Max Bennett Thrasher, Phil Waters, and others. Fortune evidently thought that the rift which had developed at Chicago was healed. The party, he told

1. *Washington Post*, August 7, 1901.

2. Fortune to Washington, September 29, 1901; Fortune to Scott, August 31, 1901, Fortune Papers; Duster, ed., *Crusade for Justice*: (Chicago, 1970), p. 266.

Scott, broke up "in the best of humor and health." But after parting with Fortune, Washington failed to write to him for two weeks—something unprecedented in their relationship.[3]

During this interval McKinley died and Roosevelt became president. As is well known, he soon invited Washington to the White House, indicating that he wanted to talk to him about possible appointments in the South. Their conversation followed lines which the two men had discussed previously of plans to build a new Republican party in the South which would be based on "character" rather than patronage and bribery. After the meeting newspapers reported that, although Washington was not a politician, he had expressed the belief that if the race question was to be settled and party lines broken down in the South, the Republican party must have a broader base of support and must seek white members. "If you want to build up the Republican party in the South and make it something besides a by-word and reproach, . . ." he was quoted as saying, "you must get the better elements of whites in it. That is best for the party and the public service. It is also best for the Negro." He was reported to have advised Roosevelt to appoint the best qualified men to office, regardless of whether they were Republicans or Democrats.[4]

Fortune, along with many other Negroes, was shocked at the press reports of Washington's remarks. They looked suspiciously like an endorsement of lily-white doctrines and a means of bypassing the regular Republican organizations in the South, which were controlled by blacks. "The statement of his

3. Fortune to Scott, September 9, September 24, September 25, 1901, Washington Papers.

4. Roosevelt to Washington, September 14, 1901, in Morison, ed., *The Letters of Theodore Roosevelt*, 3: 149; Roosevelt to Washington, September 14, 1901, Washington Papers; Henry F. Pringle, *Theodore Roosevelt* (New York, 1931), p. 161; *Chicago Herald*, quoted in *Indianapolis World*, October 5, 1901; *Boston Globe*, September 30, 1901, quoted in *Boston Guardian*, September 27, 1902.

position after seeing the President, . . . fills me with astonishment and bewilderment," he wrote Scott. "We can't give away every thing and have anything. I should have seen Mr. Washington before he saw President Roosevelt."[5] He was alarmed when, shortly after the Roosevelt-Washington meeting, John G. Capers, a Gold Democrat who had served in Cleveland's cabinet, was appointed Republican national committeeman from South Carolina, while the claims of E. A. Deas, a Negro, who had long been the leading Republican in the state, were ignored.

Like Washington, Fortune had known Roosevelt in New York. But while Roosevelt had early developed a warm admiration for the Tuskegean, it is evident that he did not like Fortune or the type of Negro whom Fortune symbolized. He had also been annoyed at the small attendance at a Negro rally in New York which he had addressed while running for governor. He held Fortune responsible for the failure of the meeting and continued to recall the unfortunate incident whenever he saw him. Fortune's own initial reactions to Roosevelt had been favorable, but as early as November 1898 he had written Washington: "He is no good, and you will find it out." Fortune's doubts about the then governor of New York were due in part to evidences of his racism, and especially to derogatory remarks he had made concerning the conduct of Negro soldiers in an article about the Rough Riders which he had written for *Scribner's*. For this Fortune had attacked him repeatedly in the columns of the *Age*.[6]

5. Fortune to Scott, October 1, 1901, Washington Papers.
6. Fortune to Washington, October 4, November 30, 1898; March 31, 1899, Washington Papers; Roosevelt to Fortune, March 27, March 30, 1899, Morison, ed., *Letters of Theodore Roosevelt*, 2: 972–73; *Cleveland Gazette*, July 21, 1900. For a summary of Roosevelt's racial attitudes see Seth M. Scheiner, "Theodore Roosevelt and the Negro, 1901–1908," *Journal of Negro History* 47 (July, 1962): 169–82.

Fortune sent off a barrage of letters and telegrams to Washington, trying to ascertain whether he had really said what the white press had reported him as saying after the meeting with the president. Finally Washington wrote a letter attempting to clarify what he had said and urging Fortune to support Roosevelt's policy in the *Age* and promising to meet Fortune in New York soon. Fortune replied that, after receiving the communication from Washington, he had found it necessary to rewrite the entire editorial page of the *Age*, which he had been making "all fight on the Southern policy." After consideration, he and Peterson had agreed that they had better go along with Washington. "But," Fortune warned his friend, "I will not endorse that policy until we have talked over the matter." He would use an editorial which Washington had sent him, but it would be in quotation marks, leaving him free to criticize it later. *"The readers of the Age will not expect me to pursue the policy outlined in your editorial note,"* he said, adding, "I am very glad that you are very sure of our friend."[7]

Fortune and Washington patched up their personal relationship, but the editor of the *Age* continued to be skeptical about Roosevelt's policies, and he received many letters from Negro politicians who were disturbed by the president's appointments, some of which, like the naming of Thomas G. Jones, another Gold Democrat, to the federal bench, were made at the suggestion of Washington. Of course, the Negro press applauded Roosevelt when he invited the Tuskegee Wizard to dinner at the White House, and excoriated the white South for its attack on the president over the incident, but otherwise Negro editors were not enthusiastic about Roosevelt.

Washington and Fortune conferred before the former met with the president to discuss his first annual message to Congress. Fortune insisted that Roosevelt would make a mistake if he failed

7. Fortune to Washington, September 29, October 8, October 9, 1901, Washington Papers. Emphasis as in original.

to condemn mob law, but the message said nothing on this subject.[8]

When Roosevelt appointed Fortune's good friend, Robert H. Terrell, as one of the justices in the District of Columbia, Fortune applauded. This appointment, declared the *Age*, "indicates more than anything he has yet done as President his determination to destroy the color line in politics."[9] Fortune's hopes for an appointment for himself, as well as his friendship for Washington, restrained his criticism of the Roosevelt administration. He hoped that with Washington's support he could secure a position which would enable him to pay for his house and straighten out his finances so that he would not have to be dependent on Washington. He was resolved to break his dependence on the Wizard and to liberate Scott as well, if he could. For Scott, while entirely loyal to Washington and serving as his alter ego, was poorly paid and overworked, and there was no prospect of improving his position at Tuskegee. He had told Fortune of his desire to break away, and Fortune had replied that his aspirations were legitimate, adding, "but W. will not stand for them *because you are more useful to him where you are*. I am willing to do what I can, but your change of base depends upon my change of base."[10]

Fortune wanted the ambassadorship to Haiti, but told Washington he would be governed by his wishes in the matter if the

8. Fortune to Washington, October 5, October 12, November 1, November 27, December 18, 1901, Washington Papers.

9. Undated clipping from *Age* (c. November 13, 1901), scrapbook, Terrell Papers, Manuscript Division, Library of Congress. Washington, who was responsible for the appointment, had evidently first known Terrell through Fortune. In 1900 Fortune had urged Washington to support Terrell who was then seeking the position of superintendent of the Negro schools in Washington (Fortune to Washington, March 12, 1900, Washington Papers).

10. Fortune to Washington, September 17, 1901; Fortune to Scott, October 1, 1901, Washington Papers. Emphasis as in original.

Tuskegeean preferred that he not take a post outside the country. He also considered applying for the postmastership at Red Bank but gave this up because the local member of Congress would not support him. He then decided to concentrate on the post of Collector of Internal Revenue in New Jersey and worked strenuously to get recommendations, although he was doubtful about the support of the two senators. He presented papers applying for the collectorship but stating that he preferred the Haitian post.[11]

On a trip to the capital he talked to the president, who seemed to be cordial and said that he expected to see Washington in a few days, which Fortune interpreted as a favorable sign. But a few weeks later Washington advised him to withdraw his papers since Roosevelt had indicated that his appointment would not be approved.[12] One of the reasons for the collapse of his prospects was that a group of Negroes, including Whitfield McKinlay, a real estate dealer who was probably Washington's closest friend in the nation's capital, expressed to the president their opposition to Fortune's appointment. What part Washington himself played in all this is not clear, but it is evident that he did not push Fortune's cause very vigorously with the president who relied so heavily on his advice about other Negro appointments. His failure to do so was undoubtedly due, in part at least, to another one of those unfortunate drunken episodes in which Fortune was periodically involved.

At least two members of the capital's Negro community wrote to Tuskegee about the incident. One of them was E. E. Cooper, editor of the *Washington Colored American*, a man

11. Fortune to Washington, September 17, November 7, November 26, December 5, December 12, December 16, December 18, 1901; January 2, January 22, 1902; Fortune to Scott, January 2, 1902, Washington Papers. Fortune had become a resident of Red Bank, New Jersey, in 1901. See below, pp. 289–90.

12. Fortune to Washington, February 1, March 1, March 4, November 10, 1902, Wshington Papers.

whom Fortune had always distrusted. He reported that while Fortune was in Washington in December he and Paul Laurence Dunbar had gone on a "holy terror" just before a meeting of the Bethel Historical and Literary Association at which Fortune was to read a paper. Fortune came late and had lost his manuscript and "made an off hand talk in a rambling way similar to the one he made at the Business League last August in Chicago." Whitfield McKinlay also wrote Washington who requested him to get all the details he could about the affair. Washington then wrote to Fortune that some of his "very best friends in Washington" had written to him of Fortune's drunkenness and he expressed his disapproval and disappointment. Fortune replied that most of his "friends" in Washington drank more than he did and that they had written to Washington because they had their own axes to grind. As usual he denied that he had been drinking excessively.[13]

Washington also wrote another—and very revealing—letter to McKinlay. He told him that the news of Fortune's drunkenness caused him a great deal of pain—that he had warned Fortune to avoid temptation in Washington and that Fortune had promised "he would not be led astray." One thing was clear, the Wizard said piously, "and that is that while it is necessary for me to be thrown from time to time with people who are not right in their lives, I am determined that no such company or influence will ever make me swerve one iota from the path of right as I see it." His position was the more difficult, he said, because some of his friends were not broad enough to understand it.

13. Washington to McKinlay, December 12, 1901, Woodson Collection; E. E. Cooper to Washington, December 12, 1901; Fortune to Washington, December 16, December 19, 1901, Washington Papers. In a second letter to Washington Cooper said: "Don't say anything about the Fortune matter for I really blame Lawrence Dunbar rather than Fortune. Fortune is bright and witty and entertaining and when two live spirits get together they are apt to do most anything" (December 1, 1901, Washington Papers).

"It is impossible, as you know, to shake off at once the old time men and old time influences." Some people in Washington were criticizing him for paying too much attention to the " 'old crowd' who, in many cases, stood manfully in the earlier and darker days." Aside from this, it was unfortunately true that public sentiment among Negroes, as among whites, was "very largely moulded and educated by the press. It will be impossible to use the press for the purpose of educating our people if one cuts loose entirely from those who control the press." He had wished frequently, he added, that there was one good strong newspaper which had behind it "individuals who were clean in their private lives and unselfish in their public utterances and influence."[14] It is evident that his friendship with Fortune had become a source of embarrassment to Washington in the large role which he was now playing in public affairs. But although he would have liked to terminate the relationship, he found Fortune and the *Age* indispensable to his purposes.

After he had been rebuffed in the matter of his appointment, Fortune told Washington that he was considering resigning his positions in all race organizations and devoting himself entirely to writing. "I have done my share of purely race and party work," he said, "and the reward has been unsatisfactory in every other respect than that of knowing that I have done my duty. I shall get out of the whole business in good humor and let my record in that department of activity stand on its own merits." When Washington, Peterson, John Durham, and others protested, he said he was determined. He had done more than his share in the race struggle, and others had reaped the rewards. He had nothing to show for his efforts "but poverty and the antagonism of people powerful [enough] to cut my throat." A few months later he wrote Washington that he was also considering selling the *Age*. He suggested that Washington might

14. Washington to McKinlay December 16, 1901, Woodson Collection.

like to buy his interest in the paper and that William H. Baldwin or Robert Ogden, two of the philanthropists who supported Tuskegee, might be willing to put up the money.[15]

But however discouraged and embittered he may have been, Fortune did not withdraw from his race activities or sell the *Age*. Nor did he cease his defense of Washington as criticism against him mounted. Some Negro papers were saying that Roosevelt's failure to mention mob law in his annual message had been on Washington's advice. Washington was also being blamed for the removal of Negro officeholders in the South and for the appointment of Lily Whites. Black politicians like Deas of South Carolina and Pledger of Georgia were thoroughly alarmed and hostile because Roosevelt was consulting Washington on matters of patronage while they were unable to reach the president. Most of the letters to the *Age* from the South were so antagonistic to Roosevelt and Washington that Fortune did not print them. He was being "hammered unmercifully," he said, for his failure to attack Roosevelt. After his failure to receive the hoped-for appointment, he did issue a few blasts. The *Age* expressed disappointment that, in dealing with the South, Roosevelt was following the example of McKinley and was, in addition, appointing white Democrats to office. Such practices would alienate Negro voters in the North, it warned, and not accomplish what the president hoped in the South. "The South will remain solidly Democratic."[16]

But in spite of his doubts about Roosevelt and his previously expressed desire to withdraw from race activities, Fortune played a leading role in the convention of the 1902 Afro-Amer-

15. Fortune to Washington, March 7, March 24, June 9, 1902, Washington Papers.

16. Fortune to Washington, January 16, February 6, February 8, 1902; Scott to Washington, July 12, 1902, Washington Papers; *Washington Bee*, February 15, February 22, 1902; *Age* quoted in *Indianapolis World*, May 10, 1902.

ican Council which endorsed the Roosevelt administration. Bishop Walters at first threatened to go after Roosevelt "hammer and tong" in his presidential address, but Fortune dissuaded him. He also anticipated an effort at the convention to censure both Roosevelt and Washington. Deas of South Carolina was planning to come to Saint Paul to attack Roosevelt, and some of the members from the Chicago area were also threatening to "swipe" both Roosevelt and Washington.[17] In the face of these threats, Washington decided to go in person to Saint Paul and meet the opposition head on.

After the meeting Scott wrote admiringly to his chief: "It was wonderful to see how completely your personality dominated everything at Saint Paul. From the moment that you reached there you were the one center of interest." The pro-Washington group overrode all opposition. The address to the country which was adopted contained the usual demands for the protection of constitutional rights and asked Congress to create a commission to investigate conditions of Afro-Americans. There followed an endorsement of the president for what he had said on the subject of fitness for appointment to public office and "the attitude of the Federal government toward all of its citizens, regardless of race or color." The Tuskegee Wizard had indeed done his work well. A slate of officers friendly, or at least amenable to him, was also elected. Fortune was elected president and Walters chairman of the executive committee. Among the vice presidents were Deas, Pledger, and George H. White, politicians who might not like the political role which Washington was playing, but whose political future seemed to depend upon his good will. Mrs. Fannie Barrier Williams of Chicago, wife of attorney S. Laing Williams, was elected corresponding secretary, succeeding Ida Wells Barnett,

17. Fortune to Washington, April 14, June 23, June 27, 1902; Fortune to Scott, July 2, 1902, Washington Papers.

who along with her husband had joined the opposition to Washington.[18]

Washington had achieved what he wanted at the convention, but some of the Negro press excoriated him and Fortune for the methods which had been used. "The 'Wizard of Tuskegee' was there," said the *Washington Bee*. "His satellites were in the saddle and he handled and groaned [*sic*] the studs. They trotted and pranced just as he pulled the reins and his ticket was elected and his namby-pamby policy . . . was incorporated into the address, which was nothing more than a pronouncement of his Nibs, the boss of Negro beggars." The *Boston Guardian*, edited by William Monroe Trotter, who was rapidly emerging as Washington's most implacable foe, condemned the election of Fortune because, it claimed, the true president would be Washington. "It is well known that Fortune is only a 'me too' to whatever Washington aspires to do," said Trotter. "These two men have long since formed themselves into one twain in their dealings with the Negro race, Fortune furnishing whatever brain the combination needs and Washington the boodle." The *Guardian* declared that the failure of the council to condemn Roosevelt's southern policy was a dereliction of duty and a betrayal since the council was formed to protect political rights. In words which Fortune might have written if he had expressed

18. Scott to Washington, July 17, 1902, Washington Papers; Charles Francis Adams, "The Afro-American Council," *Colored American Magazine*, March 1903, p. 338; *Indianapolis Freeman*, July 19, 1902. Pledger probably supported Washington because he wanted his aid in securing a political appointment which would enable him to leave Georgia. He first sought the position of minister to Liberia, then a consulate; but Washington refused to endorse him for any appointment even though Fortune urged him to do so, saying that he understood Pledger's desire to leave Georgia—that it was "a splendid state to go from" (Fortune to Washington, May 26, October 30, November 6, 1902; Scott to Washington, July 2, 1902, Washington Papers).

his true convictions, the *Guardian* declared that Negroes had a right to expect a Republican administration to enforce the Constitution and protect their rights. On the contrary the present administration was completing the work of disfranchisement by excluding Negroes from appointive offices and was "putting the finishing touches on the South's work of eliminating the Negro as a political factor." All that "Fortune . . . and Co." had accomplished by "springing" Washington on the convention, said Trotter, was to "discredit themselves and cause the Council to misinterpret the Negro people." And, he added somewhat bitterly, "We might have expected Prof. Du Bois to have stood in the breach here, but like all the others who are trying to get into the band wagon of the Tuskegeean, he is no longer to be relied upon."[19]

In spite of the endorsement by the Afro-American Council, there was strong dissatisfaction with the Roosevelt administration among black politicians. One of the few hopeful signs, to them, was Roosevelt's appointment of James S. Clarkson as Surveyor of the Port of New York, which the politically sophisticated interpreted as a move to win southern Negro delegates away from Hanna and help insure Roosevelt's nomination in 1904.[20] Clarkson, who was sensitive and sympathetic to the position of black politicians, as Roosevelt was not, took the initiative in persuading the president to repudiate the Lily Whites, who, encouraged perhaps by some of Roosevelt's ac-

19. *Washington Bee,* July 26, 1902; *Boston Guardian,* quoted in ibid.; *Boston Guardian,* July 26, 1902. A recent thorough and scholarly account of Trotter's life is Stephen R. Fox, *The Guardian of Boston: William Monroe Trotter* (New York, 1970).

20. Pringle, *Theodore Roosevelt,* p. 242. Roosevelt, who had earlier expressed a low opinion of Clarkson as a "spoilsman," called a *New York Times* correspondent who interpreted the appointment of Clarkson as a move to win southern delegates "a malicious and slanderous liar" (Roosevelt to Henry Clay Payne, July 8, 1902, in Morison, ed., *Letters of Theodore Roosevelt,* 3: 285–86).

tions, were showing unprecedented audacity. In North Carolina a Republican convention refused to seat a single Negro delegate, barring even ex-congressman George White. The convention endorsed the disfranchisement provisions of the recently adopted state constitution and agreed not to support court cases over disfranchisement. Shortly thereafter the Republican convention in Alabama expelled Negro delegates.

In private correspondence and in an editorial in the *Age* Fortune advised that in states where white men excluded Negroes from conventions, Negroes should call their own conventions—open to all good Republicans, black or white—and let the national convention of the party decide which delegation to seat. "If the purely white party is regularly recognized the situation will be simplified and we men of the North and West will know what to do, and we will do it. We urge this course because it is the only one possible by which the attitude of the National Republican party can be authoritatively obtained and because it is a matter of political life and death for the race in the Southern States."[21]

General Clarkson wrote a letter containing the same sentiments to Booker T. Washington, adding: "It is just as impossible to have negro delegates from the North and refuse legal negro delegates seats to which they have been elected in Republican Conventions in the South as it was to have in the old days men free in the North and slaves in the South." But Washington, who had recognized as clearly as Fortune or Clarkson the growing disenchantment of Negroes with Roosevelt, and who was also alarmed over the strength of the Lily Whites, had another answer. As usual he preferred to avoid a confrontation and to deal with the problem indirectly. He went to New York

21. *Indanapolis Freeman*, September 6, 1902; *Age* quoted in *Indianapolis World*, October 4, 1902; Fortune to Scott, September 16, 1902; Fortune to Washington, September 18, 1902, Washintgon Papers. "We must fight the devil or go to the wall," he told Scott.

to see Clarkson and impressed upon him the seriousness of Negro disaffection and its implications for Roosevelt's chances of securing the nomination in 1904. He gave Clarkson a letter which the latter conveyed to the president together with a communication which Clarkson wrote himself.[22] The letters convinced Roosevelt that it was necessary to act and showed him what to do.

Washington's most important advice was that the administration should dismiss a few Lily White officeholders and make it clear that it intended to withhold patronage from Republican organizations which drew the color line. In short order Roosevelt removed two men in Alabama who had been active in the Lily White movement—the United States district attorney and the Collector of Internal Revenue. In both cases they were replaced by Gold Democrats who had opposed disfranchisement and who were recommended by Washington, although the Tuskegeean's role was not generally known.[23]

Fortune sent a telegram congratulating Roosevelt on removing the Lily Whites, and in the *Age* he published an editorial, evidently dictated by Washington, explaining that a Gold Democrat had been appointed as United States attorney because the president was unable to find a competent Republican lawyer who was not a Lily White. But he did not feel that the appointment of white Gold Democrats was a sufficient rebuke to the Lily Whites or of any great benefit to southern Negroes. The appointment of the white man should have been balanced by simultaneously naming a Negro to another post. "I am not fighting the battles of white men in the South," he told Washington, "but of black men, and I see nothing but humiliation in

22. Clarkson to Washington September 17, October 11, 1902, Washington Papers; Roosevelt to Clarkson, September 29, 1902, in Morison, ed., *Letters of Theodore Roosevelt*, 3: 332–33.

23. John Durham to Washington, September 2, 1902; George B. Cortelyou to Washington, October 26, 1902, Washington Papers; *Age* quoted in *Indianapolis World*, October 25, 1902; *Washington Bee*, November 15, 1902.

the systematic side tracking of our men for Democrats." He continued to advise Alabama Negroes to hold their own convention and to send delegates to the next national convention. He feared that if they did not do this, the Lily Whites would be recognized by default.[24]

But Fortune applauded heartily when Roosevelt named his old friend, Dr. William D. Crum, as Collector of the Port of Charleston, South Carolina—one of his few important appointments of Southern Negroes. When the white citizens of Charleston and the *Charleston News and Courier* launched an attack on Crum and on Roosevelt for making the appointment, the president released a letter to the press defending his action. He said it was his policy to appoint to office only men of high character, and he would not deny appointment to such a man simply on the grounds of color. In general he attempted to respect local feelings, but, he declared, "I cannot consent to take the position that the door of hope—the door of opportunity—is to be shut upon any man, no matter how worthy, purely on the grounds of race or color." The president's letter was lauded in the Negro press and probably did more than anything he had done to restore the confidence of Negroes in him.[25]

24. Fortune to Washington, October 8, October 9, October 10, October 30, 1902; Fortune to Dr. S. S. H. Washington, November 10, 1902, Washington Papers; *Age* quoted in *Indianapolis World*, October 25, 1902.

25. *Boston Transcript*, November 28, 1902. John Durham wrote to Washington that Roosevelt's letter was "the biggest thing ever uttered by a President concerning the colored people" (November 30, 1902, Washington Papers). Crum had been in correspondence with Fortune, seeking his support, before he applied for the appointment, which was made on the recommendation of Washington (Fortune to Washington, September 15, October 8, October 17, November 11, 1902, Washington Papers; Crum to Whitfield McKinlay, November 20, 1902, Woodson Collection). For a detailed account of the Crum affair see Willard B. Gatewood, "Willam D. Crum: A Negro in Politics," *Journal of Negro History* 53 (October, 1968): 301–20.

Almost simultaneously with the publication of Roosevelt's letter, Washington wrote to the press concerning his own political activities. He had been embarrassed by stories in the white press about his role in some of Roosevelt's appointments. In the letter he emphasized that his life work was education and that any conferences which he had had with the president had grown out of his position as an educator. He had never sought "to promote political candidates or volunteer information regarding men or measures," but if requested he had and would continue to "give information about men and measures, which would tend to promote friendly relations with the races."[26]

Washington's disingenuous disclaimer, which was misleading, to say the least, may have disarmed some whites who had been critical of reports of his political power, but it did not convince his black opponents. For months the *Boston Guardian* had been berating him for his political activities and his deviousness concerning them. "The Colored People . . . do not want a sleight of hand performer for their leader," Trotter declared. It was plain, he said, that " 'the professor' was more interested in placing men in office (white men we mean) than he was in managing his school." A cartoon entitled "One Man Cannot Do Everything" showed Washington dressed as a "mammy" at an ironing board. In a fireplace were irons labeled "Tuskegee first"; "Social separation"; "No politics for Negroes"; "No Negro appointments"; and "White office holders." Underneath was a caption which said: "Auntie Booker has too many irons in the fire; some of them are bound to burn up."[27]

26. *Boston Transcript*, November 28, 1902. Washington had sent a draft of the letter to Fortune, who agreed that it would be desirable to release the letter. He said that he did not think that Washington's political role had strengthened his educational work or his position with the race, and that southern whites resented the impression, which had been given in the press, that he was dispenser of political patronage in the South (Fortune to Washington, November 7, 1902, Washington Papers).

27. *Boston Guardian*, November 1, November 8, 1902.

The *Guardian* was right as to Washington's involvement in politics, but ironically Trotter and other black critics were entirely unaware of Washington's efforts to block the Lily Whites. The *Washington Bee* declared that Washington "was responsible to a large extent, for the lily white movement South and he never changed until President Roosevelt, through General Clarkson . . . put a quietus to the movement." When Fortune indicated in the *Age* that Washington was opposed to the Lily Whites, the *Guardian* printed a cartoon entitled "Word from the Sub-Cellar Leader" in which Washington was in the cellar, talking by phone to Fortune, who was upstairs. He said: "Hello, this Fortune? This is Booker. I simply want to say that Lily-Whitism at the South is not real. Don't mention my name." To which Fortune replied: "Not real! Why—Well just as you say." In fact, the *Guardian* was saying, nothing that Fortune said about Washington could be believed because, "It is held by knowing ones that much of the fat that now greases the way for the *Age* comes out of the Tuskegee larder."[28]

Fortune no doubt smarted over the gibes in the *Guardian* concerning his dependency on Washington, and he continued to try to find a way to break loose. He wrote to Scott that he was resolved to "find a way out of the deadlock in [his] political status or bust," and that he was looking after his own affairs. In spite of previous rebuffs, he approached General Clarkson about the possibility of an appointment. Clarkson told him that the president was not opposed to him but was hesitant to nominate him for any sort of position which required Senate confirmation because the New Jersey senators would not support him. Fortune then proposed a special mission to Hawaii and the Philippines to study labor conditions. As early as 1899 he had suggested that in light of the increasingly intolerable conditions for

28. *Washington Bee*, November 29, 1902; *Boston Guardian*, September 27, October 25, 1902.

Negroes in the rural South and the slums and poverty which faced most of those who moved North, the government should investigate the possibility of helping those who wished to do so to emigrate to the Philippines. His interest in the islands was no doubt stimulated in part by the fact that T. McCants Stewart had moved to Honolulu in 1898.[29]

Through the efforts of Clarkson he received an appointment as Special Immigrant Agent of the Treasury Department to study race and trade conditions. Clarkson wrote to Washington that Roosevelt was pleased with Fortune's proposal and thought that the mission might be of great value to the country. For once, Clarkson said, Fortune was happy over his prospects. But, he suggested, someone who had "the nearness and also the courage" should impress upon him the importance of this opportunity and that "he must keep himself strictly in the middle of the road" to prove himself worthy of the trust placed in him. Washington did not see Fortune before his departure, but he relayed Clarkson's advice. After his arrival in San Francisco, where he was warmly received and where he gave an address, Fortune wrote that he was "living absolutely" up to the Tuskegeean's parting advice.[30]

29. Fortune to Scott, November 13, 1902; Fortune to Washington, October 17, November 3, 1902, Washington Papers; *New York Sun*, May 3, 1899; *Washington Colored American*, November 16, 1898.

30. Charles Anderson to Washington, November 10, 1902; Fortune to Scott, November 18, December 6, 1902; Clarkson to Washington, November 20, 1902; Fortune to Washington, November 28, December 10, 1902, Washington Papers. The *Washington Bee* was skeptical about Fortune's mission. It predicted that Fortune would write "a long winded report describing the beauties of the yellow fever country, and conclude by saying it is just the country for American Negroes. That is if he is not attacked with the yellow fever before he returns and makes his report" (*Bee*, December 20, 1902).

In Honolulu he saw his old friend Stewart, who had gained a respectable position in the legal profession of the city. The visit was marred somewhat by the lack of cordiality on the part of Stewart's second wife, who did not like Fortune and refused to see him. Otherwise everything went well in Hawaii. Fortune was cordially received by the white population and given cooperation by the Chamber of Commerce, the planter's association, and the labor unions in collecting the information he sought. He stayed longer than he had anticipated in order to make a week's trip of inspection of plantations on several of the islands. On the whole he found little race prejudice in Hawaii, which he attributed in part to the fact that many of the whites were descendants of New England missionaries.[31] In a newspaper interview he said that he thought southern Negroes might find it advantageous to emigrate to the islands, which caused the *Washington Post* to remark that Fortune was a *New York* Negro and a *journalist* and in no way qualified to judge the needs of southern Negroes.[32]

En route to Manila he visited Japan and Hong Kong, and he revisited Japan on his return voyage. He was enchanted with the country and its charming people and observed:

The fact that you are a stranger and an American makes every Japanese feel that he must be at your service. And the rudeness and vulgarity of many white Americans, under

31. Fortune to Carrie Fortune, December 28, 1902, Fortune Papers; Fortune to Washington, December 22, 1902; January 10, 1903; Washington Papers; T. Thomas Fortune, "Politics in the Philippine Islands," *Independent* 55 (September 24, 1903): 2266. In Honolulu Fortune was entertained by the brother and sister of General Samuel Chapman Armstrong, founder of Hampton Institute and mentor of Booker T. Washington. Stewart's second wife was Alice M. Franklin, who had studied dramatics in New York and Paris and had gained a reputation as a dramtic reader (*Cleveland Gazette*, April 15, 1893).

32. *Washington Post*, February 16, 1903.

such circumstances, were shocking to me, as well as the Japanese, who witnessed them. And few people on their travels are more rude and vulgar than the average white American, who seems to be thanking God all the time that he is not as other men.[33]

He reached Manila in February and remained on Luzon until May, when he departed for the United States. He took his duties seriously and tried to read as much about the Philippines as he could and to acquire a smattering of Spanish as well as observing conditions first hand. "I am after the facts," he declared, "and I am going to get them, if possible. I am determined that the papers here and in the States shall not be able to say when I get in my report that I did not see and study conditions here for myself." He went on a six-weeks expedition into northern Luzon in the company of Captain Robert Gordon Wood, a black who had spent fifteen years in the United States Army. It was an arduous trip which few Americans had ever attempted. The party started out on the only railroad which the Philippines boasted, then they traveled by horseback and steamer and, in an area where a drought had killed the pack animals, by foot. They stayed in native villages and sometimes slept on the ground. After returning to Manila Fortune went on a shorter expedition into southern Luzon, where he found a cholera epidemic raging, but he escaped with only a cold, which he caught from sleeping on the ground.[34]

He found a land rich in resources and potentialities for agricultural development but unbelievably backward in methods of farming. In Luzon the racial situation appeared to him to be quite different from that in Hawaii. William Howard Taft, the governor, seemed to be highly regarded by the natives, but For-

33. T. Thomas Fortune, "The Filipino," *Voice of the Negro* 1 (May and June, 1904): 200.

34. Fortune to Washington, February 26, April 11, April 20, 1903, Washington Papers; Fortune, "The Filipino," pp. 243–46.

tune thought that there was a disproportionate number of southern whites in positions of authority in the civil service and in the military. He attributed this to the fact that during the Philippine insurrection many southerners had come to the islands in volunteer military regiments from Kentucky and Tennessee and had remained after the end of hostilities. "No southern white man should be allowed to hold an administrative office in the Philippines," he wrote Washington. "Their conduct towards off-color people will always cause more or less trouble. The Filipinos hate the whole tribe of southerners here, and so do I. You cannot temporize with southern white men."[35]

Social patterns were not unlike those in the southern states. White Americans never married Filipino women, although many of them established illicit unions. When they returned to the United States, they assumed no obligation to the women they left behind or to their offspring. "Indeed," said Fortune, "the white American is the only white creature on earth who seems to have no abiding affection and makes no sort of provisions for his children resulting from common law relations with Negroes, Indians or Malays." The Filipinos themselves showed no race prejudice toward the few hundred American Negroes, mostly discharged soldiers, who lived in Luzon.[36]

In short Fortune was of the opinion that there were economic opportunities for American Negroes in the Philippines and that Negroes would be able to live harmoniously with the brown-skinned Filipinos. But the race prejudice of white officialdom made more difficult the problem of governing the islands

35. Fortune, "Politics in the Philippine Islands," p. 2268; Fortune to Washington, February 26, 1903, Washington Papers. Fortune was sharply critical when, a few months after his visit, the vice-governor, General Luke E. Wright, a southern Democrat, was named governor as Taft's successor. The promotion, he said, was a "crime against the Filipino people" (*Philadelphia Telegraph*, September 28, 1903).

36. Fortune, "The Filipino," pp. 200–201.

and winning the confidence of the native people. After his return to the United States, he suggested that the appointment of an Afro-American official, Booker T. Washington, perhaps, as governor of the islands might have the effect of conciliating the Filipinos and encouraging Negroes to emigrate to the islands. These proposals were met with derision in several white newspapers. The *Washington Post* suggested sarcastically that Fortune rather than Washington should be named, remarking, "We haven't the slightest doubt that a translation of all our Afro-Americans of Mr. Fortune's class to Luzon, or Sulu, would be attended by the happiest results. . . . In this way two proud and independent peoples would be brought together. . . . We are satisfied that the Filipinos and the Fortune school of Afro-Americans were made for each other." The *New York Commercial* said that proposals to encourage Negro emigration to "the land of the thin skinned, resentful and retaliatory Filipino" were foolish and mischievous. Negroes were needed in America.[37]

Fortune found that the American newspapers in Manila were "as violently Democratic and race-baiting as those of Memphis or Atlanta." They had begun attacking his mission before his arrival in Manila and continued after he arrived. He wrote a long article for the leading daily defending President Roosevelt and criticizing some of the "Rebel sentiment" which he found so pervasive. Obviously this did not endear him to the local officialdom. He assured Washington that his personal conduct was circumspect. "I am going to justify by my conduct and work the confidence of those who sent me on the mission," he said. Nevertheless, he and Captain Wood were involved in some sort of a squabble with the Manila police and arrested on charges of disorderly conduct, taken before a white judge who came from Mississippi, and fined. The incident apparently at-

37. *Brooklyn Citizen*, June 26, 1903; *Washington Post*, July 9, 1903; *New York Commercial*, June 27, 1903.

tracted much attention in the Manila press, and some white papers in the United States claimed that Fortune was "fired" from his mission because of it.[38]

The Philippine mission, like everything else in which he was involved, turned out to be a fiasco financially. He had been allotted six dollars per day for expenses but found that this was inadequate. While in Manila he asked Washington to request the president to increase the allowance to ten dollars, but no action was taken on his request. Instead, when he arrived in the United States on June 24 and reported to the Treasury Department, he was informed that his appointment had been for six months only and had terminated May 16, while he was at sea, and that he would receive nothing for expenses after that date. Fortune protested the ruling and declared that he would not submit his complete report to the department until the matter was adjusted. General Clarkson indicated his willingness to intervene on his behalf with the secretary of the treasury and the president, and Washington also indicated that he would do something about the matter. But there is no evidence that any financial adjustment was ever made, nor was Fortune's entire report ever published.[39]

"I have been through a heap in the past seven months," Fortune wrote Washington after his return to the United States, "and I don't think I am as young as I was." He was suffering from a recurrence of malaria, a disease which he had first contracted in Florida and which struck him again in the Philippines.

38. Fortune, "Politics in the Philippine Islands," p. 2268; Fortune to Scott, February 26, 1903; Fortune to Washington, February 26, April 11, 1903, Washington Papers; *Jacksonville* (Florida) *Metropolitan*, June 6, 1903; *Indianapolis Freeman*, March 4, 1904; Fortune, "Way of the World," *Norfolk Journal and Guide*, April 30, 1927.

39. Fortune to Washington, February 26, November 2, 1903; copy of a memorandum of Fortune's expenses (presumably submitted to the Treasury Department), October 15, 1903, Washington Papers.

The doctor told him he should have a complete rest, but the accumulation of work facing him and his "damned bank account" made this impossible.[40] In spite of ill health, the demands of his newspaper work, and the state of his finances, he went to the convention of the Afro-American Council in Louisville and presided over the stormiest session in the history of that organization.

Up to that time the council had done little toward the achievement of its stated objectives. This was due in part to the internal power struggle which consumed the time and energy of its leaders. But lack of funds and reluctance of injured persons to prosecute were more important reasons for the failure to bring test cases before the courts. The most important legal effort made directly under the auspices of the council was an attempt to challenge the suffrage provisions of the Louisiana constitution, but the case failed to reach the Supreme Court. As early as 1899 Fortune and Washington had been interested in initiating a case, but the Negro whom they expected to bring suit was unwilling, hoping instead that a white friend would test the law. "We seem to be a race of 'Micawbers,' " Fortune commented. Presently a local affiliate in New Orleans decided to institute a suit with the support of the National Afro-American Council. An appeal for funds was made to churches, schools, and other Negro groups. Two New Orleans attorneys were engaged, but progress in the preparation of the case was slow. The council contributed a few hundred dollars toward the legal costs. Other money from "friends of the race" was evidently raised by Washington. But the case never actually materialized, a fact which Fortune blamed on the New Orleans attorneys.[41]

40. Fortune to Washington, July 20, 1903, Washington Papers.

41. Fortune to Washington, January 25, June 23, December 30, 1899; June 4, June 21, 1901; August 4, 1902, Washington Papers; *Indianapolis Freeman,* Holiday edition, December 29, 1900, p. 16; *Age,* October 26, 1906.

The council claimed some credit for bringing the Alabama Suffrage Case, which was decided while Fortune was in the Philippines. But Washington was personally largely responsible for initiating the case, and he bore all the costs, although he was so eager to conceal his part that most of the correspondence between Tuskegee and the attorney in the case was carried on under pseudonyms.[42]

So carefully concealed were Washington's behind-the-scenes efforts at fighting disfranchisement that neither his black critics or his white admirers had any inkling of them. While Fortune was in the Far East, opposition to Washington's public statements on political activities and his role in the Roosevelt administration became more intense and vocal. Suffrage leagues hostile to him that had been organized in several cities planned to send delegates to the Louisville convention. Several newspapers, including the *Washington Bee* and the *Chicago Conservator*, had sharpened their attacks on the Tuskegeean, but the *Boston Guardian* continued to be his most relentless foe. Hitherto W. E. B. Du Bois had been careful to avoid a break with Washington, with whose views he was by no means in complete disagreement. Trotter had been critical because Du Bois had failed to speak out against Washington's domination of the Saint Paul convention of the Afro-American Council. But in 1903, in an essay entitled "Of Mr. Booker T. Washington and Others,"[43] Du Bois courteously but firmly expressed dis-

42. *Giles* v. *Harris*, 189 U. S. 475 (1903). The Supreme Court, speaking through Justice Holmes, held that the wrong complained of by the plaintiffs—refusal to register a voter because of his race—was political in nature and that relief could come only through the state legislature. Three justices dissented. In the correspondence concerning the case, Wilford Smith, the attorney, was J. C. May; Emmett Scott was R. C. Black (August Meier, "Toward a Reinterpretation of Booker T. Washington," *Journal of Southern History* 23 [1957]: 222).

43. W. E. B. Du Bois, *The Souls of Black Folk* (Chicago, 1903).

agreement with Washington's submissiveness to white prejudice, his overemphasis on industrial training, and his failure to speak out against disfranchisement and segregation. Du Bois, who was to prove to be Washington's most discerning and articulate critic, was likewise practically the only one of his black opponents who had access to white journals. This made him especially dangerous because it might enable him to damage Washington in the eyes of his white supporters.

In the feud between pro-Washingtonians and anti-Washingtonians, which was less over ideology than over the personality and methods of the Tuskegee Wizard, there was no place for divided loyalties. Because of his commitment to Washington, Fortune was denounced by Trotter and his allies as a traitor to his race. The editor of the *Guardian*, himself a teetotaller who had been president of the Total Abstinence League while an undergraduate at Harvard, also referred scornfully to Fortune's weakness for strong drink.[44] Fortune heartily reciprocated Trotter's dislike and expressed contempt for the scurrility of the *Guardian*. He sometimes spoke disdainfully of Du Bois. His hostility to both of these critics of Washington, aside from the fact that expediency dictated it, no doubt arose in part from the fact that both were intellectuals, younger and more highly educated than he. Both men were what Fortune had hoped to be in his youth, and the fact that he secretly agreed with some of their charges no doubt made his attempts to rebut them the more intense.

Just before the Louisville convention, Washington sent Fortune an article on suffrage which he had published in the *North*

44. Fox, *The Guardian of Boston*, pp. 17, 44. John Durham, Fortune's long-time friend, was almost unique in letting it be known that, while he deplored Trotter's methods and his attacks on Washington and Fortune, he nevertheless agreed with his uncompromising views on absolute human equality, which, after all, were similar to those which Fortune had always expressed (Durham to Whitfield McKinlay, September 5, 1902, Woodson Collection).

American, partly as an answer to Du Bois, with the request that he use it in the *Age.* Fortune agreed to publish it but said that while doing so he would also define his own position, which was different from Washington's. "We cannot concede anything that is ours," he said, "as the enemy is utterly unscrupulous." In the editorial Fortune said that Washington's article reilluminated his position on suffrage, which Du Bois had "badly misconstrued" in his book. Washington had always supported educational and property qualifications but believed that they should apply to all alike without regard to race. But, Fortune said, he himself had never held these views. "Our view of the matter is that the suffrage question is the basic principle of national citizenship; that it should, therefore, be controlled absolutely by the federal Government, in a fundamental act mandatory upon all the States and from which no state could deviate in the uniform and absolute equality of its conditions." If there were ignorant citizens, unqualified to vote, the fault lay with government, which should provide adequate schooling for all children. "When the State has done its duty in the matter of educating its citizens . . . it will be time enough to talk about restricting this suffrage by a property or educational qualification." He added that under existing suffrage restrictions the United States was moving away from democratic principles toward oligarchy, and "We believe in democratic government pure and simple!"[45]

At Louisville a sizeable group of anti-Washingtonians were on hand and seated. An altercation developed almost immediately when a picture of Washington was placed on the stage. William H. Ferris of Boston, a recent graduate of Yale, objected to the picture being displayed unless there was also displayed a picture of some Negro who stood "for the higher life and in-

45. Fortune to Scott, June 22, 1903, Washington Papers; *Age,* July 2, 1903.

tellectual development" of the race. Trotter followed with a
bitter attack on Washington, and the business of the convention
was delayed until a picture of the late J. C. Price was placed
beside that of Washington. But in spite of the efforts of the
opposition, the pro-Washington forces dominated the convention. Washington made one of his typical conciliatory addresses,
stressing the need for interracial cooperation. He urged Negroes
to exercise self-control and avoid extreme utterances during the
difficult period through which the race was passing. He insisted
nevertheless: "There should be meted out equal justice to the
black man and the white man whether it relates to citizenship,
the protection of property, the right to labor, or the protection
of human life. Whenever the nation forgets or is tempted to
forget, this basic principle, the whole fabric of government for
both the white and the black man is weakened." Fortune had
prepared an address on the suffrage question, but it appears that
it was not actually delivered, although it was reported in the
press. In it he declared that all the wrongs under which the race
suffered—separate coach laws, marriage laws, inequitable
school taxes, and crimes against individuals—grew out of the
denial or abridgement of the constitutional right to vote.[46]

The resolutions adopted by the convention, one of which
expressed appreciation to Roosevelt for his attitude toward
Afro-Americans, bore evidence of Washington's influence. The
majority report from the nominating committee recommended
the reelection of Fortune and a slate of other officers favorable
to Washington, but a minority report recommended another
slate. There were cries of foul play when the majority report
was adopted. Just before the convention adjourned, Trotter
arose and tried to make a speech denouncing Roosevelt for making so few Negro appointments. Some delegates shouted for him

46. *Louisville Herald*, July 2, July 3, 1903; *Topeka* (Kansas)
Capital, July 3, 1903; *Boston Guardian*, July 11, 1903.

to sit down, but he refused, shouting, "We northern Negroes are not going to sit supinely by and let the whites put their feet on our necks." He also tried to introduce some resolutions, none of which were adopted. After the meeting Fortune told a reporter that Trotter was merely a "wind bag" whose views carried no weight, while Bishop Walters insisted: "He misrepresents us all. We don't want to stir up strife." Washington, who had returned to Tuskegee, wired Fortune: "You will be doing personal favor if will write short letter to Brooklyn Eagle taking ground there was no serious opposition done policy at Louisville." Fortune complied with an article which appeared in the *Eagle* a few days later.[47]

The *Washington Bee* characterized the Louisville meeting as a "fraud," and declared, "The editor of the New York Age has at last become the obedient tool of the principal of Tuskegee." In its report of the convention the *Guardian* said of Fortune: "For as of Lord Bacon, it may be said of Fortune in this council business, that he is 'Wisest, meanest of all mankind.' " While this and later attacks by Trotter enraged Fortune to the point that he considered filing a libel suit, the comments in the *Chicago Conservator*, which usually expressed the views of his one-time friends, the Barnetts, must have cut more deeply.

T. Thomas Fortune of the New York Age is a weak man and seems to grow more so as age tells on him. Twenty years ago every intelligent Negro in this country regarded Mr. Fortune as the coming national leader of the new-born citizens that needed only to labor and wait for the mantle of the great Fred Douglass to fall upon him. Then Mr. Fortune was known all over the country as the most fearless advocate of the manhood rights of the Negro in this country, Fred

47. *Louisville Herald*, July 4, 1903; *Birmingham Age Herald*, July 4, 1903; *Atlanta Constitution*, July 3, 1903; Washington to Fortune (copy of telegram), July 9, 1903; Fortune to Washington, July 12, 1903, Washington Papers.

Douglass not excepted. . . . Had any Negro then, great or small, rose up and started to canvass the country with a view of spreading the sentiment that the Negro as a race should be trained for good servants and laborers only, that disfranchisement of the Negro was a blessing rather than a curse . . . We say, if any Negro in the days when Fortune was regarded as race loving and brave, had started out advocating these things, Tom Fortune would have met him on every corner and crossed swords with him and openly and loudly denounced him as an enemy to his race.[48]

When Fortune wrote an editorial in reply, the *Conservator* said that everybody knew that Brother Fortune was no longer capable of arguing—that he was capable only of "cussin' and calling hard names." "We pity Tom Fortune," it went on to say, "because he is a great man fallen and is no more his former self on matters touching the liberties and rights of his race than a toad frog is like a tadpole, and with his old fashioned love and fire for his race seem to have gone all his powers of reasoning and logical hot shot. Poor fellow."[49]

Ironically, while he was being denounced in the Negro press as Washington's tool, the white press continued to lump Fortune with the Tuskegeean's critics. Negroes should follow Washington in charting their course, said a correspondent of the *Chicago Tribune*, for he was right and "Prof. Du Bois and T. Thomas Fortune dangerously wrong." The *Washington Post* defended Washington's views on suffrage and declared that Negroes like Fortune wanted the vote for all Negroes, "no

48. *Washington Bee*, July 11, 1903; *Boston Guardian*, July 18, 1903; Scott to Fortune, November 23, 1903, Washington Papers; *Chicago Conservator*, August 23, 1903. Of course the *Conservator* editorial was unfair to both Washington and Fortune. It distorted and exaggerated what Washington had actually said on industrial education and disfranchisement.

49. *Chicago Conservator*, October 10, 1903.

matter how ignorant and vicious they may be, because that arrangement furnishes them with dupes and tools whom they can employ for their own personal advantage."[50]

A few weeks after the Louisville convention Trotter sought revenge in Boston at a meeting held under the auspices of the Negro Business Men's League in the A.M.E. Zion Church. Both Washington and Fortune were scheduled to speak. William H. Lewis, who had once opposed the Tuskegeean but later had become one of his converts and who had recently been appointed by Roosevelt as assistant United States attorney, presided. The audience was tense, expecting trouble. Almost as soon as Fortune had been introduced and had started to speak, a Negro named Granville Martin began to heckle. Trotter and Martin had come to the meeting with the intention of asking Washington a series of questions about remarks attributed to him in the press, especially a letter to the *Montgomery Advertiser*, in which he had said that every revised constitution adopted in the South put a premium upon intelligence, thrift, and character. Did this mean, they intended to ask, that Washington endorsed the disfranchisement of his race? Martin was soon ejected by a policeman. But as Fortune began once more to deliver his speech in which he intended to praise Washington and to deprecate divisiveness among Negroes, he started to sneeze and cough violently and realized that large quantities of red pepper had been scattered on the platform. He managed, however, to finish his remarks, but while he was doing so, Martin returned and was again ejected for causing a disturbance.

The singing of a song restored order to the meeting tempo-

50. *Washington Post*, September 7, 1903. The white press continued to contrast Washington and Fortune. The Syracuse *Post Standard*, June 12, 1906 said: "According as the T. Thomas Fortune type, with its loud insistence upon rights, is forced to subside, and the Booker T. Washington type, with its earnest effort in the direction of quiet self-improvement, gains the ascendancy, progress for the race may be expected."

rarily, but when Washington began to speak, someone in the rear of the hall shouted: "We don't want to hear you Booker Washington. We don't like you." An uproar followed in which Lewis and Fortune tried in vain to silence the crowd. As the police tried to arrest a man named Bernard Charles, who was causing part of the disturbance, Trotter, armed with an umbrella, and his sister Maude, armed with a hat pin, tried to rescue Charles, who simultaneously was attacked by another member of the audience who slashed him with a razor. A policeman finally dragged off the two Trotters. Charles was taken to the hospital; the Trotters and Martin were taken to the police station, where the two men were jailed and the girl was released. Meanwhile Washington, with his indomitable self-possession, succeeded in making his speech, which dealt with the economic condition of Negroes, emphasizing the greater opportunities for them in the South.[51]

The *Washington Bee* voiced the views of anti-Washingtonians when it blamed the Tuskegeean and Fortune for the Boston incident which, it said, occurred because they had made it impossible for the Boston group to get a hearing at Louisville. "Editor Trotter of the *Boston Guardian* has the congratulations of the country," said the *Bee*. "There is only one way to get rid of trimmers and apologists." When Trotter was given a jail sentence for his part in the disturbance, he became a martyr in the eyes of Washington's opponents. Some of his admirers held a reception in his honor in Boston, and Francis J. Grimké of Washington, one of the most distinguished Negro clergymen of the time, wrote a letter to Trotter, expressing sympathy and condoning his action. In an editorial Fortune commented that Trotter was trying to pose as a martyr but was merely making himself ridiculous as were Dr. Grimké and others who defended him. With a fine disregard of the efforts to suppress discussion

51. *Boston Transcript*, July 31, 1903; *Boston Globe*, July 31, 1903; Fox, *The Guardian of Boston*, pp. 49–54.

at Louisville, he declared: "Trotter now finds himself in jail for doing the very thing which we as a race have complained of all over the country; that is, the prevention of free and open discussion. . . . One of the charges which white people of this country are constantly bringing against us is that instead of condemning the criminal element of our race, we honor the criminal as much as we do any other class of citizen."[52]

During the months following the Louisville convention, Washington was on the alert for signs of opposition, such as the organization of suffrage leagues in various cities, which might challenge his leadership. He told Fortune: "We shall have to watch all these movements carefully during the next year in order to keep control of the Afro-American Council." In January 1904 he sponsored a secret conference of Negro leaders of all shades of opinion at Carnegie Hall to thrash out the issues over which there were divided opinions and, presumably, to disarm his critics. He wrote W. E. B. Du Bois that the main object of the meeting was "to try to agree upon certain fundamental principles and to see in what way we understand or misunderstand each other and correct mistakes as far as possible."[53]

Washington insisted that Fortune be present although some of the others who were invited opposed, perhaps because they considered him indiscreet. "The absurdity and ridiculousness of it has exasperated me," Washington wrote his friend. "For you not to be present would place me in a rather awkward position." In a confidential memorandum to Francis Grimké, Du Bois

52. *Washington Bee*, August 8, 1903; Fox, *The Guardian of Boston*, pp. 54–57; *Age*, November 5, 1903.

53. Washington to Fortune, November 3, 1903, Washington Papers; Washington to Du Bois, quoted in Herbert Aptheker, "The Washington-Du Bois Conference of 1904," *Science and Society* 13 (Fall 1949): 347. Washington had planned a conference at least a year earlier, but lack of funds had prevented it from being held. Apparently the money for the 1904 conference came from Andrew Carnegie.

classified Fortune, along with William H. Lewis, Whitfield McKinlay, George L. Knox, the editor of the *Indianapolis Freeman*, and Wilford Smith, the attorney, as participants who would be "unscrupulously for Washington." He classified himself and Grimké and three others as "uncompromisingly anti-Washington." The other participants he classified as being favorable or unfavorable to Washington in varying degrees.[54]

The conference agreed upon a series of resolutions, which all who were present signed. These declared that the right to vote was of paramount importance; that leaders of the race should be trained in institutions of higher learning, but that the masses should receive industrial training; that court tests of laws restricting travel rights should be sought; and that lynching be condemned. A committee of twelve was to be appointed which would serve as a bureau of information on matters relating to race and which would seek to unify and coordinate the work of race organizations. Just what part Fortune had in the proceedings is not clear, but Washington was pleased with his performance.[55]

Clearly Roosevelt's presidency and the part which Washington played as his confidential political adviser had put added

54. Washington to Fortune, November 5, 1903, Washington Papers; Du Bois to Francis Grimké, in Carter G. Woodson, ed., *Works of Francis J. Grimké*, 4 vols. (Washington, D. C., 1942), 4: 89–90. The *Washington Bee*, whose editor was not invited, declared that no man who had any respect for his race should attend the conference. "Mr. T. Thomas Fortune is the mouthpiece of Washington," it said, "and the report is that all Negro appointments must come through these two" (*Bee*, quoted in *Boston Guardian*, January 16, 1904). Monroe Trotter was not invited to the conference, but Washington was fearful that he would learn what went on and divulge it to the press (Washington to Dr. S. E. Courtney, January 10, 1904, Washington Papers).

55. Minutes of Conference of Colored Men, Carnegie Hall

strain on Fortune's relationship with Washington. Fortune had wanted to escape from his increasing dependence on the Tuskegee Wizard. He had protested privately against Roosevelt's southern policy and had tried to persuade Washington that it was inimical to the interests of southern Negroes, but he had refrained from criticizing Roosevelt in the *Age* because he continued to hope for a political appointment. He had compromised himself more seriously by allowing the National Afro-American Council to be used to promote Washington's leadership and by cooperating in attempts to silence or discredit opposition to Washington's power and ideology.

Parlor, New York, January 1904, Washington Papers. Washington, DuBois, and Hugh Browne were appointed to select the other members of the Committee of Twelve. Du Bois was not pleased with most of the members whom the other two men selected and was dissatisfied with the guidelines which Washington drew up for the committee. He soon resigned (Aptheker, "Washington-Du Bois Conference," pp. 349–50). Fortune agreed to serve on the Committee of Twelve but privately expressed doubts that it would accomplish anything (Fortune to Scott, January 28, 1904; Washington to Fortune, June 8, 1904; Washington Papers; Fortune to Scott, July 10, 1904, Fortune Papers).

VIII

The Uneasy Alliance
Continues

SOON AFTER THE CARNEGIE HALL CONFERENCE FORTUNE WENT
on a lecture tour for the purpose of organizing local coun-
cils and raising money for the National Afro-American Council
and, incidentally, to do missionary work for Washington and
Tuskegee. He was greatly saddened at the outset by the news
of the death of Colonel Pledger, and the tour as a whole was a
depressing experience. Fortune felt that as oratory the lectures
were a great success. In fact, as he told Scott, it occurred to him
that he had perhaps missed being a "great orator" by being an
"indifferent newspaperman." Financially, however, the trip was
a failure. "They come out to applaud to echo," he said, "but put
pennies in the cause." He nearly decided that "the effort to get
the race interested in the preservation of its rights as men is a
fool's errand." The expenses of the trip were $50 more than he

received from lectures and appeals.[1] The only bright spot of the tour was a visit with Phil Waters, the West Virginia attorney who had been a member of the camping party at the Gauley Bridge in 1901 and with whom Fortune had established a warm friendship.[2]

He returned to Maple Hill deeply depressed over the apathy of the race and still brooding over Pledger's death. He was especially disturbed because the colonel had sent a telegram just before his death asking him to come to Atlanta, but it had arrived too late. *"There was a sworn understanding,"* Fortune wrote Scott, "between Pledger and me that, wherever we should be, when the end came to either, the survivor should respond to the summons of friendship and love." But the friend had passed on, and he had not been there. "And he was true to me and with all his faults I loved him!" he cried. Pledger's death and his own confused business situation had taken the heart out of him, and once more he announced that he had decided to resign his position in all race organizations. He was tired of fighting. "I desire to get off in a corner and lead a life of privacy,

1. Fortune to Scott, January 11, January 13, January 21, January 28, 1904; Scott to Fortune, January 19, 1904, Washington Papers; *Indianapolis Freeman*, January 30, 1904; *Age*, October 25, 1906.

2. Waters, who was several years younger than Fortune, was a graduate of the University of Michigan Law School. He was active in Republican politics and had a reputation as an orator. See *Washington Colored American*, September 9, 1899; *Indianapolis Freeman*, February 2, 1907. Waters knew Washington and Fortune through Washington's sister who still lived in Malden, scene of Washington's boyhood. Waters was also an intimate of Scott's. Like Fortune he had a weakness for drink but appeared to have conquered the habit. He assured Washington that, according to his instructions, he had kept Fortune out of temptation's way during his visit in West Virginia. See Waters to Washington, January 18, February 3, 1904; Fortune to Scott, January 28, 1904, Washington Papers.

speaking my word to the world without effort to dominate anything," he told Scott. "I want to stand aside from the center of the row, and I am going to keep on striving for release."[3]

One avenue of release would be the sale of the *Age*, a possibility he had broached earlier with Washington and which Washington now endorsed. In fact, the Wizard had found a person who was eager to buy the paper, and he thought he knew a source from which the necessary funds could be secured. He wrote that he had decided that Fortune's best interests would be served by the sale of the paper. With the money received, Fortune could pay for his home and settle his other debts. At the same time he probably could be employed by the *Age* with much the same control which he now exercised. The would-be purchaser was Fred R. Moore, a man whom Fortune knew well and considered a close friend. He had probably introduced Moore to Washington. As a child Moore had sold newspapers in Washington, D. C. Later he had worked for years as a messenger in the Treasury Department before coming to New York, where he worked as a messenger of the Western National Bank and delivery clerk in the New York Clearing House. In addition, he began to deal in real estate, first in Brooklyn and later in Harlem. He was president of the Afro-American Investment and Building Company, and apparently arranged the mortgage when Fortune bought a home in Red Bank, New Jersey, in 1901. Moore was also named executor of a will which Fortune made in 1902. Hard working, unimaginative but dependable, he had won the confidence of Washington. He lacked Fortune's intellectual brilliance and literary talent, but if it was to Fortune's advantage to sell the *Age* for needed cash, Washington probably thought that it was to his advantage to have as owner of the paper a person upon whose discretion and reliability he could

3. Fortune to Scott, February 6, February 25, 1904, Washington Papers. Emphasis as in original.

count, in view of Fortune's increasing tendency to drink and his recurring ill-health.[4]

Washington encouraged Moore to begin negotiations with Fortune and Peterson and indicated to him that he thought that William H. Baldwin, Jr., one of the trustees of Tuskegee, would be willing to advance the money necessary for the purchase. But later he denied to Fortune that he had had any part in the matter. Fortune and Peterson indicated to Moore that they would sell the paper for $10,000, and Moore countered with an offer of $7,000 and a guarantee of employment to both men.[5] When Fortune returned from the lecture tour, Moore wired Scott that he thought the matter could now be settled satisfactorily—that Fortune was home "broke." Washington then tried to make arrangements for Moore to see Baldwin, but for reasons which are not clear Baldwin was unwilling to loan the money. His refusal, said Moore, "came as a stunner—I certainly thought we had the matter O.K."[6]

The other possible means by which he might hope to straighten out his finances was an appointment from the Roosevelt administration. Fortune continued to hope that this might materialize in spite of his previous disappointments and the failure of the Treasury Department to pay the claims he had

4. Washington to Fortune, January 22, January 28, 1904, Washington Papers; *Age*, January 4, 1900; *Pittsburgh Courier*, October 22, 1927. Stubs in Carrie Fortune's checkbook in the Fortune Papers show that monthly payments were made to Moore. In 1893 Fortune had made a will in which Carrie and T. McCants Stewart were named as executors. In a codicil dated November 28, 1902, Moore was named executor. The will is in the Fortune Papers.

5. Fred R. Moore to Washington, December 29, 1903; Moore to Scott, January 1904 (no date); Fortune to Washington, January 28, 1904, Washington Papers; Fortune to Moore, April 29, 1904; Fortune to Washington, February 19, 1905, Fortune Papers.

6. Moore to Scott (telegram), February 7, 1904; Scott to Moore, March 1, 1904; Moore to Scott, March 4, 1904, Washington Papers.

made for reimbursement for the Philippine mission. He wanted to be appointed stamp agent in Washington, a position which had the advantage of not requiring Senate confirmation and of enabling him to continue to do his editorial work on the *Age*. He talked to Clarkson about the post, and Clarkson agreed to work in his behalf. Washington, however, whose support was indispensable, hesitated to bother the president about replacing the incumbent agent until after the November election. He said he also thought he had made some sort of a promise to Pinchback to secure the post for him in the event that there was a vacancy. Fortune replied: "I know that the President is nervous, and would prefer to have the matter go over until after the election; but I am also nervous and don't want it to go over. Where my interests are concerned there has usually been a disposition to put the matter off to another day, so that I usually get left."[7]

But his hopes for an appointment were shattered, temporarily at least, by a violent quarrel with Washington. The two men were in Washington, where the Tuskegee Wizard gave an address and was honored at a dinner by the leading Negroes of the community. As usual, when he planned to speak before a black audience, Washington had consulted Fortune about what he should say, and Fortune's influence was apparent in his remarks on suffrage. "I do not favor the Negro giving up anything that is fundamental and which is guaranteed by the Constitution of the United States," he declared. "It is not best for him

7. Fortune to Scott, February 22, 1904; Scott to Fortune, February 25, March 5, 1904; Washington to Fortune, March 8, 1904; Fortune to Washington, March 11, 1904, Washington Papers. Part of Fortune's financial embarrassment at this time was due to the fact that he had borrowed $300 from Washington when, on his return from the Philippines, he had failed to receive the amount he expected from the Treasury Department. Warren Logan, treasurer of Tuskegee, was pressing him for repayment (Fortune to Scott, May 10, 1904, Washington Papers).

to relinquish any rights."[8] Afterwards some "friends," one of
whom was J. Douglass Wetmore, young attorney from
Jacksonville, Florida, told Washington of certain indiscretions
on the part of Fortune that made Washingtion furious. It appears that Fortune had been boasting of his intimacy with Washington and had revealed something about Washington's role in
the Alabama suffrage cases—a connection which Washington
had gone to extreme lengths to conceal. Washington confronted Fortune with the fact that he knew he had betrayed his
confidences and gave him a merciless tongue lashing. "There is
hell in the camp between me and the Wizard," Fortune wrote
Scott. Things between them could never be the same again.[9]

He returned home, "nursing the wounds made by pseudo
friends," and considering what to do about his future. He decided to resign from the presidency of the Afro-American
Council. "I want to cut loose from the whole situation of selfishness and throat-cutting and pursue my own purposes, and to
damn and praise, as the situation warrants, unhampered in any
direction," he declared. "Other men look out for themselves
exclusively, and I must do it or sink. I don't propose to sink."[10]

He wrote a long letter to William H. Steward, editor of the
American Baptist and vice-president of the council, tendering
his resignation. He reviewed the history of the Afro-American
League and Council and declared:

> I have grown old and impoverished in the long struggle,
> and I must now take heed of my age and precarious health
> and devote my time and energies to repairing my personal

8. Washington to Fortune, March 8, 1904, Washington Papers;
Washington Post, March 17, March 18, 1904; *Washington Times*,
March 19, 1904.

9. J. Douglass Wetmore to Washington, April 4, May 19, 1904;
Washington to Wetmore, April 16, May 19, 1904; Fortune to Scott,
March 26, 1904, Washington Papers.

10. Fortune to Scott, March 26, March 28, 1904, Washington
Papers.

fortune in the interest of my immediate family. . . . In my own way I shall continue to labor, as in the past, for the highest aspirations of the race, for nobler manhood and for perfect equality of citizenship of all men.[11]

When he received the letter, Steward, who was taken completely by surprise, wrote to Washington, asking him what he should do. In reply the Wizard advised him to ignore the resignation—to write Fortune some good advice but to defer any action on the resignation. "The fact is," he said, "that he has not been acting properly for the last ten days, and probably wrote you in a fit of ill-temper." But, whatever his motives, Fortune did not reconsider.[12]

When Washington came to New York, he saw Fortune, but only briefly. "We have passed beyond the stage of confidences," Fortune told Scott, "and I do not think we shall get to it again." But, he added, his own fighting instinct was "sharp as a razor." And the weapon which he could use—to the embarrassment of both Roosevelt and Washington—was the editorial page of the *Age*. He wrote Washington that he had prepared an editorial criticizing the president for recent appointments of some Lily White Republicans, for his failure to appoint more Negroes to office, and for his partiality for southern Democrats. "He has been making it hot for me for some time," he said. "I shall make it hot for him from now until the convention meets." He added: "Necessarily, as his adviser on the race question, you will come in the scope of the general criticism which I shall make . . . and this is the only regret that I have in the matter."[13]

11. The letter is reprinted in Fortune, "The Quick and the Dead," pp. 248–49.

12. William H. Steward to Washington, March 30, 1904; Washington to Steward, April 7, 1904, Washington Papers.

13. Fortune to Scott, May 3, 1904, Washington Papers; Fortune to Washington, May 1, 1904, Fortune Papers.

Less than a month later Jerome Peterson, Fortune's partner, was named for the post of United States consul at Puerto Cabello, Venezuela. Peterson had not sought the appointment and was at first reluctant to accept it. It appears that it had been engineered by Washington and Charles W. Anderson, perhaps with the hope that the recognition given to Peterson might help placate Fortune and that the salary which Peterson would receive might relieve the financial burdens of the *Age*. Anderson, who was probably the most influential Negro in New York politics and who was rapidly replacing Fortune as Washington's closest confidant, had come to New York from Ohio in 1890 and had become active in politics almost immediately. As has been mentioned, he and Fortune had traveled together in the South during the campaign of 1896. He had worked as private secretary to the state treasurer and was currently supervisor of accounts for the New York State racing commissioner. In 1905 Roosevelt named him Collector of Internal Revenue for the second district of New York—one of the highest posts which he gave to a Negro.

Fortune was pleased with Peterson's appointment, but he did not like Anderson. He told Washington that he dealt with Anderson purely on a *"business basis"* and felt none of the obligations of friendship toward him which he felt toward Washington and Scott and Moore.[14] Anderson had also tried to find some sort of a post for Fortune which would supplement his income while permitting him to continue his work on the *Age*. The appointment did not materialize, but the *Age* received funds from the Republican National Committee and advertising from candidates for state offices during the 1904 political cam-

14. August Meier, *Negro Thought*, p. 254; Fortune to Washington, September 13, 1904, Fortune Papers. Anderson assiduously cultivated Washington's good will and became invaluable to him as an informer. He purchased forty copies of *Up from Slavery* to distribute to his friends as Christmas gifts.

paign. After the appointment of Peterson, the *Age* ceased its attacks on the administration, and when Roosevelt was nominated, it warmly endorsed him and supported him throughout the campaign. Through Washington the president relayed to Fortune his appreciation for his support.[15]

Meanwhile Washington had suggested that Fortune might ease his financial plight somewhat by writing another book for him—*The Negro in Business*. Fortune expressed some hesitation because his own responsibilities on the *Age* had increased with Peterson's departure, but he needed the money and started work on the book. During the summer of 1904, in addition to doing the usual writing and editorial work on the *Age* (without even the assistance of a stenographer), he was attempting to attend to the business management of the paper, work on Washington's book, and help Fred R. Moore with the editorial work on the *Colored American Magazine*. The magazine, which had been published in Boston since 1901, had recently been moved to New York with Moore as publisher and general manager. Washington had been instrumental in bringing the publication to New York and had invested $3,000 in the venture, a fact which both he and Moore concealed even from Fortune. Washington continued secretly to subsidize the magazine in a small way, and it evidently also received some funds from the National Negro

15. Washington to Anderson, May 31, 1904; Fortune to Washington, August 1, 1904; Roosevelt to Washington, October 15, 1904, Washington Papers; Fortune to Washington, September 13, 1904, Fortune Papers. Douglass Wetmore wrote to Washington that the *Age* sang a different tune politically after Peterson received his appointment. Washington replied: "I do not see what put it into your head that Mr. Peterson's appointment was meant to smooth down the ruffles in the editorial columns of The Age, but we all congratulate ourselves that The Age has changed its tune a little" (Washington to Wetmore, May 24, 1904, Washington Papers).

Business League of which Moore had been appointed national organizer. In addition to literary and political articles, it devoted some space to news of the league.[16] Fortune was persuaded to do the work on the magazine without pay at first, with the understanding that Moore expected to receive money enough from some undisclosed source (Washington) to make it a viable enterprise. But although Washington kept making up the deficits so that the magazine continued publication for several years, he did not contribute enough to make it into the kind of publication which Fortune had envisioned, and Fortune received no remuneration for his work. Washington never admitted to him that he had any financial relationship with the magazine. In fact, he told him that he had no "business relations" whatever with Moore.[17]

Fortune liked and trusted Moore although he had evidence that Moore had revealed to Washington matters which he had told him in confidence. Moore no doubt considered himself a loyal friend to Fortune, but his loyalty to Washington was paramount. He evidently had made a promise to report faithfully to Tuskegee everything he knew of Fortune's activities, and especially his drinking. In March 1904 he reported that he was glad to say that Fortune had been "OK right along" since Washington's last visit. But a few weeks later (following the quarrel with the Wizard and Fortune's resignation from the presidency of the Afro-American Council) Fortune must have

16. Fortune to Washington, May 30 1904, Fortune Papers; Washington to Fortune, June 9, 1904; Fortune to Washington, August 1, 1904, Washington Papers; August Meier, "Booker T. Washington and the Negro Press, With Special Reference to the *Colored American Magazine*," *Journal of Negro History* 38 (January, 1953), p. 70 and passim; *Colored American Magazine*, June, 1904, pp. 458–59.

17. Fortune to Scott, August 17, 1904, Fortune Papers; Washington to Fortune, February 25, 1905, Washington Papers.

gone on a drunken binge from which Moore evidently helped rescue him. "I have got complete hold of my bootstraps again," he wrote Moore, "and aside from the d——d disgust that I should have lost my stride, I am feeling very well, although tired, and I have done an enormous amount of work this week. ... Your grateful friend ..." Moore promptly sent this note to Washington, saying that Fortune was penitent and should be "given another chance." But by autumn he reported that Fortune, who was at Red Bank working on Washington's book, was "in his cups again, indicating that too much money is coming in and he cannot stand prosperity."[18]

Shortly after the 1904 election Moore also wrote that Fortune had told him that he had stood by Washington and that he thought it was time for Washington to stand by him in the matter of a political appointment—"with the usual threats accompanying his remarks." (The threats were probably that he would throw the influence of the *Age* against Washington and Roosevelt.) Moore advised Washington that he thought it would be prudent for him to insist that a third party be present during any conversation with Fortune in which the question of an appointment or money was discussed. "This threatening attitude of his, so far as you are concerned, is not [at] all praiseworthy, and is not justified," said Moore. "It seems to me to be clearly a case of friendship that ceases in your absence, for all of the many kindnesses that you have shown him, and done for him, since my acquaintance with you seem not to be appreciated." A few weeks later Washingon assured Fortune: "You

18. Washington to Fortune, February 25, 1904; Moore to Washington, October 25, 1904, Washington Papers; Fortune to Washington, February 28, 1904; Fortune to Moore, April 6, 1904 (with notation by Moore to Washington on back), Fortune Papers. A few weeks later Moore informed Washington that Fortune was "showing up poorly"—that he was "loading himself up each day" (Moore to Washington, November 10, 1904, Washington Papers).

have no warmer or better friend" than Moore. "He is one that you can always depend on."[19]

In spite of their growing mutual distrust, Fortune and Washington maintained cordial relations during 1905 and 1906, and at times their friendship appeared to be almost as warm as ever. In a postscript in a letter to Scott in May 1905 Fortune said: "Tell the good Wizard I miss him fearfully from this town." Washington wanted him to come to Tuskegee for commencement, but Fortune refused because he wanted "to stick to the machine to keep the credit ahead of the debit side of the cash book"—a situation which usually reversed itself when he was away.[20]

Washington had begun to increase his financial support of the *Age* in order to increase the size of the paper and thereby, he hoped, to increase circulation and put the venture on a paying basis. This was done through a special fund which paid for enlarging the paper to eight pages and for adding special features. When revenues increased, it was expected that Washington would be reimbursed. R. L. Stokes, who had been at Tuskegee, was added to the staff to help with editorial work, and Moore, who was doing some of the printing for the *Age* in his shop, gave Fortune some assistance on the business end of the paper. With prospects improved, Fortune worked on the *Age* with his old-time zeal, and for several months his health improved. "I am afraid I am falling in love with the work of journalism again," he told Scott. "I have long sought to be weaned from it." He was feeling better than he had for years and

19. Moore to Washington, January 21, 1905; Washington to Fortune, February 24, 1905, Washington Papers.

20. Fortune to Scott, May 15, May 24, 1905, Washington Papers; Washington to Fortune, May 20, May 27, 1905, Fortune Papers.

weighed a hundred and fifty pounds, ten pounds more than at any previous time.[21]

All went well until late summer when attendance at the annual conventions of the National Business League and the Afro-American Council disrupted his routine. He had continued as chairman of the executive committee of the Business League, and the fact that the 1905 convention was in New York City involved him in the work of preparation, along with Moore, who was chairman of the local arrangements committee. The convention of the Afro-American Council, which met in Detroit, followed immediately. The council, which had appeared moribund after Fortune's resignation, was revived rather suddenly—perhaps, as some critics charged, as a response to the recently launched Niagara Movement. Although he had foresworn further involvement in such organizations, Fortune accompanied Washington to Detroit and evidently helped to accomplish whatever the Wizard wanted to accomplish by the meeting. The convention "went off with eclat," he told Scott. But he himself was a nervous wreck as a result of the two conventions and his anxiety over *Age* work which had accumulated during his absence.[22]

He was once more in a financial crisis, which was made more acute by the unexpected return of Jerome Peterson from his consular post. Peterson and his family arrived in New York totally without funds but determined that they would not return to the post in South America where the pay had been inadequate to meet expenses. Fortune was obliged to put some of his own salary and some of the *Age* funds at Peterson's disposal.

21. Scott to Fortune March 15, 1905; Fortune to Scott, May 12, May 15, 1905, Washington Papers; Fortune to Washington, March 16, March 22, April 1, April 8, May 20, 1905, Fortune Papers.

22. National Negro Business League, *Report of the Sixth Annual Convention, 1905*: Fortune to Scott, September 7, 1905, Washington Papers.

The situation was further complicated by the fact that the special features for which Washington provided funds had to be paid for in advance while the funds from Washington were not received until two weeks after the matter was published. The result was that both the *Age* accounts and Fortune's personal accounts were "down to rock bottom." Once again Washington came to the rescue of the *Age*, forwarding funds necessary to pay the obligations of the paper and to continue it at eight pages. But Washington expressed disapproval that Fortune was not more successful in making collections and in increasing circulation. He indicated that he was able to help with the *Age* but was unable to "accommodate" Fortune "in a personal way further at present."[23]

While relieved that the crisis was passed, Fortune nevertheless replied hotly: "You have the matter confused. You have not accommodated me *in a personal way* in any of this matter. . . . I hope I make this matter plain to you and the $250 + $52.82 have gone to the Age and not to me." Washington had done a great deal for the *Age*, Fortune said to Scott, "but I have lived on half pay in order to keep the paper up to the standard he and I thought necessary under the circumstances to maintain; and [I gave] besides my time. I don't blame him a bit, but I do blame myself for sacrificing so much of my personal interest for the mutual good."[24]

He once more asked Washington to try to help him and the

23. Fortune to Scott, September 26, September 27, 1905, Washington Papers; Fortune to Washington, September 28, 1905; Washington to Fortune, September 30, 1905, Fortune Papers. Washington himself did not have to worry about his personal financial security or that of his family since in 1903 Andrew Carnegie had given him as a personal gift an endowment which assured him and Mrs. Washington of an income during their lifetimes.

24. Fortune to Washington, October 2, 1905, Fortune Papers; Fortune to Scott, September 30, 1905, Washington Papers. Emphasis as in original.

Age by securing an appointment for him from the Roosevelt administration. If he could secure the Haitian ministry, or preferably the registership of the Treasury, his salary from the *Age* could go to support the paper. "But," he said, "you are afraid of your enemies, in one way, and therefore do nothing for your friends but impoverish yourself to help them and detract from their self respect by such help." To Scott he wrote that this was, perhaps, the last favor he would ask Washington, but he was desperate. It was necessary for him to make provision for his family. He would be forty-nine years old in a few weeks. "The Wizard may not like to go to the front in this matter," he said, "but I wish him to do it or decline to do it, because I have reached a crisis in my affairs and need his initiative and backing in it."[25]

Washington did not reply to Fortune's plea; he let Scott do so. Washington was willing to do all he could to advance Fortune's interest, said Scott, but at the moment it did not appear that the incumbent minister to Haiti was likely to resign. "I ought to go further," Scott continued, "and say that during the course of the conversation, ye Wizard stated that on one occasion when he took up the matter of yourself with the President, the latter stated his inability to do as was desired. It is painful, of course, to the Wizard to have to repeat the conversation with the President, but he was not able to change the President's intention." Scott added: "Perhaps you do not see as ye Wizard does, but he thinks there is a great opportunity in building up the Age so that it will pay handsome and satisfactory dividends."[26]

25. Fortune to Washington, September 28, 1905; Fortune to Scott, September 30, 1905, Fortune Papers.

26. Scott to Fortune, October 3, 1905, Washington Papers. The incumbent minister to Haiti, W. F. Powell, did resign two weeks later. W. F. Powell to Booker T. Washington, October 19, 1905, Washington Papers.

After this rebuff Fortune resorted to another, more desperate tactic in an effort to break out of the impasse. At his request Wilford Smith, an attorney who frequently did legal work for Washington, wrote the Tuskegeean that Fortune was anxious to dispose of the *Age*. He was willing to sell his interest for $6,000. "He wishes to offer it to you first," said Smith, "and if you cannot arrange some way to purchase it, he will then seek a purchaser elsewhere, and hints that the other party might be unfriendly to your interests. You know Mr. Fortune very well and can understand what all this means. I promised that I would lay the matter before you, and I am keeping my promise." In a postscript he said that Moore had suggested that Washington not correspond with Fortune about the matter but should attend to it when he came in person to New York. Washington replied to Smith that he did not own a single dollar's worth of interest in any colored publication, that he did not intend to depart from this policy and would not be influenced by "a threat, either implied or direct, that the interest would pass into unfriendly hands."[27]

Washington evidently followed Moore's advice. He came to New York and saw Fortune. Shortly thereafter, through the efforts of Charles W. Anderson, Jerome Peterson was appointed to a position in the office of the Collector of Internal Revenue. This relieved the *Age* of the necessity of paying Peterson's salary and made it possible to increase the remuneration which Fortune received for his work on the paper.[28]

27. Smith to Washington, November 18, 1905; Washington to Smith, November 25, 1905, Washington Papers. Charles W. Anderson wrote to Washington that he had been told that the *Age* was on the market and had been offered to "Niagara gentlemen." He said he considered this "the last play in the Cedar Street [Fortune] scheme of coercion" (December 4, 1905, Washington Papers).

28. Washington to Fortune, November 28, 1905; Scott to Fortune, December 15, December 30, 1905; Anderson to Washington, December 27, 1905, Washington Papers.

Throughout 1906 Washington continued to subsidize the *Age* through the device of the "special account," but the amounts which he spent were small, and he was sometimes dilatory about payments. The paper was once again operating at a deficit, and Fortune announced that in spite of Washington's objections, it was necessary to reduce the size from eight to four pages once more. In August he announced that he preferred to remain in New York and work and not attend the National Business League convention in Atlanta and did not think that his services were worth what it would cost Washington to pay his expenses. But as usual he attended the convention and later helped to make arrangements for the meeting of the Afro-American Council in New York in October. "We are in a bad box this week," he told Washington after the convention. He reminded him that some of the correspondents on the "special list" which he subsidized had not been paid for four weeks. At year's end he was complaining again that Washington was delinquent in his payments and that he had been left "in the very worst of financial holes."[29]

Meanwhile the founding in 1905 of the Niagara Movement by a group of black intellectuals under the leadership of Du Bois constituted an open challenge to Washington's ideology and claims to race leadership. The "Declaration of Principles" of the Niagara group, with its emphasis on suffrage and civil rights, its rejection of "cowardice and apology," and its call for "persistently manly agitation," sounded very much like the platform of the Afro-American League and Fortune's own utterances. In

29. Fortune to Washington, January 10, March 3, October 25, 1906; Fortune to Scott, January 2, August 16, December 26, 1906, Washington Papers. At this time the circulation of the *Age* was only about 6,000. Fortune thought that it would be necessary to increase this to at least 10,000 to make it possible to print an eight page paper without operating at a deficit (Fortune to Washington, August 13, 1906, Washington Papers).

[269]

fact Fortune accused Du Bois of stealing the platform of the league. The formation a few months later of the Constitution League, another protest group, which cooperated with the Niagara men, was another threat to Washington's position. The principal figure in the Constitution League was a white industrialist, John E. Milholland of New York, who had formerly been on cordial terms with both Washington and Fortune. But he had gradually become disenchanted with the Tuskegeean, and especially with his equivocal position on suffrage. Early in 1905 he had written Washington: "You will pardon me for saying it, the most enlightened sentiment is not reflected in the course you have marked out." He looked upon the formation of the Constitution League as a rejection of Washington.[30]

Fortune himself was especially sensitive to the Niagara group's demand for "an unfettered and unsubsidized press" and felt compelled to insist that he was not Washington's pliant tool nor the *Age* his subsidized mouthpiece. Through the editorial page of the *Age* he defended Washington and undertook, with apparent relish, a campaign to discredit Du Bois, Trotter, J. Max Barber (another Niagara man who had recently begun publication of *The Voice of the Negro* in Atlanta), and the Tuskegeean's critics in general.[31] In the *Voice of the Negro* in Jan-

30. *Age*, July 27, 1905; Fox, *The Guardian of Boston*, pp. 123–26; John E. Milholland to Washington, January 17, 1905, Washington Papers. A summary of the Niagara Movement is found in Elliott M. Rudwick, *W. E. B. Du Bois: A Study in Minority Group Leadership* (Philadelphia, 1960), chap. 5.

31. *The Voice of the Negro* was subsidized by Hertel, Jenkins and Co., which had published some of Washington's books. When the journal was first launched, both Washington and Fortune contributed to it and Scott was a member of the editorial board, but Scott soon resigned because he disliked Barber's policies (Meier, "Washington and the Negro Press," *Journal of Negro History* 38: 75.

uary 1905 there was an item by Du Bois which said that in 1904, $3,000 had been spent by a person who was not identified as "hush money" to corrupt five Negro papers which were not named. Fortune wrote Washington that he had decided to "go after Du Bois, the *Voice of the Negro* and Atlanta University . . . hammer and tongs" along lines which Washington had suggested. In "going after" Du Bois and Trotter, Fortune did not use the weapons of irony and innuendo which he sometimes wielded so effectively. Instead he resorted to vituperation. Du Bois's failure to name the papers which he said received "hush money," Fortune wrote, meant that he was either a coward or a liar. He should establish his accusations or retreat. He added: "Let the 'Boston Skunk' [Trotter's paper] and its allies get out in the open and reduce their insinuations to specific charges."[32] In an editorial on "The Leadership of Du Bois" the *Age* admitted that *Souls of Black Folk* was one of the great books of the generation, but asserted that his association with Trotter and his kind showed that Du Bois was motivated by jealousy of Washington and by personal venom and hysteria. He was unscrupulous because he condemned Washington's entire career by lifting out of context "two or three ill-considered sentences" which the Tuskegeean had uttered. In other editorials Du Bois became the "professor of hysterics" and the *Guardian* the "Boston Windjammer." After the Reverend Charles Morris, a member of the Niagara group, had delivered a speech in which he charged Washington with subsidizing the *Age*, an editorial declared: "The chief spokesmen of the Niagara movement all appear to be sick in their heads. Mr. Morris is about as idiotic as the editor of the *Boston Windjammer* is crazy and the editor of the inconstant *Moon* [Du Bois] is hysterical. Awake or asleep the whole befuddled outfit sees only Booker Washington,

32. Fortune to Washington, Jan 12, 1905, Fortune Papers; *Age*, February 16, 1905.

the editor of the *Age* and mountains of auriferous boodle with which to corrupt somebody." In other editorials the *Age* said that in raising the "subsidy" question Trotter and Du Bois were being hypocritical. Trotter had unsuccessfully sought a subsidy from the Republican National Committee, and Du Bois had solicited white men for contributions to his paper, *The Moon*.[33]

One substantive issue over which Fortune differed sharply with the Niagara men was their proposal to fight disfranchisement by implementing the second section of the Fourteenth Amendment, which provided for reduction in representation in Congress and the Electoral College for states which denied the vote to male citizens. As we have seen, for many years Fortune had consistently advocated federal action under the Fifteenth Amendment to protect the vote but had urged Afro-Americans not to support reduction in representation because to do so would give color to the view that a state could constitutionally deny them the right to vote. Washington, who was converted to Fortune's view, in turn presented Fortune's arguments to Roosevelt. On Washington's advice the president decided against mentioning reduction of representation in his messages to Congress in 1902 and 1904. Fortune was pleased with this but urged Washington to recommend to the president the creation of a commission to investigate the abrogation of rights of Negroes which had developed since 1876. The remedy for dis-

33. *Age*, March 2, 1905; January 11, February 8, August 2, 1906. In 1904 Washington and Anderson blocked Trotter's efforts to receive a financial subsidy for the *Guardian* from the Republican National Committee (Fox, *The Guardian of Boston*, p. 74). There is some doubt whether Fortune himself actually wrote some of these editorials, which were in a style quite unlike his usual one, but they undoubtedly had his approval. They appeared during the period when R. L. Stokes was associated with the *Age* and may have been written by him.

franchisement, he reiterated, lay in legislation based on the Fifteenth Amendment.[34]

Although on this question Washington was clearly following Fortune's advice, some of his critics accused him of refusing to endorse reduction in representation out of deference to the white South. *The Voice of the Negro* published a cartoon depicting Booker T. Washington with a padlock on his lips. The key which hung from the lock was labeled "Southern White Supremacy." Editorially *The Voice* attacked those who opposed reduction in representation as tools of the white South. The treatment of the subject in *The Voice* infuriated Fortune. "If Dr. Washington's mouth is padlocked on the question of Southern Representation, it was padlocked by me," he told Barber. "I have come to the conclusion that we can do nothing with you Niagara people because you appear to me naturally to run to coarseness and vulgarity in your treatment of men who differ from you."[35]

Fortune supported, although without enthusiasm, a call to revive the Afro-American Council, a move which the Niagara men interpreted as primarily an attempt to counteract the influence of their organization. Although the council had held

34. Washington to Fortune, November 22, 1902; Fortune to Washington, November 26, 1904, Washington Papers; *Age*, February 9, 1905. For a good summary of Fortune's views on reduction of representation see *Age* editorial, December 29, 1904, reprinted *Age*, January 26, 1905.

35. *Voice of the Negro*, March 1906, p. 243; Fortune to J. Max Barber, April 5, 1906, Washington Papers. In a letter to Washington, John E. Milholland enclosed a letter from H. E. Tremain on the subject of Washington's opposition to reduction of representation. Tremain said that Washington, "doubtless unconsciously, has absorbed the views of the financial and academic philanthropists, and their adherents, whom he necessarily cultivates" (Milholland to Washington, January 17, 1905, Washington Papers).

its annual convention in 1904, following Fortune's resignation, it had shown little vitality under the leadership of William H. Steward. It appeared unlikely that there would be a convention in 1905, but in July of that year, simultaneously with the launching of the Niagara Movement, Bishop Walters sent out a call for a national meeting of the council in Detroit in September. Fortune endorsed the call in the *Age* but expressed the opinion that the council could not succeed with its present organization. The *Chicago Conservator* said that there would have been no meeting of the council if there had been no Niagara Movement and that the only people who would go to Detroit would be those who were subservient to Washington. From Chicago Ida Wells Barnett wrote an open letter to the Negro press denouncing Walters and Fortune for the effort to revive the council in order to weaken the Niagara Movement. The *Age* responded with an abusive editorial which accused her of being an ingrate and "lying about the only friends she ever had."[36]

Gradually, however, Fortune became more restrained and less personal in his criticism of the Niagara Movement. He expressed general agreement with the platform of the movement, which he said Du Bois had taken from the declaration of principles which he had formulated for the Afro-American League in 1890. He wished the movement well but warned that it would be no more successful than the Afro-American League and Council unless it could win mass support. But he continued to accuse the Niagara men of being motivated by jealousy of Washington. When Du Bois compared the Tuskegeean invidiously with Douglass and pointed out that the legal and political status of Negroes had declined disastrously during the years of Washington's ascendancy, Fortune said it was absurd to blame the decline on him. He asserted that Washington

36. *Age*, July 27, August 3, August 31, 1905; undated clipping from *Chicago Conservator* scrapbook, Washington Papers.

opposed disfranchisement and had spent more money than ten thousand other men of the race on seeking to break the forces of disfranchisement. In another editorial the *Age* pointed out that while Douglass lived and was regarded as spokesman for the race, all of the southern states had been lost to the Republicans, and Mississippi and South Carolina had passed measures disfranchising Negroes—but on these points the Niagara men were silent. "Now why," it asked, "do not the Niagara Movement people acknowledge frankly that they are an aggregation of soreheads?"[37]

Meanwhile Fortune was becoming increasingly critical of the Roosevelt administration. As we have seen, he and the *Age* had supported the president during the campaign of 1904, partly out of loyalty to Washington and partly because of hopes of political reward. After Fortune learned that Roosevelt would never give him an appointment, however, reservations which he had always held privately began to be reflected in the paper's editorials. In a letter to Washington soon after the 1904 election, Fortune had warned that the South had set out to capture the president and that it appeared to be having success. "You want to understand that the attitude that the President adopts toward the South will be ascribed to you," he admonished his friend, "and we shall have to hold you to account if it militates against us." The *Age* expressed some doubt when it was announced that Roosevelt expected to make a tour of the South, including a visit to Tuskegee, in the autumn of 1905. But once the decision to make the tour was definite, the *Age* recommended that while in the South the president should speak out against lynching and disfranchisement. As Fortune observed, however, this advice was ignored. During the trip both the president and the white South were on their good behavior and avoided embarrassing subjects. The white South did not bring up the matter of dinner for Washington at the White House, and Roosevelt lauded

37. *Age*, May 31, August 16, 1906.

the chivalry of the South and did not mention the massacre of black troops at Fort Pillow. Both ignored the "skeleton in the South's closet"—the Negro problem—and for the most part the skeleton made itself as inconspicuous as possible. The *Age* deplored the president's "expedient silence" on disfranchisement and Jim Crowism. He had gone South, it observed, not to see his black friends but his white enemies, not to please his black allies but to win over his white opponents. Fortune disagreed with a statement Washington made to the press in which he said that the president's southern trip had helped reduce racial hatreds and had been a blessing to the country. No good had come to the black South, said Fortune. The visit simply drew the white South and the white North closer together and left "the black South to tread the wine press of wrong and outrage alone more than ever."[38]

When Roosevelt sent his annual message to Congress in December, the *Age* commented that the president had touched on every imaginable subject, including the maltreatment of dumb animals and the preservation of the bison, but had ignored "the plight of the decitizenized Afro-Americans in the South."

In Republican politics in New York, Fortune gave some support to Roosevelt's opponents and to persons who objected to Washington's control over Negro patronage. Fortune was on friendly terms with Gilchrist Stewart, son of T. McCants Stewart, who had recently moved to New York to practice law and engage in politics. Stewart was active in the Constitution League, and Charles Anderson suspected him of harboring designs for usurping his position in the Republican organization

38. Fortune to Washington, November 26, 1904, Fortune Papers; *Age*, October 12, October 26, November 26, November 9, 1905. This last editorial embarrassed Washington. He wrote to the President: "The Fortune editorial shows how it is possible for matters to go wrong when wise men are not on guard" (Washington to Roosevelt, November 15, 1905, Washington Papers).

and of using his ties with Fortune to influence the stand of the *Age* on political questions. He warned Washington to be on his guard against Stewart's machinations. After he and Washington had engineered the appointment of Jerome Peterson to the Internal Revenue Service, Anderson asked Washington to point out to Fortune that the arrangement had been made for his benefit and that he ought to see to it that "the columns of the 'Age' are not open to those little inch high politicians around here who think they are plotting against me [i.e. Stewart]." When Washington suggested to Fortune that he not permit Anderson's opponents to use the *Age* to attack him, Fortune replied hotly that the *Age* had never assailed Anderson, that he would treat Anderson in the same way he treated "all those with whom I work in accord," and that Washington's letter showed that he had no faith in Fortune's fidelity to friendship. Nevertheless, in the 1906 primary election in New York, Fortune and the *Age* supported Stewart and the anti-Roosevelt faction in the Republican party which was defeated by the pro-Roosevelt-Charles Anderson-Booker T. Washington faction.[39] By this time Anderson had replaced Fortune as Washington's closest confidant, and Washington no longer consulted the editor of the *Age* on political questions.

But in other matters Fortune continued to give loyal support to the Tuskegee Wizard, and the personal relations between the two men remained cordial. Fortune continued as chairman of the executive committee of the National Negro Business League, a position he had held since its founding. In August 1906 he journeyed to Atlanta for the annual convention of the league, which was followed by a visit to Tuskegee by some of the members. In an extemporaneous speech at Atlanta,

39. *Age*, December 7, 1905; Anderson to Washington, December, 27, 1905; January 4, 1906; Washington to Fortune, December 30, 1905; Fortune to Washington, January 21, September 20, 1906; Gilchrist Stewart to Washington, August 26, October 4, 1906; Anderson to Scott, September 13, 1906, Washington Papers.

Fortune paid glowing tribute to Washington as a *practical* leader, saying:

> If the Business League stands for anything, it should stand for industrial efficiency, for commercial inspiration, for good citizenship, and we can have no better example of that than in the grand President we have WHO IS ACCOMPLISHING SOMETHING AS WELL AS HIS ASSOCIATES WHO ARE NOT "HOT AIR" ARTISTS. . . . We all came here to Atlanta, and stand shoulder to shoulder, having confidence in him, FOR THE MAN WHO CAN COMMAND HIM-SELF CAN ALWAYS COMMAND OTHERS, and *Booker T. Washington* knows how to do that.[40]

The riot which erupted in Atlanta a few weeks after the convention brought Fortune and Washington more closely together, although each reacted in characteristically different fashion to the tragedy. The disorders came as no surprise to either man since both had been aware of the growing tensions generated in the gubernatorial campaign of Hoke Smith and the highly inflammatory onslaught against Negroes which was being carried on by the Atlanta newspapers. Washington was in New York when the riot started. Two days later he was in Atlanta, traveling alone, having rejected Fortune's suggestion that he go with him. Before leaving New York he issued a statement which was published in the *Age*, urging Negroes to exercise self-control and not to make the fatal mistake of trying to retaliate. "We of both races must learn," he said, "that the inflexible enforcement of the laws against all criminals is indispensable." After reaching Atlanta, Washington wired Fortune that he had been in consultation with leading whites and Negroes and was encouraged by the willingness of leaders of both races to meet together. He praised the courage and self-control of the black population of the violence-torn city. In making the

40. National Negro Business League, *Report of the Seventh Annual Convention, 1906*, p. 157.

telegram public, Fortune described Washington as "one of the bravest Negroes that ever lived."[41]

In editorials in the *Age* Fortune denounced Hoke Smith and the Atlanta press. "There must be some sane white people in the South," he said. "There must be some sane white people in Atlanta. But they give no sign." Instead, despicable white policemen and desperate newspapers were given free reign. In a decent society, the *Age* declared, Hoke Smith "would be tried in the proper way and convicted and sentenced and shot." In a letter to Scott, Fortune said: "I cannot believe that the policy of non-resistance in a situation like that of Atlanta can result in anything but contempt and massacre of the race." During an interview with a New York reporter, Fortune declared that in Atlanta whites had ruthlessly slain the innocent. Educated, law abiding Negroes had perished along with the lawless. They received no protection from the government although the police and militia could have stopped the massacre if they had chosen to do so. He had hoped, he said, that reports from Atlanta would show that Negroes had slain whites in retaliation. "The trouble will go on in Atlanta," he declared, "until the Negro retaliates—until, driven to bay, the Negro slays his assailant."[42]

41. *Age*, September 27, 1906; *Hartford Courant*, reprinted in *Boston Globe*, October 6, 1906. For an account of the riot and its background see Charles Crowe, "Racial Violence and Social Reform: Origins of the Atlanta Riot of 1906," *Journal of Negro History* 52 (July, 1968): 234–56; and idem, "Racial Massacre in Atlanta, September 22, 1906," ibid. 54 (April 1969): 150–73.

42. *Age*, September 27; October 4, 1906; unidentified newspaper clipping, September 30, 1906, containing interview with Fortune in scrapbook, Washington Papers; Fortune to Scott, September 28, 1906, Washington Papers. Earlier Fortune had written to Scott: "What an awful condition we have at Atlanta. It makes my blood boil. I would like to be there with a good force of armed men to help make Rome howl" (Fortune to Scott, September 25, 1906, Washington Papers).

When J. Max Barber, author of *The Voice of the Negro*, fled from Atlanta to Chicago, Fortune and Washington joined in deriding him for deserting members of his race at a critical time. Threats had been made against Barber, but threats had also been made against other Afro-Americans in Atlanta who had stood their ground and refused to leave.[43]

The editor of the *Age* and the Tuskegee Wizard also worked harmoniously, along with Bishop Walters, who was again president of the Afro-American Council, in planning the convention of that organization which met in New York in October 1906. Fortune served as chairman of the central committee for the meeting, which was more elaborate than any previous one, but Washington was responsible for securing some of the distinguished white participants, notably Oswald Garrison Villard. The only address which received much attention in the white press was Washintgon's speech on "The Requirements of Citizenship," in which he urged Negroes to remain in the South and deplored inflammatory speeches by northern Negroes. But Washington did not dominate the convention, and the general tone of most of the sessions was rather militant. In his presidential address, Walters reiterated the original purposes of the council and, without mentioning the Niagara Movement by name, denied charges that it had ever compromised in any way with the enemy. The council, he said, had always stood for the full rights of citizenship. He called for a federal law to punish mob violence. "The object of our enemies," he said, "is to make us serfs. It is nonsense to cry peace when there in no peace. We are determined to rise or die in the attempt to obtain our rights."[44]

Lynching and disfranchisement were discussed at most of

43. Draft of dispatch to *Age* from Atlanta, evidently written by Washington, Washington Papers; *Age*, October 4, 1906.

44. Walters to Washington, June 13, 1906; Walters to Scott, July 3, 1906, Washington Papers; *Washington Post*, October 12, 1906; *New York Times*, October 10, 1906; *Age*, October 11, 1906.

the sessions. Fortune, John E. Milholland, Mary Church Terrell, and ex-governor Pinchback participated in a panel on "Lynching and Its Remedy." At other sessions plans were discussed for raising funds—$50,000 if necessary—to carry more test cases on disfranchisement to the Supreme Court. One hopeful sign at the convention was the active cooperation of the Constitution League. Some supporters of the Niagara Movement were also present, and there was some talk of a possible rapprochement among the groups.[45]

But Fortune remained skeptical. At one session he declared that the intellectuals were doing their share in working to improve the condition of the race, but that the problem was that the masses did not respond to their efforts. In an editorial a few weeks later he said that there were a great many good people in the Niagara Movement and he wished that they and the good people of the Afro-American Council could work together. "We should fight the enemy and not each other," he declared, "for the enemy is strong and united, and we are weak and disunited."[46]

By the time this editorial was written, an event had occurred which had the effect of drawing Fortune and Walters closer to the Constitution League and the Niagara men and which intensified the efforts of Washington and Anderson to discredit the opposition. The event was the order issued by President Roosevelt, just after the November elections, discharging from the United States Army without honor three companies of Negro troops of the Twenty-Fifth Infantry who were stationed at Brownsville, Texas. The unprecedented action grew out of the fact that on the night of August 13 a group of armed men, whose identity was never established, "shot up" the town of Brownsville, killing one person and wounding two others. In-

45. *Indianapolis Freeman,* October 20, 1906; *Age,* October 11, 1906.

46. *Age,* October 11, November 22, 1906.

vestigations by military authorities convinced them that Negro soldiers were responsible, but it was impossible to identify the culprits. The guilty would not confess, and their fellow soldiers, if they knew their identity, steadfastly refused to reveal their names. In the face of this "conspiracy of silence" the Inspector General of the Army recommended that all members of the three companies be dismissed without honor, although they included men with records of service of up to twenty-six years and six who had won medals of honor. The president, after studying the report of the Inspector General, instructed Secretary of War William Howard Taft to carry out the recommendations for discharge, but the order was not released until the day after the election, in which the Republicans retained control of the House of Representatives.[47]

The Negro press responded to the dismissal of the troops with unprecedented bitterness, and many white papers in the North were also critical. In editorial after editorial Fortune denounced the dismissal of the soldiers as lynch law by executive order.

> It is carrying into the Federal Government the demand of the Southern white devils that innocent and law-abiding black men shall help the legal authorities spy out and deliver practically to the mob black men alleged to have committed some sort of crime. The principle involved is not only vicious and contrary to the spirit of our Constitution, but it is an outrage upon the rights of citizens who are entitled in civil life to trial by jury and in military life to trial by court martial.

47. James A. Tinsley, "Roosevelt, Foraker, and the Brownsville Affray," *Journal of Negro History* 41 (January 1956): 43–65; Emma Lou Thornbrough, "The Brownsville Episode and the Negro Vote," *Mississippi Valley Historical Review* 44 (December 1957): 469–93, passim. For details of Washington's efforts to infiltrate and discredit the Niagara Movement see August Meier, "Booker T. Washington and the Rise of the NAACP," *The Crisis* 61 (February 1951): 69–76, 117–23.

The *Age* declared that any black men who would enlist in the United States Army to fill the places of the discharged soldiers should be spurned by all Afro-Americans. No Negro should reenlist when his term expired.[48]

When Washington learned that the dismissal was pending, he urged the president to delay the action, saying that he had additional information. But Roosevelt loftily replied that he could not possibly refrain from acting as he had. "You cannot have any information to give me privately, to which I could pay heed, my dear Mr. Washington, because the information on which I act is that which came out of the investigation itself." To Taft, Washington wrote that he had never, in all his experience, observed such a reaction as had swept through the entire colored population at the president's order. Privately, because he recognized the threat to his own position in an action so objectionable to Negroes by a president with whose policies he was so closely identified, he let it be known that he had tried to deter Roosevelt. But publicly he refused to condemn the president, even though he wrote to Anderson that he knew "the enemy" would blame him for the action.[49]

Washington was apprehensive that the extremity of the Negro protest would alienate white friends in the North. "One thing the American people will not stand for for any length of time, and that is the abuse by any group of people of the President of the United States," he observed. He succeeded in persuading Fortune to publish an editorial which said that there was danger in overdoing agitation and personal abuse of the president. The wiser course, said the *Age*, was for Negroes to raise money to test the soldiers' cases in the courts. But in the same issue another editorial lumped Roosevelt and Clark Howell

48. *Age*, November 8, 1906.

49. Copy of letter of Roosevelt to Washington, November 4, 1906; Washington to McKinlay, November 7, November 8, 1906, Woodson Collection; Washington to Taft, November 20, 1906, Washington Papers; Tinsley, "Roosevelt, Foraker, and the Brownsville Affray," p. 49.

of the *Atlanta Constitution* together and declared that the president had evoked the ecstatic approval of the white South by the Brownsville order.[50]

Meanwhile Gilchrist Stewart had been appointed by the Constitution League to investigate the Brownsville affair, and J. Douglass Wetmore, legal counsel for the Afro-American Council, had been instructed by Alexander Walters to investigate the facts and to employ a distinguished white attorney, if necessary, to represent the interests of the discharged soldiers. Stewart came back from Brownsville with information which he said showed that much of the evidence against the soldiers was flimsy. His report impressed Senator Joseph B. Foraker of Ohio sufficiently that he called for a full investigation. In January, as the result of Foraker's insistence, the Senate ordered an investigation by the Committee on Military Affairs. The senator's interest in the matter was politically embarrassing to Roosevelt and threatened to create an impediment to the presidential ambitions of a fellow-Ohioan, Taft, if Roosevelt did not seek another term. Anderson wrote Washington that Gilchrist Stewart was boasting that Foraker's fight would kill the president's aspirations for another term and "thereby knock out 'The Booker T. Washington Cabinet.' "[51]

Anderson was busily investigating and reporting to Washington the actions of Negroes, including members of the Afro-American Council, which might be embarrassing to him and the Tuskegeean. In January Fortune, Walters, Mary Church Terrell, and other members of a steering committee of the council met in Washington with representatives of the Niagara Movement and other interested groups to hear a report of Wet-

50. Washington to Ralph Tyler, December 5, 1906, Washington Papers; *Age*, December 13, 1906.
51. *Cleveland Gazette*, December 1, 1906; *Indianapolis Freeman*, December 8, 1906; Tinsley, "Roosevelt, Foraker, and the Brownsville Affray," p. 50; Anderson to Washington, January 4, 1907, Washington Papers.

more's investigations. Fortune, Walters, Wetmore, and others spoke against the president's treatment of the Brownsville troops. The group adopted a resolution lauding Foraker, and a delegation called on the senator and pledged their support of him. The next day Walters, Fortune, and Wetmore addressed a mass meeting on the Brownsville question. Fortune called upon members of the race to act responsibly. "This is not a question of politics," he said, "but one of principle which involves all the people of the United States. By dismissing the colored troops without a court martial or civil trial, the President has outraged a fundamental principle of citizenship. . . . Let us not try to make this a race issue. Let us not abuse the President but differ with him with . . . firmness on the right." He appealed for money to use to fight the cause of the soldiers in court.[52]

Although publicly the Washington-Fortune alliance continued, behind the scenes tensions increased. Washington no longer trusted Fortune and was concerned about his instability and addiction to alcohol. But he continued to subsidize the *Age*, and Fortune, unable to find any alternative, became more dependent financially upon his aid. Fortune was increasingly despondent over the race and its prospects and weary of the feuding between Washington and his critics. Burdened with his own personal problems, he seemed for a time to have lost much of his old crusading zeal. But the Brownsville affair rekindled his fighting spirit, while it put new strains on his relations with Washington.

52. Fortune to Scott, January 7, 1907, Fortune Papers; Anderson to Washington, January 8, 1907; Washington to James A. Cobb, January 9, 1907; Cobb to Washington, January 14, 1907, Washington Papers; *Age*, January 17, 1907. Cobb, an attorney in Washington, D.C., was present at the meeting at the request of Washington who had asked him to attend and report to him what happened.

IX

Fortune Breaks

Fᴀᴏᴍ Fᴏʀᴛᴜɴᴇ's ᴠᴏʟᴜᴍɪɴᴏᴜs ᴄᴏʀʀᴇsᴘᴏɴᴅᴇɴᴄᴇ ᴡɪᴛʜ Wᴀsʜ-
ington and Scott, from such portions of the files of the *Age*
as have survived, and from his other published writing it is
possible to construct a fairly complete account of his race activities and his relationship with the Tuskegeean and his circle.
But, except for a few glimpses in the Fortune-Washington-Scott
letters, we know little about Fortune's domestic life.

We know that he was a devoted father who took satisfaction
in the accomplishments of his children. His son, Fred, was an excellent student, and his father was proud of the fact that a paper
which he had written, "Race War in a Lot," was printed in some
newspapers. Jessie, his daughter, was preparing to be a teacher,
and by 1901 was finishing her training course in Brooklyn. Fortune took Jessie and Fred on holiday expeditions to such places
as Southhampton and New Haven, where they enjoyed the
beaches and fresh air.

Fortune himself derived great pleasure from long, solitary rides on his bicycle, especially when he was feeling nervous. He persuaded Emmett Scott to buy a bicycle and was pleased when Scott developed a taste for this diversion.[1]

But in the correspondence which survives, Carrie Fortune is seldom mentioned, and only in the most formal way. She evidently shared in few of her husband's diversions. Like her husband, she appears to have had rather delicate health. In January 1900 she went alone on a visit to Florida to recuperate after a long illness—her first visit to her old home in more than ten years. She continued to enjoy her musical activities. Sometimes she directed the church choir. She also took part in the Federation of Afro-American Women. On one occasion Fortune stayed home with the children while his wife went to Providence to attend a meeting of the Northeastern Federation, at which she read a paper.[2]

When Washington came North on his frequent visits, he never went to the Fortune home in Brooklyn, although he was invited to do so. He and Fortune met in the city, sometimes with other men. But Mrs. Washington visited the Fortunes and was evidently on good terms with Carrie, and Jessie and Washington' daughter Portia were friends. When Mrs. Fortune went to Jacksonville, Washington expressed the hope that she would visit Tuskegee, but she was not able to do so.[3]

Although there is no outward evidence that relations between husband and wife were not happy, the pattern of For-

1. Fortune to Washington, June 19, July 3, 1897; August 30, 1898; January 25, 1899; Fortune to Scott, June 19, October 14, 1899; September 24, October 1, 1901, Washington Papers.

2. *Age*, April 22, 1897; January 4, 1900; *Boston Globe*, August 12, 1900; Fortune to Washington, January 4, February 3, August 6, August 8, 1900, Washington Papers.

3. Fortune to Washington, April 22, April 29, 1897; December 27, 1898; Carrie Fortune to Washington, December 27, 1898; Washington to Fortune, January 3, 1900, Washington Papers.

tune's life certainly suggests that he deliberately stayed away from home a great deal. During the nineties he spent several months of almost every winter in the South. He spent the summer of 1899 at Saratoga, while Carrie and the children remained in Brooklyn. He was back in Saratoga at Thanksgiving. He sometimes went off alone to Atlantic City to do his writing, and during the first part of 1900 he was in Washington, D. C., most of the time.[4]

The ostensible reasons for these long absences from New York were his precarious health and the demands of journalism. He feared the rigors of winter in New York, the more so, no doubt, because of the experience of his younger brother. He also evidently tried to get away from the tensions and pressures of the city, among them probably the temptation to drink too much. While at Saratoga during the winter of 1899, he wrote to Washington that he was glad that he had come—that he already had got "a firm grip on [his] bootstraps." He said he wished he could never see New York again. "It eats up my nerves." He left reluctantly to return to "vile New York where the slow process of undoing will begin again." After his return from his stay in Washingtgon he said, "I grow healthy and cheerful away from New York. I go to smash here every four weeks." A few days later he was complaining that he had "a slight nervous attack" as the result of overwork and " 'local provoking causes,' the same which always drives me away from New York temporarily." As to whether the "local provoking causes" included domestic friction there is no clue.[5]

But during the summer of 1901, arrangements were made for the entire family to go to Red Bank, New Jersey. While there, Fortune discovered a house with which he fell in love. It was a

4. Fortune to Washington, June 23, November 27, November 28, 1899, Washington Papers.

5. Fortune to Washington, November 27, November 28, December 1, 1899; May 7, 1900, Washington Papers.

large structure of twelve rooms on a plot of more than an acre of ground. It was surrounded by shade trees, and there were also fruit trees and a grape arbor. Best of all, it was only an hour's trip out of New York City. It could be bought for less than $4,000—a fraction of its actual value—because of the necessity of settling an estate. The whole family, including Mrs. Fortune, was enamored with the prospect of living there, and Fortune resolved to acquire it. In order to make the first payment he used a small inheritance he had received from his father and all the cash he could scrape together. Within a week the family was ready to move to the estate, which they named Maple Hill.[6]

In spite of the added financial burdens which it involved, acquisition of the new home compensated for some of the other disappointments and frustrations which Fortune had suffered. Life in the country was physically and psychologically beneficial to him. When possible, he did his writing and editorial work at home, going into the city only once or twice a week. He took pride in his garden and fruit trees. He offered to send Washington some of the products of his orchard, and the Wizard reciprocated by offering him a horse from the Tuskegee farms, a gift which Fortune declined because of the expense of caring for the animal. Carrie was also happy at Red Bank. She enjoyed gardening and played an important role in the colored Episcopal church in the community.[7]

In the spring of 1902 Washington, along with John Durham,

6. Fortune to Washington, July 2, July 9, July 22, July 27, 1901; Washington to Fortune, July 23, July 24, 1901, Washington Papers. Fortune wanted to spend August and September getting settled in the new home and concentrating on writing in order to make some money, but Washington was insistent that nothing must prevent him from attending the convention of the National Business League in Chicago and going from there on a camping trip in West Virginia. He offered to pay Fortune's expenses, so Fortune agreed to go.

7. Fortune to Washington, May 2, July 29, August 1, 1902; Fortune to Scott, June 9, 1902, Washington Papers.

came to Maple Hill for his first, and perhaps his only, visit to the Fortune home. Carrie was overjoyed that he had finally accepted her invitation.[8] Many other friends and political acquaintances came. Some of them stayed for long periods of time. Fortune loved playing the host, and Carrie too enjoyed their guests although the costs of such hospitality must at times have been a financial burden. Robert Terrell and his wife Mary, whom Fortune knew as "Mollie," and their daughter Phyllis were close friends who visited at Maple Hill. Emmett Scott and Phil Waters were frequent guests. In 1905 Mrs. Waters and her daughter Phyllis spent the summer with the Fortunes. Mrs. Scott and Emmett, Jr., were also guests part of that summer.[9]

During this period Fortune and Waters were very close, in part probably because Waters too had had a weakness for drink, which he appears to have conquered. On several occasions when Fortune was recuperating from illness or a bout with alcohol he spent long visits with Phil. In the Waters home, where there was an excellent library, he found an atmosphere in which he could relax and write.

With Scott Fortune's ties were even closer than with Waters. He ribbed him about the rapidity with which the size of his family increased. When he learned that Emmett had become the father of twins he exclaimed, "You are a positive phenomenon," and predicted that the "next news of an interesting event" would be the birth of triplets. Fortune loved Scott's children. When Emmett, Jr., visited Maple Hill, he presented the boy with a bicycle. Later, when Fortune visited Tuskegee in the autumn of 1905—his first visit there in seven years—he

8. Fortune to Washington, March 7, May 1, May 3, 1902; Washington to Fortune, March 8, 1902; Carrie Fortune to Washington, May 1, 1902, Washington Papers.

9. Fortune to Terrell, July 16, 1904; clipping, *Red Bank Mail and Express*, June 24, 1904, Terrell Papers, Manuscript Division, Library of Congress; Waters to Scott, July 5, 1905; Scott to Fortune, July 15, 1905, Washington Papers.

stayed in Scott's home and saw all five of his children for the first time. After the visit, he wrote an article about Scott and his family in the *Age* and paid tribute to Scott for the part he played in making possible the success of Washington and his school.[10]

Fortune sympathized with the younger man, who, burdened with the responsibility of rearing a large family, had little hope of improving his position at Tuskegee or of breaking away. When Scott's name was mentioned as a possible appointee as Registrar of the Treasury, Fortune was eager to help him if possible. But Scott told him to disregard the rumor. "The Wizard," he said, "would not stand for any political job for me for several reasons, and then, too, I am not hiking so strenuously as I might have been at some time in my life for recognition."[11]

To Scott, in turn, as to no one else, Fortune expressed his own growing bitterness and pessimism. After one disappointment he wrote: "I have reached the conclusion that the Fates have the cards stacked against me, and that all that is left to me is to plod on in the effort to make a fair living and to die decently at the psychological moment. . . . *All the way I have shaken the trees and others have gathered the fruit.*" He worried constantly about money and the financial prospects of his family. A few weeks later he wrote to Scott: "It is too much for me at my age and with my handicaps to hope that I shall ever be able to save up anything to properly educate Fred or to leave my family above want. . . . The fools live for others and the wise man lives for himself. . . . If I had to go over it again I would think first of myself and interests in every alliance and move."[12]

10. Fortune to Washington, September 21, 1904; Fortune to Scott, July 20, 1903; July 17, 1904; Scott to Fortune, July 21, November 6, 1905, Washington Papers; *Age*, November 2, 1905.

11. Fortune to Scott, November 25, 1904, Fortune Papers; Scott to Fortune, March 16, 1905, Washington Papers.

12. Fortune to Scott, January 2, 1905, Fortune Papers; Fortune to Scott, February 19, 1905, Washington Papers. Italics added.

One of the many disappointments Fortune suffered was his failure to interest publishers in his verses.[13] After repeated rejections, he decided in 1905 to publish his poems privately. In making the selection from all that he had written over a period of twenty-five years, he found "by far the larger part more adapted to the grate than the public eye." Perhaps, he said, some of the verses which he was publishing should have been committed to the flames "because . . . we are more partial to our own progeny, of whatever sort, than others can be, and blind to faults in it."[14] The verses were entirely devoid of the "dialect rot" which Fortune disdained, and indeed there was little in them to suggest that the author was an Afro-American. In contrast to his journalistic writing and his speeches, which nearly always emphasized race and which were likely to be bitter and satirical, the poems were romantic and sentimental. Most of them were set in Florida. Some dealt with the romantic history of his native state; others described its natural beauties. The book was not dedicated to Carrie but to "Jessie and Frederick White, my beloved children, whose affection and devotion have been an inspiring and sustaining influence in my life." Jessie, at least, must have taken pleasure in the book, because she, too, wrote verses, some of which her father published in *The Colored American Magazine*.

Indeed Jessie was Fortune's greatest joy. She finished her teacher training course in Brooklyn in 1902. Washington, who knew her as a friend of his daughter, suggested that she might like to work at Tuskegee for a time, a proposal which Fortune endorsed; but Jessie and her mother decided that she should seek a position in the New York City schools. Although there

13. Washington to Fortune, October 19, 1903; Fortune to Washington, October 28, 1903; Fortune to Scott, January 12, 1905, Washington Papers.

14. T. Thomas Fortune, *Dreams of Life: Miscellaneous Poems* (New York, 1905), p. i.

was a long list of applicants, she was selected for a permanent position in Manhattan in a school with an all-white enrollment. Her father was very pleased and proud—the more so, he said, because Jessie was the beneficiary of the fight he had joined when he first came to New York to break up the color line in the schools. "I am glad to see my daughter enter upon work in the public schools of New York on perfect equality with all others as a direct result of a fight I began when she was a baby," he told Washington. But he added, "Mrs. Fortune deserves most of the credit for the splendid education and noble womanly qualities which Jessie possesses."[15]

Although Carrie was seldom mentioned in the correspondence which Fortune carried on with Washington and Scott, the surviving letters contain no hint that the relations between him and his wife were not harmonious. Nevertheless, in October 1906 they separated. Under instructions from Fortune, Fred R. Moore made arrangements for Mrs. Fortune and the children to move to an apartment in Harlem. Fortune agreed to pay the rent and to support Carrie and Fred.

We do not know what particular development, if any, precipitated the break, and we can only speculate about the causes. Moore's letter to Mrs. Fortune describing the arrangements he had made suggests that Fortune was in a state of acute depression and perhaps was threatening some desperate action. "Please say nothing to him in the way of complaint or anything," Moore advised. "Just take matters the way I have suggested and go in for ordinary conversation [when you see him]."[16] A letter

15. Fortune to Washington, September 7, October 6, October 20, October 30, November 6, 1902, Washington Papers.

16. Moore to Mrs. Carrie Fortune, October 1, October 5, October 8, 1906, Fortune Papers; conversation of author with Miss Phyllis Waters, who visited in the Fortune home as a child. There is no mention of the separation or Fortune's marital difficulties in any of the letters in the Washington Papers, but there are few letters for this period. Perhaps some of the letters were destroyed.

from Fortune to Jessie a few months later suggests that he may have been contemplating or threatening suicide. In correspondence with Carrie and Jessie, which his wife preserved, Fortune attributed his desire for a separation simply to differences in temperament (without indicating the nature of the "differences") and indicated that for years this had caused friction.

The separation occurred just before his fiftieth birthday, and some of his depression and desperation may have been due to the dread of approaching old age, which he had always feared. At fifty he was still a handsome man, but Carrie had grown fat and had no doubt lost the physical attraction which she had possessed during the early years of their marriage. Fortune had always been attractive to women and obviously enjoyed their society. But no evidence remains that he was involved with other women or was unfaithful to Carrie during the periods when he was away from home. Several months after the separation, as we shall see, he was in love with another woman, but whether this affair was responsible for the estrangement from his wife, we do not know.

In December Fortune and Carrie saw each other, but he refused her pleas for a reconciliation. "I have weighted all that you say and I am impressed with it," he told her. "Of course there is nothing whatever between us, except the matter of incompatability, which I long ago remarked to you, and I have as high appreciation of you as I ever had, as you have always been so straight in your living and I have no cause whatever to complain. I hope and feel that our relations will always be pleasant and agreeable, and I shall spend as much time with you and the children as my engagements will allow." To Jessie he wrote that he thought a great deal of her mother and wished that matters had turned out differently. "She has a good big heart and she is honest as the day is long, but we do not agree temperamentally, and we have now arranged for the best." A few months later when Jessie again raised the question of a reconciliation, her father told her that matters were settled and that

it was not wise to reopen them. "Your mother and I," he repeated, "have temperaments so radically different that we cannot get along happily together. We had a great many years of
uncomfortable and unsatisfactory association, with much discord in it, and I do not care to have any more of it. It would
be a great deal better if we had a divorce. . . . No; I should not
be happy to take up the old relations and I desire to have peace
and to live my own life the few years I have left to me." He
added that he did not like "some phases of the situation," but
did not want to take on the old life of worry and cross purposes
again. "I should be tempted to do something desperate, as I was
often in the old days, and I would rather die an honest rather
than a violent death."[17]

Shortly after the domestic crisis that led to the separation
from Carrie, the Brownsville affair occurred, adding to Fortune's melancholy and creating a new strain on his relations with
Washington. But any reservations which Washington may have
had about his emotional stability or his loyalty did not deter him
from involving himself more deeply than ever in the affairs of
the *Age*. Early in 1907 the *Age* was for the first time incorporated, with Washington, albeit secretly, as one of the principal
stockholders. In January Scott came to iron out details of arrangements which Washington and Fortune had already discussed. In a long memorandum to his chief, Scott outlined
plans for reorganization and suggestions for developing the *Age*
into a national newspaper and making it financially successful. It
would be necessary "to preserve the personality of Mr. Fortune
on the Editorial page, for what he has stood for as much as
anything else, and to which . . . the present standing of the
paper is due," he said. In addition Scott recommended improve-
ments in the makeup of the paper, more advertising, a Washing-

17. Fortune to Carrie Fortune, December 6, 1906; Fortune to
Jessie Fortune, December 6, 1906; May 26, 1907, Fortune Papers.

ton correspondent, and more features on fashions, music, and the theater. Most important would be the hiring of a real business manager.[18]

Fortune and Peterson reached an agreement with Scott over the incorporation. Fortune had been afraid that his partner would object to making Washington a shareholder and allowing him consideration for the money he had already put into the *Age* because Peterson had previously maintained that Washington had benefited from the money he put into the paper. But Peterson agreed to give Washington stock in recognition for what he had already done. "I feel now that I have justified to you the position I have always taken with you that it was very unsatisfactory to have you place money in a property in which you had no property interest," Fortune wrote Washington. "I certainly feel better to know that you have something to show for the money you have put in the paper." Washington replied that he was pleased with the arrangements, especially with "the generosity exhibited by both you and Mr. Peterson in connection with past relations."[19]

The New York Age Publishing Company was incorporated under the laws of New York on February 4, 1907, with capital stock of $50,000, of which $15,000 was to be open to subscription in shares with a par value of $10. Fortune was designated president of the corporation, and Peterson secretary-treasurer. In addition to receiving stock for the money he had already spent on the *Age*, Washington was to receive stock for additional money invested in expansion and the purchase of new equipment. Altogether he held 950 shares, but the stock was issued in Scott's name.[20]

18. Fortune to Scott, January 8, 1907; Scott to Washington, January 11, 1907, Washington Papers.

19. Fortune to Washington, January 25, 1907; Washington to Fortune, January 29, 1907, Washington Papers.

20. Jerome Peterson to Scott, May 2, 1907; Peterson to Wash-

As part of the program of expansion, Fortune and Washington agreed that the *Age* should do its own printing. This necessitated the purchase of new presses and other equipment and the rental of new quarters. For several months Fortune was frantically busy buying equipment and moving to the new location at 7 and 8 Chatham Square. The costs, as usual, were greater than he had anticipated. By June, he wrote Scott, things were in working shape, but "I still have the old job of my life in hand in a somewhat aggravated form, of trying to do big things with small means." The investment in equipment in turn made it necessary to seek as much job printing as possible, which added to his burdens. He found it difficult to find time to do the editorial work on the paper. One week he wrote Scott:

> Here it is Saturday morning, and I have not got a line written or a page of copy edited for the paper next week, and forty columns to be got together, with a nervous condition out of which to fetch the whole business. . . . I feel bum, tired and sick today, but shall pen down to my six columns of editorial all the same. . . . Kiss the babies for me and tell dear Mrs. Scott I think often of her and her kindness to me when I was there.[21]

Because of the cost of new equipment, Fortune thought it unwise to increase the cost of the paper by enlarging it at once. He advised waiting until after the dull summer months and increasing the size in the fall. But Washington insisted upon a seven column, eight page paper beginning in March.[22]

Fortune constantly complained of the strain of overwork,

---

ington, May 9, 1907; Fortune to Scott, April 13, May 13, June 6, 1907, Washington Papers. Efforts to sell the stock to outsiders met with little success.

21. Fortune to Scott, March 26, April 4, April 13, April 19, June 6, 1907, Washington Papers.

22. Fortune to Scott, March 5, March 8, March 12, 1907, Washington Papers.

but found it impossible to share responsibility in the operation of the *Age*. E. T. Atwell was sent from Tuskegee to help with circulation and the business end of the paper. But he soon found that there was little which he was permitted to do beyond the most routine tasks. Fortune insisted upon attending to all correspondence himself. After a few days, Atwell wrote Scott that so far as the *Age* was concerned Fortune "wants to run it and his disposition is such that one has to use all the patience possible to get him to accept suggestions." Fortune treated him in the friendliest fashion, said Atwell, "but as he repeats quite often, he has been in the newspaper business 'thirty years and knows how to run it.' " Atwell left after a few weeks, and Fortune expressed regret at his departure.[23] He tried, without success, to have Peterson released for a time from his work in the Internal Revenue office, and was unable to find any other assistant who satisfied him.

Meanwhile, in addition to suggesting numerous ways of increasing circulation (none of which were successful), Washington and Scott constantly sent editorials and other copy to the *Age*. But Washington disclaimed any intention of dictating editorial policy. At one point, in an effort to soothe the editor, who had objected to something he had sent, Washington wrote:

> I hope that you will always bear in mind that anything I send you whether of a news character or editorial matter I always take for granted that you always will use your judgment as to whether or not it should go into the paper. *You are the editor and know best what to put in the paper and what to keep out of the paper.* I simply take my chances in sending you matter along with the rest of mankind.

Fortune answered that he was always glad to publish anything which Washington sent him, provided it appeared over his signature. "But," he said, "we should have an understanding

23. E. T. Atwell to Scott, January 31, February 4, 1907; Fortune to Scott, February 12, 1907, Washington Papers.

of the policies upon which we agree and disagree for editorial treatment." Washington had sent two editorial notes which were inconsistent with *Age* policy—one advising Negroes to remain in the South and one endorsing Roosevelt as against Foraker. "To adopt either and hammer it would smash the paper with its readers," said Fortune. He added that he had long ago lost faith in Roosevelt. "He has done you dirt in the soldier business and the Ohio move, as he should not have dragged you into it," he added. "But I have nothing to do with all this except that I will not subscribe to it editorially because I do not believe in it and because it would ruin the paper."[24]

The "Ohio move" to which Fortune referred was Roosevelt's decision to take a slap at Senator Foraker and to try to strengthen Taft's position in the eyes of Negro voters by appointing a Negro from Ohio to a political post. He had asked Washington for a recommendation, and the Tuskegeean had suggested Ralph Tyler, a part-time journalist and secretary to Robert Wolfe, owner of the *Columbus Ohio State Journal* and the *Columbus Dispatch*, both of which opposed Foraker. Thereafter Roosevelt named Tyler to a position as an auditor in the Navy Department in Washington. The *Cleveland Gazette* deplored the effort to use a Negro in this way and was critical of Tyler for accepting the appointment. The sentiment among Negroes in the Brownsville matter was almost universally with Foraker and against the president, said the *Age*. It declared:

> We regret exceedingly the wholly selfish use which the President is making of Mr. Washington and the colored people in his battle for political survivorship with Senator Foraker. . . . Neither Mr. Washington nor the colored people of the country can risk the hazard to be moved as mere pawns on this chess board of the President. . . . For while publicity in such a case may serve the President's purpose or scheme, it

24. Washington to Fortune, February 7, 1907; Fortune to Washington, February 12, 1907, Washington Papers. Italics added.

does not serve those of Mr. Washington but must operate instead to his hurt, to the hurt of Tuskegee and to the great cause of the race in America for long years to come.[25]

When Tyler finally received his appointment, Washington asked Fortune to "say a good word" about him in the *Age* because he was "really a fine fellow." Fortune responded with an editorial which spoke of Tyler as a "competent man of high character" and declared that his elevation was a handsome one regardless of the motives which prompted it.[26]

In May the *Age* called for the nomination of Charles Evans Hughes as the Republican candidate for president in 1908. But gradually Fortune was moderating his attacks on Roosevelt and Taft over Brownsville. Toward the end of June, Washington sent a marked copy of the *Age* to A. I. Vorys, leader of the Taft forces in Ohio, which he said would show that he was having some success in changing the attitude of its editor. "In the last analysis," he said, "the New York Age wields more influence than any other force in controlling matters." The *Cleveland Gazette* commented that the Taft subsidizers seemed to have the editor of the *Age* in their pocket. "HOW THE AGE HAS CHANGED IN THE LAST FEW WEEKS!" it gibed. "WHAT HAS CAUSED IT?" But the *Age* did not endorse Taft. In August Fortune predicted that Foraker would nominate Charles Evans Hughes and that Hughes would be elected. Throughout September the *Age* continued to urge Hughes as a presidential possibility.[27]

Fortune no doubt resented Washington's efforts to influence

25. Thornbrough, "The Brownsville Episode," pp. 479–80; *Cleveland Gazette*, February 9, 1907; *Age*, February 14, 1907.

26. Washington to Fortune, April 11, 1907, Washington Papers; *Age*, April 18, 1907.

27. Washington to A. I. Vorys, June 26, 1907, Washington Papers; *Cleveland Gazette*, July 20, 1907; *Age*, May 16, September 5, September 26, 1907.

his political position, and his bitterness toward Roosevelt for Brownsville was unassuaged; but stronger than either of these feelings was his feeling of disillusionment and weariness over the futility of protest and protest organizations. He pointed out that although the Negro press and Negro organizations had been hurling anathemas at Roosevelt and Taft, in state after state white politicians ignored them and endorsed the president and the secretary. At its national convention in Baltimore, the Afro-American Council approved an address which deplored the dismissal of the Brownsville soldiers and praised Foraker, but, as Fortune pointed out, not even the Baltimore papers published the full text of the resolutions, and the New York papers ignored them completely. In an editorial, June 27, 1908, he pointed out that not only did white politicians and press appear oblivious to protests, but the apathy of the black masses and internal dissension had caused every organization for the protection of civil and political rights to fail.

Under the leadership of Frederick Douglass, Joseph C. Price, the writer, William H. Steward, Alexander Walters, *W.E.B. DuBois,* from 1868 to the present, they have gathered in civic conventions and indignation meetings of all sorts and shown all sorts of enthusiasm and adopted all sorts of resolutions, but nothing has come of it all. . . . The great mass of people has not been touched with the fire of enthusiasm which leads to concerted effort. . . .

When the thoughtful men and women of the Afro-American people cease to divide among themselves over non essentials and [cease to] deride and slander each other to the scandal of the world, and when the masses wake up . . . there may be some hope for the preservation of their liberties under the Federal Constitution, but not before.[28]

Fortune was also weary and harassed over the burdens and responsibilities of the *Age.* He was constantly short of the funds

28. *Age,* June 27, July 4, 1907. Italics added. It is significant that Fortune mentioned Du Bois but not Washington.

necessary to pay the bills for operating and expanding the paper. In a letter to Washington asking for $200, he said, engulfed in self-pity, "I am doing the best that I can on small means, but I feel sometimes that all of the effort is hopeless and that it would be best to cut it off short and thus end it—for I have failed in all the hopes of my youth, and only work to provide for those dependent on me." In spite of the money which Washington invested in the *Age* and his ambitious plans for the paper, Fortune tried in vain to discuss with him the finances of the paper and his obligations for paying for the new equipment.[29] Indeed for one who was accustomed to preach the virtues of the business ethic and business-like practices and to deplore the lack of them in other member of his race, Washington appears to have been remarkably casual and unbusiness-like in his relations with the *Age*.

In August, Fortune, Washington, and Scott attended the convention of the National Negro Business League in Topeka, Kansas. While there Fortune tried to impress upon Washington that the *Age* was running at a deficit, that bills for new equipmen were coming due, and that there were questions about the validity of the papers of incorporation, but he came to no satisfactory understanding with him. Back in New York he wrote Scott that he had been going over the records of the incorporation and had found much confusion in the papers which had been drawn up by Wilford Smith. He said:

> It is important that you have all the facts in the business as it now stands, and for the protection of the interests standing in your name, and which now has no valid standing in law under the incorporation act of New York, and along the lines I solemnly related to you in our conference at Topeka, none of the salient features of which have been put in writing or executed by you or Dr. Washington; with the result that

29. Fortune to Washington, June 7, 1907, Washington Papers; Fortune to Scott, July 1, 1907, Fortune Papers.

nothing has been paid on account of materials we have secured or promise to cover by graduated notes, and the running revenues of the business are reduced to a balance at this
moment of less than $70.

Two days later he wrote Washington that the *Age* was "alarm-
ingly short on current running money," urging him to pay the
bill for the Jeanes Fund report which had been printed in the
Age shop.[30]

At Topeka Fortune appeared to be under great stress. He was
nervous and almost distraught. At one point he created a sensation by launching into a kind of extemporaneous sermon in
which he called upon Bishop Abraham Grant, who was about
to offer a prayer, to pay tribute to John Brown and to invoke
his spirit on the meeting and to ask God to get into the businessmen assembled there.[31]

From the time of the Topeka meeting, Fortune's behavior
was certainly abnormal, and some of those present were convinced that he had become mentally unbalanced. The most
obvious symptom of his aberration was what would probably
be considered a religious delusion. He thought that God had
called upon him to preach. In an editorial in the *Age* after his
return from Topeka, he declared: "The paramount and direct
influence of God in the affairs of men and nations cannot be
overlooked even in a meeting of business men. . . . The children
of Ham had better begin to understand this fact, because the

30. Fortune to Scott, August 26, 1907; Fortune to Washington,
August 28, 1907, Washington Papers.

31. *Age*, August 22, September 25, 1907. In a gossip column
which appeared in Negro newspapers throughout the country, R.
W. Thompson asked: "Is it really to be 'Rev.' T. Thomas Fortune?
Yet none of us need be surprised, for the very brainy editor of the
New York Age has been preaching a mighty stiff doctrine of race
salvation for lo! these many years, and his valuable missionary work
doth follow him from generation to generation" (*Washington Bee*,
September 14, 1907).

devil is hot on their coat tails." Unless members of the Business League learned to "carry into their daily life the teachings of the prophets and Christ, they [would] fail even when seeming to succeed. It is written in the book."[32]

Most of the time, except for the religious delusion, his behavior was normal, but he himself evidently felt that he was insane or becoming insane. It is pointless to try to diagnose his condition in terms of present-day knowledge of mental illness. The evidence is too fragmentary. But his earlier record and his subsequent behavior suggest a number of reasons for his "breakdown," although it is impossible to determine which were immediately responsible. For years he had been under pressures and frustrations with which he was unable to cope in almost every area of his life. Since his youth he had suffered from fits of depression. These were becoming more frequent and more severe. Chronic financial uncertainty caused him increasing mental distress as he grew older and realized that he had not made provision for his family's future. Coupled with the realization that he was a financial failure was the conviction that he had failed in the great cause of his life—the crusade in behalf of his race—and that he had wasted his talents and the best years of his life on a futile purpose. For a man of his great abilities, who had shown such brilliant promise in his youth and to whom success and applause were important, however much he might deny it, the sense of failure was especially devastating. Closely related to his sense of personal failure must have been inner conflicts arising from his relationship with Washington. Fortune knew that at times he had compromised his own principles and integrity in supporting Washington while secretly agreeing with his critics. And while Washington's fame and prestige had grown, Fortune had not been rewarded for his loyalty to him but had become an object of contempt in the eyes of the anti-Washington intellectuals with whom he was in reality psycho-

32. *Age*, September 25, 1907.

logically and ideologically more in rapport than with the Tuskegeean.

Inner conflicts over his personal life must have been even more important in causing his mental distress—but on this crucial subject almost no evidence survives. We know that Fortune had separated from Carrie in October 1906, and that by the following summer, at least, he was having a love affair with another woman. He expressed a desire for a divorce, evidently with the expectation of marrying the other woman, but there is no clue in the letters which have been preserved as to her identity, although Washington and Moore knew about her. On the one hand Fortune wanted to escape from his relationship with Carrie and seek happiness elsewhere; on the other he felt guilty over his treatment of a wife who was blameless and entirely devoted to him. Another factor about which evidence is elusive, but which was probably significant, was his fear that he had inherited a tendency to insanity. Brooding over this "hereditary taint" may well have induced the mental state which he feared. Finally alcohol was undoubtedly a factor in his mental illness. For years he had been a heavy drinker at social gatherings. As inner conflicts and fears grew more acute, he sought to escape them by resort to alcohol. And, of course, the realization that he was compounding his problems by drinking added to his mental burdens.

Probably present-day psychology would attribute his behavior to a breakdown in his usual inner defenses. To escape reality he took refuge in a world of his own—a delusion in which he felt he was called upon to preach and spread the word of God. But his contemporaries ascribed his illness to "softening of the brain." In the state of knowledge—or lack of knowledge—of mental disease in 1907, a condition such as his was regarded by some as laughable, by others as pitiful. But none of his friends offered him any meaningful assistance in this difficult period. Instead some whom he regarded as friends took advantage of his misfortune to further their own schemes.

The exact sequence of events following the Topeka meeting is not clear, but on September 4 Fortune agreed to transfer his interest in the *Age* to Fred R. Moore. He wired Scott: "Recognizing the shattered condition of my health and the imperative urgency of taking a long rest, . . . I transferred my interest in the New York Age Publishing Company to Fred R. Moore."[33] It is not clear whether the initiative for the transfer came from Fortune or Moore, nor is there evidence of whether or not at that point Moore was acting with the assurance that Washington would give him the financial backing necessary to purchase Fortune's stock.

A few days later Washington and Scott came to New York, but the visit, so far as Fortune was concerned, did nothing to straighten out the tangled affairs of the *Age*. After returning to Tuskegee, Washington wired for Fortune to come there, telling him that he had arranged with Moore for money to meet the current obligations of the *Age* and to cover the cost of Fortune's railroad fare.[34]

But by that time. plans to sell Fortune's share in the *Age* had run into a snag because Peterson claimed that the terms of his original partnership with Fortune give him an option on Fortune's stock, and he was unwilling for it to be sold to Moore. Fortune wired Washington that the deal with Moore was off:

You know, that neither Moore nor Peterson has any money and that I am striving to get away from routine grind so that I will be able to do the work God intended I should do regularly and in order. In the effort to do this it may become necessary to dump my Age interests in the gutter. When a man gets tired of being a slave God will help him to

33. Fortune to Scott (copy of telegram), September 7, 1907, Fortune Papers.
34. Washington to Fortune, September 13, 1907, Washington Papers; Washington to Fortune (telegram), September 17, 1907, Fortune Papers.

find the way to freedom. I have had 30 years of slavery to the race and I am going to have some freedom or "bust."[35]

Meanwhile Moore was actually running the *Age* office although both Peterson and Fortune tried to persuade him to withdraw and tried to return to him the $300 which he had given as a deposit when Fortune offered to sell him his interest. In spite of the fact that Fortune had obviously been in an abnormal mental state when he made the agreement, Moore insisted that he had a binding contract and threatened Fortune with a lawsuit to compel him to withdraw from the *Age*. Both Fortune and Peterson apparently tried to find out whether Moore had been in communication with Washington, but Moore had denied communicating with either Washington or Scott.[36]

Moore refused to budge, and in the end it was agreed that he would pay Fortune $7,000 for his stock in the *Age*. He gave him notes in that amount which were to be paid over a three-year period. Booker T. Washington in turn agreed to advance the money to Moore to cover his payments, but this fact was carefully concealed from both Fortune and Peterson. Moore told Peterson that a "white friend' had loaned him the money. To Fortune Washington claimed to be unaware of the source from which Moore secured the money, saying that he had evidently discovered a "gold mine."[37]

In the *Age*, October 3, 1907, there appeared a letter over Fortune's signature which said that with this issue he was sever-

35. Fortune to Washington (telegram), September 17, September 18, 1907, Washington Papers.

36. Moore to Washington, October 17, 1907, Washington Papers.

37. Fortune to Scott, October 15, 1907; Scott to Moore, November 2, 1907; Moore to Washington, December 24, 1907, Washington Papers; Fortune to Washington, November 25, 1907, Fortune Papers.

ing his connection with the paper. He left in the *Age*, he said, "my spirit of good will, where it has abided for some thirty years. During that time I strove to do right as God gave me light. I appreciate the friendships I have made and hope for the enemies I have made that they cheerfully feel that they got what was due them. I extend my hearty good wishes to the new management."

An editorial in the same issue said that Fortune was retiring "against the protests of the stockholders" in order to have more leisure for other writing.

Washington continued to try to induce Fortune to come to Tuskegee, but Fortune resisted. One reason, he explained, was that he did not want to be there at the time of Portia's wedding, which was soon to occur, because "the long nervous strain I have been and am still under requires that I remain away from such excitements." He added:

When a man has been sick in heart and head for four long months he must get very close to his Maker in his life thoughts and when he finds Him he cannot feel all at once as he has felt, especially if his past life has vastly more of evil than good in it. In the honest effort to find "the light, the truth and the way," the outcome of it may be life or it may be death. Who Knows! You must have God in your life and in your work, and if "the still small voice" has ever been with you as it has been with me, you know, as all good Christians do, that the end of it is life everlasting.

He concluded:

If you will consider the matter from this point of view you will better understand what happened at Topeka in all matters in which I took part.[38]

Washington's eagerness to have Fortune at Tuskegee appears to have been motivated less by concern for his friend's wel-

38 Fortune to Washington, October 15, 1907, Fortune Papers.

fare than by apprehension over what he might reveal of the Tuskegeean's relations with the *Age*. He began a carefully calculated campaign to forestall the effect of any revelations which the erstwhile editor might make. An occasion presented itself when Mrs. Fannie Barrier Williams, wife of Chicago attorney S. Laing Williams, who had been writing a column on women's activities for the *Age*, wrote to tell him that she had received a curt note from Peterson notifying her to discontinue her letters. She did not like the idea of being summarily dismissed and wrote to Washington with the understanding, she said, "that you have a considerable financial interest in The New York Age and possibly have something to do with its policy and business management." Washington promptly replied that he was sorry to hear of her unpleasantness with Peterson. But, he added emphatically, "I write to say especially however, that I do not hold a single share of stock in connection with the Age and have no financial interest in it. I have made it a rule from the beginning not to own any part in colored newspapers." Mrs. Williams apologized and assured him that she and her husband had never believed any of the gossip about his financial aid to newspapers but that they had heard "from one who is regarded as one of your closest and most loyal friends" that he had invested in the *Age*. She was glad to learn the truth and said she and her husband would continue to make it known that it was not his policy " 'to have any financial interest in colored newspapers.' "39

When Washington learned that Fortune planned to go to Chicago instead of accepting his invitation to Tuskegee, he wrote to two friends in that city—attorney Williams and Dr. Daniel Hale Williams, the surgeon—telling them of Fortune's mental condition and emphasizing that he could not be consid-

39. Fannie Barrier Williams to Washington, September 13, September 21, 1907; Washington to Mrs. Williams, September 18, 1907, Washington Papers.

ered responsible for anything he might say or do. To Dr. Williams he said that Fortune had been in bad shape mentally and physically for some time. "He has not been able to do any work for several months on his paper for the reason that he seems to have lost his mental balance and gone off on a religious craze," he wrote. "I understand that Mr. Moore has paid him a good sum for his paper, and I presume for this reason he has some cash. It would be a great pity for him to squander his cash, especially as it is the only thing he will have to live on the rest of his life in a fruitless effort to start a paper. . . . The danger is some unscrupulous people will get hold of him in a way to stir up trouble." He wrote in similar vein to Laing Williams and asked him to be on the alert if Fortune came to Chicago and to try to help him. "In reality," he assured Williams, "the man is not in a fit condition to enter into any enterprise. He is as weak as a child mentally." When the attorney replied that there were rumors that Fortune had been "forced out" of the *Age* because he would not support Taft and Roosevelt, Washington said that so far as he knew nobody had forced Fortune out and that he had been trying to sell his paper for a long time. "He offered the property to Moore, and Mr. Moore got a friend of his to back him with the result that after the paper was sold Fortune wanted to back out of the agreement but Moore would not let him." He added that it would be a pity for the poor fellow to squander what he had received from the sale of the *Age*.[40]

Presently both Williamses informed Washington that Fortune had arrived in Chicago and that they had seen him. Part of the time, S. Laing Williams reported, he had appeared to be in good shape and had talked rationally, but a few days later Wil-

40. Washington to Dr. Daniel Williams, October 30, 1907; Washington to S. Laing Williams, October 20, November 5, 1907, Washington Papers. The statement that Fortune had been unable to work for "several months" was patently not true, as the voluminous correspondence between Fortune and Tuskegee in this period attests.

liams had heard him attempt to deliver a lay sermon at the Institutional Church that was "wretchedly incoherent and meaningless." Both men reported that Fortune had a woman with him and that he had consulted the attorney about a divorce and had been told that a year's residence in Illinois would be necessary. Washington replied that there was indeed a woman with whom Fortune had been involved for several months. "How he can explain his religious fervor in connection with such conduct I cannot understand," he piously observed.[41]

Fortune went to Chicago intending to establish himself in journalism in that city. He first tried to buy the *Conservator* without success, and then began negotiations for acquiring an interest in *The Voice*. This was the periodical which had been published in Atlanta under the name *The Voice of the Negro*. Following the Atlanta riot of 1906, Max Barber, the editor of *The Voice*, had gone to Chicago, where the magazine was published by Hertel, Jenkins and Company. Now Fortune sought to enter into a partnership with this member of the Niagara Movement whom he had formerly castigated. Using the money from the first two notes which Moore had paid, he acquired a controlling interest in the *Voice*, while Barber and his friends retained the remainder of the stock. He wrote Washington that he intended to get the magazine, which had been poorly managed, into shape and then start a weekly newspaper. But he needed more money and asked Washington to take up the Moore note which would fall due the following August and send him the money. "I am in good health,' he said, "and am not so nervous as I have been." But both Dr. Williams and S. Laing Williams told Washington that Fortune was being swindled in *The Voice* business. The latter said that *The Voice* company was heavily in

41. S. Laing Williams to Washington, November 1, November 6, November 14, 1907; Dr. Daniel Williams to Washington, November 4, 1907; Washington to S. Laing Williams, November 19, 1907, Washington Papers.

debt and that Fortune had evidently invested without looking into the matter of corporate indebtedness.

Dr. Daniel Williams wrote that Fortune had fallen into the hands of "the wolves." The surgeon and his wife had "been watching the game here, since the poor demented friend came on the scene some two weeks ago. Poor fellow we pity him," he said. "The once brilliant mind is being gradually obliterated. . . . As to the facts the wolves have already gathered him in."[42] Washington thanked the doctor for informing him of the situation. "It is amusing and pathetic," he said. Fortune wrote him almost daily, he added, asking for money to carry out his plan to start a newspaper, but he was sending none. "The pathetic part of the situation is this: Within a few months he will have spent all he gets from the sale of The Age and then will have nothing upon which to live the remaining portion of his life. When I see him I plan to talk frankly in that direction." But it was "just as well to let him learn his lesson now as later," he said a few weeks later.[43]

While this pathetic little drama was unfolding in Chicago, Moore in New York was confronted with the problems of publishing the *Age*. He was burdened with the same financial difficulties which had helped bring on Fortune's collapse, and he

42. S. Laing Williams to Washington, November 1, 1907; Dr. Daniel Williams to Washington, November 4, 1907, Washington Papers; Fortune to Washington, October 31, 1907, Fortune Papers. Dr. Williams was interested in obtaining an appointment at Freedman's Hospital in Washington, D. C., and needed Washington's help in the matter. After telling Washington about Fortune, the surgeon assured the Tuskegee Wizard that he could place reliance on him and his wife. "Situated as you are among a pack of wolves, vicious wolves, you need to have trusted true friends where they can best serve you," he said.

43. Washington to Dr. Daniel Williams, November 9, December 5, 1907, Washington Papers.

lacked Fortune's editorial experience and talent. Without Fortune the *Age* was really not the *Age*. As soon as Moore had taken over the paper, he and Peterson and Scott had tried to persuade Fortune to write a weekly column for the paper, but Fortune had refused. What the paper needed most, said Moore, was a *known editor*. As a temporary expedient, Ralph W. Tyler, the man whom Roosevelt had appointed as auditor in the Navy Department at Washington's recommendation, was induced to write editorials. In advising Tyler about his work, Scott said he thought that at the present it would not be wise to include "too much pro-Taft or Roosevelt matter." Moore was "all right" regarding both men, but Washington and Scott thought that "on account of the position taken by the *Age* under Fortune it might be well gradually to work up, say by December or January, instead of at this time to the pro-Taft program."[44]

Nevertheless, with Scott's approval, the *Age* published an editorial by Tyler entitled "Brownsville Ghouls," which created a storm of controversy. The editorial asserted that human ghouls, like buzzards, always swooped down during a disaster, and he blamed Negro ghouls for raising the race issue over the dismissal of the Brownsville troops. "When the natural volubility [*sic*] of our race was fanned into a flame by the discharge of the soldiers," wrote Tyler, "there were those, who crouching behind inhuman avarice and selfishness, were ready to swoop down, buzzard like upon the prey." When Foraker began his investigation, the editorial went on, these buzzards flapped their wings. "These inhuman ghouls raised the black flag of Race Discrimination and moved out in search, not of justice, but of the thirty pieces of silver coined for Judases." Not Roosevelt, whose many brave and helpful acts had proved him a real friend

44. Fortune to Scott, September 30, 1907; Washington to Ralph W. Tyler, October 1, 1907; Scott to Tyler, October 12, 1907; Moore to Scott, October 12, 1907, Washington Papers.

of the race, nor Taft nor Foraker was responsible for making a race issue of Brownsville, but black ghouls, "worthless parasites," who had led the race into an ambush.[45]

When Fortune read the editorial, he wrote a reply to the *Age* which was not published. To Washington he wrote from Chicago, "The real 'ghouls' in raising the color question in the Brownsville affair were Theodore Roosevelt and William Howard Taft and credit should not be denied them. . . . I am sorry you are mixed up with Roosevelt, who is a dangerous man, even as I told you he was when we were at the Gauley River seven years ago."[46]

In the same issue of the *Age* with "Brownsville Ghouls" there was an attack on Gilchrist Stewart, Charles Anderson's political foe. Stewart replied in a letter which was published in the *Washington Bee*, adding, "You make no formal announcement to the public, Mr. Editor of the Age, that Editor Fortune has severed his connections with the New York Age. Anyone who read the editorial on the affray at Brownsville would know that it would be impossible for a race-loving man as Fortune to pen such a traitorous article." Other papers took up the cry. Several suggested that the sudden change in the editorial policy of the *Age* was evidence that Fortune had been forced out because of his refusal to support Taft.[47]

The *Age* might fail to print Fortune's letter, but other papers were eager to publish communications from him. The most sen-

45. *Age*, October 17, 1907.

46. Fortune to Washington, October 31, 1907, Fortune Papers. Washington agreed that the editorial was a mistake and wrote Moore that he thought so. To Tyler he said that he feared it had proved a boomerang as it represented too abrupt a change in editorial policy (Washington to Tyler November 4, 1907, Washington Papers).

47. *Washington Bee*, November 9, 1907; Fortune to Washington, October 31, 1907, Fortune Papers.

sational was a letter which he wrote to Monroe Trotter and which was published in the *Guardian* under the headlines "T. T. FORTUNE CONGRATULATES GUARDIAN":

> Accept my congratulations on the seventh anniversary of the Guardian. You have made a brave fight for "a square deal." Keep it up. God is in the fight for the good and He will remain in it until the end of the chapter. Don't let up on Roosevelt and Taft. Lay it on them thick, as usual. They are the sinners who have provoked the thunders and should get the lightning. . . . Publish this if you want to.

Fortune also wrote a letter to the editor of the *Cleveland Gazette*, the leading Foraker organ among Negro newspapers. "Hurrah for you and the faithful," he said. " 'It was a famous victory,' and God was there. Brownsville will down, will it? So will dear Banquo's ghost! Let Roosevelt-Taft ghouls howl. When God gets behind men, as He is behind Roosevelt and Taft he does not rest until he eats them up!"[48]

After these letters appeared, Anderson wrote to Washington that Fortune had "gone over, horse, foot, and dragoon to the enemy." Tyler wrote to Scott that he thought the *Age* should attempt some sort of a reply to the letter which had appeared in the *Guardian*. He had written an editorial that he called "Dementia-Americana," in which, while not mentioning Fortune by name, he denounced Trotter as having a "diseased" and "perverted" mind which paraded "before the public the dethroned reason of others." "By some inexplicable decree the diseased and unbalanced brain always imprecates against those who have proved a friend and support before reason was dis-

48. *Boston Guardian*, November 16, 1907; *Cleveland Gazette*, November 16, 1907. In the same issue of the *Guardian* was an article reprinted from the *Springfield Republican* commenting on the change in editorial policy of the *Age* and speculating that Fortune had left the paper because his criticism of Roosevelt and Taft was unacceptable in "certain quarters."

throned [*sic*]," he continued. "The true man . . . will cover with
the mantel [*sic*] of love, pity and charity the tottering brain of
foe or friend, rather than expose it to morbidly curious, un-
sympathetic throng." The editorial also denounced as evidence
of a perverted mind the *Guardian*'s oft-repeated charge that
Washington controlled the *Age*. Publication of the editorial,
Tyler urged, would serve to deny the charge that Washington
owned the *Age*, rebuke Trotter for taking advantage of Fortune's mental state, and "warn the public that anything from
Fortune now can be charged up to a mind that is lost." But
Scott advised against publishing the editorial, and it did not
appear.[49]

The real problem, in Washington's eyes, was not that Fortune appeared to have gone over to "the enemy" in denouncing
Taft and Roosevelt, but that he might reveal Washington's financial relations with the *Age*, a fact which he went to elaborate
lengths to conceal. Moore was instructed to keep the book
which showed the stockholders of the *Age* at his home rather
than at his office and not to let anyone see it. Mail from Washington and Scott was not sent to the *Age* office, and Moore was
warned to avoid carrying any communications he might have
from them to the office. Moore advised Washington not to
worry, that Fortune was harmless. He could be controlled because there was "too much evidence hurtful to him" (evidently
a reference to Fortune's illicit romance and the possibility of
using it to keep him quiet). But Washington did not think that
a threat to reveal this fact about his personal life would silence
Fortune. "The fact is," he said, "Mr. Fortune, I do not think
cares a rap about his wrong doing being made known to the
public." The only way to influence him, said Washington,
whose admirers so often praised him as the embodiment of

49. Anderson to Washington, November 19, 1907; Tyler to
Scott, November 20, 1907; Scott to Tyler, November 22, 1907; Scott
to Moore, November 22, 1907, Washington Papers.

Christian charity, was for Moore to hold over Fortune "the fear of selling his house from under him, if he breaks out."[50]

Washington's apprehensions were aroused because of letters which he and Scott had received from Alton H. Blake, editor of a paper called *Western Opinion* published in Chicago. Blake wrote that Fortune and Barber were planning to start a paper in opposition to Washington and that Fortune had said that Washington had bought his interest in the *Age*. Washington wrote to Blake that he did not own or control a single newspaper or publication of any sort and that he was sure that Fortune had been misquoted because Fortune knew that he had not bought the *Age*. Again he said that he had refrained from investing in newspapers because he thought a man in a public position such as his "ought not to try to influence newspapers in a financial manner."[51]

The situation had indeed become so dangerous that Washington decided to withdraw from any connection with the *Age*. Scott wrote Moore that the Wizard had decided that his stock (which was held in Scott's name) should be transferred to Moore. In turn Moore would give Washington notes which he would repay over a period of years. Washington also expected to continue to protect Moore in meeting the remaining notes which were held by Fortune. Washington did not intend to deposit the notes in a bank for collection and was disposed "to carry matters along" with Moore until the latter was "in shape to straighten out the whole situation." But this would enable Washington to announce to Peterson and to the world that he held no *Age* stock.[52]

50. Scott to Moore, October 7, October 19, 1907; Moore to Washington (telegram), October 31, 1907; Washington to Moore, November 1, 1907, Washington Papers.

51. Alton H. Blake to Washington, October 29, 1907; Blake to Scott, October 29, 1907; Washington to Blake, November 2, 1907, Washington Papers.

52. Scott to Moore, November 2, 1907; Peterson to Scott, No-

On November 21 the following statement concerning ownership appeared in the *Age*:

We wish to state . . . once and for all, . . . that it is not true as one or two Afro-American papers have industriously stated, that Dr. Booker T. Washington owns The New York Age or any part of it. He does not own it and he does not control it. The New York Age Publishing Company is a stock concern and the majority of stock is owned and controlled by the President [Moore] and the Secretary and Treasurer of the company [Peterson]. No man who is before the public, as is Dr. Washington, should own or control newspaper property for the reason that such ownership or control would carry with it influence as regards the editorial opinion of the newspaper. . . .

It is a well-known fact that Mr. Fortune has sought for a number of years to dispose of his interest in The New York Age. . . . When he found a satisfactory purchaser, he received his price, and the bargain was closed, and the most friendly and kindly relations exist between Mr. Fortune and the present ownership of the paper.[53]

Moore had received the notes, signed them, returned them to Scott, and the stock was transferred to him. "And everything is OK," he wrote Scott. "The dam niggers can now [say] what they please. Best thing to do is to retain a stiff upper lip. Pay no attention. The only way to kill a *darky* or any one else is not to notice him." But the matter was not ended. Washington sent a copy of the *Age* statement about ownership to George L. Knox, publisher of the *Indianapolis Freeman*, a paper which regularly received small amounts of financial support from Washington, with a request that he publish it "so as to refute the

---

vember 20, 1907, Washington Papers. Scott's letter to Moore showed that, in addition to the stock held for Washington, Scott personally held stock in the *Age* with a face value of $3,500 which was not transferred to Moore.

53. *Age*, November 21, 1907.

CHAPTER NINE

falsehood which has been pretty industriously circulated by a certain element."[54] The appearance of the statement in the *Freeman* caused Fortune to speak out. From Chicago he wrote a letter which Knox published and which said that statements in both the *Age* and *Freeman* were misleading. He asserted:

> The Age states a possible fact when it declares that Dr. Washington does not own a dollar's worth of stock in the New York Age Publishing Company. You say, "Mr. Washington insists that the charge (that he owns stock) is a falsehood, which has been circulated by those who know what such a charge means. . . ."
> Who circulated the "charge"? What does such a "charge" mean? . . . I have no dirty linen to wash in private or public. My dirty linen is entirely a personal matter, between God and me.
> Now while The Age was about it why did not President Fred R. Moore tell the whole truth? While Mr. Washington was "insisting" why did he not "insist" as to the whole business? What is there to conceal? Nothing but the facts. Will they hurt Mr. Washington or Mr. Moore? They appear to think so. . . .
> When I sold my 1,250 shares of stock to Mr. Moore last September and took his paper in payment for most of it, Jerome B. Peterson owned 1,250 and Booker T. Washington owned 950 shares, Emmett J. Scott being stockholder of record. . . . If Mr. Washington has disposed of his stock I don't know it and don't care about it.[55]

Other Negro papers seized on Fortune's letter, reprinted it, and commented on it editorially. The *Richmond Planet* remarked that the fact that Fortune had broken his silence was to be "attributed to the lack of judgment on the part of the edito-

54. Moore to Scott, November 23, 1907; Washington to George L. Knox, November 24, 1907, Washington Papers. Emphasis as in original.
55. *Indianapolis Freeman*, December 14, 1907.

[320]

rial management of the New York *Age*. It would have been well to pass over in silence the aspersions and innuendos concerning ownership." The *Guardian* gleefully reprinted the letter under headlines which screamed: "FORTUNE SAYS BOOKER DID OWN NEW YORK AGE STOCK." Fortune's revelation, it declared, confirmed that Washington had been trying to deceive the public. It was impossible for anyone "any longer honestly [to] eulogize Booker Washington as an unselfish, clean, conscientious man and educator of his race much less compare him in character to Jesus Christ."[56]

The sensation created by Fortune's letters soon died down. His revelation had merely confirmed what Washington's black critics had already been saying, and most of the white philanthropists whose good will Washington cultivated were oblivious of the whole affair. Fortune no doubt purged himself of some of his pent-up resentment over his dependence on Washington and his bitterness toward Roosevelt by his outbursts to the press. He probably felt that he had vindicated his manhood by publicly defying and embarrassing Washington, but the letters to the press did not mean that he was really reclaiming his independence, for Fortune was a broken man. Within a few months he was again seeking the support of the Tuskegee Wizard. But Washington no longer feared Fortune or needed his services; for when he lost the *Age*, Fortune's influence ceased.

56. *Richmond Planet*, December 21, 1907; *Boston Guardian*, December 28, 1907. It seems that John Milholland of the Constitution League also took satisfaction in Washington's embarrassment. An envelope on stationery of the League and apparently addressed by him was mailed to "Mr. Booker T. Washington, Editor and Proprietor of the Age" (Moore to Washington, December 30, 1907, Washington Papers).

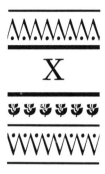

Years of Degradation

B Y THE YEAR'S END FORTUNE WAS BACK IN NEW YORK. PLANS for publishing *The Voice* in Chicago had been abandoned. We hear no more of the mysterious woman who had accompanied him to Chicago; apparently that episode was finished. Fortune's mental aberrations continued to be the subject of gossip, and in his abnormal state he was exploited by persons who called themselves his friends.[1]

1. Whitfield McKinlay wrote Scott: "I told Mr. W. sometime ago that the most fortunate thing for F would be to have someone lock him up in a sanatorium for a couple of years. For years I have dreaded the thought that he would do some foolish thing that will reach the ears of the hostile white press that will cause the whole race to wish that he had never been born. I never thought he was well balanced and recent events have proved it" (McKinlay to Scott, February 16, 1908, Woodson Collection).

He tried without success to persuade Moore to take him and Max Barber onto the *Age*. He then announced his plans to "resurrect" *The Freeman* as a monthly magazine. The first issue appeared February 1, 1908. Fortune evidently cashed one of the notes which Moore had given him to launch the venture, but the magazine survived for only two or three issues. Then, completely without funds, he begged Moore for a job, and Moore hired him temporarily to write editorials for the *Age*. Fortune was without money for food, Moore wrote to Washington, and was delighted when Moore agreed to pay him fifteen dollars a week for his work, with the understanding that he would not write anything of which Moore did not approve. "When a man *cries* to you what are you going to do?" asked Moore.[2]

But any help which the new editor gave to the former editor of the *Age* was given grudgingly. Moore evidently feared a rapprochement between Fortune and Washington and so persistently sought to emphasize Fortune's worthlessness and drunkenness and "disloyalty" and "ingratitude" in letters to Tuskegee. When Fortune first returned to New York, Moore reported that his religious obsession was a "farce" and that he had spoken abusively of Washington and Scott. He advised Washington not to see Fortune except in the presence of a third party. A few days later he wrote that he wanted to talk to Washington about Fortune, who was "the meanest man" he had ever met. To Scott he wrote that Fortune was "a bad egg." He was quiet, wrote Moore, and said he was getting along "O.K.," but he kept trying to "catch" Moore by asking him

2. Moore to Washington, December 30, 1907; Dr. Daniel Williams to Washington, January 16, 1908; Moore to Scott, March 18, 1908, Washington Papers; Fortune to Washington, March 3, 1908; Fortune to Carrie Fortune, March 25, 1908, Fortune Papers; *Washington Bee*, January 25, 1908; *Indianapolis World*, February 8, 1908. Emphasis as in original. Barber soon abandoned plans to come to New York and stayed in Chicago as a member of the staff of the *Conservator*.

questions about his relations with Washington. When he gave Fortune employment on the *Age*, Moore assured Scott that he had "again thrashed over his past disloyalty" before agreeing to hire him. But Fortune stayed with the job only three weeks and quit—to Moore's relief—after having been drunk for six days. "I am still of the same way of thinking," said the self-righteous Moore, "T.T.F. is entirely unappreciative and ungrateful."[3]

After that Fortune was virtually a derelict, without work and without money and without prospects of either. He spent much of his time sitting in parks and was reduced to begging acquaintances for money in order to eat. "As for my luck," he wrote Carrie, "it couldn't be worse, and if it sticks, so well; when I drop out I will be glad and will not be missed. As the life of me has been worthless to myself and to the rest of mankind. It looks that way and that is the way I feel about it. Who is to blame? That is an academic question." For a time he was in such an abnormal state that Carrie considered asking Washingington's assistance in having him committed to a mental institution.[4]

In this desperate state of affairs his only source of income was the notes which Moore had given him in payment for his interest in the *Age*. He was compelled to borrow against them and to sell them at a discount. Moore (who received money from Washington to pay the notes as they fell due) advised the Wizard that he could save $1,000 if arrangements could be made to borrow money to pay off the remaining outstanding notes at a discount. J. Douglass Wetmore, the attorney, who professed to be a friend of Fortune's and who had loaned him some money and had already sold some of the notes for him, wrote Washington that Wilford Smith and an associate were dickering

3. Moore to Washington, December 30, 1907; January 21, 1908; Moore to Scott, March 18, April 7, 1908, Washington Papers.

4. Fortune to Carrie Fortune, May 29, 1908, Fortune Papers; Carrie Fortune to Washington, May 7, 1907, Washington Papers.

with Fortune to sell five of the notes (which had a face value of $2,500) for $1,500 and that Fortune had agreed to pay Smith $300 for selling the notes for him. Wetmore, however, reminded Fortune that he had promised to give him first option on the notes, and Wetmore offered to get the notes for Washington for $1,500 if he would pay him $150 for his services. Subsequently Wetmore bought the notes for $1,500, but Washington did not buy them from him, perhaps because he was fearful that the transactions might be publicized; but Wilford Smith and others were eager to buy the notes from Wetmore.[5]

What Fortune did with the money he received from the sale of the notes is not clear. Some of it was assigned to Carrie to be paid to her periodically by Wetmore. Apparently there was some difficulty in compelling Wetmore, whom Fortune described as "a tough proposition," to make the payments to Carrie. But there was not enough money to save Maple Hill. When he had gone to Chicago, Fortune had promised his wife that he would give her his equity in that property and she had returned there to live, but by November 1908 a foreclosure seemed imminent. Moore proposed that the property be deeded to the building and loan association which held the mortgage and of which he was president. He promised to allow Mrs. Fortune to live there until the property was sold and to give her any money he received in excess of the mortgage, interest, and taxes. Carrie continued to live there until 1910 when Maple Hill was sold under court order.[6]

5. Moore to Washington, March 30, April 7, May 16, 1908; Wetmore to Washington, July 27, August 4, August 10, 1908; Washington to Wetmore, August 13, 1908, Washington Papers. By February 1909 all the notes had been redeemed (Washington to Moore, February 20, 1909, Washington Papers).

6. Fortune to Carrie Fortune, May 29, December 2, 1908; May 10, 1910, and an undated letter, 1910; Wetmore to Carrie Fortune, November 13, 1908, Fortune Papers. In addition to giving Carrie the equity in Maple Hill, Fortune wrote to Carrie that he had sent her

Washington's relationship with Fortune during this difficult period remained ambiguous. Outwardly, at least, he did not appear to bear any grudge because of Fortune's letter to the *Guardian* or his revelation of the Tuskegee Wizard's financial interest in the *Age*. He wrote to Fortune about the plans for the annual Business League convention. Fortune replied that he had no suggestions, but he wrote to Scott that he and Washington were in "good sympathy and understanding again."[7] But Washington evidently instructed Moore to try to get possession of the letters which he had written to Fortune during the long period of their intimacy because he was afraid that Fortune might sell them or use them in some way to embarrass him. Moore wrote to Mrs. Fortune asking her to search for the letters. The letters were returned to Tuskegee, and some of the letters which Fortune had written to Washington and Scott were in turn sent to Mrs. Fortune, but the details of the transaction are not clear.[8]

---

exactly half of the money which he had at the time and would send her more when he had it (Fortune to Carrie Fortune, May 29, 1908).

7. Washington to Fortune, February 21, 1908; Fortune to Washington, February 28, 1908; Fortune to Scott, March 3, 1908, Fortune Papers; Washington to Fortune, February 26, 1908, Washington Papers.

8. Moore to Washington, May 6, 1908, Washington Papers; Moore to Carrie Fortune, June 8, 1908, Fortune Papers. According to Fortune's recollection at a later date, Mrs. Fortune told him that a friend of Washington's whom she refused to identify had visited her and tried to buy the letters since, he said, Washington was afraid that Fortune might use them against him. Later, when Fortune saw Washington in New York, he asked him if he would like to have the letters, and when Washington said that he would, Fortune went to Red Bank and collected the correspondence, which covered a period of eighteen years, and Mrs. Fortune sent it to Tuskegee (Fortune to Scott, July 4, 1913, Washington Papers).

Washington refused to loan money to Fortune to help him pay his rent and told him he was unable to help him secure an appointment to do literary work for the Republican National Committee. But somehow, probably through the aid of Clarkson, Fortune was placed on the payroll of the National Committee during the 1908 campaign. In spite of his strictures against Taft for his role in the Brownsville affair, Fortune had announced in the short-lived *Freeman* that he would support him for the nomination. During the campaign he wrote material in support of Taft which was published in Negro newspapers.[9]

Except for this brief stint, however, Fortune apparently was without employment. In December he wrote to Carrie, thanking her for a letter which she had sent him expressing sympathy, saying:

> I am very grateful, . . . [for] the sympathy you express for me in the desperate situation I am [in]. I am very grateful for your sympathy. We none of us live unto ourselves alone. . . .
>
> Let us hope for better times and that we all shall have more to eat and more peace of mind. I also have had a hungry stomach many times since the storm began to blow and haven't change for food for a day ahead now. The storm must spend its force after a while. Let us pray as we hope.[10]

A few months later he wrote her: "I am feeling a shade better than when I last wrote you and am still striving to be placed so as to help you as well as myself. *It is a desperate* job but I must succeed, and I hope soon to land something." In the

9. Washington to Fortune April 20, July 16, 1908; Anderson to Washington, September 29, October 12, 1908; Moore to Washington, October 14, 1908; Washington to William Howard Taft, March 7, 1908; Taft to Washington, March 10, 1908; Scott to Fortune, November 3, 1908, Washington Papers.

10. Fortune to Carrie Fortune, December 2, 1908, Fortune Papers.

same letter he told her he was sending her the deed to one of the small lots in Florida which they still owned, hoping that it might be worth something to her someday.[11]

During 1909 he worked briefly for various ephemeral Negro newspapers and intermittently wrote articles and editorials for the *Age*. But Moore resented his presence. He wrote Washington that Fortune was always "nosing" into everything and that "feeding him and giving him carfare" kept Moore's pocket empty. Fortune begged everyone for money. In August he and Roscoe Simmons planned to start a paper called "The National Voice," with Fortune as editor and Simmons furnishing the capital. But this evidently came to nothing. A few weeks later Phil Waters wrote Fortune that a group was interested in starting a new Negro paper in West Virginia, and he urged Fortune to inquire about work on it. "You know where you can eat and sleep indefinitely, ha, ha, need no money along this line," Waters added. This job, like many others, did not materialize, but Fortune continued to hear from Waters, who was one of the few old friends who did not forsake him in these troubled times. Waters told him that he had seen Emmett Scott and that Scott had spoken highly of him. Fortune wrote to thank Scott, adding: "Very few of the old friends have anything good to say of me; on the contrary they dog me so persistently everywhere I go with evil reports that I cannot make bread and butter." Scott replied that he was pleased to hear from Fortune and was distressed that Fortune was having such a hard time and wished that it was in his power to be of some service.[12]

11. Fortune to Carrie Fortune, March 9, 1909, Fortune Papers. Emphasis as in original.

12. Moore to Washington, July 9, August 3, 1909; Fortune to Scott, February 4, 1910; Scott to Fortune, February 10, 1910, Washington Papers; Waters to Fortune, September 25, 1909, Fortune Papers. John E. Bruce also wrote to Fortune to encourage him in his efforts to reenter journalism (Bruce to Fortune, November 2, 1909, Fortune Papers).

Another friend was Chris Perry of the *Philadelphia Tribune*, whom Fortune had known since his earliest days in journalism. Early in 1910 Fortune's luck and mental health took a turn for the better when Perry offered him a job on the *Tribune* as associate editor. He entered upon the work with small pay but renewed hope. He would try to make the editorial page as good as he had made that of the *Age*, he said. He had also begun to write occasional signed articles for the *Age* again and was pleased when Washington wrote to compliment him on one. "The pleasure of hearing from you again is like the pleasure of knowing that I am coming to my own again," he replied. In July Perry sent him to the annual Hampton Institute Conference, which he had attended regularly in the nineties. Here he was heartened by the cordiality of old acquaintances. He hoped to supplement his income from the *Tribune* by writing regular contributions to the *Age* but was unable to persuade Moore. Late in 1910 he began writing for the *Amsterdam News*, which had begun publication in 1909 as a rival of the *Age*.[13]

Meanwhile, as a reporter for the *Tribune* he had accompanied Booker T. Washington on a trip through Delaware which was made in behalf of the Business League. As a reporter for the *Tribune* he also attended the annual convention of the Negro Business League in New York City. At one session he sat on the platform, and after an address by Oswald Garrison Villard, Washington, who was presiding, presented him to the audience and asked him to speak. Fortune replied that he had come to the convention, after three years' absence, to see rather than be seen. After "three years of sickness and disability," he said, "I thought I could come again and look into the faces of

---

13. Fortune to Washington, May 9, July 18, 1910; Fortune to Scott, November 8, 1908, Washington Papers; Fortune to Carrie Fortune, May 26, 1910, Fortune Papers. He told Carrie that it was good to be on the *Tribune* and that he hoped to make good so as "to command a living wage before snow falls again."

those who are becoming veterans in the good work." He congratulated the league on its progress, endorsed what Villard had said, and sat down, after saying: "Now I do not want to begin to talk, for I have done my share during the thirty years or more of my activity in behalf of this people. I have no message to bring except one of encouragement."[14]

During these years when Fortune was enduring the torments of mental illness and was financially destitute, there must have been many times when Booker T. Washington regretted his decision to back Fred R. Moore financially in acquiring control of the *Age*. In the first place the usefulness of the *Age* as an instrument for propagating his views and reinforcing his position as race leader was weakened by the revelation of his financial relations with the paper, which confirmed the suspicions of many that he controlled the editorial policy. Secondly, under Moore the *Age* did not maintain the literary and journalistic qualities which had made it the most distinguished race paper. And although as national organizer for the Business League, Moore had expounded on the principles for developing successful Negro business enterprises, he failed to make the *Age* a business success.

Both Washington and Scott, who were interested in the quality of the *Age* as well as in using it to strengthen Washington's position, were chagrined at the appearance and content of the paper. One week the front page looked like a huge handbill, Scott commented. He wrote to R. W. Thompson, an experienced journalist (subsidized by Tuskegee) who wrote a newsletter from Washington which appeared in many Negro papers, about the editorial problems of the *Age*. Thompson agreed with

14. Fortune to Carrie Fortune, June 20, 1910, Fortune Papers; Fortune to Washington, July 18, 1910, Washington Papers; National Negro Business League, *Report of Eleventh Annual Convention, 1910*, pp. 12, 138.

him that Moore's ideas of journalism were "pitched too low" and that some of the material which he featured was "cheap." Moore failed to appeal to "the superior class of readers" whom the *Age* had always sought to attract. "The loss of Fortune is indeed a great loss," said Thompson, although he thought Fortune was too extreme an individualist to fit into the large outfit which Washington and Scott hoped to make of the *Age*. But, Thompson emphasized, the *Age* needed an editor. Washington later observed to Moore that the latter was publishing editorials by so many different people that "it is getting noised abroad throughout the country that the *Age* is edited by anybody who wants to write an editorial."[15]

In September 1908 George W. Harris, a graduate of Harvard, was employed as editor-in-chief of the *Age*, but this arrangement did not last long. The quality of the paper, in Scott's view, continued to deteriorate, and he protested to Moore over the increasing sensationalism of some of the contents, which Moore hoped would increase circulation. Moore could not even be relied upon to follow the political line which Washington expected him to follow. By 1910 Charles W. Anderson was denouncing Moore as "the messenger boy editor" and accusing him of perfidy to Washington and to the faction of the Republican party with which Washington and Anderson were identified. Washington replied that Moore would have to adapt the tone of the *Age* to Anderson's views, but in spite of Moore's financial obligations to him, the Tuskegee Wizard was not able to control Moore's political vagaries.[16]

15. Scott to Moore, March 3, 1908; R. W. Thompson to Scott, March 10, 1908; Washington to Moore, August 29, 1908, Washington Papers.
16. Washington to R. W. Thompson, September 17, 1908; Scott to Moore, September 28, 1910; Anderson to Washington, April 10, 1910; Washington to Anderson, April 15, 1910, Washington Papers. Anderson continued to complain to Washington about Moore's editorial policies and the publication of materials

Moreover, the business management of the *Age* and Moore's financial relations with Washington were chronically in an unsatisfactory state. Early in 1908 Wilford Smith submitted a proposed "declaration of trust" to Washington which he recommended that Moore execute in order to protect Washington's interests. The paper showed that all the money which Moore had used to purchase Fortune's stock had been furnished by Washington and Washington had promised to advance the money to redeem the notes which Fortune still held. It also showed that the stock held in Scott's name which had been transferred to Moore was in reality the property of Washington and that Moore had paid nothing for it. The paper said that Moore merely held the stock in trust and that he was obligated to transfer this stock any time that Washington directed him to do so and that he could not sell or transfer the stock except at Washington's direction. After executing the instrument, Moore was to be paid a monthly salary.[17]

Washington instructed Moore to have Peterson make out a weekly report showing receipts and expenditures and circulation of the *Age* but said that Peterson should not know that the report was to be sent to him. Moore was frequently delinquent in filing the reports. In September Washington complained that for the third time the report had not been filed. "There must be something wrong with an office that does not look after matters more systematically," he said. "We gain nothing by dilly dallying with people who do not do their

which he considered to be in bad taste. On one occasion Washington replied: "I have done my best in every way to get Mr. Moore to see the wisdom of his publishing a high-tone paper along constructive lines that should be free from anything that savors of personal journalism. I shall not give up my efforts, but I confess that it is a pretty hard task" (Washington to Anderson, June 11, 1911; undated latter, 1911, Washington Papers).

17. Smith to Scott, January 23, 1909; undated draft of declaration of trust, Washington Papers.

duty." He also complained to Moore over the state of house-keeping in the office of the *Age* and over various other delinquencies.[18]

Finally Washington employed a certified public accountant, Daniel C. Smith, to look into the business affairs of the paper. Smith found much to criticize. One practice which he deplored as contributing to the inefficiency of the operation was the employment of four of Moore's children on the staff of the *Age*. One daughter was the bookkeeper, a second the stenographer, while one son worked in the printshop and another was in charge of agents and distribution. Smith considered the staff incompetent. He discovered great confusion in the lists of subscribers and found that many persons were not notified when their subscriptions expired. He reported that he thought that the paper was operating at an average deficit of $200 a month.[19]

In a later report he said that subscriptions had declined considerably. When Washington sent Moore his salary one month, he said: "I very much hope that hereafter you will be able to make the business earn this salary," and urged radical changes in the operation of the office. But at the end of 1909 Moore told Scott that he was broke and urgently requested a loan of $250. Meanwhile Washington considered having a mortgage executed in his favor on the holdings of the *Age* in view of the money which he had been advancing. But Moore protested the proposal of a mortgage since he had been telling Peterson that he had been borrowing money at the bank to make up deficits and that

18. Washington to Moore, April 22, September 7, 1908, Washington Papers. On July 7, 1909, Washington again wrote to Moore, complaining that the monthly report had not been filed.

19. Daniel C. Smith to Washington, September 11, November 8, 1908, Washington Papers. The *Age*'s deficit was offset part of the time by a subsidy from the Republican National Committee. A memorandum in the Washington Papers shows that during the campaign of 1908, the *Age* received $200 a week, the *Indianapolis Freeman* $50 a week, and other papers lesser amounts.

the execution of the mortgage would reveal his indebtedness to Washington—a fact which both Washington and Moore wanted to conceal. Moore was not humbled by Washington's rebukes nor apparently embarrassed by his financial dependence upon him. Instead he expressed resentment and dissatisfaction with the Wizard's attitude. He insisted that he was operating the *Age* economically and pointed out that Washington should feel indebted to him, saying:

> In the purchase of Fortune's interest I saved you money, both by discounting and getting his interest at a smaller sum than anyone else could have gotten. . . . You have been protected, you have been able to say whatever you pleased without being known and I think this is a valuable asset to you. . . . You could not do this before and you could not say what you say now because the man at the helm [Fortune] was untrue. Now it strikes me that I am deserving of better consideration and better treatment, parsimony does not help anyone.[20]

By 1910, when Fortune had been humbled and had presumably "learned his lesson" and paid for his "disloyalty" to him, Washington was ready to be charitable. The fact that Fortune seemed to have recovered much of his mental vigor and was wielding his pen in the service of the *Amsterdam News* and the *Philadelphia Tribune* may also have caused him to decide to make a gesture in Fortune's behalf. Whatever his motive, the same Booker T. Washington who had connived at the purchase of Fortune's interest in the *Age* at a time when Fortune was unable to act rationally and responsibly, who had suggested to Moore that he hold the threat of foreclosing the mortgage on his home over Fortune's head to prevent him from telling the

20. Washington to Wilford Smith, January 7, 1909; Washington to Moore, May 11, July 5, 1909; Moore to Washington, January 19, 1909; March 23, 1910; Moore to Scott, December 20, 1909, Washington Papers.

truth about the ownership of the *Age*, this same Washington now proposed a public tribute to Fortune and his services to journalism. This was to take the form of soliciting subscriptions of money which would be presented to Fortune![21]

In January 1911 a form letter from Washington was sent to a long list of potential contributors. It said:

> A number of friends of Mr. T. Thomas Fortune are of the opinion that in some substantial way the Negro people should record the appreciation of his service to the Negro people during a season extending over more than thirty years.
>
> It has been suggested that a testimonial subscription fund be raised and I am of the opinion that such testimonial should be large enough to adequately express the deep sense of appreciation which I think the masses of our people everywhere feel.

Later a second letter was mailed which was identical with the first but included the assurance that the name of each contributor would be presented to Fortune and later would be published. About fifty persons responded to the appeal, contributing a total of $288.55, and Washington himself gave $16.40 to make the total slightly over $300! Washington assigned his two lieutenants, Charles W. Anderson and Fred R. Moore, to take charge of arrangements for the presentation. He sent the money to Anderson with instructions to use his own judgment as to the manner of presentation. Embarrassed perhaps that the amount was not greater, he wrote: "It was thoroughly understood by the donors and all concerned that this money is given not because of its intrinsic value to Mr. Fortune, but simply as indication of the race's indebtedness to him for his long and hard service in behalf of the progress of the race."[22]

21. Apparently Washington had conceived the idea of the testimonial during the summer of 1910 (Scott to Fortune, November 3, 1910, Washington Papers).

22. Copy of form letter, January 4, 1911; Moore to Scott, Feb-

When Scott had first mentioned the testimonial to Fortune, the latter had replied: "As to the Testimonial, I have nothing to say, because I do not know what to say. *I have starved so long,* losing home and everything else while doing so, so that the heart to feel anything but pain, has gone from me." After the money had been collected, he told Anderson that he preferred a private presentation, but Moore insisted upon a public ceremony. Anderson, with whom Moore was now at odds politically, declared that Moore was very much opposed to the whole business and insisted upon taking charge so that he could insure that the affair would be a failure. To Scott, Anderson expressed the opinion that Moore opposed the testimonial because "it seems quite possible that Fortune has braced up, and will be a force which must be reckoned with hereafter in this city." Moore, he said, hated Fortune with "that intensity which is only felt by a man who feels that he has wronged another, and that that other has the sympathy of a great many people who have no private axes to grind."

Meanwhile broadsides were distributed which announced:

A TESTIMONIAL TO
T. THOMAS FORTUNE
will be given at
Abbyssinian Baptist Church
242–46 W. 40th St.   Rev. A. C. Powell D.D., Pastor
Thursday Evening, March 9th, 1911
at 8:15 o'clock
Fred. R. Moore Will Preside

. . . .

The Public Are Cordially Invited!

_____

ruary 2, 1911; Anderson to Washington, February 17, February 20, 1911, Washington Papers. Emphasis as in original. A book in the Washington Papers labeled "Fortune Testimonial Fund" shows that 348 letters were sent and 64 replies received. Scott wrote to Fortune, March 2, 1911, that the amount contributed was not as large as it should be (Washington Papers).

But Moore devoted only five lines in the *Age* to the testimonial and refused to cooperate with the *Amsterdam News* in publicizing it.[23]

Fortune told Scott that he was reluctant to attend the meeting since Moore apparently intended that it should be "a frost," but was persuaded by Anderson and others to appear. Anderson reported to Tuskegee that the ceremony was poorly attended and that Moore, who presided, "knew he was guilty of making it a frost." When Wilford Smith, one of the speakers who paid tribute to Fortune, spoke of him as an uncompromising race champion, Moore interpreted this as an implied slur against Washington and launched into a long harangue in defense of the Tuskegeean, whom no one was attacking. Several other speakers praised Fortune as the foremost editor whom the race had produced, and, according to Anderson, Fortune replied in "a very sensible and discreet speech."[24]

Scott agreed that Moore must have deliberately tried to kill the meeting. "He is not a very inspiring person to have to work with," he remarked to Washington. To Anderson he said that it was unfortunate that the meeting had been "attended by so much that detracted from its dignity and real importance." It could have been, Scott went on to say, an occasion of "surpassing interest and one that would have knit Mr. Fortune to us much more strongly than is likely to happen as the result of the bungling way it was handled."[25]

23. Fortune to Scott, November 8, 1910; Anderson to Scott, March 6, March 11, March 13, 1911; Scott to Washington, March 10, 1911; Washington Papers. A copy of the broadside is in the Washington Papers. Emphasis as in original.

24. Fortune to Scott, March 8, 1911; Anderson to Scott, March 11, 1911, Washington Papers. Washington had wired both Moore and Anderson that he was anxious that the meeting be a great success (Telegram, Washington to Anderson, March 8, 1911, Washington Papers).

25. Scott to Washington March 10, 1911; Scott to Anderson,

Although Fortune's mental health was greatly improved by 1911, employment opportunities were so limited that he was barely able to subsist. The work on the *Tribune* evidently terminated because Perry could no longer afford to pay him. For several months the only steady income which he had was five dollars a week for writing for the *Amsterdam News*. He went to Rochester for a short time to work for the *Sentinel*, which had begun publication there but which soon collapsed. He wanted to return once more to the *Age*, but the wages which Moore offered were so small that he could not accept. In September 1911, however, after he had reestablished some of the ties with Washington, he returned to the *Age* as associate editor in charge of the editorial page, a position he held until September 1914. Moore reported to Scott that Fortune was "down and out" and that he had given him employment but had impressed upon him that he would "not stand for any antagonism to our friend [Washington] and that he of all men can little afford to be otherwise than friendly to him." Publicly the *Age* announced that Fortune was once again a member of the staff, that his health had been restored and that he was "now better equipped than ever before to deal with the living questions of the day. He always desired to be associated with his first love again, and we are glad to have him."[26]

March 13, 1911, Washington Papers. Washington did not attend the testimonial to Fortune, but a few days later he came to New York on one of his periodic visits. It was during this visit that the "Ulrich affair" occurred. Washington was assaulted by a white man, Henry Albert Ulrich, who claimed that the principal of Tuskegee had made advances to his wife. The episode created a sensation in the press, both white and Negro, but, so far as the author has been able to discover, extant papers contain no comments by Fortune on the affair. For a full account see Willard B. Gatewood, "Booker T. Washington and the Ulrich Affair," *Journal of Negro History* 55 (January 1970): 29–44.

26. Fortune to Scott, April 3, May 19, July 12, 1911; Fortune to

As editorial writer, Fortune did not have the same freedom which he had enjoyed when he was owner and editor, but some of the old Fortune was evident in his editorials. In 1912 the *Age* supported Taft over Roosevelt and the Progressives. This gave Fortune an opportunity to revive Roosevelt's responsibility for Brownsville and to call him "two-faced" on the race question. The Progressive party in the South was branded as a Lily White party. During the campaign a number of Negro intellectuals, including Bishop Walters and Du Bois, announced their support of Wilson. The *Washington Bee* made a particularly vicious attack on Walters for endorsing the Democratic candidate, but in the *Age* Fortune defended Walters as a great and good man. Chase responded with an attack on Fortune and his record, including his alcoholism. This caused Fortune to comment that if Chase wanted to discuss the whisky question he should begin with his own private bottle which he kept on the shelf in his office concealed in a dummy volume of Blackstone. Mr. Fortune had had "plenty of misfortune and trouble in the past seven years," the editorial concluded, "but he has met them all and conquered them all as he got to them."[27]

The *Age* was bitterly critical of the Wilson administration for segregating government employees in offices in Washington and for failure to appoint Negroes to office. Some of the Negroes who had voted for Wilson were also chagrined over evidences of his racism. The *Age* commented ironically: "Now we would not have Bishop Walters and his organization [NAACP?] feel for a second that we do not sympathize with

---

Washington, May 30, 1911; Moore to Scott, September 18, October 7, 1911, Washington Papers; *Age*, October 11, 1911. On the editorial page of the *Age* Moore was listed as publisher and editor; Lester A. Walton, Moore's son-in-law, as managing editor; Fortune as associate editor; Jerome Peterson as treasurer; Eugene L. Moore as advertising agent.

27. *Age*, 1912, passim; January 2, 1913.

them in the sack cloth and ashes wherewith the force of circumstances has clothed them. We still think that Bishop Walter's
white grandfather and not his colored father in heaven led him,
by the voice he said he heard, into the Democratic slaughter
house."[28]

Fortune took issue with Du Bois, who said in *The Crisis* that
the Wilson policy of segregating government employees was
bad, but "Bad as the Democrats may prove, they cannot outdo
William Howard Taft." And when Du Bois spoke of *"The Old
Age* of New York" as a "disreputable paper," Fortune chided
him. The *Age* was old, he said, but not disreputable. "Dr. Du
Bois peddled the Age when he was a boy in Great Barrington
and was glad to do it, and wrote some of his youngest and most
joyous smart things for it when he was a student. . . . But that
was a long time ago."[29]

With the return of his old vigor and editorial thrust, Fortune
also began to take to the lecture platform once more. Late in
1913 he went on a tour of Maryland, Virginia, and North
Carolina, speaking on "The Black Man's Burden."[30] The lectures were no doubt an attempt to supplement his income from
the *Age,* which failed to pay him a living wage as Moore continued to flounder in his efforts to make the paper a viable
business enterprise.

In February 1913 Washington wrote to Moore: "You must
realize by this time, as I have told you before, that it is absolutely
necessary for the *Age* to improve its financial standing, and I
think you will agree with me in stating that it will be impossible
for you to go on much longer carrying the burden of personal
debts which you are carrying without injuring your personal

28. *Age,* August 7, 1913.
29. Ibid.
30. Ibid., November 6, December 4, 1913. Fortune also appeared on the program of the National Negro Press Association in
August 1913, reading a paper on "The Press and Public Opinion."

reputation to such an extent that it will be impossible for you to have much influence as a newspaper editor." In May, Fortune wrote to Scott that he was leaving the *Age* once more because Moore could not afford to pay him for his work. Since his return to the paper in 1911, he said, his copy had been in every week two days ahead of the deadline and there had never been any complaints about his work. He was supposed to receive ten dollars a week, but the *Age* was $193.50 in arrears in paying him. He needed twenty-five dollars desperately to pay Fred's school expenses. "My lines are very hard," he said. "What am I to do? The Negro papers are not able to pay for extra work and the daily papers do not care for Negro productions of any kind. Under such circumstances I face the future with $5 in hand and 57 years as a handicap." "I don't need any more work," he said. "I need more pay for the work I am doing." Moore assured him that he did not want him to resign but was forced to reduce his pay to eight dollars a week, which Fortune was compelled to accept because he had no alternative.[31]

Scott attempted to intervene with Moore on Fortune's behalf. He had seen Fortune on a trip north, he told Moore. "I wish I could put into words how deeply touched I was to find Mr. Fortune coming back to his old self mentally, but somehow or other altogether 'off-gear' financially." He added:

> Mr. Fortune had been a friend to all of us for many, many years, and if it were possible for me to do anything at all for him, I would count it a privilege, but there is nothing that I personally can do. I feel like making a plea for him, but I know very well how you resent what you regard as outside meddling and hesitate to say anything at all beyond making the statement that I am sure that the fine editorial work that he is doing is surely worth Fifteen (15) Dollars per week. ... He needs all he can get, and he is "delivering the goods."[32]

31. Washington to Moore, February 17, 1913; Fortune to Scott, May 6, May 15, July 17, 1913, Washington Papers.
32. Scott to Moore, July 15, 1913, Washington Papers.

By the beginning of 1914 Fortune felt that the worst was past. "I feel . . . I am equal to more and better work than in the old days. The thing is to get the work, and I am gunning for it," he wrote Washington, asking him to let him write a signed column for *The Negro Farmer*, which was published at Tuskegee. He was also, he told the Wizard, planning to work for the *Advocate-Verdict* at Harrisburg, Pennsylvania, "a paper which does not seem very friendly to you at this time," while continuing to write for the *Age*. Washington replied that there was no opening on *The Negro Farmer*, and the job with the Harrisburg paper did not last long.[33]

In September 1914 Fortune severed his connection with the *Age*[34] and went to Washington as publisher and editor of the *Washington Sun*, a paper which had been launched a few months earlier. Where he got the money, if any, to assume this responsibility is not clear. The *Age* was still in arrears in paying his wages, and Moore refused to give him a note or other evidence of his indebtedness. Fortune had hoped to use the money which Moore owed him as a basis for credit for expenses incurred in connection with the *Sun*. He entered upon the new work with zest and optimism and expected to make the *Sun* pay its way although it had been badly managed and was operating at a deficit before he took over.[35]

33. Fortune to Washington, January 23, 1914; Washington to Fortune, January 28, 1914, Washington Papers.

34. Moore to Washington, September 30, 1914. On the recommendation of Charles W. Anderson, Moore employed James Weldon Johnson to write editorials when Fortune departed. Johnson it was understood, agreed to follow a "conservative and constructive" editorial policy (Moore to Washington, October 7, 1914, Washington Papers).

35. Fortune to Scott, September 19, 1914, Washington Papers. The *Sun*, which had offices at 1234 U Street, N.W., had begun publication early in 1914. The principal financial interest in the paper appears to have been held by Dr. Julia P. H. Coleman, but Fortune was listed as editor and publisher.

As editor of the *Sun*, Fortune was free to speak his own mind as he had not been since selling his interest in the *Age*. The *Harrisburg Advocate-Verdict*, with which he had been briefly associated, was an anti-Booker T. Washington publication, and through its columns Fortune himself had made some bitter comments about Washington and his associates. When he took the job on the Harrisburg paper, he had written to Washington: "You will have to acknowledge that Villard and Milholland have made off with the Negro in his civic rights sentiment, the gist of the whole business in all ages, and left us the husks, the educating of men in school and church and business for them to lead"—a reference to the rising influence of the NAACP, which Washington continued to oppose but whose program was close to the objectives which Fortune had enunciated in the Afro-American League and through the columns of the *Age*. But in the *Sun* Fortune defended Washington and Tuskegee. Soon after he took over the editorship, Washington wrote to tell him that he was grateful for the "many acts of kindness and interest" which Fortune was manifesting in the columns of his paper.[36]

Fortune replied that it was gratifying to know that Washington was appreciative of the policy he was pursuing and intended to continue to pursue concerning the Tuskegeean and his work. To Scott he implied that his editorial support would be advantageous to the Wizard because the city of Washington was a "hot bed" of the NAACP and opposition to Tuskegee. He blamed Chase of the *Bee* (which was evidently receiving a subsidy from Tuskegee) for his "vile and vacillating support of Dr. Washington and his policies." In later correspondence Fortune and Washington expressed implied criticism of the Negroes in the NAACP for their dependence on white leadership. "The white leadership is not after my way," declared Fortune, "and I say so in The Sun and out of it." Washington said

36. Fortune to Washington, January 24, 1914; Washington to Fortune, October 6, 1914, Washington Papers.

that the nation's capital was full of Negroes who had been educated by white people in northern institutions and who continued to worship at the feet of white men. "This type of black
people are mad in the first place," he said, "because God made
them black instead of white, and it is very hard to reconcile
them to anything that is rational."[37]

Washington invited Fortune to come to the annual Tuskegee Negro Conference, but Fortune replied that he was unable
to come because of lack of funds. Apparently Washington made
no effort to subsidize the *Sun* in spite of Fortune's avowals of
support, and by the end of 1914 the paper was in dire financial
straits and Fortune was again in ill health. He went back to New
Jersey, where living was cheaper than in Washington, to recuperate. In March 1915 it was announced that he was resigning
as editor of the *Sun* although he would continue to contribute
a column to it as he was doing for other Negro papers. Soon
after this he went west to join the *Indianapolis Ledger*, but the
demise of that paper came even more swiftly than that of most
Negro papers. By summer he was back in the East again, writing
editorials for the *Philadelphia Tribune*.[38]

In June of 1916 he also took charge of the editorial and literary departments of *The Colored American Review*, which
had begun publication a few months previously. It was a
monthly periodical which included editorials as well as articles
on such subjects as education, literature, the theater, and business. The announcement of Fortune's appointment said that he
had not been an active editor for nine years but had been laboring to recover from a nervous breakdown. The *Review* would

37. Fortune to Washington, October 8, November 4, 1914; Fortune to Scott, October 14, 1914; Washington to Fortune, November
2, 1914, Washington Papers.

38. Fortune to Washington, December 28, 1914; Fortune to
Scott, March 5, 1915, Washington Papers; *Washington Sun*, March
5, July 16, 1915; *Indianapolis Recorder*, August 16, 1915.

afford him "the best possible medium for the elaboration of his ideas on national and race questions." "We are sure," the announcement said, "that the race at large will benefit more from Mr. Fortune's future work than it did from his work from 1879 to 1907, as an active factor in race thought, agitation, organization, and material uplift."[39]

The first editorial which appeared after Fortune took over his duties was "President Wilson's Narrowness of Prevision," in which the president was attacked for failure to fulfill the promises "of broadness, fairness, and generosity," which he had made during his campaign. On the contrary, the editorial declared, he had gone farther than any president to adopt a sectional outlook toward Negro citizens and to turn public opinion against these citizens. "President Wilson has shown in all that he has said and done during his term of office that he has no place in his statesmanship for Colored American citizens, except one of subordination to white men such as the master class had before the War. He had his opportunity to make good as a broad American statesman and he failed." But another editorial spoke approvingly of the nomination of the humanitarian Louis Brandeis to the Supreme Court. When the Senate Judiciary Committee reported favorably on the appointment, every Negro who knew of Brandeis's record "lifted up his voice to heaven and from the depths of his heart cried Thanks unto Him who giveth us the victory."[40]

During the political campaign of 1916, with the support of Charles Anderson and Emmett Scott, Fortune was given the task of compiling a campaign booklet called "The Republican

39. Frontispiece, *The Colored American Review*, vol. 1, no. 9 (June 1916). The *Review* described itself as "a national monthly magazine of inspiration." Fortune was listed as editor, F. M. Robinson as president, E. T. Toussaint Welcome as vice-president and circulation manager, Louis Harris as secretary-treasurer and business manager. The offices were at 2305 Seventh Avenue.

40. *Colored American Review*, 1, no. 9 (June 1916): 245, 283.

Party and the Negro." In it he reviewed the benefactions which Negroes had received from the Republican party since the Emancipation Proclamation. On the other hand, since 1860 the Democratic party, especially in the South, had been consistently, maliciously antagonistic to Negroes, striving to undo what Republicans had accomplished. Democrats were responsible for disenfranchisement, segregation, and intimidation of southern Negroes. More recently they had been responsible for the enactment of residential zoning ordinances, and a Democratic president, Wilson, had adopted the policy of segregating government employees—a policy unheard of under Republican administrations. "As a matter of principle the Negro is a Republican, born and nurtured in the Republican Faith, and is against the Democratic party because it is and always has been against him."[41]

The work on *The Colored American Review* lasted only a few months. Thereafter, Fortune attempted to subsist by occasional contributions to the *Amsterdam News*, the *Age*, and other papers. Early in 1917 he was in Washington on some sort of work—perhaps an attempt to set up a Washington bureau for the *Age*—but this soon collapsed, and he was destitute again, asking Scott to loan him money to tide him over until he could find more work. But a few months later his fortune took a turn for the better when he was appointed assistant director of a Negro welfare bureau which the governor of New Jersey was setting up in response to the greatly increased migration of southern Negroes which had recently begun. The bureau, which was the first of its kind, was intended to help immigrants find employment and housing. Since there was a great need for farm

41. A draft of the introduction which Fortune wrote is in the Emmett J. Scott Papers, Soper Library, Morgan State College. Correspondence in the Scott Papers between Fortune and Scott during July and August 1916 deals with the preparation of the booklet. The segregation of federal employees in Washington had actually begun under Taft.

labor in the state, part of Fortune's work was to divert some of the newcomers from the cities to agricultural work.[42]

During these dark years Fortune lived alone—most of the time in a room in Trenton or Lawrenceville, New Jersey, where his expenses were minimal. In solitude he endured periodic fits of depression and nervousness which made it difficult to do his writing—if he was employed. He also had a tendency to chills, which, he told Carrie, he attributed to "the long nervous horror" with which he had to struggle. In 1912 he had proposed a reconciliation with Carrie, but she gave a negative answer, in part, apparently, because she feared assuming responsibility for him in his disturbed mental condition. He replied that he accepted her decision and the reasons she gave and appreciated her frankness. "You have done wisely in consulting your best interest in the decision you have made," he said. "It is not necessary for you to run the chance of being in any way responsible for me in the uncertain nervous condition which I inherited from my father and which has made my life an agony since we separated in 1906. . . . The high esteem in which we hold each other, the cordial relations of friendship and helpfulness we have sustained since the separation I hope will be sustained to the end."[43]

He visited Carrie occasionally, and they wrote long letters to each other in which they mentioned such trivial matters as what she should plant in the garden while she still lived at Maple Hill, and a new kitten which she had acquired. When Fred considered leaving the high school at Red Bank to go to work to

42. Fortune to Scott, March 21, 1917, Scott Papers; *Trenton Daily State Gazette*, October 31, 1917.

43. Fortune to Carrie Fortune, May 26, June 20, 1910; September 27, 1912, Fortune Papers. So austere was his life that the expenditure of 20 cents for carfare from Philadelphia to attend the commencement exercises of the Bordentown School was an event worth mentioning in a letter to Carrie.

supplement the family income, his father insisted that he must graduate from high school and make plans to attend Rutgers. He was very proud of Fred. "He has a very high order of intellect," he told Carrie. He also took satisfaction in the fact that Fred made a brilliant record in track meets during his high school days. He was even more pleased that Fred was selected to give an oration when he graduated from high school. Both Carrie and Jessie sent him pictures of Fred and long letters about the graduation exercises, but Fortune was unable to attend the graduation, nor did he see any of the track meets in which Fred distinguished himself.[44]

To Carrie he wrote: "I am very sorry that I could not have seen him in at least one of the meets. You deserve full credit for what you have done for him in the matter of his education, as in that of Jessie, and I very freely grant you the credit due you. If I have had any part in it, in the case of Fred or of Jessie, I am not able to put my hands upon it at this moment. What it has been stands for itself and will count for itself. We can mutually rejoice that they are as good and accomplished as they are, and indulge in the pleasing hope that they may grow progressively better and more accomplished with the passing of the years."[45]

Somehow Fred was able to continue his education beyond high school and to graduate from Meharry Medical College. Some of the money for his education came from the sale of some real estate which Fortune had inherited from his father. Some of it Carrie scraped together, though how she did it is not clear, and some of it Fred earned himself. Jessie, who was teaching in the New York City schools, probably made a contribution to Fred's education as well as helping to support her mother during these lean years.

With Jessie, Fortune's relations were always warmer and

44. Fortune to Carrie Fortune, March 25, December 2, 1908; May 26, June 20, 1910, Fortune Papers.

45. Fortune to Carrie Fortune, June 3, 1910, Fortune Papers.

more affectionate than with Carrie or Fred. While she was teaching, Jessie met Aubrey Bowser, a young Harvard graduate, who was also a teacher and for a time the New York correspondent of the *Boston Guardian*.[46] Fortune was pleased when Jessie and Bowser were married, and his relationship with his son-in-law was cordial. During the summer of 1913 Jessie spent several weeks with her father at Lawrenceville, New Jersey, recuperating after the birth of twin babies who died. "Mrs. Bowser is with me," Fortune wrote Scott, "and it is a great comfort. She is intensely literary, musical and companionable."[47]

In spite of the cooling of relations with Booker T. Washington—Fortune told Scott that he considered his friendship with Washington dead—his relationship with Scott remained affectionate, and he probably poured out his troubles to the younger man as he did to no other person. Sometimes he asked Scott for money, and Scott responded to these pleas when he could and was distressed when he was unable to help his old friend. Whenever Scott came to New York, Fortune would try to see him, and once or twice Scott visited Fortune in New Jersey. After one of these brief visits Fortune wrote that it had been good to see Scott again and to hear his voice. "I have had no friends and associates since 1907," he said, "having fought out alone in sickness, poverty and solitude the demons of nervous disorders that make men poor indeed." Scott told Fortune that it lay very strongly on his heart that he was unable to help him in his financial difficulties. "I can only repeat what I have often said," he wrote, "and that is that my ship will never come in bringing me any treasures, which shall not also be for you. A debt of grati-

46. Fortune to Carrie Fortune, September 12, 1912, Fortune Papers. In the *Guardian* Bowser wrote an attack on Fred R. Moore, blaming him for taking the *Age* away from Fortune (Anderson to Washington, October 29, 1910, Washington Papers; interview by author with Aubrey Bowser, January 1956).

47. Fortune to Scott, May 15, July 12, July 22, 1913, Washington Papers.

tude I am under to you far out-weighs any possibility of my ever properly discharging it."[48]

The feeling that he was an outcast, the humiliation of his poverty and inability to hold a job, the guilt which he felt over his failure to fulfill his obligations to his family—all these undoubtedly made Fortune's recovery the more difficult. His experience was the more painful to a person as proud as he had been and one who had been hailed as brilliant and had become accustomed to admiration and applause. He evidently felt that his illness was some sort of punishment from God. In 1914 he wrote Scott that *"the seven years* have been lived in death," but he believed that now that they were past he would once more be able to make his way as he had before 1907. But the punishment did not cease after seven years although his mental vigor was restored. In 1917, unemployed, with no prospects of a job, he cried: "What a desperate condition I have had the past ten years. It would have been better to be dead!" A few weeks later he told Scott that he thought the agony was about finished and that the Comforter was about to come, and he was glad. He treasured Scott's sympathy and efforts to help him the more, he said, because most of his former friends, as well as his enemies, had been against him "actively or passively." "I have learned more and more," he said, "during the past eleven years, while working my way out of spiritual and physical darkness, how to value kindly expressions, because so many unkindly and ungenerously [*sic*] ones have pursued me."[49]

When he wrote these words to Scott, the worst was over and better times were to come, although Fortune was unaware of this. During the years of mental illness and degradation, he had learned much and seems to have gained a tolerance and

48. Fortune to Scott, October 21, 1912; Scott to Fortune, February 11, February 25, 1914, Washington Papers.

49. Fortune to Scott, February 25, 1914, Washington Papers; Fortune to Scott, March 21, April 9, 1917, Scott Papers. Emphasis as in original.

humility as well as stability which he had lacked in the years when he was editor of the *Age* and ally of Booker T. Washington. He never again enjoyed the prestige of his earlier years, but he regained his self-respect and in his last years became once more an esteemed member of the journalistic profession.

XI

"Dean of Negro Journalists"

IN SPITE OF HIS PREMONITIONS OF AN EARLY DEATH FORTUNE lived beyond the allotted three score and ten years, dying in 1928 at the age of seventy-one. During his last years he appears to have experienced a complete mental recovery and to have found a peace denied him earlier.

Booker T. Washington died more than twelve years before Fortune—in November 1915. Following his death Fortune wrote an article, "The Quick and the Dead," which appeared in the *A.M.E. Church Review* in April 1916. In the article, which was a kind of apology for his own life, Fortune reviewed his relationship with Washington, evaluated Washington's role as a race leader, and sought to establish his own place in history. He divided the history of race leadership into three periods. The first period was that of the preeminence of Frederick Douglass, which extended from 1841, when Douglass made his first address, to 1884, when he lost much of his influence as the result of his marriage to Miss Pitts, a white woman. The years of Douglass's ascendancy were characterized by Fortune as the period of the "Colored American." Douglass had been the *spokesman,* he said, but not the *leader* of the race, and in the years following the Civil War his position had been contested by John Mercer Langston and others. The "Afro-American" period of leadership had begun in 1880, when at the age of twenty-four Fortune began his editorial career in New York. The years from 1880 to 1900 had been devoted to agitation for political independence among northern Negroes, civil rights, and elimination of discrimination in transportation and places of public accommodation. In trying to achieve these objectives Fortune had the advice of Douglass, Langston, George T. Downing, and others. The organization of the National Afro-American League in 1890 had been an important step in the struggle. But the race had not supported the league, and devotion to it had been a drain on Fortune's financial resources and had left him impoverished.[1]

During the 1890s he and Booker T. Washington had become close friends and coworkers. They had developed a working understanding that Fortune should continue to pursue "the radical course" which he had always pursued and that Washington should "pursue the course of diplomacy he had mapped out for himself," but that he would not write or say anything which Fortune regarded as injurious to Washington or to the race. The first quarrel between the two men had occurred when Washington became involved in politics as "adviser extra-ordinary of President Roosevelt" and endorsed a southern policy which Fortune did not approve. Washington had also protested against Fortune's "unsparing condemnation" of Roosevelt for the discharge of the Brownsville soldiers. In 1904, Fortune recalled,

1. Fortune, "The Quick and the Dead," *A.M.E. Church Review,* April 1916, pp. 247–48.

his health had begun to fail, and it "failed utterly" in 1907. After the Topeka meeting of the Business League his health had compelled him to dispose of the *Age* and begin the long struggle to recover his "nervous control," which was now, ten years later, quite complete.

In 1904, Fortune continued, after his health had begun to deteriorate and he had resigned as president of the Afro-American Council, Washington had become the active leader of the "Negro people" but not of the "Afro-American people," as Douglass had been the leader of the "Colored Americans, who have neither race nor people, being eth[n]ical non-descripts, derelicts of the undistinguishable mixed multitude no man can number." Washington had been leader of the "Negro people" until 1915, "but without their selection or election, and because white men labeled him leader after the Atlanta address in 1895, and gave him plenty of money to carry out the purposes of his leadership." Fortune added: "I helped make him leader, . . . and if I had to go over it all again I would do for him just what I did do, because I thought then, and think now, that we needed to build up the educational and business interests of the race, so that it might have some intelligence and money to back up its much-talked about justice and equality in the citizenship of the nation." Dr. Washington, he said, was a very great man who had done a very great work, but it was not the same work as Douglass had done from 1841 to 1880, nor such work as Fortune had done from 1880 to 1904. "I had everything in common with Mr. Douglass and his methods," wrote Fortune, "and nothing in common with the policies of Dr. Washington, especially his personal and political ones. His work was necessary to be done, and I helped rather than hindered him in the doing of it."[2]

After he had lost his health and the *Age*, Fortune said, Washington had had no further use for him. They had seen each other only five times after the sale of the *Age*. "We did not

2. Ibid., pp. 249–50.

fall out and quarrel"; he said, "we were on speaking terms to the last, but he had no further use for me in his business because I had lost my health and my newspaper, and because with my assistance he had been able to reach the point of leadership where he did not want friends to advise him, but persons to do what he wanted done."[3]

In the years following Washington's death Fortune continued to live by his writing. He was associated with so many papers for short periods of time that it is impossible to compile a complete list. In 1919, when he was more than sixty years old, he considered taking a course in operating a linotype machine to escape the uncertainty and poverty of living by work on Negro papers, but there is no evidence that he actually took the course. He contributed regularly to the *Amsterdam News* and a short-lived paper, the *Washington Eagle*. During the early 1920s he was in Memphis, editing the *Negro Outlook*. In 1919 he began writing for the *Norfolk Journal and Guide* and continued that association until his death. From 1922 until his last illness he wrote editorials and features, and in 1923 his name began to be listed as contributing editor in recognition of his editorials. Later he began writing a weekly column, called at first "The Way of the World" and later "The Passing Show," in which he expressed his opinions on all manner of current issues and reminisced about the past. Among his last contributions was a series of articles, "After War Times," in which he recalled his boyhood in Florida. During the twenties he also became a contributing editor of *The Hotel Tattler*.[4]

But his most important journalistic work during the last years of his life was once again in New York as editor of *The Negro World*, the publication of Marcus Garvey's Universal Negro Improvement Association. Fortune assumed the position of editor in 1923 and held it until his death.

3. Ibid., p. 250.
4. Fortune to Scott, May 5, 1919; May 18, 1920, Scott Papers; *Norfolk Journal and Guide*, October 6, 1923.

The Manhattan of the twenties, in which the UNIA flourished, was a very different place from the city in which he had launched the *Globe* forty years earlier. By 1920 two-thirds of the burgeoning black population lived in Harlem, in an area between 130th and 145th Streets and Fifth and Eighth Avenues. By that time every major Negro institution, including the *Age* and the *Amsterdam News*, had moved northward. The offices of *The Negro World* were at 52 West 135th Street, in the heart of the business district and near the One Hundred Thirty-Fifth Street Library, which was becoming the cultural center of Harlem.[5] It was the era of the Harlem Renaissance and the New Negro.

Fortune's association with the Garvey movement was rather remarkable in light of his earlier record. In the nineties, as we have seen, he had heaped scorn upon Bishop Henry M. Turner and other advocates of Back-to-Africa movements. His own goals, frequently reiterated, had been the winning of the rights guaranteed by the United States Constitution and the assimilation of Afro-Americans into American society and institutions. In later years he had certainly become increasingly skeptical about the good will and cooperation of white Americans in the achievement of these goals and more convinced that Afro-Americans would have to fight their own battles. As the Negro population in the urban North had increased, his own life had become increasingly segregated and his contacts with white Americans fewer, but he had never shown any sympathy for the kind of racial separateness which Garvey advocated. Although he was not a convert to the ideology of Garvey, however, he had confidence in the latter's honesty and admired him for his ability to arouse and mobilize the Negro masses as no other leader had done.

Emmett J. Scott, who had become registrar of Howard University, was a Garvey convert, as was John E. Bruce, with

5. Gilbert Osofsky, *Harlem: The Making of a Ghetto* (New York, 1967), pp. 120, 128–30, 180–82.

[357]

whom Fortune remained on friendly terms. Both Scott and Bruce were awarded the rank of KNON (Knight Commander of the Distinguished Order of the Nile) by Garvey.[6] Fortune's contacts with Garvey appear to have come primarily through Bruce. For Bruce, who, unlike Fortune, had always opposed racially mixed schools and interracial marriages, conversion to Garvey's ideology was a logical step, although he at first opposed Garvey's schemes as chimerical and impossible of achievement. But after he heard Garvey address throngs of Negroes on his visions of brotherhood, mutual protection, and the fostering of black business enterprises, Bruce decided that his ideas were not only good, but practical. The interest which Garvey inspired among Negroes all over the world showed, said Bruce, that Garvey had

caught the vision; that the people of color throughout the world, believe in his leadership and want him to lead them. . . . The old leaders were not able or were too lazy or indifferent or both, to work out a plan for the redemption and regeneration of the Race, as attractive and practical from any angle in which it is viewed, as that of Marcus Garvey.

Bruce considered Garvey scrupulously honest and had a higher opinion of him than of other "professed race leaders" whom he had known. He wrote a column for *The Negro World* and wrote for the *Daily Negro Times*, another Garvey paper which was published in 1923 and 1924.[7]

In 1922 an editorial in the *Norfolk Journal and Guide*, probably written by Fortune, spoke charitably of Garvey and said that most of his business schemes had turned out badly not because they were inherently impractical but because the race

6. Fortune to Bruce, February 24, 1923, Bruce Papers; E. David Cronon, *Black Moses: The Story of Marcus Garvey and the Universal Negro Improvement Association* (Madison, Wis., 1955), pp. 47, 48, 69–70.

7. Undated manuscript, Bruce Papers.

was not able to finance them. After Garvey was convicted in federal court on charges of using the mails to defraud, another editorial declared: "Marcus Garvey is down and out, but he taught us that mass organization of African people is possible because he accomplished it."[8]

Later the same year (1923) Fortune became editor of *The Negro World*. During his association with the paper, Garvey was either in prison or in exile. While Fortune was listed as editor, Garvey continued to be listed as managing editor, and his wife, Amy Jacques Garvey, as associate editor. Every issue of *The Negro World* carried a front page editorial which was either a message from Garvey or something taken from his writings, or a message from the editors urging Garvey's followers to appeal to President Coolidge to pardon their leader, or some other plea on his behalf. But of necessity there was less emphasis on Garvey and the movement than earlier, and the publication became more of a general newspaper. There was news of branches of the UNIA and other matters of race interest in the United States and news of colonial and oppressed peoples all over the world. There was a page in the Spanish language which was of particular interest to Spanish speaking immigrants from the West Indies, and a woman's page edited by Amy Jacques Garvey. Fortune was in charge of the editorial page and wrote most of the editorials, which ranged over a wide variety of subjects—from Coolidge's efforts at governmental economy to the threatened breakdown of the League of Nations. But the emphasis was on subjects of interest to Negro readers, such as the United States' policy in Haiti.[9]

In an editorial in the *World*, Fortune spoke approvingly of an article in the *Nation* by E. Franklin Frazier in which the latter said that other race leaders, including Washington and Du Bois, and organizations like the Urban League and the

8. *Norfolk Journal and Guide*, July 29, 1922; June 30, 1923.
9. *Negro World*, May 21, 1927.

NAACP had failed to attract mass support because they lacked the "dramatic element" of the Garvey movement. Wrote Fortune:

> What was the dramatic element lacking in these contemporary organizations, as it was also in the National Afro-American League, the forerunner of them all, organized by T. Thomas Fortune, in 1890? The lacking dramatic element was the direct and insistent appeal of Mr. Garvey to the race, nationality and self interest of the Negro people—the conservation of their social, civic and economic values, with the redemption of Africa from white rule and exploitation and the building of an African State by the Negroes for the Negro in Africa.

The editorial compared Garvey to other anticolonial leaders. He was doing for Africa what Ghandi was doing for India and what Sun-Yat-Sen had done for China. He was sowing "the seed of racial integrity and the seed will come ultimately to fruitage." In other editorials, however, Fortune stated that, while working for the redemption of Africa, the main objective of the Garvey movement, Negroes in the United States must not sacrifice the rights guaranteed them by the United States Constitution. "The more we value our opportunities, the more we save and have, the better able will we be to assist the Universal Negro Improvement Association in its program of race upbuilding and national rehabilitation."[10]

In lauding the role of Garvey, the *World* took some jabs at W. E. B. Du Bois, who, while seeking to promote Pan-Africanism, was disdainful of Garvey. One editorial accused Du Bois of stealing Garvey's thunder. Fortune attended the session of the Pan-African Congress in New York City in September 1927. He said that he was unable to agree with the opinions expressed by Professor Rayford W. Logan, who said that it was not to be expected that Europeans could be driven out of Africa and that

10. Ibid., July 3, August 28, 1926; May 14, 1927.

the natives should go along and learn from the white Europeans. This, said Fortune, was the old theory "of the lion and lamb lying down together without a row because the lamb was inside the lion." But Du Bois was the most important figure at the conference; in fact he *was* "very largely the Pan-African Congress," and Fortune attacked him bitterly for his attitude toward Garvey. "Dr. Du Bois," he observed, "has no love for Marcus Garvey, and, naturally, Mr. Garvey has no love for Dr. Du Bois." While Du Bois was reading a list of resolutions which had been presented by a committee, someone introduced a resolution from the floor, expressing sympathy for Garvey and asking Coolidge to extend executive clemency to him. Many persons in the audience applauded the suggestion, and one speaker lauded Garvey, but Du Bois insisted that the resolution must go to the committee for consideration, and thus killed it. *The Negro World* attacked this action of Du Bois as evidence of his pettiness, but declared: "We think that Dr. Du Bois will grow to the point of bigness to realize that Africa and the Negro people are very large problems which should have the active sympathy and cooperation of all the thinking persons of the race, to whatever organizations of racial uplift and betterment they belong."[11]

When Garvey was pardoned by Coolidge, Fortune wrote in the *Journal and Guide* that he was of the opinion that Garvey had never been proved guilty of fraud.

I have been very close to Mr. Garvey, as editor of the newspaper. . . . He is a man of unusual ability, strength of character and determination of purpose, and strictly honest. He is a fanatic on the redemption of Africa from white over-lordship and exploitation, a great big job, and he has done more than any other Negro to unify race sentiment and cooperation under Negro leadership upon an international basis. He has constrained the Negro to think Negro, as the

11. Ibid., September 23, 1927.

Jew thinks Jew, and that is a very great achievement, something no other Negro ever did. . . . To redeem Africa, to unify Negro sentiment and cooperation, to teach the Negro to conserve his social, civil and economic values, under Negro leadership and financed by Negroes—that is a worthwhile program.[12]

Fortune served Garvey and the UNIA well, although there is no evidence that he actually "joined" the movement or belonged to any of the various orders associated with it as John E. Bruce and others did. He continued writing editorials for *The Negro World* almost to the day of his death. An editorial following his death expressed gratitude for what he had done. At the time he became editor, it said, Marcus Garvey and the UNIA were passing through Gethsemane, and Fortune had "towered a mighty bulwark against the pettiness and prejudice and chicanery of those Afro-American enemies of the movement." In addition,

his seasoned counsel, his stirring faith, and the balance and nice judgment that come only with the years were of inestimable value to the Universal Negro Improvement Association, while fear of the pen—which could excoriate and crush amazingly, when occasion demanded—in the hands of a man to whom the earliest deeds or misdeeds of contemporary leaders, in whatever walk of life, were as an open book, mitigated the fury or silenced the waspish tongues of many who longed for Marcus Garvey's head.[13]

In spite of his services to the Garvey movement and his admiration for Garvey himself, Fortune certainly did not subscribe to the separatist doctrines and abdication of demands for Negro rights in America which caused Garvey to give at least tacit support to the Ku Klux Klan and to meet with some of the

12. Fortune, "The Passing Show," *Norfolk Journal and Guide*, December 13, 1927.
13. *Negro World*, June 9, 1928.

Klan leaders. To the end, he retained his contempt and defiance of white supremacy doctrines and white supremacists. The same *Negro World* editorial which praised his devotion to Garveyism also praised his personal courage and spirit. "T. Thomas Fortune, at three score and ten, would have grappled with an insulting 'cracker' on a farm in Florida," it said. He also retained his political independence and skepticism about the good faith of both major parties so far as the rights of Negroes were concerned. He supported John W. Davis, the Democrat, rather than Coolidge in 1924 because Davis "came out manfully" against principles endorsed by southern Democrats, while Coolidge remained silent on the subject of the Ku Klux Klan.[14]

As the campaign of 1928 approached, Fortune declared that Al Smith was the only possible Democratic nominee. He did not think that Democrats should be concerned about the possible defection of southern voters because of Smith's stand on Prohibition. He pointed out the inconsistency of the South's insistence on the enforcement of the Eighteenth Amendment. "If Southern whites insist upon the enforcement of the eighteenth amendment and the Volstead Act," he asked, "why do they squirm so when the fourteenth amendment and its enforcement is slipped under their nose? Consistency ain't always a jewel." He had no faith in the Democratic party. "It is simply a party in opposition, an opportunist party, which thrives only on the mistakes of its opponents," he said. Nor did he have any faith in the Republican leaders—Coolidge, Hoover, and Hughes—none of whom had any genuine interest in Afro-Americans and their rights.[15]

He never retreated from his insistence that Negroes, as United States citizens, should claim and fight for all the rights

14. Ibid.; Fortune, "The Passing Show," March 24, 1928. For Garvey's relations with the Ku Klux Klan see Cronon, *Black Moses,* pp. 187–90. Garvey supported Coolidge in 1924.

15. Fortune, "Passing Show," March 10, 1928.

guaranteed them under the Constitution. In a column written a few months before his death he said:

> There are so many privileges and immunities denied us as citizens, which we are entitled to enjoy equally with others, that we would be discouraged at the prospect of the long fight we have before us to secure them, if we did not stop to reflect that, by our history as well as the history of others, they only succeed who refuse to fail and who fight all the time for theirs whatever the obstacles. I feel that way about it now at the age of seventy-five [sic] as I did at the age of twenty-one. I want all the young and the old people of the race to feel about it in the same way.[16]

During his last years, as a venerable practitioner of the journalist's trade for almost half a century, he was warmly admired by some of his younger colleagues. In 1926 his appearance at the convention of the National Negro Press Association (which in the days of his preeminence had been the Afro-American Press Association) created a stir. It was reported that "the beloved dean of Negro journalists" was greeted and applauded by the assemblage as "the ablest and most forceful editorial writer the race has ever produced." The following year he attended the meeting which celebrated the one-hundredth anniversary of the founding of the first Negro newspaper in the United States, Russwurm's *Freedom's Journal*. In addressing the gathering, he was critical of some of the recent trends in journalism, especially the amount of space devoted to sports and entertainment. He emphasized "the supreme importance of the editorial page." His younger listeners disagreed, insisting that the editor should give the public not only what he considered important but what the readers wanted, so long as it was not harmful.[17]

16. Ibid., February 11, 1928.
17. *New York Age*, quoted in *Negro World*, September 11, 1926; *New York World*, June 15, 1928.

Most of the old friends were dead, although he and John E. Bruce saw each other occasionally and wrote to each other, exchanging views about politics, commiserating with each other over their ailments, and taking satisfaction in their ability to obtain an occasional pint of bootleg whisky. But the passing of his contemporaries was compensated for in part by his associations with some of the younger members of the newspaper fraternity. He liked to talk to them about his past struggles and achievements and was anxious to justify to them the role that he had played. The publisher of the *Journal and Guide* urged him to write his memoirs, which Fortune would have liked to have done, "but," he said, "only they can write such who have leisure from the daily bread grind."[18] But in his own newspaper columns and in interviews with young journalists, he tried ro set the record straight, as he saw it. An article by Vinton Plummer, entitled "Retrospect of Negro Journalism and Life and Times of T. Thomas Fortune," which was published in the *Hotel Tattler* and reprinted in the *Journal and Guide*, reflected Fortune's views. In discussing his misfortune which began in 1907 it said:

> The friends of Dr. Washington freezed on Mr. Fortune after he lost control of the New York Age through the direct connivance of Dr. Washington, after there appeared to be a break between them, which Dr. Washington, for his purposes, was responsible for and not Mr. Fortune, and the friends of Dr. Du Bois freezed on him because of his friendship for Dr. Washington and his policies, and between the two Mr. Fortune came nigh being crucified in his bread and butter, but he has always remained on the firing line and is very much on it right now.

The current "New Negro" school of writers also ignored Fortune's role as agitator and organizer and the importance of his literary work; but, said Plummer, no adequate history of the

18. Fortune to Bruce, February 24, 1923, Bruce Papers; Fortune to Scott, April 21, 1924, Scott Papers.

Negro in America could be written "which ignores the agitation and constructive work of Timothy Thomas Fortune. This view of the matter may shock Dr. Du Bois, Dr. Carter G. Woodson, Mr. James W. Johnson and W. S. Braithwaite, with Mr. George W. Forbes and Mr. Fred R. Moore thrown in for good measure, and other historians, anthologists, and publicists, but it is truth and can't be rubbed out."[19]

Younger men admired not only Fortune's journalistic talents but also his indomitable spirit and his refusal to make concessions to the physical limitations which came with advancing years. "He fought old age by refusing to recognize its weaknesses," one of his associates on the *Journal and Guide* recalled. In spite of failing sight he remained a prodigious reader, and with his alert and disciplined mind kept a good grasp on current affairs. In performing his journalistic duties he was persistent and industrious and, in his last years at least, not given to fits of temperament. He had suffered from rheumatism for many years, and by the 1920s pains in his back and shoulders made it increasingly difficult to use a typewriter. Finally the time came when he could no longer use that instrument, and he resorted once more to writing his copy by hand. "Time and again, his powerful and courageous spirit would drive his frail and failing body past the point of endurance until he could hardly move from sheer fatigue."[20]

By the summer of 1927 he himself admitted his increasing frailty. In August he went to the Catskills for a holiday but was unable to do any walking or climbing with other members of the party. He had to be content simply to sit on the veranda and gaze into space. "I was not well enough to think normally or to work," he said. "The pencil and sheet of paper had lost their allurement for me, and the only pleasure I got out if it all was in

19. Plummer, "Retrospect of Negro Journalism," *Hotel Tatler*, reprinted in *Norfolk Journal and Guide*, January 12, 1924.

20. *Norfolk Journal and Guide*, June 20, 1931; Fortune to Bruce, February 24, 1923, Bruce Papers.

seeing others have an enjoyable time. But it was awfully dull and stupid not to be able to do anything but stare into space or shift into the shade when the sun got too hot in the place I was." He recalled that when he had been in the Philippines he had seen many men stolidly sitting in the doors of their bamboo huts, gazing into space, doing nothing, and apparently getting infinite pleasure out of utter relaxation. "I learned a long time after that," he said, "that you have to be born and cannot be made that way, and that in the making you are likely to go all to smash, especially if you are mentally and physically active."[21]

During the following months he spent most of his time in the country, away from the noise of the city, but he continued faithfully to write his editorials and other copy for *The Negro World* and the *Journal and Guide*. Early in April 1928 he suffered a collapse while in New York City and was taken to the home of friends for a week. Then he was taken to Philadelphia by his son Fred, who was a surgeon at Mercy Hospital. After a time, as he showed some improvement, he was moved to his son's home. During his last illness he and Fred established an intimacy and rapport which had formerly been lacking in their relationship. He had always been close to Jessie and her husband and children. Now he told Fred that he regretted that there had been barriers between them and that he had never permitted his son to be very close to him. Although confined to his bed while at Fred's, he continued to dictate editorials. He suffered a relapse and died on June 2. His last editorials appeared in *The Negro World* on June 9 in the same issue which carried the news of his death.[22]

After his death Fortune was widely eulogized in the Negro press. Perhaps the most discerning tribute was an essay in the *Amsterdam News* by Kelly Miller, dean of Howard University,

21. Fortune, "Passing Show," January 14, 1928.
22. *New York Age*, June 9, 1928; *Negro World*, June 9, 1928; letter of Dr. Frederick W. Fortune to the author, July 30, 1957. Fortune was never reconciled with his wife. Carrie Fortune outlived

who had known Fortune since the 1890s. "After all has been said and done," wrote Miller, "Timothy Thomas Fortune represented the best developed journalist that the Negro race has produced in the Western World. His pen knew but one theme —the rights of man. His editorials were accepted throughout the journalistic world as the voice of the Negro."[23] During the interval between the decline of Frederick Douglass's greatest influence and the rise of Booker T. Washington, wrote Miller, Fortune had been the most influential Negro in the United States.

A record of his life would be an adequate history of the Negro race for the past fifty years. He knew intimately and influentially every upstanding Negro who participated in the dramatic episodes of Reconstruction. He was not merely an onlooker but a participant. In 1876, when the Negro was in the heyday of his political firmament Tim Fortune was entering into his twenty-first year. There were Negro Senators, Representatives, Governors, judges and influential administrators. Fifty years later everyone had been driven from the seats of power and even the seats destroyed. So great has been the apostasy from the days of Grant to the days of Coolidge. Fortune saw and experienced all this with an inward groaning, too deap for utterance.

Furthermore, said Miller, "Fortune witnessed the exploitation and failure of every theory propounded for the solution of the race's problems." In attempting to find solutions, "Frederick Douglass said, 'Get White,' Marcus Garvey said, 'Get out,' Booker T. Washington said, 'Get along.' "

In his declining days Fortune's despairing soul, after being baffled and buffeted by all other expedients, inclined to the theory of Marcus Garvey. But here again he found that it is as hard for the Negro to get out as it is to get white. And, so, in the final analysis there remains only the expediency of

---

him by more than a decade, dying in Brooklyn in January 1940 at the age of 78.

23. *New York Amsterdam News*, June 13, 1928.

getting along, which Fortune's dying soul witnessed and quaked.

Mr. Fortune's life measures the progress and regress of the race during the past half a century, but it tells us little or nothing of the future. He found the race with a faith and philosophy, and leaves it with neither.[24]

Miller's own pessimism was reflected in his interpretation of Fortune's career, and he may have exaggerated the depths of Fortune's disillusionment and despair during his last years. The person who wrote the tribute in *The Negro World*, on the other hand, certainly overemphasized Fortune's commitment to Garveyism and the redemption of Africa, but perhaps he caught Fortune's spirit better than Miller had when he said: "He was a young old man, a New Negro, who loved America, while recognizing much in it to hate," and who kept his fighting spirit to the end.[25]

As Kelly Miller observed, Fortune lived in an era when acceptance of the "get along" philosophy, best exemplified by Booker T. Washington's pragmatic, accommodationist stance, seemed to be the only way for black people to survive. But Fortune's personal misfortune was his inability to accept the "get along" philosophy. In some respects he was an opportunist, and for reasons of personal expediency he had made compromises, particularly in his long support of Washington. But he lacked Washington's capacity to rationalize, to accept and adjust, and to insist that things were getting better when they were in reality getting worse. Fortune had always been more skeptical than Washington about the good will and cooperation of whites, and he had never gone to the lengths to which the Tuskegean had gone to placate and conciliate. He was simply unable to adopt a patient, compromising, pragmatic position on questions of human rights and human dignity. Whatever his other vagaries and inconsistencies, on this fundamental question he was consistent throughout his long career. This is the reason

24. Ibid.
25. *Negro World*, June 9, 1928.

that what he wrote and said remains relevant to a later generation—but it was also his personal curse. Unable to bend as Washington had, he was broken. But by the 1920s, after years of mental torment and degradation, he seems to have come to terms with life. He no longer despaired over his personal affairs, and perhaps he saw signs of hope for his race. In such widely different movements as Garvey's UNIA and the National Association for the Advancement of Colored People he certainly saw signs of a movement away from the acceptance of the "get along" philosophy and the racial apathy which had for so long discouraged him. Although he was not himself identified with the NAACP, of which Du Bois was the symbol in those days, its program and methods were those which he had envisioned in the founding of the Afro-American League. By the time of his death, the NAACP had begun to win some significant cases in the United States Supreme Court and was carrying on a vigorous campaign against lynching.

The much publicized, militant "New Negro" of the 1920s was by no means an entirely new creature. Fortune must have felt an affinity with him because he bore a marked resemblance to the "Afro-American agitator" of the 1890s whom Fortune had lauded and exemplified. Fortune's earlier writing had not emphasized the racial cultural heritage of Afro-Americans as had the writers of the Harlem Renaissance, but his pride, his defiance of white oppressors, and his protests against racial injustice anticipated what later writers said. Claude McKay's poem, "If We Must Die," which appeared in 1919, is frequently cited as epitomizing the "New Negro" and the spirit of protest which characterized the Harlem Renaissance. But when McKay urged that Negroes "nobly die" so that "the monsters" they defied should be compelled to honor them, and when he declared, "Like men we'll face the murderous cowardly pack" and die "fighting back," he was echoing in verse what Fortune, the Afro-American agitator, had said years before in editorials and speeches.

BIBLIOGRAPHICAL NOTE

MANUSCRIPTS

Booker T. Washington Papers, Manuscript Division, Library of Congress.

The correspondence between Fortune and Washington and Fortune and Emmett J. Scott gives a detailed picture of the Fortune-Washington relationship and also contains much material on other aspects of Fortune's life. Some of the letters in the collection are original; others are carbon copies of letters written by Washington and Scott. In 1908, after Fortune sold the *Age* and broke his ties with Washington, most of the letters which Washington had written to him over a period of eighteen years were returned to Tuskegee and are in the collection.

In addition to the Fortune-Washington-Scott letters, the correspondence of Fred R. Moore, Charles W. Anderson, and other persons associated with Washington and Fortune contains important information.

T. Thomas Fortune Papers, a private collection in the hands of Fortune's descendants.

This is a small collection but very important for the purposes of this book. It contains some of the most intimate and revealing letters which Fortune wrote to Washington and Scott and which were returned to him in 1908 in exchange for the letters which he returned to Tuskegee. There are also several letters from Fortune to his wife, Carrie, which throw light on his estrangement from her and on his mental illness.

Emmett J. Scott Papers, Soper Library, Morgan State College.

This collection contains several letters between Fortune and Scott which were written in the years after Scott left Tuskegee.

Little other manuscript material has survived. There are a few letters in the Carter G. Woodson Collection and Robert and Mary Church Terrell Papers, both in the Manuscript Divison of the Library of Congress, and in the John E. Bruce Papers in the Schomburg Collection of the New York Public Library.

NEWSPAPERS

Fortune's preeminence as an editor occurred during a period when personal journalism was flourishing. The editorial pages of the *New York Globe*, the *New York Freeman*, and the *New York Age* are the best sources for a study of his racial thought. The news columns of these papers also contain important information about his activities. Unfortunately, except for scattered numbers and clippings (mostly in the Booker T. Washington Papers), the files of the *Age* from 1892 until 1905 have disappeared.

From a scrapbook in the Fortune Papers, from clippings in the scrapbook in the Booker T. Washington Papers, and from signed articles it has been possible to locate and identify a substantial amount of what Fortune wrote for the *New York Sun* and the *Boston Transcript*. In his later years he wrote signed columns for the *Norfolk Journal and Guide*, and it appears that he wrote most of the editorials in the *Negro World* during the period when he was editor.

Negro newspapers other than those with which Fortune was directly associated are very valuable, especially for the years when the files of the *Age* are not available. Among the most useful were the following: *Washington Bee; Cleveland Gazette; Indianapolis Freeman; Washington Colored American; Richmond Planet; Boston Guardian;* and *Amsterdam News*.

Fortune attracted a considerable amount of attention in the white press. The scrapbooks in the Washington Papers contain numerous clippings which have been useful. The scrapbooks were also valuable in furnishing leads which helped in locating other newspaper articles.

BOOKS AND ARTICLES

Black and White: Life, Labor and Politics in the South (New York, 1884), an exposition of his current views on politics and economics, contains some of Fortune's best writing. In *The Negro in Politics* (New York, 1886), a pamphlet which appeared two years later, he further expounded his views on political parties and the role of Negroes in relation to them. Fortune wrote a chapter entitled "The Negro's Place in American Life at the Present Day," for the book, *The Negro Problem: A Series of Articles by Representative Negroes of Today* (New York, 1903), which also contained articles by Washington, Du Bois, and Chesnutt. In 1905 he published privately a book of his verses, *Dreams of Life, Miscellaneous Poems*.

Fortune wrote the introduction to the first book of Washington's published speeches, *Black Belt Diamonds: Gems from the Speeches, Addresses, and Talks to Students of Booker T. Washington. Selected and arranged by Victoria Earle Mathews; Introduction by T. Thomas Fortune* (New York, 1898). Later Fortune did a substantial amount of ghost writing, revising, and editing of other books and articles appearing under Washington's name, but this was not recognized in the publications.

Fortune was the author of numerous articles published in periodicals. These include: "Why We Organized a National

Afro-American League," *Afro-American Budget*, vol. 1, no. 8 (February 1890); "Civil Rights and Social Privileges," *A.M.E. Church Review*, January 1886, pp. 105–31; "The Quick and the Dead," ibid., April 1916, pp. 247–52; "The Afro-American," *Arena* 3 (December 1890): 115–18; "The Race Problem; The Negro Will Solve It," *Belford's Magazine* 5 (September 1890): 489–95; "Industrial Education: Will It Solve the Negro Problem?" *Colored American Magazine* 7 (January 1904): 13–17; "False Theory of Education," ibid. 7 (July 1904): 473–78; "Intermarriage and Natural Selection," ibid. 12 (June 1909): 379–81; "Mob Law in the South," *Independent* 49 (July 15, 1897): 900; "Good Indians and Good Niggers," ibid. 51 (June 22, 1899): 1689; "Politics in the Philippine Islands," ibid. 55 (September 24, 1903): 2266–68; "The Latest Color Line," *Liberia*, no. 11 (November 1897), pp. 60–65; "Afro-American or Negro?" *Outlook* 62 (June 10, 1899): 359; "The Kind of Education the Afro-American Most Needs," *Southern Workman* 27 (January 1898): pp. 4–6; "Haytian Revolution," *Voice of the Negro* 1 (April 1904): 138–46; "The Filipino," ibid. 1 (May–June 1904): 199–202, 240–46; "The Voteless Citizen," ibid., vol. 1 (September 1904); "Who Are We? Afro-Americans, Colored People, or Negroes?" ibid. 3 (March 1906): 194–98.

Books, articles, and unpublished dissertations by other authors which have been used in the research and writing of this book are cited in the footnotes.

INDEX

[375]

Index

Fortune, Emanuel, Sr. (father), 3–5, 7, 10–19, 22, 151, 172, 178

Fortune, Fred (son), 99–100, 287, 292–94, 342, 348–50, 367

Fortune, Jessie (daughter), 97, 99–100, 287–88, 293–96, 349, 350, 367

Fortune, Sarah Jane (mother), 3–4, 7, 15, 22

Fortune, Stewart (son), 97, 98, 99

Fortune, Thomas (grandfather), 3

Fortune, Timothy Thomas: as agitator, 46–54, 106, 110–11, 178, 188, 370; as author, 43, 69–78, 89, 157, 165, 170, 207–13, 261, 263, 346–47, 353–55; criticism of, 49–50, 57, 178, 183–84, 186, 246–48; death, 353, 362, 367; dependence on Washington, 215, 228, 234, 252, 267, 285, 303–4, 305, 321; depression, 171–74, 211–12, 254, 258, 292, 294–95, 305, 348; description, 31–32, 159, 295; differences with Washington, 192–95, 217–21, 244, 305, 344, 355, 369; drinking, 175n, 214–15, 223–24, 243, 262–63, 285, 289, 291, 306, 325, 340; early employment, 17–24, 32–33; early life, 3–9, 17–33; economic philosophy, 43, 54–56, 78, 81–82, 158, 162; education, 7, 22–28; educational philosophy, 53–55, 73–75, 168, 196; employment on newspapers, 23–24, 37, 41–61, 95–97, 102–4, 307–9, 330, 334, 335, 339–47; exploitation of, 234, 267, 305, 306–7, 309–13, 321, 323, 325–26, 335–36, 365; family, 3–22, 31, 97–100, 174, 287–96, 306, 348–50, 367; financial problems, 43, 57, 66–67, 79–80, 95–96, 103, 104, 120, 170–74, 178, 207, 210, 212–13, 215, 217, 222, 240, 257n, 265, 267, 269, 285, 292, 302–4, 305, 324–26, 328–29, 341n, 342, 345, 347, 348, 354; friendships, 81, 100–102, 150, 163, 172, 236, 288, 291–92, 329, 350–51; and Garveyism, 356–62, 368–70; ghost writing, 170, 173, 207–10, 261, 263; health, 172–75, 178, 180n, 181, 191, 209, 212, 213, 240–41, 264, 289, 345, 366; hopes for political appointment, 154–56, 172, 190n, 205–6, 215, 217, 222–23, 225, 226, 234–40, 252, 256, 263, 267, 275; interests, 97–102, 288; marriage, 31, 294–96, 306; mental breakdown, 304–6, 310–11, 323–25, 351–53; militancy, 48–50, 106, 182, 198–99, 215, 218, 279, 369; old age, 364–67; "other woman," 306, 312, 317, 323; personal friendship with Washington, 137, 156–61, 163, 171–72, 175, 213–14, 264, 277, 290–91, 327, 354–56; Philippine mission, 235–40, 367; poetry, 98–99, 102, 172, 179, 211–12, 293; politics, 57–66, 72, 77, 85–95, 103–4, 146–49, 151–57, 163–64, 205–6, 226–30, 275, 363–64; racial ideas, 71–73, 128–35, 145–46, 157–59, 362–63; and religion, 25, 56, 74, 83, 98, 304–5, 306–8, 312, 324; rift with Washington, 217–21, 257, 259, 277, 285, 315–16, 320–21, 350, 335–56; separation from wife, 288–89, 294, 295–96, 306, 325, 348, 367n; speeches, 59, 95, 105–6, 178, 181–84, 186, 188, 197–201, 253, 277–78, 341; support of Washington, 190–92,